Copyright 2019, Kent T. Foreman

ISBN 9781645509882

Edited by Ryan Archer.
Credit to Dr. Marianina Olcott, for her invaluable patience, sagacity, and support.

A Labor of Love

Food for Thought for Future Generations

By
Kent Foreman

Edited by
Ryan Archer

Bi-conditional reciprocity

This concept finds a place in several entries of the text, though it could, plausibly, be involved in nearly all of them. Bi-conditional reciprocity is the logical case that refers to the influence exchanged between variables in an equation, or context. Influence, power, or energy, etc. is exchanged, in lieu of a one-sided, non-reciprocated, or unilateral offering. Simply, *every* element, including the personal subject, the individual – YOU, the reader – is participating in relationship. An awareness of the possibility of, or the opportunity for, relationship facilitates the greater development of not only the self, but the greater context, or community, as well.

Contents

CHAPTER 1	**1**
ABILITY	1
ABSOLUTE	2
ABSOLUTION	3
ACQUIRE	4
AESTHETICS	5
AGRICULTURE	5
ALCOHOL	8
ALONE	9
ALOOF	10
ALPHA	11
ALTERNATIVES	13
ANGST, ANXIETY	14
ARCHETYPE	15
ARROGANCE	16
ART	16
AUDIENCE ANALYSIS	17
SITUATIONAL AWARENESS	18
CHAPTER 2	**20**
BABY	20
BAD	21
BEAUTY	21
BEGINNING	22
BEHAVIOR	23
BELIEF	24
BELONGING	26
BENEFIT	27
BETRAYAL	27
BEYOND	29
BODY	30
BOUNDARIES	32
BOYS	33
BREATHING	33
CHAPTER 3	**35**
CAPABLE	35
CARING	36

CHAKRA	37
CHANCE	39
CHARACTER	39
CHARITY	42
CHOICE	43
CLEANLINESS	43
CLOSURE	44
COMFORT	45
COMMUNICATION	46
COMPASSION	47
CONCENTRATION	48
CONFIDENCE	48
CONSCIENCE	50
COUNSEL	51
CONSEQUENCE	51
CONTINUE	52
CONTROL	52
COURAGE	53
COSMOS	54
CRAFT	56
CREATE	56
CREDIBILITY	57
CRITICAL	57
CULTURE	59
CURIOSITY	65

CHAPTER 4   66

DAD	66
DARING	67
DARKNESS	67
DATING	69
DEATH	70
DEBT	72
DECISION	73
DEITY	74
DELIVERANCE	76
DEMEANOR	76
DEPRESSION	77
DESTRUCTION	78
DEVELOPMENT	78
DEVOTION	79
DIGNITY	80
DISCERNMENT	80
DISCIPLINE	82

DISILLUSIONMENT	83
DIVINE	84
DREAM	85
DRIVE	88
DRUG	88
DUALISM	90
CHAPTER 5	**92**
EASE	92
EDUCATION	93
EGO	98
ELATION	99
ELEMENT	100
ENDING	100
ENERGY	101
ENLIGHTENMENT	104
ESOTERIC	110
ETIQUETTE	111
EXCLUSIVE	112
EXPERIENCE	112
EXPRESSION	113
CHAPTER 6	**114**
FAILURE	114
FAITH	115
FALLACY	117
FAMILY	117
FEAR	118
FLOW	122
FREEDOM	122
FRIEND	126
FRIVOLITY, FUN	126
FUTURE	127
CHAPTER 7	**128**
GAME	128
GENETICS	129
GIVING	130
GLORY	130
GOD, GODDESS	131
GOOD	133
GOSPEL	134
GRACE	135

GROUNDING	135
CHAPTER 8	**137**
HAPPINESS	137
HEALTH	138
HEART	141
HELP	144
HISTORY	145
HONOR	147
HOUSE VS. HOME	149
HUMILITY	149
HUMOR	150
HYGIENE	151
CHAPTER 9	**153**
ID	153
IMAGINATION	154
INCLUSION	156
INFERIOR	157
INFORMATION	158
INITIATE	161
INNATE	163
IQ	164
INTELLECT	165
INTENT	166
INTIMACY	166
INTUITION	168
CHAPTER 10	**169**
JEALOUS	169
JOB	172
JOURNEY	174
JOY	176
JUBILEE	177
CHAPTER 11	**179**
KARMA	179
KNOWLEDGE	179
CHAPTER 12	**182**
LABOR	182
LAUGHTER	184

LAW	185
LEARNING	194
LEVEL	197
LIBERTY	198
LIFE	206
LITERATURE	212
LONGING	214
LOSS	215
LOVE	218
LYING	227
LYSISTRATA	228

CHAPTER 13 — 231

MAGIC	231
MAKER	233
MARKET	234
MATERIALISM	235
MEANING	236
MODERATION	238
MORALITY	239
MOTIVATION	241
MUSIC	243
MYTH	245

CHAPTER 14 — 248

NATURE	248
NIGHT	251
NIRVANA	251
NURTURE	253

CHAPTER 15 — 255

OBSTACLE	255
OCCULT	256
OPINION	257
OPPORTUNITY	258
OWNERSHIP	259

CHAPTER 16 — 260

PARTICLE	260
PATRIARCHY	261
PERFECTION	263
PERSEVERANCE	264
PERSON	264

PERSPECTIVE	267
PHILOSOPHY	268
POLITICS	270
POPULAR	273
POWER	275
PRACTICAL	278
PREPARED	279
PRESENT	279
PROFANE	280
PROMISE	282
PROPRIETY	282
PSYCHE	286
PUBLICITY	291
CHAPTER 17	**294**
QUALITY VS. QUANTITY	294
QUANTA	297
QUEEN	299
QUIET	302
CHAPTER 18	**305**
RACE	305
RATIONALITY	310
READING	313
REAL, REALITY	315
RECEPTIVE	316
RELATIONSHIP	317
RELIEF	319
RENAISSANCE	320
RESPECT	324
RESPONSIBILITY	331
REST	333
REPAYMENT	334
RESTRAINT	335
CHAPTER 19	**337**
SATIETY	337
SECRET	338
THE SELF	340
SERVICE	342
SETTLING	343
THE SHADOW	344
SHARING	347

The Soul	348
Spells	352
Standards	352
Sustenance	353
Symptom	354
System	356
CHAPTER 20	**358**
Tact	358
Taste	359
Terror	360
Time	366
Touch	371
Tradition	372
Transcendent	373
Trauma	375
Trouble	377
Trust	378
Truth	379
CHAPTER 21	**383**
Underlying	383
Unity	384
Utility	386
CHAPTER 22	**388**
Valor	388
Values	389
Vibration	391
Violence	393
Virtue	397
Vivacious	399
The Void, The Abyss	400
CHAPTER 23	**401**
Warrior, Warriorship	401
Water	405
Wholeness	405
The Will	406
Wit	408
Wonder	409
Work	411
Worry	414

SELF-WORTH	**414**
CHAPTER 24	**416**
X-FACTOR	**416**
CHAPTER 25	**417**
YOU	**417**
CHAPTER 26	**418**
ZEAL	418
ZENITH	419
ZOOPHILOUS	420
CONCLUSION	**422**

Preface & Acknowledgements

This text is an alphabetical encyclopedia of socially pertinent concepts. Primarily written with my daughter, Deia (DCKF), in mind, I recognized how it had a wider appeal and a general, positive application to others. I note how her education amounts to crass indoctrination - a disappointing combination of a regurgitation of facts and common-core methodologies that are presented with a view towards standardization tests, alone. This concerns me greatly, for such experience amounts to no sort of holistic or comprehensive platform. The general quality of product generated by such a disappointing institutional and cultural offering is a lazy mind, a larger scale of dumbed-down individuals, and so much wasted as far as heads, hearts, and hands. This system is not encouraging people to develop their best selves, and that approach negatively affects our own persons, but also our neighborhoods, the greater national community, if not the global scene, as well.

This particular labor of love amounts to an educational resource for my child, if not any reader who cares to benefit from an approach to concepts, and systematic thinking, generally. For perspective is always limited by how much one knows. When we expand our knowledge base, we can transform our minds! Written with a view towards pique-ing curiosity, advising as to alternatives, and structuring a virtuous ethos, this is offered as guidance and support. In my opinion, today's public education system is a disaster, and should we, as United States Americans, have any hope for the well-being of future generations, we need do what lies in our power to bring about improved circumstances. This is a facet of my own greater social effort, a portion of a contribution as a concerned human being, a part of the satisfaction of my role as a loving father.

The powers that be desire a non-critical mass of consumers in order to maintain the status quo. I would be a failure as a person if I did not apply myself meaningfully, and what is more: I would fail this magnificent innocent as a father if I did not strive to supplement, if not oppose a structure that robs individuals of their greater dignity, and subjects them to such a woeful excuse for an education.

Over the course of nearly two years spent writing the text I experienced a significant amount of personal growth and development. The text became the product of a fair portion of what I have studied and experienced over the course of forty plus years. That said, much of what is offered is culled via my own academic notes - recollections and ideas garnered via my own readings and exploration. This should provide ample material to critique and engage; the point of the text is to elicit engagement.

As a business owner, I made use of available time to structure, research, and script the text. I grasped how there was viability to the project, and I persevered to complete it. Importantly, I recognized how I need continually study and research not only topics and concepts for inclusion, but I had to focus on my own development and progress. I had to implement what I encouraged in the text, and practice what I preach. I continually questioned whether I was knowledgeable or talented enough to bring this text to fruition. This was a feat to accomplish – a definite test of character and self-worth.

Significant sources and quotes are footnoted. I made use of Webster's Encyclopedic Unabridged Dictionary of the English Language, New Deluxe Edition (Thunder Bay, San Diego, 2001) as a start to each entry then fleshed out the concept using what my own experience, notes, and assorted texts provided.

This text could not have been realized were it not for the invaluable contributions of some remarkable people. I need first recognize Deia's mother, Amanda, for being an amazing Mother.

I am so thankful that we have You in our lives.

My own Mom encouraged and supported this, and all other efforts in myriad ways and I am rather pleased that I get to share significantly with that amazing lady. I owe my father for his directive to "look it up," among other pertinent servings of guidance and counsel. That first advice has proven invaluable.

Many thanks go to Fonzi as he provided for an improved quality of life, and the ability to meaningfully pursue goals and dreams. The support of my editor and friend Dr. Marianina Olcott is nothing short of incredible. She believes in what I am doing, and demonstrates as much by meeting on a routine basis to help filter my head and heart. I am touched, honored by her presence and contributions.

Last, but not least is Deia Celeste. This is for her. She pushes me to do that much more with what I have, as a Father, and as a person. I see her shining face and recognize her amazing potential - I am motivated to be the best man and Father I can. The lessons contained here are meant to guide her, to save her from unnecessary loss, heartache, and pain – experiences that can be avoided altogether, given mindfulness and preparation. If I can save her, or anyone else significant loss or misery – much less instead add to their experience with joy and worthy resources – this text is a success. I am thankful that she is my daughter: my muse, my source of constant joy, the Angel of my Heart, the Goddess of the Heavens.

The specific words of Don Henderson, Kellen Durose, Martin Lee, Sandy McKeithan, and Tom Dewan all found places here, and they deserve credit for conversations, ideas, quotes, and encouragement, too. Many thanks to Julia Brandow for cover work. Jennifer Soutas was unnervingly productive – and is simply incredible. I am so very grateful for her contributed efforts.

As for how to read this book, I recommend several tactics. Please, engage critically. Discern those elements and features that pose some truth or relevance, and apply those worthy portions. Secondly, I wrote this for my daughter. Forgive the tone, but again: extrapolate what is pertinent and valid. Please look past my personal tone and that particular approach. I have used an incredible array of dashes, CAPS, and italics to emphasize and impart *my own character*. Because she is a competent reader, I wrote to her in a mature way, though there *are* affectionate, and familiar remarks. If you are a parent, consider adjusting or structuring the lesson to your own child, or audience. Be critical and explore my position. Counter my narrative with a fuller perspective. Realize that this is not meant to be a page-turner. This is a concept book. The segments are to be read in no particular order, because the concepts are stand-alone entries. Consider adding pertinent concepts to the list. Help facilitate the emergence of compassionate, critically engaged individuals who make use of an inclusive moral compass. Finally, do try and enjoy the experience.

Introduction

A significant portion of our North American United States population is lacking critical thinking skills, self-respect, as well as respect for others. This text serves as the foundations of a greater cultural project, one that is meant as a foil to so many unnecessary consequences of our culture. By presenting a diverse array of concepts, the reader will have an introduction to many ideas that are largely absent from public education. Drawing from cultural practices here in the United States, historical precedent, and my own experience, this labor of love encourages self-respect, fosters consideration of others, and, with a remarkable element of fortunate engagement, facilitates the emergence of a critical, curious, interested and engaged audience! While it is not meant as a comprehensive approach, this is meant as a learning resource for my child, other parents and their children, and whoever desires to extract, and savor something positive from its pages.

By engaging this book, you will be better able to engage concepts systematically, logically, and cogently. This text's scope will benefit you by providing a lengthy spectrum of issues, and ideas for your personal investigation and application. This alphabetized array of concepts is meant to complement one's experience and provide insights as to ideas that remain outside the woefully static realm of public schooling. While I *am* a product of that same system, and I *did*, in fact, receive what I deem to be a quality education, this text is more a product of my own self-guided investigations, readings, and experience.

I wrote the book because our United States character and culture needs revision. We need revisit ideas, revise practices, and encourage within people the emergence of an improved ethos. We need consider the idea of characterization; we can not apply terms like 'free' and 'brave' if our actions do not substantiate their use. It is time to birth an ethos born of curiosity, critical engagement, and self-respect. Many cultural elements, and public education methods, specifically, are failing us. It is long past time to discuss and implement alternatives. Presenting concepts provides readers with a chance to identify some consequential variables that might be overlooked, de-emphasized, if not ignored by greater cultural institutions and edifices. A grasp of concepts gives rise to able thinkers, and we are in desperate need of them here and now, ever forward and always.

Consequences borne of our culture are more and more apparent to the engaged, or discerning perspective. Our participation in a predatory system encourages its continuance. Its possible fulfillment culminates in degeneracy, slavery, disappointing waste, and such staggering degrees of loss. Our standards are comprised largely of lesser applications of inferior concepts and practices. Should we, as a people, desire improvements, we need make better use of an astounding array of conceptual options as resources. We are not confined to this arrangement, and we need not suffer unnecessarily. A grasp of *these* particular concepts makes for a fuller representation of character; learning generally improves the circumstances of the learner! Making use of these conceptual instruments can elicit self-respect, improved self-worth, and the wherewithal to engage with others openly, and respectfully. Diligent study equates to a meaningful investment in the self, and the greater community. Should we truly entertain the possibility of improved conditions, we need prioritize methodologies that elicit new, and positive results. *A Labor of Love* is posed as a means to the improvement of social, economic, and environmental conditions in the United States.

Chapters are alphabetized. There are 27 chapters (a Conclusion serves as the last), and concepts follow suit. And guess what? Chapter 1 features concepts that start with the letter 'A,' of all things! It includes abilities, absolute, aesthetics, etc., and the chapter ends with situational awareness. Definitions are provided, with examples of the concept at play. Then a demonstration is offered as to how the concept is pertinent, or how it might best be applied should she/the reader care to make a place for it in their life. At the end of some concepts I listed some poignant quotes that facilitate the message, as well as provide suggestions for further study and research.

Please forgive its shortcomings. Please help substantiate its worth by contributing to the list of concepts. This country needs people engaging together to bring about an improved national community, and we do that by educating - by leading people from ignorance.

Concerning the Audience

As I began *A Labor of Love*, I came to the point as to how I should address readership as my Daughter, alone, or if it should adopt a more generalized approach. How was I to address feminism, approach women's rights, or impart a perspective that means something to women, generally? I decided upon a route that treats of information that is applicable to people sans gender differences. These concepts, ideals, and values apply to anyone, regardless of gender. Their exploration and implementation *can* elicit returns, should they be included and applied deliberately, prudently.

Regarding 'The Hater'

There is a significant, and disappointingly healthy and established character of anti-intellectualism in the United States. It leads a significant portion of people to label as 'the hater' those voices that offer protest and critique. I strive to impart means that encourage the presence of wonder, a desire to investigate and examine. The alternative is a lackluster perspective: self-assured and ignorant, one that effectively limits the occasion for meaningful interaction, and growth. Close-mindedness is the refuge of limited minds. By providing some morsels for consideration, perceptual limitations can be exceeded, if not perhaps eliminated. I accept the designation of critical theorist, in lieu of general malcontent, or hater. I certainly offer the text with Love. It is a heartfelt appreciation of mankind, and the recognition of so much opportunity, that I maintain significant hope for the people of this country, and the world. The Hater is the antithesis of who I am, and what I offer. I do not expect, nor desire, full agreement.

"The public is wonderfully tolerant. It forgives everything except genius."
Oscar Wilde

Explicit credit to Tom Dewan, for his humor and insightful critique concerning all things.

"The basic tool for the manipulation of reality is the manipulation of words. If you can control the meaning of words, you can control the people who must use the words." – **Philip K. Dick**

Chapter 1

Ability

Ability is possession of the means or skill to do something. It is talent, or proficiency in a particular area. Faculties can be equivocated as abilities. There are different types of abilities; among them are emotional, physical, and mental. Emotional abilities are feelings. Mental abilities include critique, discernment, perception, and strategy. Physical abilities refer to doing exercise, playing sports, performing martial arts, or even making love.

Diversify your abilities. Discover what you enjoy and develop those skills and talents. Hone tools so that you have an expansive array of abilities to make use of when particular needs arise. Make it so you have a conceptual utility belt, analogous to what the comic character Batman applies during the course of his investigations. Have skills at your disposal so you can behave or participate appropriately in your own adventures.

Work on yourself - invest in yourself - such that you have something worthwhile to offer. Differentiate your skill set so you stand apart with a unique array and a greater sense of self. In *Time Enough for Love*, author Robert Heinlein wrote, "A human being should be able to change a diaper, plan an invasion, butcher a hog, conn a ship, design a building, write a sonnet, balance accounts, build a wall, set a bone, comfort the dying, take orders, give orders, cooperate, act alone, solve equations, analyze a new problem, pitch manure, program a computer, cook a tasty meal, fight efficiently, die gallantly. Specialization is for insects."

Heinlein's list is a solid one - nearly exhaustive, but incomplete, still. The point is to recognize basic skills and commit them to memory. Generally, become aware of yourself. Develop basic skills and abilities such that you can provide for yourself after your Mother and I are gone. By investing in, and working on, yourself you obey the command of the Delphic Oracle: KNOW THYSELF. As Plato/Socrates advised, "The unexamined life is not worth living."[1] Examine yourself: shape worthy character - build a comprehensive skill set. Know your strengths and weaknesses. Play to your strengths and improve on your abilities such that your weaknesses do not impede you unnecessarily. Discover the abilities that bring you joy - those skills that make your heart SING! Create yourself by applying abilities that demonstrate a worthy character.

If something is worth doing, it is worth doing well. Build your skill set. A good primary ability is being able to learn or being teachable. Have an open mind and explore the world. Continually refine your person. Communicate efficiently, effectively, eloquently, and express yourself in such a way that you can not be misunderstood. Feel, with passion and depth. Lead compassionately. Love fully, plan carefully, and live fully, and well. Work on yourself, and develop those abilities that serve you.

Absolute

Absolute refers to being not qualified or diminished in any way - a totality. An absolute is neither relative nor comparative and it implies an unquestionable finality: "an absolute success."

Consider your full day as you conclude it. The Romans used a concept called memento mori: Remember that you have to die. It is a reminder that you will someday perish and leave this material plane. Make good use of your time, whether it is one singular day or the sum of all of your years. When you end a stage…a project, a day, a week, a relationship, a conversation, a trip, even a shower…consider that the action stands as an event that is absolute. It stands alone as a singular event. Was it an absolute success, or even an absolute failure?

Consider your actions: your thoughts, your feelings, and your words. Strive to build on the total of absolute successes. Work on you so that at the end of your life you can rest content knowing that you put forth quality thoughts, feelings and actions. You are an awesome individual, of amazing quality. When your end comes, you will want to look back with minimal regrets, and recognize how your life was an absolute success. I believe in You!

Keep in mind: you learn more from failure than you do by success. Do not be afraid of failure because it is an opportunity to learn. Further, do not be afraid to fail amazingly, in new and huge ways.

Absolution

Absolution is the 'formal' release of guilt, obligation, or punishment. The formal component of absolution speaks to an external institution, like a church or a government. That formal element can be contrasted with the necessity of the application of your own internal apparatus. In much the same way, praise can be offered by an external source. This text is a guide that can facilitate or inform your own decisions and experiences. While external judgment, in the form of absolution, praise, blame, etc. *is* important, it can only serve as a contrast to the more important internal moral faculty.

You need be a responsible judge of your own actions and character. Sculpt yourself and your values such that you behave well and can maturely critique, forgive, or praise yourself. Living a life premised solely on external blame or praise is very dangerous. Your own ethical faculties need guide your behavior, and you need to take responsibility for your own actions. Measure your actions and strive to lead an honorable life. In doing so, you will be able to forgive yourself whenever necessary. Also, your self-confidence will deliver in very important ways.

Acquire

Acquire means to buy or obtain an object or asset and to learn a skill, habit, or quality. Make plenty of space for consideration of the immaterial. Certainly, material goods are a necessity in this life - Aristotle said as much. But be aware of your emphasis and focus. The intangibles you acquire highlight your life. A piece of jewelry should not bring the joy that meaningful friendships impart. Some of these intangibles include experiences, skills, friends, and concepts like peace, and wholeness. Seek out new experiences. Try to do as much as possible so that you can relate with people and offer something worthwhile. Travel and see different cultural practices and traditions. Find the means to contrast with your own life. Abilities and skills are important, as relayed earlier. Round out your character by seeking new information and contrasting perspectives.

Experience will inform your own ethos, values and behaviors. Make certain those acquisitions - that which is acquired - benefit and improve you, for not all experiences are necessary. You do not need to do everything that is available in life. Sometimes, though, experience thrusts things upon you. Sometimes you are forced to participate in contexts or scenes that you may not choose or enjoy. Car accidents, or maybe witnessing a natural disaster (like a dangerous flash flood), serve as examples. Whatever they may be, make sure your life's acquisitions amount to more than baubles and 'stuff.' Make sure they serve your highest good. Move toward those skills, experiences, materials, or personal relations that improve your life.

Aesthetics

Aesthetics are a set of principles concerned with the nature and appreciation of beauty, especially in art. In the philosophical realm, the question applied is, "what is beauty, or what is beautiful?" This question can be applied in many different realms. The next pertinent question might be, "what is art?" Might there be situations or contexts that have no beauty? I maintain that animal abuse can not be beautiful. Perhaps a particular bodily function is not beautiful, either. There are many applications of the term 'beautiful.' Can the flag of Japan be called beautiful? What of the equation: "2+2=4"? Is it beautiful?

An understanding of terms allows us grasp certain forms of knowledge and hopefully, helps us to utilize terms with precise, applicable meanings. In some circumstances, beauty may not apply. Consider what you perceive and be critical as to how you are judging the context. To behold beauty is a wondrous event. For example, your own birth was a beautiful moment. Hearing you say, much less mean the words, "I Love You," is nothing short of amazingly beautiful.

Contrast the term with others, so they maintain meaning and significance. Investigation and being knowledgeable of aesthetics is an important skill and practice. It informs values, communication, and perspective.

Agriculture

Agriculture is the science or practice of farming, including cultivation of the soil for the growing of crops and the rearing of animals to provide food, wool, and other products. I have worked in agriculture for the duration of your entire life. It is important for you to understand why I have invested so heavily in the sector. In this segment, I will present a personal account of why agriculture motivates me, and why it elicits my continued attention. I have paired it with a historical examination of the significance of agriculture so you grasp why I persist with my personal goals.

Put simply: everyone eats. People benefit, and more than just survive - they thrive when they consume the freshest of organic produce. When people settled land in the Neolithic Period, the larger community was responsible for food production. Nearly everyone took an active role in the maintenance of his or her own food shed.

One of the concepts that stimulates me is the ancient idea of the *polis,* or, as I understand it, the community meeting place. Ideally, in the center of each Greek city-state would be situated a polis. Not just the aristocratic, land-owning politicians would meet there to discuss the variables of their land, but *everyone* would assemble and discuss the condition and health of their town, city, etc. Outside of the polis was what was known as the *agora,* or the marketplace where merchants would congregate to sell their wares, and where people would assemble and mingle publicly. Dwellings and homes were situated outside of the agora. Crops and produce were grown around the perimeter of all of the community.

Because of the threat of invasion and external threats, personnel erected walls and protected the people in castles or fortified cities. The agriculture was left unprotected, outside of the walls. Hopefully growers produced enough food to be stored within the city, should the threat be prolonged or severe. Otherwise, those in the city would starve and suffer due to the food shortage. During feudal times, people received protection from authorities by providing goods, money, or produce. But in the case that the protecting authority was displeased, or could not arrive to help in time, peasant growers would lose their homes, the crop, farms, and perhaps even their lives to robbers, roving bands of marauders, invading hordes, etc.

The American colonists were comprised of a large portion of farmers and ranchers. They would settle land

and hopefully produce enough food to feed their families and then sell what surplus they had in order to make a living. As technological innovations improved living conditions, people left the land and moved to cities. Farm work remains a difficult task, even given remarkable leaps of technology. There is now a disappointing decreasing amount of family farmers, but there is hope! A new generation of growers is emerging; young people, among a significant swath of diverse people, are returning to the land and addressing agricultural arts. I am another face of the organic, local, small farm initiative, and the greater 'slow food' movement.

Corporations do not necessarily provide the best produce, nor engage in the safest methodologies in terms of logistics. Wasteful inefficiencies corrupt food systems all over the world. In terms of mileage, storage, processing, handling and packaging, food is old, distant, and dangerous. But this is not a necessary condition.

Remember that just because something is in a bad state or condition does not mean that it is forever in that same condition.

Local, organic family farms are a most viable means of helping feed, employ and even house people across the country. Local economies benefit from dynamic local food systems as does the greater environment. I have invested a lot of time and energy into improving California's diverse food systems because the effort benefits an ever-increasing amount of people.

It is important to showcase what it takes to pursue a worthwhile goal. That effort can be most difficult, and usually involves hard work, dedication, diligence, and perseverance. I believe in the viability of my goals. You mean a tremendous amount to me. I believe in the necessity of us enjoying an inclusive, significant and loving relationship. Just as I believe in our relationship, so too do I believe in my food project. Put forth that effort to realize your own big, exciting, wondrous dreams. Make certain they are worth the loss of sleep. That said, I hope they keep you up at night, giddy with excitement! NEVER GIVE UP! I believe in you, and I know you can achieve anything when you put your best energies forward.

AND! Importantly: eat plenty of ripe, local, organic and fresh wares from local family farmers whenever possible. Buying directly from the source is the best way of ensuring quality, as well as meaningfully engaging a local economy, in several ways.

Alcohol

Alcohol is an intoxicating agent found in beer, wine and liquor. It is a depressant. Excessive consumption can sometimes lead to abuse of alcohol; alcoholism is an addiction to the consumption of alcoholic liquor or the mental illness and compulsive behavior resulting from alcohol dependency. Alcohol, and by extension, alcoholism, can weaken the body and can even result in death. Excessive consumption over one session can have lasting, if not permanent consequences. It weakens both cognitive and physical faculties. Your mind is impaired such that proper judgment is affected. Your bodily functions are maligned, and your reaction time is seriously slowed, hence why so many folks suffer car crashes while they are driving under the influence of alcohol.

It taxes the liver and kidneys. If someone drinks excessively and does not eat or drink a sufficient amount of water before going to bed, the result is a hangover. It is a painful experience, typically involving a painful headache, if not body pains, too. It is your body's way of communicating discomfort due to the amount of work it need perform in order to cleanse itself. Alcohol is an ancient commodity. Beer, wine and liquor have been consumed since even before the establishment of agriculture in the Neolithic period. It is used in informal social situations, as well as more formal institutional rituals and traditions.

People go out for beers after work, or they drink at a baseball game or at backyards barbeques. People visit vineyards in Paso Robles, Santa Cruz, Napa, Italy, France or even Australia to enjoy regional wines. Alcohol has a worldwide presence. Churches use wine as a symbol, as a sacrament. Other religions and belief systems make use of alcohol in their own special rites.

As with so many other things, moderation with alcohol is recommended. Because alcohol impairs how your brain and body perform, it is a good idea to practice self-restraint, or self-control with it. Alcohol can be enjoyable in many different contexts. Its presence influences gatherings as diverse as dinner parties, or dances, or very consequential business meetings. Approach it respectfully and responsibly. It can affect your entire life if not handled with care and maturity.

Alone

Having no one else present, or being on one's own is what is known as being alone. The state of being alone is solitude. One can be sad because no one has friends or company. Conversely, one can be lonely in a group of people as well. It is important to be comfortable when by yourself. You have the ability to make friends, for you have a compassionate heart, a considerate mind, and a caring character. You will never truly be alone. But be willing to have some alone time so that you can re-center and focus on you.

I suggest eating alone, watching a movie alone, perhaps even traveling alone. The buddy system is recommended for some activities, but focus on being self-sufficient. You need not be reliant on the company of others in order to be happy. Along the same lines: make friends of those who make you feel like you belong with them. A solid starting point is being comfortable with your own self. It is most disappointing to be in the company of others and still feel alone, if not isolated. Prioritize being comfortable with yourself so you can then recognize how you want to feel in the company of others. You will be in a better position to welcome the good people in your life when you understand how specific values overlap, and sync with your own principles.

Aloof

To be aloof means to be conspicuously uninvolved and uninterested, typically through distaste. It might be the case that one enjoys solitude excessively. People might identify this behavior negatively. Truly, some folks eschew human contact, and live like hermits devoid of greater human experience or interaction. Some individuals minimize human interaction because of their own spiritual needs as well. But being aloof at the social level usually occurs because an individual views people as below them. They might regard themselves as worth more than their fellow man, and 'look down their nose' at others, in a negative, judgmental fashion. Other times, though, people may not understand someone's reticence or hesitation to engage with others. Some folks prefer to enjoy their solitude. Some might be disappointed by people, and maintain distance. Still others might have a lot going on internally - with their emotions or thoughts - and need time and space apart, to sort them out. Still others might not communicate well or be nervous around people. Being aloof can be positive for the person doing it and also result from negative things that have happened, or that are happening to them. Conversely, people may understand the reasons why someone is aloof, or also view the same behavior as negative – like the case where someone distances themselves from people because the group is so critical that their judgment motivates the person to maintain distance.

Engage others as you are comfortable. Sometimes it is necessary to be aloof, as in the situation where you do not want to participate in a petty argument. Some people *are* abrasive, crass, and obnoxious. Find the people that are worthy of your company and associate with quality individuals. Also, keep in mind that good times are to be enjoyed, despite the sentiment that you do not want to engage or participate. I can recall incidents where I was reticent to be involved in a social situation, yet certain events turned out to be some of the best occasions of my life. Have an open mind and be willing to exert courage via interacting with people. Balance that with the understanding that good people are usually available, present, and willing to interact with you though good people are so hard to find. Make use of the moment: *carpe diem!* And again: sometimes it is better, if not necessary, to be aloof and/or distant.

Alpha

Alpha is the first letter of the Greek alphabet. We are addressing the more urban definition of the word, referring to the head animal in a pack, and by extension, an unofficial leader. You will encounter those who want to lead, and those who prefer to follow. In my experience, it is the majority of people who prefer to be led. They desire to be guided, if not told what to do. As far as leaders go, though, it takes a good individual - one of worthy quality - to lead well. Many people seek attention, or worse - power, hence their interest in leading or serving as the lead in a project or organization. Be able to identify different components of quality leaders.

What makes a good leader, then? Heed those individuals that are transparent – those that are open as to their goals, intentions, and plans. Make certain they are respectful of others; a leader should take others into consideration as they serve, or yield power or authority. A good leader might be compassionate though some leaders elicit results because they are the very opposite. Some folks get returns by being harsh and even abusive. Further, some people are motivated by either of these two manners: love or fear, the proverbial carrot or the stick. A good leader will utilize clear communication and include the members of the team. Further, a worthy leader will work hard. Sometimes an individual just barks orders and benefits from the toil of others. These types of leaders are sometimes viewed with contempt as they are not working with those who are actually performing. But oftentimes a leader will work hard in a way that is not readily apparent. The boss of the factory works in the office, not necessarily alongside the laborers in the actual factory. Be aware that there are different responsibilities but a leader demonstrates that he is working with and for the team, though possibly in a dissimilar fashion. Using another analogy, a leader on the battlefield does not *just* send troops into combat. A worthy leader sometimes fights alongside his troops on the field. And yet another analogy: a construction foreman sometimes constructs trenches instead of just instructing others to do the hard work. Make sure the leaders you follow are working with and for the team, rather than just benefitting from the latter's work. Seek out those leaders who complement and improve their teams, instead of behaving like parasites.

Finally, a good leader will recognize the results and efforts of his team – the contributions of the players involved. This is *most* important. When one knows they are recognized and appreciated, they perform better. This goes for all social dynamics. Family members, team members, business peers all put forth more effort when they know that their efforts are acknowledged. Be mindful of the crowd that wants to be led. Pay attention to those that move to a position or role of power and how they lead. The portion of your last name of *Foreman*, does not make you a leader, much less a good one. I recognize how you care about people, how you are considerate and respectful

I admire your strength.

When you are in a leadership position, be sure to lead honorably and respect your team. Also, give way to those who are better leaders. Do not seek power merely because it remains available. Those worthy and able folks typically ascend to those positions. Therefore, as recommended previously, shape a worthy character, complemented by an expansive array of skills and abilities. In the case that you choose to lead, you will be equipped to do the job well.

"Choose your leaders with wisdom and forethought. To be led by a coward is to be controlled by all that the coward fears. To be led by a fool is to be led by the opportunists who control the fool. To be led by a thief is to offer up your most precious treasures to be stolen. To be led by a liar is to ask to be told lies. To be led by a tyrant is to sell yourself and those you love into slavery."
– Octavia Butler, 'Parable of the Talents'

Alternatives

Alternatives refer to one or more available possibilities. Life is all about strategy. That is not the same as saying that life is a game. But one must have a plan or a policy in order to achieve goals and general aims, or pursuits. Given that you will meet with interruptions, obstructions, distractions, detractors and opposition, it is wise to keep options open. Always have alternatives in mind. So while you try to formulate the best possible plan, you also need a Plan B. Consider, then: you might also formulate Plans C through M (if not through Z!) while you are at it. It is important to realize that there are always alternatives, even if you do not like them. Along the same lines, it is never too late to dream a new dream or birth a new goal. Sometimes plans, or people, for that matter, do not work out as well as you could have originally hoped. Grasp the fact that you are *never* stuck. Format back up or contingency plans such that you can flow, given obstacles or life's curve balls.

Angst, Anxiety

Angst, and/or anxiety are emotions experienced when one is under stress with worry, dread, or anticipation. When individuals are under pressure, they either respond or react. Responding involves refined ability, while a reaction is more base – lacking a balanced, measured, rational element. Some physiological results do not have anything to do with a rational, logical element. But an important note is to recognize how, in all of your life, you can be in control of your answers to life, and all of its challenges.

Experiencing angst or anxiety typically involves a helpless feeling. When one feels like they are stuck, they can make seriously bad decisions. Alternatively, when one takes the time to make a considerate and measured response, alternatives are identified, and better decisions can be made. You will deal with adversity in life. Whether you respond or react to challenges will make a considerable difference with what follows. The more you are able to practice self-control, and implement a balanced approach, the better the results. Take heart! Breathe, and breathe, and breathe some more. Take several seconds to breathe and get centered, in order to address the situation or the ills at hand. It is better to be on firm footing than by reacting haphazardly.

Remember that problems are never final; there are solutions available, even if they are not immediately recognized. Take your time. Breathe some more! Consider meditating. Get some food, water, or rest. Ask for help if it is available. Remember that the world and people, generally, are good! You are good! Do good deeds, and sew good seeds.

Archetype

An archetype is a universal symbol. It may be a character, a theme, a symbol, or even a setting. Archetypes serve as a typical character, action or situation that represent universal patterns of human nature. The Greek and Roman Gods all serve as archetypes. Roles such as the hero, the sage, the innocent, the lover, the caregiver, the citizen, the sovereign, the magician, the creator, the explorer, the jester and the rebel all have traits that characterize the archetype. Importantly, an archetype is never fully good. There is a balance of traits within each archetype. The lesson of archetypes is to balance conflicting traits in order to emerge as the best.

The hero is strong, courageous, has great faith and competes against great odds. Negatively, the hero (or the female: heroine!) is challenged by arrogance or delusions of grandeur. The lover belongs to a group, and is willing to sacrifice for others. The lover is challenged by a lack of their own identity, by obsession and jealousy. The rebel is a leader, a risk taker, and a brave and honest individual, but challenged by negativity, lawlessness, or even fanaticism.

You will form your character as you develop, via experience and learning. What are you aiming at, and what are the models that guide or inform you? Myths, literature, religion, music and various forms of popular culture can inform and influence your person. Peruse media in order to encounter as wide an array as possible. Be critical as to the characters presented, for every single one is beset by their own particular challenges. Hercules dealt with obstinacy and anger, and Achilles had arrogance, among other lesser traits. Medea was strong, and compassionate, but in the end she dealt with her helplessness in a horrific fashion: by killing her children. There is an amazing spectrum of examples though history to be aware of in order to shape your own standard. Book up, and investigate this marvelous world.

Arrogance

Arrogance is the opposite of humility - immoderate confidence. It is close to self-importance, egotism, and being overly prideful. The concept of balance is very important here. While confidence is a necessary component of a strong and mature person, taking it to extremes (as in the case of so many other concepts) is disastrous. In mythology, Oedipus was arrogant. His story speaks to how it was his weak spot. Arrogance was addressed and corrected by the Gods, and importantly, by his fellow man. Most folks neither approve of nor accept the standards of a braggart spouting their own quality and worth.

It is advisable to demonstrate and showcase worthy character by way of performing good actions and behavior. Your words *never* mean as much as actions do. Rely on your behavior and demonstrate skills to showcase your qualities and character. Time spent talking about how good or talented you are is a waste. Focus your talents and use them to present instead a worthy presentation of your own unique range of skills.

Art

Art is the application of human creativity, skill and imagination, typically (but not exclusively) in visual form. We addressed aesthetics earlier in this text. Arts can be visual, like drawing, painting, making ceramics, doing photography, designing or engineering architecture, sculpting, or performing/offering conceptual arts. Literary arts are plays, books, poetry, and also epics, legends, myths, ballads, and folktales. Performing arts include music, theatre, and dance. Different elements of food can be categorized as art, as in the case of gastronomy or culinary art. Martial arts are combative practices used by the military, law enforcement, or even civilians, like you and me, as well.

What comprises an art? Art is a documented, public expression of a sentient being through an accessible medium so that people can view, hear, or experience it. The act of producing an expression can also be referred to as a certain art, or as art, in general. An art requires study and dedication. Art is no trivial or haphazard activity and it is not something that is taken lightly. Fromm said that Love should be considered an art. It, too, requires dedication and a sustained, focused approach.

You are encouraged to treat your life as a work of art. Dedicate your time to making your life into a work that you can be proud of, that you are proud of sharing. At your age, your Mother and I recognize how you have a remarkable skill and character set. Build on the foundation that you have now. Invest the time, effort, and energy in order to flourish and develop still more.

Audience Analysis

Assessing or gauging your audience while being mindful of age, culture, and their knowledge base is called audience analysis. Every person that you interact with, or have experience with, is your audience. You may not even be aware that you have an audience. While in that particular case, the best course of action is to behave as if people *were* watching. Generally: behave honorably, with dignity and respect for others and yourself.

In the cases where you are addressing a discrete group, it is best to have an understanding as to your audience. Tailor your message to the audience that is receiving it, and again: express yourself such that you can not be misunderstood. Your audience will change radically as you shift or move between contexts: as you get coffee, or speak to your class, participate in sports, or coordinate with people at work. Communication is a very detail-oriented process, requiring effort and concern. You will want to address people well, and offer your message efficiently, if not eloquently. Take the time to prepare for a successful communicative transaction by researching your audience and formatting your message to them, specifically.

Situational Awareness

The ability to identify, process, and comprehend the critical elements of information about what it is happening to you, your team, or your surroundings with regards to the satisfaction of a goal or mission is known as situational awareness (SA). SA pertains to who, what, when, where, why and how on a moment-to-moment basis. Who is involved, or present, or even nearby? How are you? How do you feel? What parts of your life, outside of the task at hand, are affecting the outcome of the immediate process, goal or mission? What is the goal? What is the primary plan? What are the contingency or back-up plans? What elements need be safeguarded or structured such that they perform adequately, like people, places, tools, etc.? What time is it? How is the lighting, or the weather? What are your exits?

SA consists in knowing what is going on around you. It also involves being aware of events or conditions that could possibly affect your own environment. Maybe a local sporting event is ending and those leaving the game will influence your travel plans. What about a political rally's participants behaving erratically, or even violently, as they depart their event?

There are many ways to develop SA. Authors Brett and Kate McKay wrote an article entitled, "How to develop the situational awareness of Jason Bourne."[2] In it, the authors offered a long list of tools to help develop the skill.

-Observe, Orient, Decide, Act (OODA). Take note of your surroundings.
Identify key variables. Make a plan and execute.

(Situational) Awareness

-Be relaxed and open, yet alert and focused. Scan your environment and continually play "I Spy." Position yourself for optimal observation and performance. Put your back to a wall. As a good practice, question others regarding the scene. Ask your team questions along the lines of context: How many people were behind the counter? How many exits were there? Was it a man or a woman sitting next to us? How many people had short-sleeved shirts?

-Practice memorizing things. Establish baselines and anomalies for the environment. Note mental modes of human behavior: dominance/submission, comfortable/uncomfortable, and interested/uninterested.

-Look for shifty hands, or someone trying too hard to act naturally. Things that do not belong in a context will stand out. You can note these perceptually, using your physical senses, or you can sense them intuitively. Hone all senses.

Generally, have a plan, and behave such that you do not appear vulnerable or an easy target. Move with purpose. As with all other skills: practice, practice, practice.

Chapter 2

Baby

A baby is everyone's starting point after departing the womb. A baby is innocent, defenseless, needy – requiring help in order to receive the food, shelter, maintenance, and importantly: LOVE! The ancient philosopher Plato remarked how the soul, or the baby in utero (within the uterus) is connected to absolute Perfection. It is At One with nothing but the Good. As the baby makes its appearance and begins to be independent, it is moving away from that Perfection. It is colored, guided, influenced and affected by humanity: people, culture, media, and traditions.

Keep in mind, then, when you hold such a precious individual, that they are embarking on their own journey. Convey good feelings and words. Speak to the best part of them. Remind them how they are loved, and LOVE, itself. Remind them how they are beautiful, safe, and needed – if not necessary, too! Ease their way into this world. There is nothing like holding a baby, or even better: being a parent. Supporting and encouraging something so pure and innocent is one of life's many treasures. Your entrance and presence in this world makes my life so much more special, and I am so much more of a person for your presence. I Love You! (Just a reminder…

Bad

Something that is of poor quality, inferior/lesser or of defective quality is what's known as being 'bad.' This discussion concerns the application of that particular term. For starters, both people and institutions apply the term. It can have a simple adjectival use: that player is bad at playing third base. Or, the term can have a moral aspect: he is a bad man. We will discuss the spectrum of morality in detail, later. But the spectrum of good and bad is not so clear cut, not strictly black and white, as simple as yes/no. That spectrum is a complicated one. As stated previously (it bears repeating), be aware of the broadest spectrum of choices variables such that you have as much good information as possible before settling on a decision.

Beauty

A combination of qualities, such as shape, color, or form that pleases the aesthetic senses, especially the sight, comprises the concept of beauty. We have already addressed both aesthetics and art, but the concept of beauty itself is broad, applicable across a vast array of realms.

Beauty that is of such excellence or grandeur such that it inspires great admiration or awe is known as sublime, as in the case of Mozart's sublime piano concertos. Be able to discern that spectrum of beauty. Forms, substances, behaviors, persons, music, words, art, feelings...beauty touches upon nearly all walks of life, and even an aspect of death, as well. Identify the sublime: feel that awe and exhilaration. Create and bring about beauty in your own life.

Beginning

The point in time or space at which something starts is the beginning. THIS is the beginning of the sentence. Just as the baby is the beginning stages of a human journey upon the earth outside of the womb, beginnings are arrayed across the spectrum of growth: infants to toddlers, juveniles to young adults. Relationships, days, and jobs, among many other things, all have their respective starting points.

It is a simple concept, but here we are focusing on perceptual practices. Consider your next step, breath or the next time you blink (especially) as a new beginning. Approach your next activity as a stand-alone new beginning – a threshold to what follows. Nietzsche asked, "If you could have things all over again would you do anything different?" and " Do you want *this* again and again, times without number?" [3] I suggest a fresh perspective, an open-mind for your thoughts, feelings, words. Mind your actions, and start each beginning, anew.

A blink is meant to moisten your eye - it is a means of lubricating your eye so that it functions efficiently, given all of the work and activity it does. I was posed an interesting question some years ago and it changed how I thought. Consider every blink as an entry into an entirely new world, one that you are creating – you engage the world every time your eye opens, post-blink. That means that when you open your eye YOU are influencing, if not actively creating, the world around you - you are participating in the creation of the world as soon as you re-open your eye. Thinking of that creative role gives the act of blinking so much more dynamic vitality. Take your moments to heart, and engage creatively, passionately, with vigor! The world is a waste if it is all just the result of biological and chemical processes. You play a part, so play it responsibly, fully, and well!

Behavior

The ways in which humans, animals, or natural phenomena act or conduct themselves is called behavior. It is outward actions, and internal thoughts (because thought is an action, a 'do-ing'). Behavior can be social – between individuals, or within a group, like a crowd. In rhetoric, and by extension, (nearly) everything human: values underlie (nearly every) behavior. Humans are a special entity in that we utilize logic/reason, and we apply meaning. Behaviors showcase the values and meanings of the performer committing an act. That you read this demonstrates that you apply some significance to the deed. Breathing and passing gas do not necessarily denote meaning, but how one breathes, or passes gas, does. Commit to behaving in ways that showcase your quality and your values. Be aware of your actions, and how they speak to who you are. Also, be aware of how your behavior is affected by your associations - by your family, your friends, by crowds at sporting events, political rallies, or even while sitting as part of an audience at the movies.

Some behaviors are swayed quickly, affected by a larger group. Powerful energies of a larger group can move folks to behave in a variety of ways. While it does not necessarily need to be bad behavior, larger groups exert a powerful influence over the individual members of a group. If you perceive or sense that the group in which you find yourself does not reflect your values or ethics, it is most wise to extricate yourself and find a better group, one that represents you adequately. Be wise to the fact that you are judged by the company you keep. So while you may not behave similarly, that you are associated with them means you will be judged by others for their actions, as well. A similar phrase is "you are guilty by association." Simply, be mindful of your peers and group associations.

Belief

An acceptance that a statement is true, or that 'it' exists is a belief. Trust, faith, confidence in something or someone are forms of belief. Beliefs can either build and improve upon a condition, or they can serve as limiting, negative beliefs. Some beliefs are about what we call objective statements like those found in mathematics. 2+2=4 is generally recognized as a true statement because we generally accept similar values for the variables of '2', '+', '=' and '4'. Other statements are subjective. These subjective beliefs are based on or influenced by personal feelings, tastes, or opinions. Personal experience, the family, and larger cultural groups to which we belong, shape subjective beliefs. They include conclusions about God, death, beauty, and sports teams.

Beliefs comprise and shape character. Identifying core beliefs is how one embarks on a path of changing them and associated emotional reactions and behaviors. For example, Rachel believes that she is a good person. She recalls that she behaves well. She treats her peers honestly and fairly. She is kind. She has a perspective that is inclusive, and broadly experienced. Finally, Rachel *feels* that she is good. This last portion is key.

Emotions play a large role with beliefs. If you have a bad experience, emotions shape the belief that is formed afterwards. For example, when I was a very young child I went to a barbeque, and at one point I thought my parents had left me there. This terrified me, as I did not know what to do! The truth was that my parents had only moved the car so they could load it more efficiently. The facts did not match my beliefs. My parents did not leave me, and they did (and do) care and love me enough to remember me, and they reassured me of that fact. I had an emotional reaction to a belief that was not true. If I remained connected to that belief, I could have remained fearful, moving forward. Instead, facts demonstrated otherwise, and I was able to release that fear, because it was irrational, and proven to be false.

It is emotion that causes a great amount of misery. We can keep or drop an idea without any problem. Emotional attachments make ideas or beliefs that much more difficult to change. When changing a belief, one needs to change the corresponding emotion. Identity is part of a belief. If you engage negative, or limiting beliefs, your mind makes a movie, and runs a particular narrative comprised of negative/limiting beliefs. If you consider yourself a loser, for example, you give yourself an identity that is false - a distorted image based on one emotionally charged thought. It is a lie and we sometimes do not notice it. Our mind does not give proper credit to all of the past good behaviors and experience that demonstrate otherwise: that we are not, in fact, a loser. When we focus on these 'loser' moments (for example, a failed test, or a bad relationship), our memory calls on the 'loser' character to show up on our memory and our imagination.

In order to shed any limiting belief, one must change their identity, or at least the mind's false version of identity. One need change their emotional memories. Put in its place another sense of identity that you can associate with, instead. Shift your emotions and your belief by feeling good. Remember how you have good people in your life that love and value you - people that recognize your worth. Remember that you behave well, generally, and how you benefit from doing good deeds.

Some people utilize affirmations to dispel limiting beliefs. Feelings, thoughts, and words all have different power, or energy associated with them. With that in mind, it is a good idea to utilize the best energies to change your life. Remind yourself of your worth by feeling, thinking, speaking of the Good. Consider using affirmations that include the 'I AM _____' formula, with a positive adjective following the subject portion of the phrase. "I am <u>worthy</u>. I am <u>valuable</u>. I am <u>Loved</u>." You need not be limited, nor need you limit yourself or others. Remind yourself how limiting beliefs about others is a projection of your ego, and has consequences for yourself as well as for the person you are judging. Be mindful of your beliefs and manage them in a considerate fashion.

Belonging

Belonging refers to being in a place, environment, or group. Things can be belongings, rightly placed in a position, or group, or as a possession.

Humans are social animals – they want to be a part, or belong, to a group. They live in cities, as part of a community. Many belong to a family, as a part in a larger whole. An important aspect of belonging is having a grasp of your self. Recall the saying, 'Know Thyself'; it was the instruction carved over the threshold of the doorway of the Oracle at Delphi. When you are familiar with, and own your personal beliefs and values, you can readily identify groups or associations to which you belong.

When you hold yourself in high esteem, consider yourself to be of value, and worthy of respect, you will aspire to belong in associations that reflect and respond to those values and beliefs. Conversely, if you insist on maintaining limiting beliefs or negative values, you will gravitate to lesser groups that behave accordingly. The concept of resonance is pertinent here. Your ideas and beliefs will resonate with those that share that sentiment. Resonance speaks to the 'lasting effect' of a shared frequency, or power. Truth has a resonance. Satisfy your human urge to belong by associating with quality people, those whose values and beliefs match your own. Discover your own values and priorities by knowing yourself, through discernment, meditation, and introspection. Invest in yourself by engaging in meaningful work.

Benefit

An advantage, profit, or reward gained from something is a benefit. A benefit might also be a payment or a gift. What is the benefit of your actions, goals and desires? Make sure to align your aspirations with worthy benefits. This is important in that not all benefits serve your greatest needs. Every action has a goal as its posed benefit. This is also known as the means one employs to obtain a particular end. Consider if the ends are worthy ones, if they satisfy greater/higher ambitions, or if they address base/simple desires and pleasures.

Just because a benefit is perceived as available does not mean that its worth your attention or pursuit. The value of a perceived benefit will correlate with the particular beliefs of the perceiver. Be mindful of whether the benefit poses a short-term gain or long-term merit. What of the costs involved? Do the means require a large amount of resources? Put another way: do the ends justify the means? Conversely, again: do certain means justify ends? The investigation of values and beliefs involves discovery and identification of benefits with goals and ends. Consider perceived benefits and weigh them against consequences in order to marshal resources appropriately and well.

Betrayal

The breaking or violation of a contract, trust, or confidence that produces moral or psychological conflict within relationships between individuals, between organizations or between organizations and individuals is called betrayal. Betrayal typically means an exposure. That exposure could be to an enemy. An exposure - in this sense - is an act of deliberate disloyalty. Not all exposures have the same negative connotation, in that an exposure can be a revelation, or a discovery.

Betrayal

Throughout time, humanity has been influenced, if not marked, by an innumerable list of betrayals. Rulers have betrayed one another or their people. Lovers have betrayed their spouses. Businesses and organizational peers turn on one another regularly in order to pursue other benefits. You will encounter betrayal. In fact, you most likely have already been betrayed. You might be tempted to betray people in your own life.

This is a complex concept like so many others. You may be expendable to some who regard benefits elsewhere as outweighing your own trust and confidence. In order to protect yourself, provide quality by living a good life. Worthy people will recognize and seek that goodness you offer. The saying: 'like with like' applies here. Similar people will desire that same good character in their lives. Still, there might be the occasion for people to act impulsively and betray you regardless of whether you have done everything right. And that serves as the grounds for the afore-mentioned psychological conflict.

To be betrayed can hurt your head, your heart, and even pain you physically. Some betrayals result in injury if not death. Associate with good people. Insist on loyalty, trust and confidence shared between members of your groups and associations. Should a betrayal occur, they are exposing and demonstrating their own beliefs and values. You need choose if someone who betrays you is worth your continued presence in their life. Beware of those people who discard relationships easily, though also: do not offer yourself freely to people. Make certain that others honor and respect you. You can recognize that by seeing how well they treat themselves. If they can not respect and honor their own person, it is highly unlikely that they can, or will, respect others.

Sometimes there is no protection from betrayal. More often than not, it is sudden, unexpected, and it is these elements that cause the most hurt. When we trust and have confidence in a particular person and they act contrary to those expectations, it is a serious breach of the relationship. Imagine a ruler turning on the very people that elected them – the people they are supposed to serve and protect. Or, in a more intimate setting, what of the betraying spouse? When someone you are counting on to build a family and spend a lifetime with betrays the relationship, sometimes there is no solution save for ending the dynamic and moving on. Each betrayal, and relationship, for that matter, is very particular. Know yourself. Associate with good people. Be able to respond adequately. Have a contingency plan and act appropriately as variables come into play.

Beyond

Every human will reach their own end - meet with their demise. For as long as humans have walked the earth, they have been exploring what lies beyond life. Different cultures and philosophies have formulated ideas as to what happens objectively. It is the responsibility of every individual to come to terms with his or her own mortality. No one has any definite proof as to what exists after life, or if there is anything at all. But it is a human exercise to extrapolate and imagine – to ponder the possibilities of an existence after life. Just as with so many other concepts, it is wise to comprehend the spectrum of information that is available. But even with a thorough and exhaustive inquiry into the beyond, the result is only academic. No one has any grasp of the objective realm of an afterlife until they reach that point. The best preparation for the beyond is life well lived. In fact, Plato said that all life is spent in preparation for death.[4] Do not reach the end of your days and be wholly unprepared - racked with guilt or regrets, second-guessing your experience here on earth. In Tolstoy's novella, *The Death of Ivan Illytch,* the main character comes to terms with a life wasted, as he nears his death. He prioritized things - material gains and successes - instead of building a worthy character and quality relationships. He is piteously remorseful but something remarkable happens that eases his tortured head and heart. He understands the consequence of wasting his life, and grasps the lesson; he understands how he has wasted the experience and he then reconciles with death. We can not wait for an event that might make everything acceptable. Instead, living a full and worthy life prepares us for our passing.

Make the most of your time here. Develop your character by behaving well - be a good person. Build relationships; earn the friendships and favor of worthy, good people. Serve your fellow man by acting nobly, for the highest and best good of all involved. Make life meaningful. Travel, read, and do not let fear impede your growth and development. Make people's lives easier and leave this life in a better condition or state than when you entered it. Experience joy among all other available, beautiful sentiments. I hope life both delights and surprises you with its depth and mysteries. Live well and know that I believe in the good that is You.

Body

A body is a tangible, physical structure. It is the material contrast to the conceptual or abstract, in the case of the spirit/soul. Because it is material, the body is the self's most accessible means of manipulation and control. Cultural and physical means work to manipulate and control the body. It is advisable to treat your body well. The body houses 'You,' the abstract that is DCKF (reminder: DCKF is the author's daughter). It is the temple that houses the Goddess. Honor your own Godhood by nurturing and protecting that temple. Keep it healthy, functional, and strong. It will serve you as long as you care for it.

Keep in mind that the body is a means to a greater end. Your primary focus need not be on the aesthetic appeal, or the strength of the body. For you have much more to offer than simple corporeal substance. You are more than good looks, or a beautiful physique. Your body does not represent your totality. Beware of those that focus on that aspect of you, alone. Also, be mindful of those that try to use it to manipulate you. You are more than the sum of those simple body parts.

A term pertinent to this discussion is that of objectification. Our culture moves to manipulate both bodies and minds. By making objects of women, as a specific practice, men seek to control or even abuse women because they see them as inferior, as objects – not people. The same is true of men – they are objectified similarly, though not to the overwhelming extent that women are. It is important to be critically engaged in order to discern this trend, and the perspectives of those who employ it. You are not a beautiful object to be used or discarded at the whim of others. You are not a means of others' ends - *unless you volitionally accept that premise.* Respect your entire person. Honor your body; insist that others follow your example.

Culturally, you will note how institutions move to objectify women. The media presents images of women that are thin and fit, able to wear skimpy clothes and model their bodies. Overwhelmingly, media portrays women as objects of sexual desire, in lieu of capable, skilled, whole people. You need not comply with their suggestion. Consider the contrast! A one-dimensional woman, who focuses on but one of her facets - the physical body - does not compare with the woman who honors and respects herself by developing her entire character and greater skill set. A woman who can communicate, who can create meaning and apply significance to the experiences of her life, instead of working solely on her form, is someone who is truly attractive.

Boundaries

The limits of an area are its boundaries. They typically are physical, as in the cases of walls, fences, signs and other tangible constructs. They can be conceptual, as well. There are boundaries that exclude items, or limit ideas, such as the boundaries of a possible discussion. Regarding your own person, you need boundaries of acceptable behavior. These boundaries might pertain to your own body, or how you are treated. Different boundaries refer to different roles and relationships. Whether it is a relationship with friends, a boy or girlfriend, or between peers at work, clear boundaries define what is welcome behavior and distinguish them from unwelcome activity.

This concept pertains to control of You, or more specifically: self-ownership. While boundaries might be context specific, you need be vigilant as to how people behave with you. Be willing to trust and be open to people if and only if they respect you and your values. Do not let folks take advantage of you and be mindful that you do not fall victim to ploys or subterfuge. You are the ultimate authority as to what is acceptable. Realize that some do not care for your authority and they might use force or violence to press their intent. You need be able to substantiate your authority and self-ownership by protecting yourself. Communicate well with your hands, if need be, to ensure your safety and well-being.

You need not suffer due to the trespasses of others. You need merely say no, as the first display of your authority. Consider: some may not heed your voice. If someone then tries to control or endanger you with physicality, you need protect yourself, and demonstrate forcefully that you are in charge of your self, and your body.

You are allowed and encouraged to protect your person using anything at your disposal.

Be able to recognize the dangers or threats of a situation, using the afore-mentioned skill of situational awareness and take the necessary steps to avoid being vulnerable. You are allowed to levy considerable force and harm, up to and including death, upon those that utilize force or physicality to impose their will.

This is, again, a complex discussion, one that we address over the course of our martial arts training together.

Boys

A quick list about boys:
No boy is above you, or better than you, merely because they are a boy.
Boys are not bad, generally. Behavior showcases specific cases of quality.
Be aware of the influence of hormones.
Boys can not complete you, nor can you complete them. Beware of those who say otherwise.
Watch for kindness, awareness, compassion, and a cultured perspective.
Boys have insecurities, too.
Protect yourself. Minimize your vulnerability.
Do not let fear impede you. A little caution, though, works wonders.
Be kind, but not at the expense of your safety or self-respect.
Include me – let me help you with counsel from my own experience.

Breathing

One of the most important skills, though neglected or minimized, is that of breathing. Breathing is not as simple as inhaling and exhaling. A more disciplined approach connects your brain waves with your heartbeat, which facilitates greater results in meditation. This practice of yogic breathing is an ancient skill and most worthwhile.

Breath is most significant across time and a wide array of different cultures. The English word spirit comes from the Latin *spiritus* (breath). In the Hebrew, God's breath gives life. By their holy text, the Bible, the word refers to 'wind, breath, mind and spirit.' It is intimately connected with God, him/herself. Life force and holiness are aspects of breath and its importance is reflected across rituals and holy texts. Developing your breathing skills helps control and regulate your heart rate, generally. In specific times of stress and agitation, this is a very important ability. Given how prevalent stress is in this culture and society should motivate you to address it and achieve some level of mastery. That mastery speaks to still greater achievements, among them metaphysical ascension, according to some traditions.

In meditation, focused yogic breathing aids in the emergence and development of greater spirit. I recommend you being open to the possibility that investment in developing breathing skills is a worthwhile endeavor. Breathe Deeply!

"There is one way of breathing that is shameful and constricted. Then there is another way: a breath of love that takes you all the way to infinity." – **Rumi**

Chapter 3

Capable

Having the ability, fitness, or quality necessary to do a specific thing is known as being capable. Capable runs parallel to the term 'able.' Part of the rationale of offering this text – and serving as one of your parents - is to help you to be a capable human being. As mentioned previously, you will need to live your own life, and be on your own after your Mom and I pass. I entreat you to be self-sufficient and live by your own merits and abilities. By building an expansive skill set, you will be capable of navigating all of life's challenges and pleasures on your own.

I consider a list of capabilities as being comprised of the following elements:
A) Communicative efficacy - know how to communicate in different contexts with widely disparate audiences;
B.) being in possession of an open/teachable mind – remaining open to new possibilities and contrasting information or perspectives without being so dogmatic or closed due to your own experience or upbringing; and
C.) being resourceful – know how to find and critique information pertinent to building skill sets or accomplishing different goals. Truly, this last element is so very important. I consider many institutions to have the same responsibility. Schooling is not to teach you what to learn, but *how* to discover and 'play' with different modes of information. When you invest in yourself in this way, you will be better prepared for much of what life offers you.

As far as other elements on that capability list, I offer only general advice: make use of your head, heart and hands. Commit to worthwhile thoughts, meaningful feelings, and good behaviors. As another general guideline, expand your list of abilities such that you are not at a loss given extreme challenges or obstacles.

Caring

The provision of what is necessary for the health, welfare, maintenance and protection of someone or something is called caring. Your Mom and I, your siblings, your extended family, and also friends, and even some acquaintances care for you. Caring is an integral element of a functional community. Caring can take many forms. It can be physical, emotional, and even intellectual. A hug (or 12, daily!) demonstrates care. Sharing your enthusiasm, or even sadness shows that you care to let someone know and become familiar with your emotions, and is a special form of caring. Writing a note or extending a call to someone is an intellectual form, as it is sharing how the recipient is in your thoughts.

Caring is a component of belonging. It is an active process. Relationships thrive on continual caring. When care is withdrawn, a relationship deteriorates. Consider the act of gardening. If you do not water the plants, they will suffer, if not die. Extend care considerately. Do not offer it lightly, or falsely. As discussed earlier, everyone is on his or her own subjective journey. Care means a lot to *everyone*, save perhaps the hermit or specifically, the misanthrope (a hater of man).

Consider how most people want to belong, or be included. Eye contact (a wink!) can mean much to someone who is suffering under the weight of his or her own thoughts. Asking how someone is can be a rote practice, a means of commencing any typical transaction in passing. For example, you interact with people as you order food, sit in your classroom, or stand in any line. But instead of offering a "How are you?" as filler, use it authentically, as a bridge towards significant dialogue and learning. Do not offer the question unless you care, unless you want to connect. For all too often, people use it only as a means of getting to their own needs. A person and their time are not for your own usage. They have feelings, value, worth independent of your needs and wants. They deserve the same care and consideration that you expect, if not demand. This is not to say that you need care about everyone. But consider: opportunities become available as you extend or offer the best that is within you. When you care, you relay good energies, and are most likely to receive similar, in kind. Sometimes you are rebuffed with a negative response, but be aware how some people are not ready for, or desirous of caring. Strive to offer the good, and it will be exchanged with or provided for you.

Chakra

The Sanskrit word chakra translates to wheel, or disk. This term refers to wheels of energy throughout the body. While typically referred to as 6 or 7 in number, other practices and cultures identify a great many more. For the purposes of this discussion, we will focus on 7. Chakras are aligned along the spine. They are centers of energy. They are positioned from the end of the spine to about 2-3 inches above the crown of the head. Each of the seven chakras contain bundles of nerves and organs and present the condition of psychological, emotional and spiritual states of being. It is very important to care for your chakras such that they remain open and flowing. Blockages denote imbalances. Chakras denote the connection between spirit, body, and mind. Awareness plays a large role in their maintenance. If you can connect events of your life affecting you emotionally, you can pinpoint the symptoms as they manifest in your body as an affected chakra. Chakras are either pertaining to matter, to the connection between matter and spirit, or to spirit, solely. The first through third chakras are chakras of matter, the fourth pertains to the connection between matter and spirit, while the fifth through seventh pertain to the spirit.

The first chakra is the root chakra. It is the chakra of stability, security, and our basic needs. It covers the first three vertebrae, the bladder, and the colon. When this chakra is open, we feel safe and secure if not fearless. The second chakra is the splenic chakra, and it honors the creative aspect in each of us. It is above the pubic bone but below the navel. It is responsible for our creative expressions. The third chakra is the solar plexus. It covers from the navel to the breastbone. It honors the life force and is our source of personal willpower. The fourth chakra is located at the heart center. It is the middle of the seven and connects the lower with the higher. It is a bridge between our body, mind, emotions, and spirit. This chakra is our source of love and connection. The fifth chakra is the area of the throat, and includes the neck, thyroid, parathyroid glands, jaw, tongue and mouth. It is our source of verbal expression, and the ability to speak the highest truth. The sixth chakra is located between the eyebrows. It is referred to as the third eye. It is our center of intuition. The seventh chakra is located at the crown of the head. This is the chakra of enlightenment, and pertains to our spiritual connection to our higher selves and to the divine.

The most basic form of maintaining your chakras is meditation and/or visualizations. Managing your energy centers requires working with good energies. Spend time in the morning, as you rise from sleep and in the evening, just before you retire, in a comfortable position, meditating. This will affect your entire life. I can not recommend it enough. You will find that purity and purification will be crucial, if not very influential to your health, and the flow and balance of your chakras. A dedicated and diligent practice of maintaining your chakras will then address your thoughts, your food and diet, your friends, and principles you hold most dear. If you decide to prioritize your energetic and spiritual health, you will structure your life around values that facilitate your continual growth and development.

Chance

A possibility of something happening, absent of any design, is called chance. There are no certainties in life. You are not guaranteed that the sun will even rise tomorrow (read and grapple with the words of David Hume). Every strategy is a gamble - every initiative in this life has risk. The best we can all do is survey the available information to make the best possible decisions with what resources are available. Much of this life is left to chance, though that is not the worst possible structure of variables. It helps us take care of ourselves and develops character and courage. It is best to leave as little to chance as possible. But every day will offer a new challenge, or the unforeseen 'curveball.' It is chance that delivers much of the color and joy to life. If everything were routine, we would not be given the opportunity to grow and develop our personhood. Humans are, by nature, risk takers. The presence of risk gives us the opportunity to showcase our worth, and our character. Accept what is offered – TAKE RISKS! – and grow with each opportunity.

Character

The mental and moral quality distinctive to an individual is what is known as character. It implies attributes including the presence, or lack thereof, of such virtues including empathy, courage, fortitude, honesty, and loyalty. Character may also refer to good behavior or habits. Character is a set of qualities that distinguish one individual from another. It is a result of, and shaped by, experience. It is an old question whether people are born with qualities - if characteristics are innate: a result of genes, among other causes – or if traits are shaped by experience alone. Some mothers convey how they can discern certain traits while their baby remains in utero. That specific discussion is extraneous for the purposes of this entry. The key aspect of character, here, is that of being a developmental process requiring investment and work.

Character distinguishes one from others of the same culture or group. While as a species (also between species, for that matter) there is an amazing overlap of DNA/genetics, learned traits separate us. Some are of strong moral character. Others give in to temptations, or do not bother to inquire, much less behave, ethically and, thankfully, there are precious few who revel in behaving amorally, regardless of the consequences they elicit.

It is important to establish your own unique set of character traits. And along those lines, it is especially significant that you develop worthy character. Unfortunately, a significant portion of our culture and media provides a lot of attention to lesser skills and traits. This is done to promote viewership, ratings and profits for TV programming, but in a greater sense: their emphasis on these characteristics promotes these behaviors, much to the detriment of those who give such behavior their attention and viewership. People follow the example of others. When poor or lesser behaviors are presented, the likelihood is that people will follow suit. This begs the question as to why a culture would allow the presentation or the modeling of behaviors that are not contributing to the betterment of the society or its people. Again, values underlie these behaviors. That bad/lesser behaviors are so prevalent in today's media means that these are, in fact, valued to some extent in our society.

Different religions, cultures, institutions, families, and other assorted groups instill and teach character elements that are deemed worthy or acceptable for their own purposes. That spectrum will vary according to context, but it is recommended that you pursue virtue in lieu of vice. Despite the cultural inclination to praise or glorify the baser levels of behavior, developing higher ambitions will serve you over the longer run. Those pursuing lesser skills, behaviors and values will find their own kind; an applicable saying is 'water finds its own level.' You are better with virtue in your life, and people who recognize the same value in the pursuit of virtue and a refined quality. Develop the good in you by pursuing and keeping worthy company. Shape and build strong, good character.

John Wooden said, "The true test of a man's character is what he does when no one is watching." When you are alone, you demonstrate your worth. Resist the lesser inclinations to be lazy or to engage vices. Immoral or wicked behavior is not something to promote or to be proud of. You have tremendous good in you and it is your own responsibility to bring it to the fore by engaging good habits and building for yourself a worthy character. Along the lines of how behaviors influence others, some maintain that all behavior is rhetorical, or persuasive. The philosopher Aristotle identified 3 essential elements of character that deliver a successful persuasive entreaty.[5] They are ethos, logos and pathos. The first term is that of character itself, something also defined as the result of habitation. You develop good character by participating in good habits. Logos is the second word, and it refers here to logical *reason*. Your argument must consist of solid logic and provide firm evidence to convince an audience as to your case. Finally, pathos refers to the emotions. A speaker must prepare the audience by putting them in a proper emotional state. While you need not focus on persuading folks with every waking moment, the point is that a solid portion of your behavior will have a persuasive facet. Utilizing good character, solid reasoning, and proper emotional support will not only convince others as to your quality, but you will earn like-minded associates and friends. Finding the balance of these elements is a formula that is most dynamic: very fluid given the contexts of social interaction. However, you character is *always* on display, and it is your opportunity and responsibility to present the level you want others to recognize.

Charity

The voluntary giving of help to those in need is called charity. While there are institutions established to aid the less fortunate, I beseech you to adhere to the words of Mahatma Gandhi, who said, "Be the change you wish to see in the world." Aid the less fortunate. Help the elderly. Look out for or defend those who are defenseless. Consider aiding an elder as they cross the street. Help as you are able. If you see someone struggling, help to make that moment, or their life, easier. Something to keep in mind, though, is how you can not fix someone else's house until your own is in order. Now, this is particular advice. For example, if you can give someone a lift to the store if you are heading in the same direction, you might do so. Sometimes, though, the cost of providing aid is prohibitive.

Sometimes you may only have the resources for your own use. It is important to recognize if and how you can help. It is no use rescuing a drowning person when the cost of their rescue is your own harm or death. Your aid should not be at the expense of your own well-being. For some people, there is no sufficient aid. Many will continue to make bad decisions, or forever be in need. You must not waste your resources offering resources to those whose condition will not be bettered. Perhaps your provision of material goods will not allay their own underlining condition, and instead result in an unnecessary loss of your own resources. While it is important to assist others, your ultimate responsibility is to your own well-being, and that of your family or close inner circle. It is painful to witness suffering and some states or conditions of people or greater: peoples. But it can amount to a grave error to try and save the world or cure myriad ills. Some woes are necessary ones. Do what you can, with what you have and make sure the costs involved do not outweigh the benefit of the deed.

Choice

Choice consists of selecting between options. A key element of choice is awareness. An awareness of alternatives provides real choice. A selection between merely two options is a dilemma. When you get to a point where you must decide between limited options is when you need carefully discern whether those are the only selections possible. To ensure the possibility of choice, space must be made for visible options. Make certain that you create the means of ensuring options. When you encounter situations where you are forced to select between limited, if not bad, variables is when you 'choose between the lesser of two evils.' But settling on an 'evil' option is no sort of real solution.

Decisions take time to make. They require deliberation – proper, measured thoughts. Make certain you provide enough time to allow for the discovery of pertinent variables. As relayed earlier, identify the most information possible about the situation. Using what information is available, you can distinguish a viable plan of action. Making use of time and information provides a greater likelihood of the availability of an array of choices. Conversely, flippant decisions made with no time afford very little as far as real choices. Do not operate by choosing when you are between the proverbial rock and a hard place. Afford yourself the means of selecting between worthy options and do your best to make good decisions with your life.

Cleanliness

'Cleanliness is next to godliness' is an old saying, yet still applicable today. The condition of being clean makes a difference as to health and social circumstances and its importance should not be underestimated. Making a clean home, comprised of clean pets, kitchen, bathroom, bedsheets, clothes, PEOPLE, etc. helps minimize the presence of bacteria and the greater likelihood of infection or sickness. When you or your material goods are clean, others take notice. The response is a pleasant one, when someone beholds with pleasure good hygiene, including clean teeth, your clean home, or a pleasant scent. When the public notices the opposite...! The response to the unclean can have consequences. Whether it is a special relationship, a job setting, or whatever else as far as social interaction goes, cleanliness reflects and establishes your reputation. Maintaining cleanliness is an important behavior, both for self and for others. Demonstrate your self-respect and, moreover, your confidence and self-esteem by being clean and insisting on cleanliness in your life.

Closure

Closure is a sense of resolution, or conclusion. Closure is a necessary component of ALL activities, for if you are not yet 'done' with something, it is difficult to proceed to the next activity or stage in your life. Closure is generally a firm answer as opposed to an ambiguous sentiment. It is a centered presence in the Now, whereas regrets, guilt, or second-guesses allude to unresolved issues with the past and with what-was. It is important to have a finale with relationships, activities, and projects. You need proceed with your life. Attachments to the past, or to things that no longer serve you, need be eliminated such that you can take your next steps.

Make certain to be present, unobstructed, unfettered by the elements, memories, and issues of the past. By making the best decisions you can, you will live a life that is deliberate, even-keeled and mature. By planning for the future, you can allow for closure with those variables of the past. It is only by achieving closure that you can be ready for new experiences. Clear your plate of what has past, so you can prepare for your next course.

Comfort

The physical ease from pain or constraint is known as comfort. It is an alleviation of emotional ills including grief, stress, or general malady. Despite comfort being a general good, it has a contrasting aspect. Comfort can retard or impede other growth and development. For some people prefer the condition of comfort to the difficulties or perceived hardship of introspection and development. Change and growth is the result of a pressing sensation, the feeling that development or something different permeates the scene, or the person. Whether it is a psychological urge or a material discomfort, a challenge invites or motivates the individual to change. This healthy drive is always stimulated by discomfort. The philosopher Soren Kierkegaard spoke to how one would proceed through achievements, and end at a plateau after the satisfaction of each goal. Man's sense of anxiety or dread - balanced or even opposed by freedom - motivates individuals to aspire still higher.[6] His rationale being that man *must* continually grow, ascend, and develop.

An individual's character is shaped by work, and that work is sometimes very difficult, but exercise makes a body stronger. We can not develop in a worthwhile fashion if not for discomfort and pressing onwards. Comfort delivers but a temporary repose. Be aware that it can be stagnating if total and complete. This does not mean that you need eschew comfort in order to grow. The life of an ascetic is not meant for all of us! But as with so many other concepts, enjoy comfort in moderation. Let it not impede your growth and development. This is particularly applicable to job positions and even relationships. Some comfort is enjoyable, but to the extremes only serves as a possible deterrent to meaningful development.

Communication

Communication is an exchange of mutually agreed upon meanings and symbols. Humans communicate with every action, for as we discussed earlier: values underlie behavior. Communication thus has a very important role in nearly every single social interaction. Some key elements of the communicative practice include preparation, self-knowledge, respect, openness, breath, patience, timing, release, confrontation and practice.

In order to ensure a successful communicative transaction, one need be prepared. Speakers need to be able to identify their own goals or aims. They need be ready to compromise, as the needs and wants of their fellow interlocutors are worthy and valuable in a dynamic, as well. They need have a grasp of self-knowledge and a sense of respect for their counterpart, as well. They need be able to recognize the other's perspective and find a way to include it, given its relative merit. For one need not make way for an aggressive, disrespectful, or an inappropriate point of view.

Communication is very particular. Willingness to engage, or even disengage, given success or cues, is an important component of communication. While maintenance of breath may be seen as an obvious facet of all activities, its presence in communication is also very important. Measured, even breath is a portion of a balanced approach to any communicative endeavor. Take your time: exert self-control by breathing in deep, regular intervals. This goes hand in hand with patience. Do not rush to realize your own goals when communicating with others. Communication is an exchange that requires time and presence.

Communication is an art. Meaningful effort is necessary; if something is worth doing, it is worth doing well.

Communication serves as a release, and it contributes to health. While there are some who eschew human interaction, a greater number of folks embrace it. It is that sharing between individuals that is a release for what is held inside. Some of those internal thoughts and feelings can be far from pleasant. Confrontation is not necessarily pleasant, nor comfortable, but it helps elicit understanding. When someone takes the opportunity to share those passionate thoughts and feelings, they are imparting their own meanings and significance to an exchange. People need to be heard (given they have something truly meaningful to offer), and, generally, they wish to be understood. With practice, you will be able to distinguish respectful, and efficient communicators – those who want to achieve a goal via inclusive methodologies and clear terms. As in the case of writing, speak and communicate such that you can not be misunderstood. When, and if a misunderstanding occurs, find the means to clarify in order to successfully realize your objectives and connect with other people.

Compassion

Compassion is a concern for others. This connects with the afore-mentioned concept of charity. Compassion for others must not detract from your own self-care; it need not exclude your own self-maintenance. You need not sacrifice your true self as you try to care for another. This is particularly poignant when it comes to relationships. You need always make certain, or ensure that you are respected and valued in a relationship. Do not let people take advantage of your compassion.

Concentration

Concentration is the action (or power!) of <u>focusing</u> one's attention or mental effort. Concentration is focused power. You get results when you develop this skill. It is not an automatic human ability. There are different levels of concentration. Amazing gifts, if not power(s) result from practice. There are individuals that can withstand freezing temperatures, levitate, communicate using their thoughts (telepathy), move objects with their minds (telekinesis), set fire to objects (pyro-kinesis), and make use of other skills simply by using this highly developed skill. These are not typical skills that are taught by the public education system, especially here in the United States. Some of these skills and powers are, in fact, a part of education systems elsewhere. Some communities and cultures want their people to have these real abilities developed and put to good use. These skills are the result of specialized instruction and diligent, prolonged effort. Even beyond the concentration needed to do your homework, or navigate a treacherous trail as you are hiking, a properly trained and concentrated mind is an amazing resource. Develop that skill and harness your own powers and greatest abilities, and then put them to good uses for yourself, and your community!

Confidence

A firm trust, or self-assurance is confidence. It, too, is the result of work and applied effort. Without that work, it is empty bravado or arrogance. One's confidence is demonstrated in the ability to perform a skill, or by how one's words match their deeds. It is not enough to say one is skilled, they must demonstrate as much. Confidence comes from *feelings* of well-being, acceptance of your body, mind and the belief in your own ability, skills, and experience.

Plan and prepare for experience. Build a skill set and apply it. Learning and research broadens that foundation of abilities and helps us to feel more confident about our ability to handle situations, roles and tasks. Positive thoughts are also a very powerful means of improving confidence. Helen Keller said, "Optimism is the faith that leads to achievement. Nothing can be done without hope or confidence." Highlight your strengths and learn from your weaknesses, and your mistakes. Use your mistakes as learning opportunities to help your growth and development. Limit negative or limiting thoughts as they are damaging to confidence and the ability to achieve goals. Generally, stay cheerful and have a positive outlook on life.

Vince Lombardi said, "Confidence is contagious. So is lack of confidence." Confidence is one of the main characteristics of charisma and people are attracted to confident people. Seek out knowledgeable opinion and have contact with those who are solid role models. Speaking with and associating with people who are confident will help you to feel and be more confident. As you grow, be sure to return the favor and serve as a role model or mentor to someone else. Experience delivers results, so achieve goals, tasks and obligations to build your confidence. Break these tasks and roles down into smaller, manageable goals. Realizing those goals and objectives builds confidence.

Stand up for what you believe in and maintain your principles. As you develop, you will gain experience and abilities. You will discover and implement principles that inform and guide your actions. Keep virtue in mind and be consistent with their application. You can change your mind if you believe it is the right thing to do, but you need not change it because you are under pressure from someone else. Usually people become more naturally assertive as they develop their confidence. Lastly, remain humble. Arrogance is detrimental to interpersonal relationships. Avoid feeling or acting as if you are superior to others. Nobody is perfect and there is always more to learn. Be open to those opportunities and seek to develop your character. Also, be willing to laugh at yourself! When you make mistakes – and we ALL make mistakes – sometimes the best response is easy laughter. Strive to keep learning and growing. Your confidence will develop as a necessary component of that process

Conscience

The inner voice or feeling as a guide to the rightness or wrongness of one's behavior is conscience. It is important for one to recognize and distinguish between virtues and vices, between right and wrong actions. This is a lifelong practice, and is very contextually based! A sense of ethics and morality is necessary and an educated and knowledgeable opinion about that realm is even better. An intelligent grasp of the concepts of ethics and morality guide and inform as to the complexities of life. Having an understanding of right and wrong between cultures, institutions and individuals is most certainly a good thing.

Your inner self is solely your own. It is most important to listen to your conscience as it is the disembodied voice of your own values and principles. It is there for your own protection and well-being. It speaks to everything you do, regardless of whether you are in the company of others or not. Conscience both contrasts and coincides with intuition. The former is comprised by experience, whereas intuition is an innate feeling. They are very related. Conscience is formatted upon one's experience with the world, and intuition colors all experience. Simply, it is worthwhile to guide your conscience by examining the variables and contexts involved in the realms of ethics and morality. Feed your curiosity of the world by being open and seeking out information by which to make educated, good decisions. Realize that morality is not so clear: not so cut and dried as yes or no, and/or even black and white. The spectrum between the extremes of right and wrong is a very colorful one and it is a worthy subject to examine.

Counsel

Formal advice is counsel. It is the application of knowledgeable opinion. As you proceed through life, you will want worthwhile advice from experienced opinion. Seek those that are worthy. Make certain they have real life experience to make use of, for not all opinions are equal. Make use of the good perspectives and opinions. Intuition, meditation, and prayer can guide you. When offering counsel, make certain you are contributing something worthwhile, for it is bad form to offer inconsequential or non-substantial material when someone has a dilemma and needs help.

Consequence

Consequence is a result or an effect of an action or condition. It also refers to the importance or relevance of an event, like, "that information is of no consequence." A consequence is not necessarily a bad thing. More so, it is a result of *any* cause. It is something that follows from something else. There are both intended and unintended consequences. The former are those you want to see occur, while the latter are unforeseen, or unanticipated. The concept of chance overlaps with consequence. Despite being prepared for an event, role, or task, unintended consequences can and do occur. There is only so much preparation and foresight available, and some consequences arise seemingly *ex nihilo* (Latin for: from nothing). The best anyone can do is prepare for the worst and hope for the best.

Continue

To continue is to persist through interruption. Some activities are better suited for continuation, while others do not deserve the persistence. Consider whether the ends or goals are attainable. In some cases, we must discontinue plans, dreams and even relationships. There might be a cut-off, or point of termination for pursuits that are greatly desired. Gauge and analyze the likelihood of success for all endeavors and engage those pursuits you can actually achieve. Otherwise, the participation in or the pursuit of unrealistic aims amounts to folly, and is called a fool's errand. Make proper use of your time, energy, head, heart and hands such that you pursue viable aims. Continue pursuing those until you realize their ultimate success! I believe in You!

Control

The power to influence or direct people's behavior or the course of events is what is known as control. It is most important to recognize who wields external control, and if your own person is practicing self-control. An authority is always posed, either formally or informally. It can be in the form of government, a police officer, or a boss. Informal authorities can be God, or even a bully at school. One differs from the other (formal v. informal) as far as the public acknowledgement or recognition.

Regarding external control, identify who does what kind of controlling behavior. Ascertain whether that control is onerous and unnecessary or if it actually serves your own self-interest. Just because someone or something is in control does not make it right. Control and authority are dynamic, fluid. Be ready to contest control and power. When external control/authority exerts undue influence, it is your responsibility to confront, oppose, or shed it. Your life is your own. You need not be oppressed or have your rights trespassed. As far as self-control, act in moderation; again: you need not live as a harsh ascetic – consider the total spectrum of behaviors. Exercising restraint and keeping your composure is a sign of self-ownership, a portion of self-mastery. It is imperative that you serve as your own master and authority, else someone or something (consider vices) can only too willingly move to exert power and influence upon you and yours.

Courage

The ability and willingness to perform or act in the face of fear, danger, pain, or grief is courage. Along with prudence, justice, and temperance, courage is a cardinal virtue. It is a virtue necessary to living a good life. It takes many forms.

It takes courage to:
- do what is right
- to face a personal fear
- to be unpopular
- to tell the truth
- to trust
- to Love
- to persevere through pain, or hardship
- to change
- to act
- to commit

It takes courage to do a great many other things, too ...

> It means doing what we know we need to do for the sake of a good deed, or, using a longer perspective, in order to live a good life.

> Recognize that living courageously is a worthy pursuit. It can be very uncomfortable, as courage is in opposition to difficult tasks, people, and events. Take heart! When you act courageously, you empower others to do the same. It is a necessary component of your community, for if the members shrink from the responsibility, or shirk the opportunity, the proverbial wolves get the sheep and win the day. Instead, the day can be won by the courageous! Be in that number of sheepdogs who guard the

community and keep watch over the sheep. Rise to the challenge: be courageous and do the right thing!

Cosmos

The cosmos is the world and beyond! – the universe regarded as an orderly and harmonious system. Some of man's most pertinent philosophical investigations concern both the subjective and objective purpose and place of man in the world and beyond. Namely, people ask: "What is my place, and what is man's place in the cosmos?" The cosmos covers reality, more orless.This covers our own planet, solar system, through the Milky Way Galaxy as a part of 50 or 100 BILLION (!!!) other galaxies in the universe.

Perspective is very important in this life. Thoughts about context, timing, and scale provide structure to our perspective. Keep in mind that your faculties – your perspective, your lenses, your greater person – have a much greater significance than the accidents connected to a sense of fashion, the judgments of your peers, how well you scored on a recent test, to whether you will be married, have kids, and achieve success, or greater human fulfillment. All that said, our planet is a tiny,

...miniscule...

speck in a void of interplanetary space. This sun is but one of a hundred billion other stars in the galaxy. That we are but this one fraction of the cosmos that is nearly incomprehensible, human concerns are almost trite and superficial when compared with the greatest of backgrounds.

We are wise to remain humble in the face of this enormous reality. "I assert that if you were depressed after learning and being exposed to this perspective," says the astrophysicist Neil deGrasse Tyson, "you started your day with an unjustifiably large ego."

Worry not! Consider your amazing relevance in the scheme of the cosmos. Carl Sagan, from his book, *Cosmos*: "…the nitrogen in our DNA, the calcium in our teeth, the iron in our blood, the carbon in our apple pies are made in the interiors of collapsing stars. We are made of starstuff."[7]

The provided definition features the term, 'harmonious.' This refers to a pleasing or congruous whole. Given your willingness to explore this particular concept of the cosmos, you will encounter, if not become familiar with, the aspect of order, ratios, math, scale, and even music. The wonders of the stars are present in the neuro-synapses of the brain, or even in the splitting of the cell during mitosis. The more you study, the more the cosmos unfolds, delivering startling beauty and even more profound mysteries. You need not be depressed with the occurrences in your life. Look to the stars and take comfort that you are comprised of out-of-this-world stuff! Truly, you ARE a Goddess of the Heavens!

Craft

A craft is an art, trade, or occupation requiring a special manual skill. Along the same lines of the discussion of beauty, art or aesthetics, I advise you to develop your own special craft. Your Mom is a talented cook, and is quite crafty, generally. She is an adept seamstress, and she can be considered an artist, of sorts. Develop a specialty that brings you happiness if not greater joy! I enjoy word-craft and martial arts; writing and my physical skills get to the core of my creative being and they differentiate me from others. While you may be skilled at sports, seek out still other distinguishing activities that establish your person as unique in the field. You are a special individual. Showcase your character and shine like no one else!

Create

To create is to cause to come into being as something unique that would not naturally evolve, or that is not made by ordinary processes. Every person is a creator, or poet (the word poet means creator, and it comes from the Greek, *poetais*). While we can procreate to make babies, the activity itself is only biologically based…simpler animals do the same, based on evolutionary necessity, or genetic diversity. But to create as humans is akin to taking of the divine. We *can* attribute significance to procreation; a couple *is* attempting to bring about the best possible genetic combination and elicit an angel. But aside from procreation, creation speaks to birthing those things that animals can not. It is an activity that connects us with our highest aspects of humanity. It motivates us to write sonnets and symphonies among so many other notable products like architecture, technology, etc.

Contribute to our human heritage and bring about something noteworthy with your own creative power.

Credibility

The quality of being believable or worthy of trust is credibility. Credibility is established when someone is routinely *believed*. It is acknowledged when the speaker's words match their deeds. Being credible is a matter of convincing or being able to be believed. So, ethical behavior need *not* be an element of credibility. A person can lie and still be regarded as a believable source. It is how fraudulent individuals, confidence men, and even some salesmen have established themselves. Their use of logos, ethos and pathos affects their audience, despite the fact that virtue, or truth, may be lacking from their greater presentation. Be mindful of the possibility that just because a credible source offers information does not mean that they are right or truthful. A person can have an established reputation of credibility over many years despite the fact that they offered untrue or biased information. It is very important to be critical as to information and all speakers, generally.

Critical

To be skilled in criticism, or to exercise skillful judgment as to truth or merit, is what is known as being critical. It is in your own interest to be critical of every speaker, and every form of information. People take initiative to further their own ends. Those goals may or may not have your own interests in mind. Parents, and family members – generally – have your well-being in mind but there are exceptions to every rule. This is not meant to make you suspicious of everyone or everything. But the more you can adopt a critical perspective, the less vulnerable you will be. As you engage or critique speakers, or media, keep the following questions in mind:
-Who is the speaker or the entity offering the information?

-How does the speaker stand to benefit or gain from successfully persuading their audience? Who benefits?
-Who has hired this speaker? Who is funding the production and advancing this particular message?
-What is being offered? What is the message, product, or purpose of this rhetorical appeal?
-Does this make sense? Does this oppose, or run contrary to other speakers, or information you have encountered?
-Is this moral or ethical? Do the values of the speaker match your own values and principles?
-What is omitted? What is not being said, what is left out of the message?
-Who might suffer, lose, or otherwise be negatively affected because of this message?
-What is affected by this message, and for how long?
-Is this an inclusive enterprise? Who is excluded, and why?
-Is this a transparent and simple endeavor?
-How many people, entities, or institutions are involved?
-How is money involved?
-Is justice served, or present in this activity?
-Is this for the highest and best good for all involved? Are there superior alternatives to the activity proposed?
-What realms are affected: social, economic, or environmental? Are other realms or spheres affected?

Many folks consider being critical as a negative character trait. They liken being critical to being a 'negative Nancy.' Some people do not appreciate different, much less contrasting, opinions. Never shy away from asking questions of speakers, institutions, or media. Engage and look deeper into things. Truly, gold and treasures are almost always hidden away, buried under layers! They require some digging – some work – to achieve worthy, considerable results.

"I have no respect for a man who Googles himself." –
Abraham Lincoln, Gettysburg Address

Culture

Culture, a system of beliefs and a set of behaviors characteristic of a particular group, is one of the broadest concepts to discuss. In lieu of attempting to cover its totality, we err on the side of brevity, and restrain our focus. A general discussion of culture precedes a segment concerning cultural vitality and longevity as our central focus, before concluding with an entreaty to engage, and participate with culture actively, critically.

Cultural concepts, like these featured in this text, structure how people live their lives from birth to death. Different principles and beliefs give rise to different ways of living. For example, a culture allows for choice regarding whether a baby is kept or not. What is eaten, and how (forks, chopsticks, or perhaps via hand) is decided by culture. Culture allows for choice when selecting a marriage partner or facilitates pre-arranged transactions. It demarcates who can show their face in society or whether cultural participants can decide as to their own sexual preferences. Culture decides whether or not front doors are locked at night. It also controls and manages nonverbal behavior; it establishes how people smile, how they stand, and also the etiquette of bodily noises and releasing gas. Culture also has a temporal element. As it pertains to *all* groups, it has been important since the first human associations, or collectives.

Culture is significant for how it reinforces dominant values and norms. Social norms, or what comprises acceptable behavior, are demonstrated, modeled, and reinforced *everywhere*. The model is overwhelmingly consistent, echoed among social institutions including media, arts and entertainment, business/finance/economics, education, religion, government, and the people serve as a reinforcing institution, too! Additionally, these realms are arranged in different ways through time and space. The ancient Egyptians, Greeks, and Spartans addressed components of their culture and structured their own particular human products via similar institutions but utilized quite disparate methodologies. The same holds true today: social institutions mold the constituency to live according to communal values and norms.

Importantly, culture is *relationship*. It addresses how you relate with your own person, with others in the same community, and with the wider world. All significant relationships require attention, investment, and work if they are to develop and improve. As culture encompasses and pertains to so many diverse concepts, we need pay special attention and work to improve it. Our relationship with culture: as cultural participants, and perhaps also as cultural creators, can only be healthy with diligent investment.

A culture's health, or vitality, concerns the condition, or quality of its people. A culture is only as good as its constituency. The longevity of a culture – or how long a culture lasts, or persists in time – is predicated, in part, by how well the people coordinate. History demonstrates how cultures that facilitate volitional enterprise are certainly better received, but also last longer than those regimes that compel association via threats or oppression. People want to coordinate voluntarily instead of being coerced to do so. A culture's health, then, is based also on how well people voluntarily participate in the community.

Voluntary, critical engagement as a cultural norm is important because the people are the operative force of the culture. By contrast, passive engagement, which aptly characterizes our own present day culture, elicits a spectrum of unnecessary factors including heteronomous, or external, applied authority, war, and emphases on scarcity, and aggression. The relationship between a people and its culture need be actively engaged, else the culture subsumes the people; conventions rule agents – cultural components steer the people, instead of the other way around! Critical cultural engagement makes culture an instrument of the people, whereas passive consumptive culture delivers the reigns of culture – the many heads of the hydra: the social institutions – to external, and not necessarily benevolent or even positive interests. It is most apparent that we are not guided, led, nor represented by the wise, for that matter. This is a result of our passive cultural engagement. We settle for inferior modes and methodologies, as far as cultural conventions, in lieu of mastering culture.

When people manage their own culture, they operate with their own subjective and collective interests in mind. Conversely, when external authority manages the culture, the people are utilized as means to ends. The culture, and cultural leadership, uses the constituents as human resources. Culture serves as a positive, inclusive group if cultural participants are critically engaged as a cultural practice, or norm. Three things that ensure the vitality of the culture include structuring learning as a cultural norm, interacting with others, and providing assistance to fellow community members in need.

In order for a culture to have health, or vitality, its participants need to know and be aware of factors that influence their lives. An understanding of pertinent systems of culture, like its particular social institutions, enables cultural participants to engage adroitly. For knowledge increases options, and facilitates access to a fuller spectrum of available activities. Being informed as to how a culture treats truth, expression, business, or the specific material aspect of earning a living, education, and the presence, and use of power in myriad forms is very important. All of these realms have significant consequences for *any* cultural participant, for most, if not all cultures, coordinate the management, shaping of their constituents by these, or similar institutions. Hence structuring positive behavior, like learning/critical engagement as a social norm, has tremendous impact. For learning improves the learner, and, by extension, improves the community of which he/she is a part. In Plato's Republic, the philosopher identified how the condition of the individual parallels the condition of the state. The implementation and reinforcement of inclusive, beneficial activities serves the individual and the culture. So fostering the opportunity for the development of the individual directly via situating learning as a cultural norm improves the condition or quality of the group.

An aware, engaged, and knowledgeable populace serves the larger culture: the community is comprised of those who strive to improve as a cultural standard, or social norm. Such a practice allows the participants to make decisions born of good information. Imagine enjoying the benefits elicited by the guidance, leadership, and representation of the virtuous or the wise! Experience, elicited by awareness and knowledge as foundational components of culture, benefits the greater collective. Constituents would recognize consequential situations in which they are involved, and then discern, arrange, and order those elements that are applicable. Social norms that impart or facilitate a knowledgeable awareness create a consistent if not impressive standard of intellectual ability within the culture. Learning facilitates knowledge and awareness and makes possible understanding, intelligence, and even wisdom. Structuring a social norm of learning enriches the culture and maintains it as a positive, inclusive group.

Another important methodology that maintains a culture as a positive, inclusive social group is interacting with others. It is the crucial component that undergirds our society, as communication among constituents gives rise to shared, communal values. Learning or critical engagement, as a social norm, works only so far. Lacking the interactive or the communicative element, constituents are isolated and culture fractures. Interaction among peers connects and bridges the divide of subjectivity with the goal of building and reinforcing community in mind. Learned, aware people who communicate create those aspects or values that undergird the culture. This active element is such a remarkable contrast to those cultural platforms that peddle values and norms for the passive consumption of the people. The Catholic Church is an example of an organization that is hierarchically structured and offers only top-down directives for its adherents. Fascist, totalitarian regimes, like Italy or Germany in World War II, are examples of similar non-inclusive, non-derivative cultures, as well.

Interacting with community members elicits perception checking, a necessary portion of being-in-the-world and living as a member of the community. Perception checking occurs when ideas or ethos is contrasted with alternatives. It generally improves the level of discourse by including not only more data but also perspective and information that is disparate and likely to add greater amounts of substance, by virtue of it being different: outside of the subjective box, or a cultural echo chamber. For example, take into consideration the idea of a contrast of cultures. Differentiating between our culture and that of Ancient Egypt, Greece, Persia, and Sparta, one notes how the social values, norms, and institutions all perform noticeably different per respective culture. The forms of government or authority were dissimilar, how they structured gender roles showcases a stark contrast and how they worshipped was radically different. Still, we can analyze their methodologies, and compare them with our own. Contrasting various cultural schemas against our own yields incredible results: we become more aware of who we are by considering precedent. We also apply those approaches among diverse instruments and tools of different cultures in order to address conditions of the present day. By interacting with heterogeneous elements from other cultures of the present, or the past, we can gauge and contrast cultural practices, perspectives against our own norms and ways of life. The same holds true of interaction between community members. Communicating with others facilitates exchange. It provides access to perspective and experience, and is invaluable. We build our character and shape both subjective and collective cultural identity via coordinating with others. A culture is only as good as its people, and the quality or condition of a people is demonstrated by how well they communicate and interact with one another volitionally. Structuring a diversified assortment of opportunities for interaction and personal exchanges between constituents enables shared values and helps ensure cultural vitality.

Finally, giving aid, or providing assistance for your fellow human beings as a cultural norm structures the culture as a positive, inclusive social group, and sets it on a course to achieve vitality in perpetuity. Giving aid, or providing relief, connects us with our peers in a *very* important way. Caring strengthens consequential communal bonds, and via perpetuation, makes a priority of those bonds of mutual support. The more we commit to such a habit, the more the caring becomes engrained as specific cultural character. The structuring of care as a cultural norm means that the participants will tend to one another, and, by extension, to the culture. Culture that features constituents caring for their peers is a demonstration of an ascendant culture. Such unity and cohesion showcase also significant bonds of fraternal strength. A culture that cares for its constituents as one of its foundational premises elicits a coordinated structure of inclusivity and positive reinforcement. A culture lasts when the participants care for one another. When community members care for one another, they not only provide for but also safeguard the greater culture. Making a standard or norm of offering either material or intangible support to those in need is a most viable way of ensuring the vitality of your culture.

Culture is one of the broadest structures of association and relationship. It is vital to critically engage and participate within your culture. The quality of a people is demonstrated by how they prioritize learning, interact with and care for others, and that level of quality will contribute to or detract from cultural vitality. Either the people are united, striving together *critically* to better their community, or they are conditioned as passive consumers.

It is your responsibility to improve the quality of your culture.

You are encouraged to apply your own personal agency and initiative to *all* contexts and situations. By striving to learn in a moment-to-moment basis, by seeking to interact with and understand others, and by caring for yourself, and your fellow human beings, you can elicit a meaningful change in your community and the world. Structure your culture to serve as a positive, inclusive force!

Curiosity

Inquisitiveness, or the desire to learn or know about anything, is also called curiosity. Delve into different and scattered subjects. Investigate more than you are taught or offered via formal instruction. Humanity develops and improves when people are curious and investigate after heeding their hunches or intuition. Some learning, or topics are a threat to specific individuals, groups, or institutions. Some entities do not want their motives, identities or actions examined. Feed your curiosity by seeking Truth and knowledge. The discovery of those goods sustains your soul - if not your higher self - and can benefit all of humanity.

Chapter 4

Dad

This section pertains to me being your Dad.
Simply, the best gift I ever received was your presence.

When your Mom relayed how she was carrying a baby, I was quite excited. Also: nervous, pre-occupied, concerned, happy, and overjoyed. When we learned that we would be having a girl, I was overcome. To witness your arrival was awe-inspiring, for several reasons. First, your Mom was (and, present tense: IS) amazing. Her demonstration of strength was nothing short of <u>powerful</u>. Secondly, to hold your little hand and witness absolute goodness, purity, innocence, and Love was a *holy* moment. The world has benefited from your presence for years now! It is very rewarding to experience your growth and development. I admire how you have an open mind and a teachable demeanor. It warms my heart to see how compassionate you are, how you care. I enjoy seeing your determination, how you persevere through adversity and challenges.

I am very proud of you. I encourage you to continue on your amazing path. Rise to challenges and develop your character in meaningful ways. Always remember that I am in your corner; I am here to help. Include me in your realm, and I will apply and offer all that I can in order to help you achieve your goals. I am a very proud Papa, and you are a very special Lady, indeed. Keep at it, PLEASE; the world needs your type of goodness and contribution.
I love you immensely. Your presence is so welcome in my life, and I am grateful for the light you bring. Keep shining, Child of Mine! You are the Angel of my heart!

Daring

Adventurous courage or boldness is what is known as daring. The concept of chance plays a role here. The application of daring lies in the face of uncertain odds or an unknown outcome. A little bit of daring goes a long way as it is balanced by the practice of prudence. You need not be daring all of the time and gamble with every action. One need not live as a daredevil. But just as chance plays a role with your growth and development, so does 'adventurous courage.' DARE TO DREAM BIG! Dare to act defiantly as the occasion warrants the behavior – notably in the face of your own limiting insecurities, irrational fears or even onerous external control or unnecessary restriction. Dare to live gloriously: bravely, ethically, compassionately, and aware! Dare to shape your life as it pertains to you and your own subjective perspective. Do not waste years on a boring, mundane existence. Mark your years with a healthy dose of daring.

Darkness

The state or quality of being dark is darkness. Darkness is very symbolic. It can mean wickedness or evil. It can refer to things that are hidden from view, or concealment. It also is a part of a balance as it is contrasted with light (as in the case of the Yin-Yang). Darkness is thus a very complex concept – like so many others. One can combat darkness when it is symbolic of evil or ignorance. But consider: darkness also needs to be accepted, for its presence makes possible the perception of stars. Similarly, a shadow is not wholly a bad thing. Generally, I advise you to dispel the darkness that is evil; to apply light or knowledge to address an ugly ignorance that comprises a dark, limited perspective. On another note, become aware with your own darkness: your temptations, or experiences that you may not be proud of. These remain foundational to your specific person, still.

"Darkness cannot drive out darkness: only light can do that. Hate cannot drive out hate: only love can do that."
Martin Luther King Jr.

"We can easily forgive a child who is afraid of the dark; the real tragedy of life is when men are afraid of the light.
- **Plato**

"Everyone is a moon, and has a dark side which he never shows to anybody." - **Mark Twain**

"Someone I loved once gave me a box full of darkness. It took me years to understand that this too, was a gift."
— **Mary Oliver**

"A man must dream a long time in order to act with grandeur, and dreaming is nursed in darkness."
—   **Jean Genet**

"What hurts you, blesses you. Darkness is your candle."
—   **Rumi**

"I will love the light for it shows me the way, yet I will endure the darkness for it shows me the stars."
—   **Og Mandino**

"We cast a shadow on something wherever we stand, and it is no good moving from place to place to save things; because the shadow always follows. Choose a place where you won't do harm - yes, choose a place where you won't do very much harm, and stand in it for all you are worth, facing the sunshine."
—   **E.M. Forster, A Room with a View**

I have been one acquainted with the night.
I have walked out in rain—and back in rain.
I have outwalked the furthest city light.

I have looked down the saddest city lane.
I have passed by the watchman on his beat
And dropped my eyes, unwilling to explain.

I have stood still and stopped the sound of feet
When far away an interrupted cry
Came over houses from another street,

But not to call me back or say good-bye;
And further still at an unearthly height,
One luminary clock against the sky

Proclaimed the time was neither wrong nor right.
I have been one acquainted with the night."
Robert Frost, West-Running Brook

"Long is the way and hard, that out of Hell leads up to light."
John Milton, Paradise Lost

Dating

You will all too quickly reach the age in which you start dating or making special appointments with people. Dating is the process where people get to know one another as they assess the suitability as partners in a relationship and for mating. While dating can be very informal, and a whole lot of fun, there are some things to keep in mind as you engage the process.

-Respect and honor one another by sharing meaningfully. Do not waste time with those who are not engaging at a similar level.

-Be safe and minimize your vulnerability.

-Be present. Enjoy the time, and make the most of it. As you learn about others, you need be also learning about yourself. Discover what interests and attracts you, what excites or even what disgusts you. What traits will you accept or require in a partner or a mate? Is the relationship a short-term fling, or a long-term commitment? Are you or your partner exclusively dating one another, or other persons at the same time? Be certain, and safe. Make certain specific parameters of exclusivity and the other significant conditions of the dynamic.

-Communicate clearly. Do not play games.

-Insist on your values and principles. Demand respect and do not settle on inferior people or behavior that is beneath you. Conversely, demonstrate your quality with worthwhile, if not classy, behavior.

Death

Death is the end of life. All mortal entities will perish and die. People and cultures approach the concept in myriad ways. Generally, the body becomes lifeless. Whether that is soul, spirit, or energy is a matter of how life force is understood. Simply, as vitality departs, dissipates or is finally extinguished, the body – or substance – remains. In my life, I have lost pets, family, friends and acquaintances. I have witnessed people die in the street in car accidents. I have seen someone drown in the ocean. I have watched as someone dropped dead from a heart attack. One never knows when death will visit. There is no guarantee of the continuation of life. With luck, one gets a full life and makes use of their time such that they enjoy it - by having relationships and creating meaning of their experiences. But there is no telling that we have our next moment.

Therefore, it is very important to be present with yourself and with others. Make use of your own time and resources. Norman Cousins wrote, "Death is not the greatest loss in life. The greatest loss is what dies inside of us as we live." Don't suffer from the tragedy of living an unfulfilled life. Take chances, and be brave. Explore, love, and investigate the unfamiliar - the many realms this life has to offer. Travel the world. Live as if what you are doing is significant and IT IS! You will never get time, and the same opportunities, again. Consider: you will never live the same moment twice. The ancient philosopher Heraclitus remarked, "No man ever steps in the same river twice; for it's not the same river, and he is not the same man." Time and occasions - the specific contexts of your life - offer specific variables. When you choose one route, activity or behavior, others are excluded. You can not do all things in all occasions; they are exclusive of certain people, times, and actions. While you can make use of the resources at your disposal, you can not control the actions of others, nor can you control what happens to them.

Sometimes death arrives unannounced. We were fortunate to know about our own dog's failing health instead of suffering her immediate and untimely demise. We were given the privilege of saying our goodbyes and helping her pass peacefully. We have lost people suddenly. Those losses were painful as there were things left unsaid. We assumed they would be with us, that we would have more time to enjoy one another. Maybe we wanted to tell someone how much we honored, loved, and cherished their presence in our lives. Plato said that life is spent in preparation for death. That said, prepare for your own end and for the mortality of others by demonstrating your immediate care and concern. Make use of time and present yourself meaningfully in the lives of others.

One of the worst realizations we can have is to recognize at the end of our days is that we wasted our lives. In such an event, there is only tremendous regret, as there is no going back to repair the mistakes we have made. We are not able to address the past after the moments are gone. Keep this in mind and make use of your time such that you need not experience a life wasted. Studying history, culture, religions and philosophy is very educational as to how people view and prepare for death. It is a worthwhile investment in your own life to come to terms with your own definitions and meanings of death, spirit, soul, and the afterlife. Do not wait until the end of your days to begin examining these concepts. They will guide much of what you do with your years.

Debt

A liability or obligation to pay or render something is a debt. It involves getting something now in exchange for a delayed payment. The cost awaits satisfaction, or fulfillment. In some cases, debt need not be a negative or a bad item. Generally though, it is best to manage your resources so as to minimize debt if not eliminate its presence, entirely. Some folks utilize credit and delay payment for so long that the satisfaction of the debt amounts to an inflated cost. Stay current with your bills and obligations and make every attempt to avoid debt. If you need take some on, address it as fast and as directly as possible. Do not let it wait or become a burden or impediment to plans or goals.

Be aware that those who allow you to use credit or issue a debt to you are in control of those future resources. They own that which you owe them. Take on only that debt that you can repay and eliminate entirely. Otherwise, someone else is a master of at least a portion of your own resources. One aspect of living within means involves cutting your expenses so you have money left over at the end of addressing responsibilities and basic needs. Budget your expenses and make it so you have a sufficient, if not significant amount of money left over after addressing your expenses and obligations.

Otherwise, you run the risk of operating on credit and taking on debt. This is largely unsustainable. Do not spend more than you earn.

Decision

Making a judgment, or the art of, or need for, making up one's mind is known as a decision. We all need make decisions, ranging from trivial issues like what we will have for lunch, right up to life changing decisions, like who to marry. Decision-making involves choosing between possible solutions to an issue. One makes decisions by using intuition, reasoning, or a combination between the two. Intuition is your feeling about an issue, whereas reasoning involves data - facts and figures - to make a decision. Examine possible information over the course of available time. It is generally a bad idea to rush important decisions. Effective decision-making allows a viable solution to be implemented. Some impediments to proper decision-making are too much or an insufficient amount of information. Too many people involved can tangle or hinder the discovery of options, or the implementation of the chosen route. Finally, emotional attachments, or even the lack thereof, can affect the process. In the case of the former, maybe people do not want to change and are fixated on maintaining the status quo. Conversely, sometimes people do not care one way or the other as to the outcome of the decision. Examine pro and cons of all options before implementing any available, perceived solution.

Steps of efficient decision-making
-identify the decision that needs to be made or the issue to be resolved -gather information
-weigh evidence
-choose from alternatives
-take action and implement
-review the decision; receive feedback and revise decision, tactics/strategy or stay the course.

Deity

The deity refers to God, or the Goddess, a divine nature or character, especially that of the supreme being or divinity. In the Bible, Psalms 82:6, it is written, "I said: you are 'gods'; you are sons of the most high." In the New Testament, the figure Jesus stated in John 10:34, "is it not written in your law: I have said you are gods?" Despite the text's emphasis of original sin, the Bible – and many other religious or spiritual books – denote that humanity has a divine element. Whether it is because of a visual similarity (being made in the same image of God) or the same spiritual composition, the sense of the divine, or the awareness of, or a reverence for a deity is an ancient facet of many cultures. As people began populating the world, they attributed many natural occurrences, like floods, lightning, and earthquakes to Gods. They made earth goddesses and gods (chthonic) and then sky gods followed. This is an interesting shift, in itself, but it remains outside of this entry's scope (See **Patriarchy**).

Deities took on names and communities adopted them to preside or protect specific regions. They were archetypes – meant for a certain sole purpose. It was not until monotheism that God took on an all-encompassing, if not very contradictory, or just inconsistent spectrum of opposing values or traits. How could a God be both wrathful yet kind; peaceful but vindictive or vengeful? These are important questions to both ask and to try and answer. Typically, though, specific portions of humanity move to emulate whatever God they worship, and that, generally, is a benevolent deity. Every deity is portrayed as powerful, so they are prone to making violent use of said power, but people and cultures generally aim to be good, honest, pure and upright. That bit of the deity that is positive is what we pursue as a goal of character development or life experience.

The first provided quote from the Bible is meant as an encouragement, an invitation of sorts, to you. When your mother and I decided to name you 'Goddess of the Heavens,' we encouraged you. By naming you, we supplied you with that immediate resource (the concept of naming is a most interesting, if not powerful one to explore). Aside from your name, we encourage you to flesh out and substantiate that bit of your own divinity. Rather than pursuing or obeying an external deity, I suggest you develop your Self, and your own sense of the divine. I am not suggesting refraining from worship, much less eschewing completely the possibility of the presence of an external deity. Do what is best for your own spiritual growth and greater enlightenment. Consider and investigate the Goddess as the temple houses the God within. Protect your noggin', and more: become familiar with both the pituitary and pineal glands.

The former is connected to the 6th chakra, while the latter is connected to the 7th. The pineal is to the pituitary what intuition is to reason. They must operate together, in sync, in order to open the Third Eye. The Third Eye is an occult, or esoteric, concept that provides perception beyond ordinary sight and senses. It can lead to higher levels of consciousness. Hence, everyone can attain that level, or connect to the God, within. I entreat, beseech and encourage you to treat yourself well. Engage those concepts, activities and people that serve those highest elements of your Self. Have reverence, a deep abiding respect and honor for your person and for others. Recognize the good – that specific form of Holiness - in others with your own divinity. This is what the Hindu salutation, "Namaste," means; the divine in me recognizes the divine element in you.

The Christian concept of sin applies here. The original sin occurred when Adam and Eve disobeyed God in the Garden of Eden and ate from the Tree of Knowledge. The Bible marks out a path of redemption. I advise you to adhere to those values and behaviors that align with the divine. Respect and honor your Self, and others. Pursue the Good and help your fellow man. You are not in need of redemption when you walk a good path. You are good...but we can all strive to grow, develop and build still better character of ourselves.

Deliverance

The formal, authoritative pronouncement of salvation, or liberation is called deliverance. It is the action of being rescued or set free. This concept is a simple, but important one. No one can take responsibility for or extricate you from the ills of your own life, or those of your own making. Make those decisions that do not conclude with your detention or imprisonment. Review the concept of attachment. Be not a prisoner to vices or bad habits. Control yourself and behave such that you need not suffer the confines or constraints of others. Handcuffs are not fashionable accessories nor are jail cells comfortable abodes. Live your life such that you limit your vulnerability and exposure to negative controlling elements. Be self-sufficient, and do your best so you need not be delivered from the control of others.

Demeanor

Your conduct, behavior, or comportment is demeanor. It is how one carries his or her self in the moment. It is behavior toward others and therefore context specific. An audience assesses one's demeanor. Others are always gauging or at least witnessing your demeanor. Demonstrate, then, a demeanor that is suitable to the moment, or to the activity at hand. Your demeanor will change whether you are in a classroom or speaking publicly. Sometimes, you will be walking to a meeting, or simply passing time. Even when you are not engaging someone, you have a demeanor when someone is viewing you. A dog notices your demeanor. They see your stride, how you move, and they can even sense your fear or confidence via the pheromones you exude unconsciously, too. Manage your demeanor appropriately. Carry yourself well: with dignity, strength, and vitality. Adjust your behavior to pertain to the task, role, audience, or context in which you are engaged.

Depression

Depression is a condition of general emotional dejection and withdrawal. Generally, an emotion like sadness is greater and more prolonged than is generally warranted by any objective. It occurs in 1 of 8 women, and in nearly 1 out of 12 men.[8] It involves a number of emotions, especially grief, fear, anger, and shame. These emotions loop back on themselves and people have feelings about feelings, sometimes without limit.

Life offers its share of curveballs, challenges, travails and obstacles. We get a portion of highs and lows. It is essential to moderate your feelings and to be aware if you are unable to do just that. Some events can absolutely paralyze us. Perhaps a death in the family, or any number of different forms of trauma can throw us for a loop. It is important to note when your emotions are extremely severe, or cyclical. If you happen to engage a non-intentional routine of feeling low, and having those sessions overtake your regular life, you may need to seek counsel if not medical help. Genetics, drugs and alcohol and external occurrences or events can all cause or elicit depression. Be mindful of how often you are that low, for how often it lasts, and importantly: if it is a regular occurrence. Unless your life is punctuated or affected by a perpetual routine of radically traumatic events, you can control your emotions and energies. I suggest both providing, and keeping good company with good people. Do not abuse drugs or alcohol. Limit your time with television, or popular culture. Develop your character and be strong or at least emotionally balanced and energetically fit. You can shape and control your own moods by maintaining your own realm. Be conscious of what you ingest. It becomes a serious, debilitating event if you are powerless to avoid or limit depressive episodes. Seek help if such conditions become regular or routine.

Destruction

The action or process of causing so much damage to something that it no longer exists or can not be repaired is called destruction. Sometimes, destruction can be creative. This can be an economic concept or refer to something we practice in the martial arts. Aside from these two applications, I suggest destroying your bad habits. Annihilate limiting thoughts, or those ideas that hold you back from goals or the life you want to live. Destroy the negatives in your life or at least remove them such that you can continue to grow, develop, and improve.

Development

Growth, progress, or a significant consequence of an event is development. Development can be incremental or can occur over a longer period of time. You will note that you ascertain knowledge or skills quite suddenly and you will also notice how you have developed over years. This is a simple concept yet it deserves your attention. Be open to the opportunities to learn and grow at each interval – in each moment – and also serve a longer view. Pick goals and establish a standard that fits you. You will look back and contrast different parts of your self as well as different selves. For you are not the person you were yesterday, much less several years ago. Develop your character. Refine your person, hone your abilities, and seek to improve and grow consciously.

Some developments are the results of chance events, accidents, or luck. Others result from dedicated, diligent exercise and effort. ALSO! I give you this text as food for thought. I want you to enjoy your life. Constant work on the self can be difficult and very tiring. You can develop your character by relaxing, by vacationing, by being silly, too. You can learn something from any activity, or by doing nothing at all. More food for thought: what is 'doing nothing?'

Keep track of your growth, achievements, and developments. When we workout, we log what we are doing, how we have improved our repetitions, or diversified our activities and routines. A journal can catalogue your activities and record your significant developments. It helps you to understand the present by remembering what you did to obtain your worthy results. Also, you can learn much by engaging in your own narrative: recording events, or the significant thoughts and feelings of your circumstances allows you to review and analyze them from a distanced time and perspective - after their occurrence.

Devotion

Devotion speaks to profound dedication or consecration – an earnest attachment for a person, activity, or cause. One who is very devoted is devout. Devotion can also refer to a form of serious worship. It is deeming something to be sacred and being very committed without fail to that object or purpose. Not everything can be an object of devotion. It might be strange to be devoted to the practice of tying your shoelaces, or the worship of purple plates. Some things are worth devotion. Make certain, when the occasion presents itself, that the object of your devotion is a worthy person, cause, or activity. Some might take advantage of the good intentions of the devout. People become confidence (con) men, causes can be cults, and activities can be bad habits or addictions. Measure the efforts against the reward, and the merit of the recipient or object. Apply yourself devotionally only to the most special of people, causes and activities. Maintain a critical perspective and be very selective about your devotion. When you find that special someone, I hope you are devout - engaged, committed, and loyal. If the cause benefits you and your fellow man, I entreat you to put forth meaningful and significant effort. When you find an activity that stokes your brilliant internal fire, by all means, address it with vivacity and earnestness.

Dignity

Dignity refers to bearing and conduct or speech indicative of self-respect or appreciation. It is your sense of self-worth or pride and one loses their dignity when they behave in a way that is a disservice to them. The question that follows, then, is, "What is worth the loss of dignity?" This is so very important.

There is nothing more important than your own sense of worth.

Be most cautious if you are encouraged to participate in activities that devalue your dignity. There is no activity that is worth the sacrifice of your dignity. As you age, dignity is a different part of mortality. Consider: you live a life as an independent, self-sufficient adult but as you age, you need help with some basic activities. You may need help getting around; someone may need to drive you to appointments, or to the grocery store. You may need help bathing, or feeding yourself, or even going to the bathroom and cleaning up after yourself. You might feel as if you were losing your dignity in those conditions. But this is a part of mortality, and it is important to understand what it entails, instead of being ashamed. Generally, do not let someone or something take away your self-respect, and also: do not give it away for anything.

Discernment

The ability to judge well, or the quality of being able to grasp and comprehend what is obscure is known as discernment. There is much that is unstated – much that exists to be discovered and deciphered – in this life. It is most essential to exercise a critical faculty to uncover strategy, cues, meaning, and options as you progress. Discernment is applied in many different realms:

spiritually, intellectually, socially, and culturally. Spiritually, you will contend with variables that deal with death, your soul, and heavy concepts like love and trust. Intellectually, you will need discernment to strategize and gauge persuasive appeals. This is applicable in every realm. In the social realm, you need be sufficiently aware to identify cues in order to ascertain meanings - subtle or otherwise. As we discussed earlier, the communicative process is a very complex one. Discernment is a necessary component of most, if not all communicative transactions.

In the workplace, for example, the social element is coupled with the presence of power. Power is involved in *any* dynamic and typically results in a hierarchical ordering of elements, roles, and obligations. You need abide by rules of the organization, and heed directions or commands offered by a boss or leader. Your ability to discern information will have consequence and bear upon dynamics within the workplace. Politics require careful analysis as well as adequate critique and the appropriate response. Discernment goes a long way when navigating the complexity of people and power. In terms of culture, the element of power is always present. Discernment helps identify the prevailing cultural trends, fashions, and modes of the day and how power influences *everything* within that culture.

Discernment is comprised of openness, awareness, critique and investigation, as well as a fair portion of intuition. One must be open to receive information. They must be aware of what variables are connected to, or influence/color that information. Myriad underpinnings, meanings, tangential bits may play a role. The process of discerning is investigation at both the broadest and at the most minute level. It is situational awareness with every realm, aided by intuition and all else an investigation brings to bear. Be inquisitive, knowledgeable, and able to grasp how concepts overlap and form greater structures and systems. Exercise proper judgment, be alert, moral, courageous, and seek to connect and delve deeper when information is provided. Of utmost importance is to apply your intuition. Your inner voice will guide and protect you for as long as you develop and apply its perspective, ability, and formidable power.

Discipline

Discipline is training others or the self to obey rules or a code of behavior. Not included in this discussion is the element of punishment (See Foucault, esp. his text: *Discipline and Punishment*). Discipline is the suppression of base desires and is synonymous with restraint and self-control. It uses reason instead of feelings or desires. Discipline helps you achieve your goals and the best things in this life. It requires focus and concentration and the exclusion of those temptations or extras that serve as distractions.

Discipline is a matter of control of emotions and impulses. Our culture seems to be absolutely fixated on instant gratification: pleasures NOW NOW NOW, and a lack of self-regulation. Discipline is like a muscle; it needs exercise and strengthening to work its wonders. In the short-term overuse will lead to depletion. Hence, extended long-term use will strengthen and improve discipline over time. Our media offers fast food that is far from healthy, products that promise immediate beauty aid, TV shows that merely please us in the moment. Our culture does not do much to promote discipline, because companies benefit from the people's reaction to various forms of persuasion by indulging in the moment. Chuck Palahniuk, in his Book *Fight Club*, states: "We buy things we don't need with money we don't have to impress people we don't like." It supposes that pleasure in the moment outweighs the investment in the future.

Living in such an undisciplined way is unsustainable and has consequences across several realms. Imagine a bear sitting around eating honey all summer, refusing to eat sufficiently so they could last the winter, hibernating.

They would be struck by the hard reality of a lack of food during the winter, and they could quite possibly starve. A more applicable human presentation: when someone insists on immediate pleasures in the form of candy, TV shows, shallow relationships, or drug and alcohol abuse, they reduce the benefits that accrue from entertaining a longer view of life and applying self-discipline. Indulging in pleasure is a definite good, but it is best enjoyed in moderation. Eschew, or at least minimize, those distractions that impede or delay progress towards your best and highest goals. Worthy development and growth takes time, effort, focus and a sustained approach. Excessive short-term pleasures only get in the way of meaningful progress and discipline requires your solid self-control. Significant goals and dreams require the same significant effort. Marshal the best within you to obtain your highest aims and to realize amazing dreams.

Disillusionment

Disillusionment is a feeling of extreme disappointment resulting from the discovery that something is not as good as one originally believed it to be. This sentiment can appear in many realms: in the workplace, in relationships, in regards to larger culture, or even when you are reading a book. Disillusionment can appear suddenly, when one realizes in a moment that the realized benefits are not as worthwhile as they first appeared. It can also result after a prolonged period. A new job or work opportunity may show itself to be more of a burden than a benefit. The same goes for relationships. Your partner may present traits that persuade you to question the dynamic. They might also behave in one manner that persuades you to end the relationship immediately, as in the case of abuse. It is important to gauge the merits of people, causes, and activities. Contrast risk and rewards. Consider how things might change over time and maintain a list of benefits and deal-breakers. Remain vigilant as to how you are served by continued participation or if ceasing involvement is the better route.

Disillusionment can occur with everyone at any age. You can only minimize it by carefully maintaining your involvement and investment in activities, with people, or causes. As is the case in life, chance events transform situations. People change their minds and their behaviors. Keep in mind that are you are never stuck permanently. Take initiative to elicit better results or change your setting if and when conditions do not improve. Disillusionment is not a permanent state, either; insist on happiness and fulfillment, instead. Go to what serves awesome sentiments, instead of lingering in those scenes that lower your vibe or your self-esteem.

Divine

The divine is of, from, or like God, or a god. It is the absolute standard of excellence or what is most delightful. Here we refer to divinity or those elements that are pure, good, and virtuous, and not the application of the sublime in more adjectival terms ("this chocolate is divine"). This concept overlaps with the previous discussion of the deity. Divinity distinguishes the deity from the ordinary or mundane. It elevates its role to a stature above the common landscape. It consists, then, of higher elements and characteristics. The divine is not common, base, superficial, or inferior, generally. It is instead comprised by only the best elements: those traits like goodness or virtue, purity, wisdom. Incorporate these traits and characteristics in your life by maintaining focus on worthy ideals, principles, and values. By doing so you invite those people, causes and activities that offer similar qualities. Engaging or seeking those higher characteristics encourages the presence of other divine elements and entities. The representative heuristic of 'like with like' illustrates this concept. While it is not necessarily the case - there are always exceptions - like character associates, generally, with similar quality, and causes; effects should resemble one another. So by being good, or maintaining a worthy standard will elicit the company and presence of good friends. Maintaining a standard of excellence - of the divine - encourages like-minded people to be a part of your life. Again, there are exceptions, but only insofar as you allow for them, in this particular case. In short: connect with the divine, with what is excellent, good, pure, and virtuous. Create and live a standard of life that is elevated and worth your attention and energy. Structure and protect your self-respect by engaging in worthy activities and causes with equally worthy - or divine - individuals.

Dream

To contemplate the possibility of doing something or that something might be the case is to dream. Dreams are more than passive visuals and scenes generated by our minds during the REM cycle of sleep. Dreams can also be an active activity; something one does with intent, focus, clarity, and diligence. Eleanor Roosevelt said, "The future belongs to those who believe in the power of their dreams." A question that results, or follows is: How do you dream, or envision a dream? Dreams are borne of experience and imagination. Your experience colors your imagination, and vice versa. Your imagination will definitely impact your experience. To start, come to know your world. Investigate history and different cultures. Explore the multi-faceted array that is this life. Then, consider possibilities. Think about what you want to see or do, and who you want to meet, where you want to travel, or how you would like to contribute. Generally, consider how you want to live your life, and how you would make use of your time, given little impediment or restriction on that experience. Structure a grand vision of what you want your life to look like, given your presence and active participation. Dream BIG, and make plans that are unique to you and your person. Then, put your dreams in motion by organizing a plan and acting. What steps are necessary to achieve your dream? What time is necessary? How much does the dream cost, in terms of energy, effort, material resources, or money? Format a plan and then start that process. Worthy dreams require significant discipline and focus. Consider: achieving a dream of being a couch potato is fairly easy and anyone can do it. But it is not very special. It is not uniquely suited just for YOU.

Something interesting about dreams is that there is a small difference between our waking state and our sleeping/dreaming state. Inside a dream is a complete universe. It has the nearly complete and similar depth of experience that the waking state offers. The laws of physics differ, and we might even interact with the deceased. But inside the dream, these things appear normal. It is all created by our mind – but the same is true of our waking state, too. When one studies quantum mechanics, they come to grasp that objects in the real world are not really solid, but are a result of mind operations. Both the dream state and the waking world are products of the mind. Taken further, the presence of mind is, itself, just a dream, too. Simply: bodies, things, brains and minds have no objective reality outside of the mind that is dreaming them.

Acceptance of the waking world as another dream is an essential aspect of permanent peace. In lucid dreaming, one participates in the dream – takes full advantage of that world and controls the development and events of the scene. Conversely, then, we can live a lucid life in our waking state by applying our minds and dreaming what we want to live. Our concept of self - the ego, the "I" - is a product of the mind, which is, again, a product lacking objective reality outside of the mind. You need not worry about a dream while you are asleep, having a lucid dream…the waking state need not be that much different. This is not encouragement to jump off a building in an attempt to fly, nor is it a suggestion to test your superhuman strength or speed on a freeway. I am advising you to apply your head, heart, and hands responsibly so as to realize and achieve your highest dreams and goals.

"As soon as you start to pursue a dream, your life wakes up and everything has meaning." – **Barbara Sher**

"A dream doesn't become reality through magic; it takes sweat, determination, and hard work." – **Colin Powell**

"If you can dream it, you can do it." – **Walt Disney**

"Hold fast to dreams, for if dreams die, life is a broken winged bird that can not fly." – **Langston Hughes**

"A single dream is more powerful than a thousand realities." – **J.R.R. Tolkien**

"Little girls with dreams become women with vision." – *Unknown*

"You are never too old to set another goal or to dream a new dream." – **C.S. Lewis**

"Happy are those who dream dreams, and are ready to pay the price to make them come true." – **Cardinal Leon Joseph Suenens**

"Dreams are illustrations for the book your soul is writing about you." – **Marsha Norman**

"Don't be pushed by your problems. Be led by your dreams." – **Ralph Waldo Emerson**

"Dream big and dare to fail." – **Norman Vaughan**

Drive

A determined urge to obtain a goal or satisfy a need is a drive. There are several ways of conceptualizing what drives an individual, or even greater humanity. As a start, we can think of a drive as a motivator. We could then apply Maslow's Hierarchy of Needs (physiological, safety, love & belonging, esteem & self-actualization), intrinsic and extrinsic motivators (inner satisfaction and desires; external rewards and payoffs), drives to achieve autonomy, mastery and purpose, or a theory of self-interest (rational self-interest motivates all human behavior). There are many theories of behavior, and they all make sense at some level.

Be aware of and consciously maintain a grasp of your drives and motivations. What are your goals? What ends are you pursuing? Consider if they serve either a short, or a longer-term need or want. Are they inclusive, or exclusive of others? When you grasp the motivation – the why, the reason underlying your pursuit of goals - your perspective can take into account a broader spectrum of variables, time, and options. Be vigilant as to what drives you. Prioritize higher versus lower order drives but structure your motivations such that you both survive AND thrive. What is the fuel to your fire, and how does it ultimately serve your best self?

Drug

A drug is any substance that, when inhaled, injected, smoked, consumed, absorbed via patch on the skin, or dissolved under the tongue, causes a temporary physiological, and often psychological change in the body. Psychoactive drugs are chemical substances that affect the function of the nervous system, altering perception, mood, or consciousness. They include alcohol, nicotine, and caffeine; these are the three most widely consumed psychoactive drugs worldwide. They are also known as recreational drugs since they are used for pleasure, rather than strictly medicinal purposes. Other recreational drugs include hallucinogens, opiates, amphetamines, and those varieties that are designated as sacraments for use in spiritual or religious settings.

Drugs have maintained a presence with humanity since ancient times, when they were utilized as cultural artifacts, or sacraments. Use of drugs during ceremony provided access to the divine, deceased elders/ancestors, and elevated consciousness. It is only since the 1960s that drugs have been largely forbidden, and made illegal here in the United States. Despite their taboo status, certain drugs including psilocybin are being incorporated in studies concerning post-traumatic stress disorder (PTSD) and depression. Recent evidence indicates that higher consciousness results from the use of drugs including LSD and ketamine. The diversity of brain activity increases as a result of these particular drugs.

Drugs are intimately connected with the ideas of the self, subjectivity, consciousness, and control. Save for those drugs that are manufactured and distributed by the pharmaceutical conglomerates, an incredible array of drugs are outlawed and distanced from public consumption. While the state contends that this is an understandable protection of its human resources, and the greater community, it is best to identify such paternal rationales for what they are: limited, short-sighted means of state trespass and oversight. Controlling the access to drugs means that the people are limited to those resources the state identifies as negative, or illicit. Drugs can be meaningful instruments in the hands of those who opt to harness them. That is not to say that all drugs are worthy of inclusion or application. More to the point, the state uses restriction as a means of controlling the people unnecessarily. The state implements prohibition, as it does not trust its citizens. In this case, the people are not trusted to examine or investigate a portion of their self;

we are forbidden from exploring altered states of consciousness. We can not format the fullest of personal narratives for our own selves while we are so limited and controlled. Should we come to honor the self, and a meaningful notion of freedom and human agency, our culture will allow for the presence of drugs. That the state keeps them distanced from the people as if they were cookies in a tempting cookie jar demonstrates how they consider it their responsibility to control resources, instead of cultivating a disciplined, experienced, and respectful constituency.

Drugs are but one way to explore consciousness and meaning. Should you elect to explore them, do your diligent research beforehand. Read about them, seek knowledgeable opinion, and be mindful of very real consequences. Take note how a great number of pharmaceutical concoctions are nothing short of dangerous. Our country is beset by a lack of moderation, self-respect/self-control. This is demonstrated objectively by a paternal nanny state, and an opioid crisis that is manifested in an absolutely stupefying amount of lives across the nation. A strong foundation of moral values and self-respect will facilitate your subjective investigations into consciousness and reality. Apply self-control and a *very* cautious perspective specifically to the inclusion of drugs in your life.

Dualism

The division of something into two opposed or contrasted aspects, or the state of being so divided, is what is known as dualism. The Latin root *duo*, meaning two, comes into play here. Dualism breaks a concept down into but two components: yes/no, black/white, good/evil, mind/body, on/off. It is an either/or dilemma, a dichotomy – only the two options exist. This is sometimes very problematic as the spectrum of available selections is only situated between extremes: right/wrong, 0/1, paper/plastic, life/death.

Dualism has historical and philosophical significance – far beyond 'simple' academic discussions, as well. But life is not so cut and dried. The 'take it or leave it' approach is far too limited and simplistic. Life is a rainbow, not just a contrast of black on white. Life has body, depth: vivacity. Our political system is currently comprised of two major political parties that offer woeful, shameful excuses for candidates. Truly, they do not adequately represent the best of the nation. The media and the larger cultural institutions insist how voters need select between 'the lesser of two evils.' But a choice for evil, however 'lesser' it might be, is still a vote for evil, nonetheless. This is what is known as a false dilemma. In logic, this is a fallacy - an error in reasoning that renders an argument invalid. There are more than two options available, but considering them amounts to a loss of power by the political parties that control the political realm, presently.

Discuss options, and be aware of proffered intentional limitations when only two choices are involved. When only two are available, the chance of a worthy solution is slim. Realize that the narrowing of options to two might be a viable route. But when you are confined between such a limited number to start with, you might be situated between the proverbial rock and a hard place.

Chapter 5

Ease

Ease is the absence of difficulty or strenuous effort, to make less serious or severe, or to move carefully, gradually, or gently. Life is not the easiest of endeavors, nor is it meant to be. Challenges build our character, and help us to develop and become better, stronger. But there is much one can do to both make life easier and ease your greater human existence. Some live life as if it is a burden, a chore, or an encumbrance – something they are stuck with. Others live their life as a sacred responsibility, as if they were tasked with a holy opportunity to live with passionate purpose in the best possible way. Still others live a life of mirth, joy, and abandon – they seek to enjoy moments with glee, freedom, and spontaneity.

You have choices as to how to live your life, and you are not restricted to choosing between the aforementioned three standards. Utilize a combination of elements of all three, but find, or even better: create your own formula. To live a life of ease is to be in harmony with your own self. When you are at harmony with yourself, you are satisfying your soul by utilizing skills and abilities, by pursing dreams and ambitions, by working with the very best aspects of your subjective self. When you are in harmony with yourself, life meets that particular standard and contributes more to the scene you are creating. The opposite is true, too. If you behave against your best self, life will provide you with that same disharmony. Living a life of ease is synonymous with being at peace and harmony with yourself.

Seven Steps to Harmony
-Breathe Love into your Being. Breathe deeply, slowly, meaningfully. Practice yogic breathing. Remind yourself to love with each breath.
-Establish your own self-worth. Do not let others decide what you are worth.
-Accept your loved ones for who they are. Do not try and change them. Change yourself first and only try to change yourself.
-Do not allow others to make you feel low, insecure, afraid, or ashamed.
-Do not give others power to make you feel less than how you want to feel.
-Expand your heart and mind with books, education, and learning.
-Collect experiences, instead of prioritizing material belongings or possessions.
-Do not be too hard on yourself. Be gentle, instead.

Education

The process of receiving or giving systematic instruction, especially at a school or university, is education. It is meant to be an enlightening experience – one that lends insight or awareness. Formal, institutional education has always served those who rule or wield power within a society or culture. It shapes the character of the student such that they perform in line with what is dictated by the greater social setting. For those offering the education want a finished product that supports, if not contributes to, its continued presence, or rule. Why would a system or its leadership, create products that buck the established trend and shirk the power structure? Education always serves a specific purpose of shaping its students to fit within the confines of the leadership or ruling class.

There are many different forms and styles of education. It is transformed to fit different needs for different cultures through history. While the ancient Greeks utilized *paideia,* at roughly the same time period, the Spartans eschewed the liberal arts and instead prioritized athletic/militaristic abilities and fighting prowess for both their men and women. They wanted their citizens to be able top defend their country by serving as warriors, primarily. Leadership will identify their needs and implement the format that best serves and protects the established status quo - the existing state of affairs. Culture, and education are two contributing factors as to why people are different across time and space. People identify different needs as to the society, and structure their architecture, beliefs and foods to distinguish themselves from others.

Education serves the mind, body, and spirit, too. Universities influence the mind, gymnasiums strengthen the body, and churches, synagogues, and temples (hopefully) tend to the spirit. To what end is education focused; what is the comprehensive goal of an education? While institutions want satisfactory consumers, employees or citizens, the best judge of education is the student. What good is an education if it does not serve the best interests of the pupil? An individual can be a decent participant, but what if they are dead inside? What of the student who has no joy or sense of expressing his or her own unique skills, talents and abilities? A student is not a passive vessel to be filled only with the means of serving as a further means to another's ends. Education has the responsibility to comprehensively improve the entire person: that pertains to the complete package of one's head, heart, and hands.

We can critique the value of particular education systems by profiling value:
-Who benefits from the education? Is the learning going to benefit the learner/student or the instructor/institution?

On a related note, if an instructor is a good one, they enjoy teaching; they help to bring about those insights or a greater sense of awareness in the pupil. A worthy instructor cares immensely for their pupils.

-What is the skill/lesson provided? What is the purpose of the education?
To what end is this instruction based/aimed?
-How is this lesson based on time? When is this education pertinent? Is this a short-term lesson or something that can be applied over an extended period? Does this education lose its pertinence or value over a passage of time?
-Where is this education valuable, or where does it pose minimal value? Is this education forbidden in certain realms or is it maybe unwelcome? In what realms is the application of education unwarranted? Are there restrictions as to 'this' education, or education, in general?
-Why is this education applied, taught, or even mandated? Why is this education important? What is the point, value, or intention of this instruction?
-How is the education taught, received, applied, or implemented? How is the education formatted, or offered? How is it available: exclusively or inclusively? How does one stand to benefit from that particular form of education?

Re: Generality & Specialization

In another section, a Robert Heinlein quote addresses specialization ("Specialization is for insects"). There are some lessons that influence if not comprise a significant portion of human cultural foundations and practices while other lessons or instructions pertain to one's own subjective path. For example, everyone should know how to dress him or her self, should know how to eat well, and should know when to come out of the rain and elements. They should be able to grasp how to live in a society with other people. They should be disciplined, and be able to control themselves. Specific forms of education lend themselves to human culture while specialized realms or portions of education address specific skills, abilities and particular contexts and realms. Studying art, history, philosophy and mathematics lends to a fuller human character while learning mechanical engineering, marketing, or brain surgery builds a specific skill set.

Some education is a good, in and of itself - it is of intrinsic, broad value - while other forms are a means to an end: they are designed with a goal in mind. The former is applicable in the most general of settings and has relevance across a wide spectrum while specialized education is meant for a more exclusive application. It is a balancing act for each individual to garner a broad understanding of humanity - to be cultured (aware of global, human concepts) while also attaining and refining an education consisting of specific skills and abilities that lend themselves to practical living. It is important to have a foundation of skills that will sustain you - that will feed, clothe, and house you. Every individual needs a skill set that will provide for the necessities of life. The general aspects of education will flesh out nearly everything thereafter, as far as culture and society is concerned.

Influencing all of this still further is how an education makes an individual feel! It is not enough for education to deliver information or offer skills and abilities. Education need impart identity and, even more, humanity - the humane element. A robot can make use of software and programming. It can conduct operations and perform actions, but it will not identify its subjective self, nor will it act ethically: with others in mind. It is the responsibility of the student to make sense of data and apply it. The way education and cultural programming makes an individual think and feel leads to behaviors that establish the greater social identity of the self. If the education or cultural instruction is lost on an individual, or does not resonate within the student, the institution loses that resource. It is the opinion of this writer that today's United States' education and cultural formatting is not helping people to recognize nor develop their own subjective worth. When someone is unable to see him or herself as worthy, they will see others similarly. This leads to a breakdown of mores and social cohesion. Therefore, the people need be critical as to what is being a taught, for the good of themselves, for others in the community and future generations. Currently, we are ceding a lot of responsibility to the state and to the media among other social institutions. Community members are not coordinating with one another to ensure the coordination of shared values; this affects morality and standards. This leads to subjective isolation and the greater breakdown of society. This, in turn, leads to the greater likelihood of a police or 'nanny' state. When an education fails to structure or rear a critically engaged and self-sufficient audience, the more state apparatus will be applied to discipline or coddle the people. A system that makes the state necessary weakens the people by imprisoning its mind, enslaving its heart, and restricting its hands.

Be aware how education serves a purpose of shaping your character within a community, but take responsibility for your own education by remaining critical. Seek out those elements that deliver a whole, creative, and considerate perspective.

Assorted Thoughts include:
"Teach them early about who they are."
- Consider the idea of the Zone of Proximal Development, or the 'subjective sweet spot' for learning. How can we:
a.) prepare each and every individual learner to be receptive as to lessons and
b.) structure lessons via these subjective modalities? If we want to honor and also make efficient use of individuals as resources meant for inclusion within and development of/for the community, how is centralized education at all viable, unless the suffering of learners amounts to necessary, acceptable loss? Keep in mind how that standard is already established; look to the manifest consequences of the policy.

Many thanks to Sandy McKeithan for this idea.

Ego

Your ego is your conscious mind, the part of your identity that you consider your "self." When one says that an individual has a "big ego," it means that he/she is full of themselves or arrogant. The ego is one's self-image or persona. Everything one does is predicated by ego. As we discussed previously, values underlie behavior. So positive, inclusive, good behavior speaks to an equally positive array of variables and a healthy ego.

A healthy ego makes growth and development possible. The self, or the 'I,' is the sum of habits. Habits are made by recurring thoughts. Once this format of thoughts is developed, habits take over. They reflect the relative condition of the thoughts. They demonstrate how the self feels about itself, as good/bad, valuable and worthy, or useless and unworthy. Habits then reinforce the thinking and structure how similar thoughts are produced. Individuals control their thoughts, habits and behavior, or they allow their habits and values to be formed subconsciously, captive to the vagaries of chance. Addressing the ego is a lifelong endeavor, and this text is meant to facilitate its positive development. Take charge of your mind and consciously develop! Practice self-control and heed the words of the philosopher Plato: "The first and best victory is to conquer self. To be conquered by self is, of all things, the most shameful and vile."[9]

Your ego is healthy when you have mastered your self, when you constantly exercise restraint and self-discipline. When one strives to develop their person, they eschew limiting beliefs and inferior or negative thoughts, habits, and people. To implement those steps that improve and positively shape the ego means that lesser concepts and practices need be reduced, minimized, or eliminated. And the self responds to such encouraging practices! When one embarks on the path of development, they strive to win a battle of ego. The first step is self-acceptance. When one behaves in harmony with their ego, they are achieving an important victory, and are grasping their most important resource. The relationship with the ego -

with your self - is the most important relationship. When one has a healthy dynamic, the individual can live a healthy life with others. A life that is inclusive, significant and loving is predicated on the healthy ego and it is definitely worth your investment of resources and care.

Elation

Elation is great happiness, exhilaration, bliss, joy, or ecstasy. While this text is not designed nor meant as a thesaurus, dictionary, or encyclopedia, it *is* formatted to complement your experience and subjective initiative. So, the inclusion of the term elation serves as a bookend, an extreme on that adjectival spectrum of emotions. Sometimes, the notion of 'good' does not suffice. Sometimes words can not adequately grasp a sentiment. Indeed, elation can not begin to describe what it was like falling in love, holding you as a baby, sharing time with you now, as you progress and mature into a lovely, aware, communicative human being. Elation stands as an extreme; it is unsurpassed as a sentiment. It is an absolute, it is untouched, or unrivaled as a description. It stands alone, at a pole of experience and emotion.

I entreat you to read, and apply the terms and vocabularies of the world. Come to terms with the description of the human experience and what is more: experience life and apply those terms that encompass or grasp significant occasions. I hope you have remarkably positive events that leave you agape – speechless - overjoyed – stupefied in awe. This life is a beautiful, wondrous experience. I hope you take the time to rise to its challenges in order to live a fulfilling, meaningful, and memorable life. I Love You. I hope you experience the heights of elation, and marvel at its scale!

Element

A part or an aspect of something abstract, especially one that is essential or characteristic, is an element. Elements are primary components. They are applicable to a broad spectrum of situations; elements are present in crime scenes, relationships, paintings/art, and recipes. Every composite or combination is comprised of elements. It is a very important skill to be able to identify or discern respective elements of different contexts. Every moment of your life contains or features them: time, place, a subject: YOU! – among still others. Being able to grasp and recognize the elements at play helps identify available options and routes of action. The better you are able to discern variables or elements, the more refined your behavior, and values! Refine your awareness and consciously apply a keen, critical perspective in order to identify pertinent points in order to make good decisions for the highest and best good of all involved.

Ending

An ending is a final part of something, especially in regards to a period of time, an activity, a book, movie, etc. Everything ends, whether it is a day, a breath, a job, a relationship, or even a life. Nearly everything is finite or limited. Make use, then, of the discrete availability of experiences. Apply your skills and your perception, your intellect, and emotions, skills and subjectivity to make use of what is at hand. When something ends, that occasion or experience is over and done. Too often an ending occurs, and we are left with regret, guilt or sadness over our inability to be fully present or to have engaged that context with our fullest self. Apply yourself significantly in order to create meaning and engage fully with the time and resources at your command.

Energy

The strength and vitality needed for sustained physical and mental activity or the power derived from the utilization of physical or chemical resources, especially to provide light, heat, or to work machines, is energy. Energy is addressed as prana, qi, manas, divine breath, jiva, ousia, and pneuma, which speaks to its importance and significance across *many* different cultural groups. The concept of energy is one that plays a role in nearly everything. Energy is delivered, in part, by sleep. For when we rest a sufficient amount, we are rejuvenated and able to address life's tasks after waking. As we rise, the sun energizes our cells and metabolism, contributes to the growth of our food, and its energy facilitates nearly all life on the planet. Food is the substance that will be converted by our bodies to be used as energy. People have an energy about them. Some contribute to our own energy while others sap our energy resources.

Our minds, hearts and bodies all make use of energy. Our greater selves are amazing systems that regulate the ebb and flow, or the give and take, of energies. It is most advisable to maintain and control our energies and put them to the best possible uses. The general point of this concept is that everything has energy: energy is included in nearly every structure, system or context. Our thoughts, our feelings, and most definitely our visible behaviors and activities all include some aspect of or relation to energy. Recognizing the specific form of energy at play and how to properly utilize it is a unique skill. Keep in mind how everything one encounters and every action one does has an energetic aspect or consequence. We would be very wise to be very cautious and considerate as to what we allow in our lives and how we behave. Energies can either aid our development or hinder our growth and negatively impact our health - or those around us.

The interaction between energy and perception is very interesting. Lacking a perceiving observer - or a *percipient* - energy lacks form, and remains in wave form. But once an observer begins to perceive and influence a context, energy coalesces, and contributes more refined scenes composed of particles. That said, per modern quantum physics, the form energy takes, and indeed: all of objective reality (!) is predicated on mind. We reviewed this earlier in the section pertaining to dreams. The waking state is formed, and shaped by mind; *there is no objective reality sans mind.* There's a philosophical question that asks, "If a tree falls in the woods, and there's no one around to witness it, does it still make a sound?" Modern empiricists maintain that nothing exists without being perceived. So, what element or context exists independent of human perception? If we have not discovered a planet, does it exist before we discover it? Does a piece of lint exist under the couch until we encounter it?

This is all just food for thought.

Simply, your perception - your own self - contributes to and influences energy, just as energy comprises your surroundings, your food, your body, the sun, etc. This is what is known as a bi-conditional reciprocity. An item, an element, variable, subject - an individual - influences something, just as it is influenced or affected by the very thing it is influencing. The same goes, again, for food, relationships, and your own self. This dynamic is present in many relationships, and informs us as to specific aspects or degrees of influence; not everything is independent, or one-sided, isolated from the actions of other variables, causes, and quanta.

Energy is vibration, or the frequency at which energy takes form and moves. Higher energies move faster, and are positive while lower frequencies are slower and negative. The former benefit the self, and serve to positively affect and aid the health of an individual. Everything has an energetic value. Everything affects something else, so it is our responsibility to safeguard our own person by being ever vigilant as to the consequences of allowing energies of all levels within our subjective realms. What does not affect our mind? Further: what, of our own person, is unaffected by the power or energy of our thoughts?

Food, people and media are all significant factors that affect our mind's health and general condition. We need be very discerning as to how things affect our thoughts. Though not all negative thoughts are bad, per se. Some fears keep us safe. Frustration and sadness are instructive; they guide us to the fact that a particular circumstance, strategy or relationship may not be the best utilized to fulfill goals, ambitions, or aims. There is a rough parallel with our heart and our feelings. Not everything we feel will aid us or help us to maintain the highest energy or vibrational frequency. Be aware of how things affect your emotions. A lowered vibration means low energy which, in turn, speaks to stagnant vibes or even depression. The energy of people is especially significant. We have addressed chakras and developing the kundalini energy, or facilitating the flow of energy along the internal energy centers. People have a specific energy and, when you become sufficiently aware, you can discern that vibration either visually or via discernment and intuition. People emanate an energy color, or an aura. Should the visual representation not be perceived, your intuition can guide you when you choose to heed that inner voice.

Much of popular culture, mainstream media, and establishment institutions are not structured to offer the best of energies. If you are critically engaged, you will notice how the presentations they offer are, generally, meant to elicit a reaction. They want a reaction to the stimulation they offer. At best, their persuasive entreaties are meant to play with or manipulate your emotions. Be vigilant as to how these, and other cultural products address your total person. Unfortunately, much of our own society is not structured to facilitate or nurture the emergence of strong, self-sufficient people. We discussed earlier how culture and education is structured to create products that both support and perpetuate the status quo. Recognize how your energies run similar or how they differ from others in your own society and immediate communities. It is not necessarily a negative if your particular vibration does not sync or mesh with others in your family, or with other social groups. Your energy will ALWAYS match its own frequency; the phrase "water seeks its own level" depicts this occurrence. People will seek (and find) individuals like themselves, with similar character and values. It is essential to know your own Self and to filter energies with which you are in contact. Develop your discernment, mindfulness, and your own energy by engaging meaningfully with worthy people, activities, and causes. Protect yourself by distancing or insulating yourself from the ill effects of lesser energies or vibrations.

Constructing positive visualizations and meditating are two methodologies that process and structure energy. There are other forms of energy manipulation that can benefit your health, as well. Chi gong, tai chi, acupuncture and reiki can facilitate energy flow and process internal energies. Become familiar with different tools and processes that can serve you and contribute to your greater well-being.

"Our hearts resonate at the same frequency of the earth and the universe. Therefore, we are all valuable instruments in the orchestration of the world and its harmony." – **Suzy Klassen**

"All thoughts produce energetic vibrations, even though you can not see these frequencies, the airwaves are full of who you are." – **Unknown**

Enlightenment

Enlightenment is insight, or awareness, but it also has several forms, too.

In the late 17th century through the mid-18th century, there was the Age of Enlightenment, in which individualism contested tradition; it signified how people and cultures were breaking away from orthodoxy and forging new paths. Spiritual enlightenment refers to full comprehension of a situation and complete, total presence in the moment. Education and self-discipline deliver a specific degree of general enlightenment. Specific training and dedication designate an individual to be at a more refined level or of a greater enlightened state. But there is no telling about the ceiling or the limits of enlightenment. There are accounts of people pursuing enlightenment using a broad array of methodologies. Spiritual enlightenment is dedicated to the mastery of the self. When one exercises the discipline and restraint to overcome significant distractions or obstacles, enlightenment is reached, or obtained. Various cultures and religions address enlightenment differently. Generally, the Christians identify the Christ, and the belief in him as the path of salvation/enlightenment and everlasting life. Eastern perspectives, like Buddhism, and Hinduism, address enlightenment as *Bodhi, kensho, satori* and *moksha.*

This is an interesting point of the concept. I am not enlightened, so I am far from being a knowledgeable opinion about the subject, specifically. I have no mandate from heaven; God gave me no specific instructions. Being familiar with philosophies, cultures, religions, and my own spiritual experience, I can only share those lessons and results. Some maintain that the three-dimensional (3D) reality in which we live - comprising height, width, and depth - is an illusion, one is which we are somewhat imprisoned due to our attachment to the human experience. So once an individual reaches/obtains enlightenment, they might grasp a fuller reality, a world in and of itself, with the fullest sense of liberty once a condition of non-attachment is achieved. The state of enlightenment connotes a sense of purity - one that facilitates connection with the broadest universe, with

Enlightenment

Truth, and also with a form of divinity, as the enlightened individual transcends the world of forms in 3D, and unites with God and the larger multiverse - that which is distanced by our specific limitations wrought of human experience and perspective. But this is theory and hypothesis, conjecture and suggestion. In a simpler, and more direct manner of speaking, sages, philosophers, wise men, and paradigmatic figures across history and cultures admonish the common man to work on themselves. They suggest and advice people to grasp the potential, if not the reality of a world beyond that of our own senses. They are not speaking of reaching a far-off planet through space travel, either. These historical figures, including Plato, Jesus, Buddha, Lao Tzu, Suzuki, Mohammed, Dante, and Blake among others, recommend various practices in order to obtain a purity, or a mastery of self in order to become enlightened. A concept that they all have in common is that of mastering or controlling the mind. Generally, exercising control of the mind, heart, and body is an essential element of the enlightenment process. By restraining all three, one is not attached to the human experience. And that also does not mean that these individuals eliminated their friends, and family, either. The human experience, with the concepts of fraternity, cooperation, and love, all have a part to play within the process. For it is not the case that all elements of the human experience are distractions. We still need social interaction, family, food, exercise, and even fun. Those elements compose portions of enlightenment too, as they supply the opportunity to apply an enlightened perspective to the routine, even mundane, experiences of life.

The portion of thoughts, feelings and behaviors that are identified as unnecessary, or even unwelcome in the quest for enlightenment, are those that do not contribute to greater degrees of mindfulness or the health and purity of the mind, heart, and body. The concept of enlightenment has much to do with the concepts of separation and attachment. Separation refers to a mental state whereby

Enlightenment

the individual perceives a lack of unity. This perceived disunity means that the individual is an entity that is separate from all else - it is not others, or everything. They are also not the dog, a hamburger, or a random grain of sand in Egypt. Because an individual sees him or her self as separate, they form attachments, for they view all else as outside of them, different than their own self. So, individuals dwelling under the misconception of separation suffer from attachments to those materials that serve as temptations or as forms of the greater illusion. To address if not minimize or even eliminate attachments, different spiritual guides, philosophies, or religions recommend practicing techniques that bring about mindfulness. This state of consciousness is a presence in the Here and Now. A consequence of the separation mindset is a preoccupation with anything but the present and immediate context or setting. So, again: there is neither the past nor the future, there is only here and now. Mindfulness helps facilitate a greater awareness with a view toward doing away with the mistaken assumption of separation. Full and complete mindfulness delivers the understanding or truth that All-is-One. We are not disconnected, separate entities, but rather different forms of the same energy having different experiences via disunity and an illusion of separation. The French philosopher Pierre Teilhard de Chardin said, "We are not human beings having a spiritual experience; we are spiritual beings having a human experience." It is not the realization of this truth that delivers the enlightened state. There is no objective enlightenment threshold. Rather it is the case that you change as a being. Once an individual enjoins in the process, they are walking a decidedly different and remarkable path. The achievement of the goal is rare, indeed, hence the precious few that are deemed 'enlightened.' The process of enlightenment refers to insight and awareness. There are stages of progression. Patterns of thoughts, feelings and behaviors evolve and transform. Given persistent dedication, the entirety of one's being is radically different. Consider those who obtain the status; they are not the typical standard of person. They have shed the characteristics or avoided altogether many of the activities of regular, ordinary people. They do not live the common life of everyone else, nor can they. Given their aims and goals, they eschew the routine of the common man to achieve amazing aspirations. The realization of these goals is within everyone's grasp, though – given an exceedingly high standard of focus and diligence.

A concentrated self-discipline need be exerted in all walks of life to reach enlightenment. Developing sustained mindfulness, presence, and the character able to forego the life typical, ordinary people understand and live requires an address of everything; those on that path focus on all influences upon the mind, heart, and body. By focusing on our mental faculties and controlling our thoughts, we obtain a better grasp of our mind. Meditation aids in this process, as does reading and studying those works that contribute to the greater endeavor. Selectively engaging popular culture and media aids in the development of our passions and our emotions: our hearts. The more we can be in control of our feelings, the more we are able to balance much of our lives. This also extends to the company we keep. Those with whom we have extended interaction heavily influence our emotions and our thoughts.

Keeping company with positive, encouraging people facilitates a healthy life, not just one directed towards realizing enlightenment. Proper food and exercise deliver worthwhile results for our body, that temple that houses the God and Goddess within. Fresh, seasonal, organic foods (consider locally grown goodies, produced by growers that you know, in your own community) are the best options to enjoy optimal health. Minimize processed foods and those wares that contain ingredients whose names you can not pronounce or identify with ease. Practicing yoga and maintaining a routine of rest and exercise helps your body process the stress and wear of our modern lives. Yoga has been a prescribed practice for thousands of years and, when coupled with meditation, offers powerful, dynamic benefits for the motivated and focused participant.

Some Suggestions

-Be Here and Now. Let go of the past; leave the future to its proper encounter. Breathe and focus on the moment. Heed your thoughts and utilize your senses to fully experience 'this.'
-Seek wise counsel and read the ancients if not the original source material offered by knowledgeable opinion.
-Take pleasure in the moment. Again: be here and now...and enjoy it! -Meditate. Make a concentrated effort to refine and develop this skill. Couple it with yoga, if not yogic breathing.
-Study the 4 Noble Truths, and the Eight-Fold Path.
-Be mindful of all activities: eating, sleeping, ...even using the restroom. All events and experiences contribute to mindfulness and development when you are engaged, open to the opportunity of learning.
-Examine your unconscious and facilitate the process of 'integration.'
-Develop virtue, concentration, and wisdom.
-Remain humble. The enlightened did not look down their noses at others, and also did not publicize their growth or accomplishments. They did not readily announce how they are an 'old soul,' or that they were pursuing the actual goal of enlightenment. They put forth the effort and connected with their fellow man on an ethical and humane level

-Beware of the rules of cause and effect and that of karma. Keep your consciousness and intent in mind at all times.
-Focus on higher consciousness. Keep your goals in mind, saturate your thoughts with a view to the Good, and greater unity.

Esoteric

"People are afraid, very much afraid of those who know themselves. They have a certain power, a certain aura, and a certain magnetism, a charisma that can take out alive, young people from the traditional imprisonment. The awakened man can not be enslaved – that is the difficulty – and he can not be imprisoned. Every genius who has known something of the inner is bound to be a little difficult to be absorbed; he is going to be an upsetting force. The masses don't want to be disturbed, even though they may be in misery; they are in misery, but they are accustomed to the misery. And anybody who is not miserable looks like a stranger. The awakened man is the greatest stranger in the world; he does not seem to belong to anybody. No organization confines him, no community, no society, no nation." – **Osho, 'Awakened Man'**

Esoteric

Esoteric information is intended for or likely to be understood by only a small number of people with a specialized knowledge or interest. Esoteric knowledge usually pertains to the abstract, obscure, arcane, or the occult. Much of this field is on display, in public view, though the majority of people do not know enough about culture, history, religion, or spirituality to recognize it. Symbols are at play everywhere we look, and their benefit of their significance and meaning is for us to discover and harness, given applicable value or worth to our own lives and worldview.

While the symbols themselves are at hand, their consequence, or even their greater power, is not. It is in your best interest to be mindful, aware, and curious. Investigate your world and see what you can discover. The more you can uncover, the more you can make use of. Recall previous discussions of culture and education: everything is structured to benefit those in power, or to maintain the status quo. While some content is obfuscated, limited, or restricted, some important content remains accessible. Much is available for those who are diligent and persevere with their investigations. Invest in a wide array of studies and see what you can uncover 'behind the veil.' Realize that much of what serves as cultural foundations are often symbols for the esoteric; there is a reason why such information is distanced from the public's grasp or use.

Etiquette

The code of polite behavior in society is referred to as etiquette. It includes table manners, social graces, and the basics of decorum, or good/proper social form. More than civility or politeness, etiquette is what distinguishes individuals as classy from those who are base, uncouth, or vulgar. How one carries their self is consequential in the personal and professional realms. A person's bearing, or punctilio, is remarkably significant. Etiquette is more than just suggestions for dealing within polite company; it is also a framework for coordinating with all others. While some may not practice structured etiquette, their own behavior does not free you from the responsibility of behaving well and in consideration of others.

Etiquette covers communication, in the situations involving introductions, responses to invitations, or as 'thank you' notes, or when (or how) to make use of a cell phone in the company of others. It also includes handshakes, basic hygiene, and also how to behave when bodily functions/needs arise. Etiquette addresses punctuality and how to coordinate with others. A list of suggestions would be exhaustive and too much for the purposes of this greater effort. Consider how you would want to be treated, and how you could perform such that you set a standard of class and upbringing. It has been my goal to raise a daughter that carries herself in a refined, mature fashion. Belching at a dinner table, acting inconsiderate of others, or being overly harsh, if not mean, are not favorable characteristics. Be kind, well mannered, and a force of incredible good in the world by maintaining worthy values and behaving with others in mind.

Exclusive

To exclude, or to not admit other things, or limit inclusion to specific persons, groups, or areas is what is known as being exclusive. The term has been utilized several times over the course of this text. Time limits options so it has an exclusive element to it. Relationships can be either exclusive or inclusive. It is a concept that pertains to a remarkable array of other ideas and notions. As you make plans, consider how exclusivity plays a role. Question who or what is left out of rhetoric, plans, etc. Something is always excluded, but that is not solely a negative aspect. A critical thinker keeps in mind that which is affected in a broad sense. Be aware how this concept is at play, of how it influences dynamics or relationships between variables.

Experience

Practical contact with and observation of facts and events is experience. The moments to which you have access or participate in comprise your own experience. An experience you share with others is known as shared experience. The more you can broaden your experience by diversifying your skill set of knowledge, activities, languages, awareness, etc., the more able you are to interact and inter-relate. For it is not enough to just do something with people; it is vital that you be able to share and create meaning and significance with others. The more you know, the more you can connect and really experience the joys that result from meaningful exchanges with others.

Some people can connect with folks anywhere. That is primarily because they have an open mind, and a good heart. Their own experience may inform them that all people experience the same spectrum of human emotions. Nearly all folks can feel anger, sadness, happiness and even joy. Realizing that all have different experiences of similar emotions and thoughts makes it fairly simple to create a bond with a stranger and connect. Sharing those experiences and creating meaning by forging relationships shapes character that much more. Seek to broaden your experience and share it such that you help your fellow man. Your own personhood - your own experience - may brighten someone's day or even save someone's life. Make your experience meaningful in this life.

Expression

The process of making known one's thoughts and feelings is expression. It is the public offering of our inner selves. Expression demonstrates what we think or how we feel. Just as with all else, moderation is best. For the fullest expression is not necessary given the dynamic conditions of an audience; you will not address your boss as you would your closest peers. Live your life such that you have worthy thoughts and deep emotions to share appropriately, as the need arises.

Chapter 6

Failure

A failure is a lack of success. We will encounter challenges, obstructions, and serious delays of goals. At worst, we experience the failure of the realization of plans. Everyone fails at some point in his or her lives. Yet failure is not a purely negative occurrence. In fact, we learn more through failing than through continual or perpetual success. Thomas Edison once said, "I have not failed. I've just found 10,000 ways that won't work." Dealing with failure, and overcoming adversity, generally, is a most important life lesson; it is through the experience of temporary setbacks or disappointments in life that we get the privilege of challenges. Without the chance to develop, then demonstrate qualities borne of adversity, we would never get to realize our potential, and many of our best traits. Through difficulty we get to discover more about ourselves; we receive the opportunity to confront and overcome the obstacle and hopefully we emerge that much better for the experience.

Failure is temporary. It is a momentary occurrence. It can and will pass given time, proper attention, and consideration, too. It is imperative to note how one can never be a complete and total failure, forever. Given proper, incremental steps, we can achieve the worthwhile goals we set for ourselves. Obstructions and failures are delays that can be resolved or summarily dealt with when we realize their temporary character. That they will eventually pass does not mean we have the comfort of waiting them out; issues deserve prompt and direct attention. We need take initiative, for we are neither hopeless, nor without means. We can bring resources to bear on situations in order to mitigate the effects of a failure. We apply resources at our disposal to remedy circumstances. By engaging critically, we can identify pertinent variables, organize a plan and implement a strategy, if not an entirely new course of action. In the case of a catastrophic failure - one in which the original plan is utterly beyond hope or successful accomplishment - the same process comes into play, albeit variables are significantly changed.

In the face of failure, it is best to accept responsibility for our role or participation in the situation and proceed with next steps. Do not let failure impede the opportunity for growth or change your spirit. Put forth effort and purposely identify positives from the situation. Make the most of the failure and heed these words of WC Fields: "If at first you don't succeed, try, try again." By addressing the failure, lessons gleaned from the experience serve not only you, but others, as well. Addressing an issue - facing failures with resolve and dedication - exposes possible solutions or remedies. When others face a similar conundrum, your experience or knowledge can be applied. Giving up in the face of failure denies us the experience of personal growth. Do not fear failure. Recognize it, address it, then move past it. Learn and grow from it.

Faith

Complete trust or confidence in someone or something, or a strong belief in God or in the doctrines of a religion, or, that which is based on spiritual apprehension rather than proof, is faith. Faith is generally opposed to reason, or the presentation of logical proofs and evidence. The applications and limits of faith are important to examine. Everyone exercises faith in some way or another; we all have faith that the sun will rise in the morning (Again, explore the work of David Hume), and that the theory of gravity will remain valid, or present with the falling of our next steps. Faith is nearly synonymous with trust. It is a concept employed by Buddhism, Hinduism, Christianity, Islam, and Judaism. All of these perspectives differ as to what is worthy of faith and how to apply it.

Faith is applied to items that warrant some degree of confidence, whether they can be proven objectively or not. In large part, faith is an array of concepts that structures or, at least, influences life and how it is lived. Trust, commitment, and action demonstrate how faith is applied. We first form or encounter a belief we agree with or feel strongly about and commit to holding it. Given that the belief has meaning or is pertinent to the larger world outside of our own mind, our actions reflect that belief. So whether we believe in the objective reality of a deity, or that we maintain the sun will shine, we employ a similar, general process of faith. The belief held firmly in mind, we commit to that faith in the deity, or the sun's continued presence. Actions and behaviors then substantiate that faith. Lives are spent honoring or serving the deity, and people continue with their routines because through their faith they believe and then subjectively commit to the thought of the sun rising. The implementation of faith transforms some people's beliefs into facts. They are subjectively certain of the reality of their deity or they accept as fact that the sun will rise tomorrow. That they hold these things on faith does *not* mean that the beliefs are true, however. They are true enough, to the holder of the faith, or belief.

The Stages of Faith offered by James Fowler is worth some investigation. Fowler maintains that, corresponding to the human life span, there are stages of faith development[10]. One need not progress through all stages and some stages may be in place, or accepted, for the span of a complete lifetime. There is no objective summit or final stage of faith. Generally, faith is a radically subjective experience. People rely on it. It allows for connection and a form of internal-intellectual-emotional support. Examine the concept of faith and decide how it will have a presence or play a role in your own life.

Fallacy

A fallacy is a failure in reasoning that renders an argument invalid. An argument is an exchange of diverging or opposing views, or a reason or set of reasons given with the aim of persuading others that actions or views are right or wrong. We encounter different, conflicting views and information every day. Making sense of and utilizing data is essential to the success of endeavors, for mistaken beliefs and wrong information can greatly influence events and plans. Recognizing logical fallacies of argument help us sort perspectives and information. They allow us to critique reasons, arguments, and strategy.

Some people utilize fallacies without intending to, while others intentionally apply them because the fallacious reasoning escapes the audience; the audience may not recognize the fallacy at play or why it is a failure in reasoning. Being able to engage logically, and discern the presence of fallacies aids discussion and facilitates greater understanding. It is an *essential* skill to think well and to communicate cogent, salient thoughts. Being able to identify fallacies sharpens mental faculties and contributes to a more meaningful and precise exchange of information. This is vital to a functional, rational, and communicative society. Given the overwhelming presence of mass media, and the fact that we live in the age of information, we are benefited immediately when we apply the ability to identify the strength or weakness of different arguments and rationales.

Family

What is a family? There are many standards as to what the relationship actually *is*. A family could be comprised of only two people; children are not a necessary component of a family dynamic. Grandparents, uncles, and aunts sometimes serve as the heads of a household or family. Oftentimes, pets are included as family members. Standards have changed over time and cultures. Now a family need not even consist of blood relatives. Harper Lee once wrote, "You can choose your friends but you sho' can't choose your family, an' they're still kin to you no matter whether you acknowledge 'em or not, and it makes you look right silly when you don't." We are at a time, though, when we can - and do - choose our family. Children formally emancipate themselves from their parents in some situations. Some children simply run away from their families. Family consists of those people who are important to the person calling them family. That importance is demonstrated by inclusion, respect, care, love and a broad spectrum of other possible concepts.

Regardless of the family structure or setting, ensure that it is a worthy relationship. Families, just as in the case of all other relationships, require commitment, trust, and work. It is a consequential responsibility of maintaining a family as the values at play in the home are important, have consequence, and contrast in the greater outside realms. The family affects the community just as the same community affects and influences the family's own situation. Though maintaining a family and participating as a member is a notable responsibility, it can be quite a meaningful joy, as well. Care for yourself such that you can care for your family - whatever that relationship entails.

Fear

The unpleasant emotion caused by the belief that someone or something is dangerous, likely to cause pain, or is a threat is called fear. Fear can be rational and serve a positive purpose, or it can be irrational and impede productivity or meaningful development. A healthy fear keeps us safe from real, verified threats to our well-being. We need heed those fears as they protect and serve our self-interest. Fear causes a change in metabolism and organ functions within the human body. Some reactions to fears include fleeing, hiding, or freezing - becoming paralyzed. These reactions are a result of fears that are perceived in the present or yet to occur in the future. The fear response allows us to confront or avoid the threat (known as the fight or flight response). Extreme fear responses, as in the case of encountering horror or terror, can elicit the freeze or paralysis.

Rational fears are appropriate and the opposite is true: irrational fears are inappropriate. Training our minds to recognize the differences between the two is an invaluable life skill. Rational fears are natural, healthy occurrences. Given proper education and well-rounded experience, one should have little difficulty in identifying those concerns that bear concern and warrant a specific course of action. Irrational fears start with the mind. They are the symptom of mental faculties that are out of control or undisciplined. A convenient tool to differentiate between the two types of fear is to apply an acronym: F.E.A.R. (False Expectations Appearing Real). Given that false (as opposed to realistic) expectations are identified, the thoughts can be revised and the fear can be dispelled. But in the presence of a real, substantive threat or danger that needs be confronted or avoided, fear is a very healthy instinct.

About 70 thousand years ago, we experienced a cognitive revolution with the advent of Neolithic times, and again, with the onset of the Industrial Revolution. Life became noticeably easier with both occasions. The difficulty level of the environment became lower and lower. Terror and extreme fear has now been replaced with boredom. William James noted how there was a "decrease in frequency of proper occasions for fear." A study shows how people born after 1945 were ten times more likely to be depressed than those born at the turn of the century.[11]
It could be said that we are suffering from too little stress,

or more particularly: we are not testing our mettle and it is affecting us negatively. Viktor Frankl identified how suffering was a human achievement; tension and anxiety are necessary for mental health. Our cultural avoidance of significant challenges that would shape or impart worthy character is an ultimate detriment to the health and wellness of the people.

While various advances in technology or medicine have made life easier for billions across the globe, we have yet to keep pace with quality, for ease does not necessarily correlate with quality. People remain grappling with meaning and purpose in their lives. That people live easier lives does not mean that they are living better ones. In fact, studies show the challenge of boredom to have severe existential consequences. Lacking the structure, or even the impetus to explore or test our subjective mettle, we languish in survival mode instead of investigating what it means to thrive - truly *live*. A lack of significant encounters with fear has left us bereft of substantial and important aspects of character.

Some fears warrant the direct confrontation while others deserve distance and cognition. One can mitigate the consequences of facing fears; spiders and snakes can be handled, or kept distanced, but facing the fears of a runaway, out-of-control vehicle is another matter entirely. Gauge whether the fears you hold are rational or inappropriate. Do not let fear cripple you or force you to lose the opportunity for growth and development. Be wise as to which fears you face and which fears are meant for your protection and well-being.

"If you know the enemy and know yourself you need not fear the results of a hundred battles." – **Sun Tzu**

"The only thing we have to fear is fear itself." - **Franklin D. Roosevelt**

"Only when we are no longer afraid do we begin to live."
- **Dorothy Thompson**

"Thinking will not overcome fear but action will." - **W. Clement Stone**

"The oldest and strongest emotion of mankind is fear, and the oldest and strongest kind of fear is fear of the unknown." - **H. P. Lovecraft**

"Avoiding danger is no safer in the long run than outright exposure. The fearful are caught as often as the bold." - **Helen Keller**

"A nation that is afraid to let its people judge the truth and falsehood in an open market is a nation that is afraid of its people." - **John F. Kennedy**

"We fear the thing we want the most." - **Robert Anthony**

"So then learn to conquer your fear. This is the only art we have to master nowadays: to look at things without fear, and to fearlessly do right." - **Friedrich Durrenmatt**

"Ultimately we know deeply that the other side of every fear is freedom." - **Marilyn Ferguson**

"One can choose to go back toward safety or forward toward growth. Growth must be chosen again and again; fear must be overcome again and again." – **Abraham H. Maslow**

Flow

To move along steadily, continuously is to flow, or be fluid. Energy and water flow. When they meet an obstruction, they change routes, adapt, and continue. We will meet with obstacles, obstructions, challenges, and woes. We need be like energy and water: flow just as they do. The great Bruce Lee once said, "...be like water. Empty your mind. Now you can put water in a cup; it becomes the cup; you put water into a bottle, it becomes the bottle; you put it in a teapot, it becomes the teapot. Now water can flow, or it can crash. Be water, my friend." Flow in the face of life's challenges. Be able to respond and act. Be mindful of how extraordinary situations *can*, in fact, cripple or paralyze you. Train and discipline your head, heart and hands in order to behave appropriately as you encounter all forms of stimuli in the world.

Freedom

The concept of freedom maintains a special place in United States culture. It is one of the foundational premises of the nation, and it is enshrined in different cultural institutions and media in order to demonstrate its significance. Freedom is the power or right to act, speak, or think as one wants without hindrance or restraint. It is the absence of subjection, either to foreign domination or despotic government. It is the state of not being imprisoned or enslaved. The concept has consequence in the realm of ideas as it is associated with free will and self-determination as well as moral responsibility. Freedom has a presence - or lack thereof - in every single behavior or activity. The question of freedom concerns if thought is innate or that a deterministic brain is engaged every time. It is connected with ideas of liberty and autonomy, living by one's own laws. In a broader communal sense, political freedoms amount to having rights and civil liberties to exercise without undue interference. Political freedoms include the freedom of assembly, association, choice, and speech.

Freedom takes many forms. One might state that they wish to be free of servitude, wants/desires, or conditions. People want to be free of hunger while ascetics and other disciplined individuals strive to be free of attachments. Politicians make use of the term, 'the free world.' Freedom can be internal or external. Internal freedom consists of one's thoughts, feelings, and personality. It is affected or maligned by dogma, fear, and habits. Balance, moderation, and will-power influence internal freedom. What and how we feel and think influences all else. Internal freedom is remarkably consequential, for without it, there is no self-control. Lacking self-control, opportunities for learning decrease and possibilities for growth diminish. Those who experience significant upheaval, trauma, or loss can be conditioned to fear. Fears give rise to insecurities that deride internal freedom. If there is no internal freedom, external freedom becomes impossible.

External freedom refers to what one has or does. Injustice and the environment curtail it. When one experiences safety and security, they generate confidence. Confidence allows for action, and initiative – participation with the greater public or communal spheres. Confidence works significant wonders for both internal and external freedoms. The balance of the two equates to health. Internal freedom is composed of and elicits responsibility. The individual serves as his or her own mental master. The confidence generated makes possible agency and the application of power in the external realm, encouraging external freedom. The responsibility of the self in internal and external realms is correlated with power; the more responsibility one wields, the more power is available.

The phrase 'freedom from…' is an example of negative liberty, which is freedom from external restraint. It is the liberty one person may have to restrict the rights of others. It contrasts with positive liberty - the possession of the power or resources to fulfill one's potential. Liberty concerns the absence of arbitrary restraints and takes into account the rights of all involved. It is subject to capability and limited by the rights of others. Freedom and liberty overlap; some contend that they are equivocations. However, the usage of the terms demonstrates an important difference. We note the use of freedom to do something, or 'freedom from' something else. Liberty is not understood similarly; there is no liberty 'from' something. Further, liberty applies to humans, while freedom can pertain to nearly all living, sentient creatures. See **Liberty**.

Freedom affords successes differentiated among actors. This variable spectrum of success elicits inequality and people often resent how some suffer, while others earn or gain more. Some identify how employees of Wal-Mart survive on food stamps and government aid, while the CEO earns more than 400x the rate of a standard worker. Others acknowledge that there would be no job were it not for the initiative and applied freedom of the CEO or management. As a different aspect of freedom, consider when slaves are released from bondage. How free can they be when they lack the necessary means of advancing their self-interest? This is not to say that slavery is preferred - definitely NOT - but the pertinent question is: what can they do, in their subjective circumstance, with their freedom? Or: what sense does freedom make in light of a lack of perceived or real/tangible resources (the means of applying and exercising freedom)? Significant thinkers have addressed freedom. The philosopher Rousseau contended that individual freedom is achieved through participation in the process whereby one's community exercises collective control over its affairs in accordance with a majority perspective, or a 'general will.' Hegel, in his *Science of Logic,* said, "Will without freedom is an empty word." FDR identified four freedoms that elicit the ultimate human freedom: freedom of speech and worship, as negative liberties, and freedoms from want and fear, as positive liberties.

Libertarians including Ron Paul disagree with the idea of positive liberty and he maintains that the individual owes nothing to society if they are not doing anything to harm others. This is but one response to the idea of wealth distribution as recourse to differentiated levels of success owing to individual freedom. Paul contends that two people can not be free if one would take from the other. Paul's specific approach to liberty and freedom is well worth the investigation and engagement.

Circumstances and conditions of freedom have changed since 1776. In the past, individuals did not need to ask permission from the government to:

- collect rainwater
- hunt
- go fishing
- own a weapon
- own a property
- start a business
- protest
- cut hair
- set up a lemonade stand
- renovate your home
- build a home
- use a transportation vehicle
- get married
- grow food on your property
- sell food.

The list of activities requiring governmental oversight and involvement has grown immensely. Should the country be *truly* free, this list would decrease in size and number. Freedom of both internal and external varieties deserves special investment in order to produce meaningful returns. Being one's own master of thoughts, feelings, and actions elicits health, balance, power, and responsibility - all as benefits, or positive consequences of the activity. Freedom requires work and substantial effort in order to perpetuate and further its presence. An investment in the Self yields worthy results - freedom being a significant one among them.

"If the freedom of speech is taken away then dumb and silent we may be led, like sheep to the slaughter." – **George Washington**

Friend

A person whom one knows and with whom one has a bond of mutual affection is a friend. People with close friendships are happier; it is not the quantity of relationships that is important, but the quality of those dynamics. There are many forms of friendship. Some vary per setting, or context. But certain characteristics are present regardless of the situation. Among those characteristics are affection, trust, honesty, loyalty, sympathy, empathy, understanding, compassion, enjoyment, communication/expression, and acceptance. Friends make this life worthwhile, memorable, and significant. Be the type of friend you want to have and contribute to the well-being of meaningful relationships. Invest in them and work on them - by putting forth diligent effort and those resources that deliver a mutually beneficial and reciprocated enjoyment.

Frivolity, Fun

Lightheartedness, levity, or lack of seriousness is frivolity, or fun. While the former term is also synonymous with the word 'unnecessary,' fun is anything but unnecessary. Life is to be enjoyed. It is here for us to make use of, and it might as well be a pleasure. We need not engage hedonistically, but fun is awesome in moderation and it is a necessary component of a balanced life.

Future

The time that is regarded as 'still to come' is the future. It is wise to take the future into consideration. Prepare for future needs and situations. Balance that view toward the future by remaining grounded in the present moment. Do not forego the significance of the Here and Now by looking down the line. Presently, we need not exclude living a life that is considerate of practical, future concerns, but we should mind the requirements of the moment while behaving as if time will continue, and that the future will come to pass.

Chapter 7

Game

A form of play or sport, especially a competitive one played according to rules and decided by skill, strength, or luck is a game. Games are intended to be fun distractions from consequential, serious endeavors. Concepts of competition and cooperation, rewards and consequences, and game theory guide this particular discussion.

Games are designed to pass time. They are recreation - meant to refresh and rejuvenate. Games are a necessary balance to responsibilities, yet they serve important functions, too. They develop physical, social, intellectual, and cognitive skills. They improve judgment. The concept of fairness helps build or implement noble moral quality. By coordinating with others, we learn the value of teamwork and the importance of individual sacrifice for a group or communal effort. Unity is an important concept for a society, and team games help implement or demonstrate it in action. Further, teammates need follow instructions from a captain or leader.

A victory in a game builds self-esteem and confidence. That it is a game insulates the participants from the stress or concerns involved in meaningful, consequential life decisions. Defeat offers some positives, as well. Defeat serves as an impetus or a motivator of greater effort. It teaches humility, and the ethics of taking greater defeats in the 'real world' in stride. Jim Nash's work with game theory demonstrates how, given coordination of participants, a loser need not be distinguished. Among different outcomes, when participants serve not only their own best interests, but also work to achieve the best good for all actors included, none need be excluded from winning or be designated as the losing party. All too often, this fact is eliminated from the realm of possibility. Games designate an outcome containing solely winners and losers. Consider games or other situations as opportunities for coordination and cooperation. While competition can serve some good, those greater rewards elicited by cooperative enterprises, games and activities have yet to be realized - in both the recreational realm and beyond.

Genetics

The study of heredity and the variation of inherited characteristics from one generation to the next is the field of genetics. Genetics studies how organisms obtain their variations, their mutations, or general differences. Living things inherit traits from parents. People and cultures noted how crops and animals could be selectively bred in order to elicit specific traits and create worthy/strong/lasting products, or varieties. Genetics is the study of the most basic components of living organisms: genes, nucleotides, amino acids, proteins and DNA. It involves how genes (discrete hereditable units) are passed from parents to progeny.

Genetic processes work in combination with an organism's environment and experience to influence the development and behavior of an organism. This is the nature versus nurture discussion. Genetics explores how basic components coordinate in an environment to shape or influence a particular entity. This realm covers an immense amount of material and a school's science department will provide a fuller explanation of the many facets of the field. One of the most important questions of genetics is to consider how biological components and/or an environment shape and influence an organism. This is a fascinating investigation and there is no solid, definitive, and objective answer pertaining to all individuals/organisms/species. This becomes a most enjoyable inquiry to see how variables play out per study.

Giving

Giving pertains to the transfer of possessions, materials or energy. Laws are given, as is money, along with things like colds, shits, and damns. For the purpose of this section, we focus on the gift of the self. Just as you are a gift to me, and the greater world, you also have the opportunity to apply/give yourself to people, activities, and causes. Your foundation, or platform of skills and abilities, can be of service. Your personality and attitude can provide someone with care and concern. The intent underlying your gift or offering is significant; what do you intend by giving yourself by participating in a context, or by applying your own self?

Gifts and giving typically denote care or demonstrate generosity. Giving makes a difference. When that generous or considerate character is absent, one is said not to 'give a shit' or to not 'give a damn.' When giving, care enough to give something worthwhile, something virtuous, of good. Your gifts and provisions can be reciprocated in exchange, so associate with those who appreciate, recognize, and grasp those same worthy qualities and effort. Give your best and make a difference with your gifts, and the ability to give.

Glory

High renown, honor, or praise won by notable achievements, magnificence or great beauty, and taking great pride or pleasure in something, is glory. This concept is another that is unrivalled, unparalleled. Glory serves as an extreme concept on a spectrum. It is reserved for only the most remarkable of achievements. One is not glorified for living a mundane or trivial existence. Glory is bestowed on those who contribute greatly for those who substantially improve a context or create/invent something of great distinction or merit. When you consider who receives glory, the values of a community are demonstrated. Athletes, war heroes, and those who save lives are all examples of those who receive glory. How and why does a community or organization glorify someone or something?

Some scenes in nature are glorious; the sight of a child's birth, or that of an amazing athletic performance, or a spectacular sunrise/sunset inspire the concept or deserve the sentiment. Similarly, when one beholds a stunning work of art, or an astounding expression of music, perhaps, they can enjoy that object in "all its glory." Put forth your best effort – your best thoughts, feelings and actions. While some seek glory, worthy actions and contributions are valuable regardless of whether they are publicly acknowledged or attended. Be more concerned with behaving well than receiving praise or recognition. A life lived well is sufficient reward, in and of itself.

God, Goddess

A masculine God, or a female deity, a Goddess, is a supreme being. They are deities which religions and cultures describe with powerful attributes and special characteristics. They serve as the ultimate source of moral authority. They have power over nature or over human fortunes and are sometimes immortal. Gods are objects of faith, though some maintain that perceived cosmic order or the incredible, awe-inspiring magnitude of nature and the whole of creation are the proof of their existence.

The posited reality of deities is a facet of philosophical investigation referred to as metaphysics. It involves first principles of things such as being, knowing, substance, cause, identity, time and space. A God is typically referred to as beyond these concepts; Gods are denoted as primary - preceding even existence. So a God presumably created time, space, and serves as the first cause of all else. God is a spiritual being. While the deity has relevance in and influence over the material plane, their own reality and place concerns a higher transcendent realm. A God is immaterial, an abstract being that can take on characteristics of form or substance to make itself known or coherent to man's own limited perspective. Otherwise, a God (in and of itself) is beyond the reckoning of man and our own base, material sense faculties. It is for this reason that people are skeptical as to the reality of a God or Goddess. While miracles, extraordinary beauty, or amazingly precise natural ratios motivate believers to hold faith or conclude that the existence of gods is necessary, others are not similarly persuaded. The latter are reluctant to accept such claims given the possibilities of other causes. That some skeptics do not believe in a deity also does not mean that they lack or even ignore their own subjective spiritual needs. Instead of believing in or relying upon a deity, some address their spiritual needs as other forms, whether it is in the form of energy, pantheism, or paganism. There are numerous approaches to spirituality, and a belief in a monotheistic God is but one. The Western conception of God is monotheism, meaning that God is one sole deity, and He is the first cause and supreme authority. In contrast, some Eastern perspectives employ no God, while in India, adherents select as to which form of Krishna to worship.

A belief in God has resulted in the institutionalization of worship. In some cases, salvation, redemption, or enlightenment is via the leadership of the institution, be it a church, a synagogue, temple, etc. Religion is the belief in and worship of a superhuman controlling power, especially a personal God or Gods. It is a particular system of faith and worship. A religion is a facet of some forms of culture and it conveys an education as to the foundations, history, rites and general rationale concerning the worship and service of the particular deity involved. As we have discussed in previous sections, culture and education feature an element of or association with power. What is perpetuated or conveyed serves a status quo and, in most cases, those holding power or serving as leadership. Religion is a cultural structure, a social institution, which wields tremendous power and influence. Wars and atrocities have been committed in the service of beliefs. That millions of people adhere to religious institutions means that those serving as their leadership hold tremendous sway over their audiences and congregations. It is important to be critically engaged as to the belief in, or worship of deities or Gods. Critical discernment is applied to the realm of spirituality just as in all other realms. Make certain that a meaningful evaluation of beliefs is not over-ridden by the passive acceptance of a dogma (a belief or set of beliefs that is accepted by a person or group, without being questioned or critiqued and analyzed). Your spirituality is your own.

Spiritual values inform nearly all realms of life. Engage meaningfully, and critically to construct and maintain worthy spiritual values. Decide for yourself whether a belief in God or Goddess is in your own best interest.

"All the Gods, all the heavens, all the hells are within you." – **Joseph Campbell**

Good

That which is morally right or righteous, is 'the Good.' Considering the Good involves an investigation of what is ethical or moral. This is a philosophical analysis that involves systematizing, defending, and recommending concepts of right and wrong. Every act has a moral or ethical component. That an action affects the actor doing the deed, or serves to influence a wider public realm, invites an inquiry as to the relative worth of the behavior. We ask, "Is this good? Why or why not? Are there better behaviors, or does this stand as the best standard or policy?" Too often this critical investigation is absent. Individuals or groups/institutions behave irrespective of the morality of their actions. Their ethics then demonstrate how they are concerned for the gains or advantages elicited by their own actions, instead of being considerate of broader ramifications or consequences. The examination of the good is wholly necessary. Though it may delay an immediate action or result, investigating the morality of behavior is always a worthy inquiry. Make certain you critique contexts as to the ethical precedents involved and seek the Good, the best in all situations. How do your behaviors facilitate the presence or the realization of the highest and best good, for all involved?

Gospel

A gospel is an account describing the life, death, and resurrection of Jesus of Nazareth. The most widely known examples are the form of canonical gospels of Matthew, Luke, Mark and John. These are included in the Bible's New Testament and serve as the substantive foundation of Christianity. There are also apocryphal gospels, non-canonical gospels, Jewish-Christian gospels and gnostic gospels.

Christianity places a high value on the canonical gospels; they are central or essential to its belief system. Many historians do not believe in the historical reliability of the books and oppose the concept of Biblical inerrancy. It is important to study the gospels for the lessons, morals, and cultural references contained therein. Understanding different spiritual beliefs helps us comprehend different cultures, people, and their behaviors. Studying Jesus, the gospels, and the larger text of the Bible informs as to many critical elements of Western history, religion, psychology, and one of the most powerful institutions in the world, the Catholic Church.

Grace

Grace, in Christianity, is divine dispensation, or God's spontaneous gift to man. It is not something earned nor a created substance. God alone initiates grace in the relationship between God and man, and it is most often represented as salvation, redemption, or forgiveness of sins. The believer need first have faith, but also it helps to address their own disposition by performing virtuous acts or remaining humble. The Catholic Church's sacraments serve as representations of, or vehicles for grace. The common use of grace in everyday language is meant to describe the provision of some material or event that occurs without human cause or intent. As an example, one might say, "By the grace of God, we escaped that disaster."

Grounding

Grounding, or earthing, is about awareness that we act from a physical body as well as endeavoring to develop spiritual awareness and development. Grounding can be synonymous with centering or focusing, but the distinguishing characteristic is that of connecting to the actual earth (hence the term, earthing). An array of symptoms may denote the need for grounding.
-Dizziness
-Daydreaming
-Feeling sick
-Heart palpitations
-Weight gain
-Clumsiness
-Static shocks
-Falling asleep when meditating
-Noise and light sensitive
-Forgetful
-Arguing and unable to get your point across.

Grounding

Some grounding/earthing techniques include:

-Eating healthy & balanced meals
-Sports, yoga, tai chi etc.
-Drinking water
-Walking/Hiking especially in natural surroundings
-Gardening
-Have contact with Animals eg. walking the dog
-Being purposeful
-Visualization

Chapter 8

Happiness

Happiness is *the* moral goal of life. For philosophers, it is a state of mind or a product of a life that goes well. Plato and Aristotle contributed meaningfully with their approaches to the concept. For Plato, the only truly happy individuals were those who were moral actors. To be moral, they needed to understand the virtues, especially that of justice. Control of the self amounted to happiness, while a greater element of social justice pertained to the community. When an individual performed one's social function with applied/implemented morals and virtues, the satisfaction of the particular duty elicits happiness. As for Aristotle, happiness is equated to human flourishing via his idea of *eudaimonia*, which for him stood as the goal of human thought and action. Eudaimonia was activity that made use of virtues and propriety. It is a chief good, in and of itself, as opposed to lesser, if not false forms of happiness like leisure, wealth, or pleasure.

Later thinkers attached or associated happiness with God, making happiness an external good that was predicated of others, rather than an internally regulated and volitional phenomenon. We note how predicating happiness on externals is folly. People, places, and things will change or cease and, should our happiness be intimately connected with them, it would unnecessarily change or cease, just the same. Happiness can be constant for as long as the effort and mindfulness is committed to perpetuating the state. This means that happiness - a meaningful, considerate condition of happiness, at that - is available wherever, whenever and to whoever desires to enjoy the state. Keep happiness in mind and watch as your external reality coordinates with that internal state.

Health

The complete state of mental, physical, and social well-being, and not merely the absence of disease or infirmity, is health. Health refers to the general conditions of the head, heart, and body of an individual. Spiritual wellness is also a form of health. Health typically includes the concepts of balance, and moderation. When activities or variables are operating harmoniously, a condition of health if achieved. Elements out of balance, or exercised immoderately, beg or invite correction. Given the same prolonged state, faculties break down, and health suffers. Spiritual, intellectual/emotional and physical health have different components, and are maintained using various methodologies.

Spiritual wellness provides a sense of subjective purpose. One maintains spiritual health by being focused on the Good and maintaining their own subjective path. Those who are spiritually well have a grasp of their own unique sense of the divine. They know how they are connected to the greater universe and they structure their beliefs, thoughts, and actions towards maintaining or realizing the fullest of connections. The spiritually healthy are strong and determined in their focus, and that spirituality itself is wholesome, positive, and good. Can a strong and determined focus of belief in a negative or evil spiritual practice be called healthy?

Mental health is a person's condition with regard to their psychological and emotional well-being. The World Health Organization (WHO) defines mental health as, "a state of well-being in which an individual realizes his or her own potential, can cope with the normal stresses of life, can work productively and fruitfully, and is able to make a contribution to their society."[12] Psychological health is important with respect to how one functions, adapts, and whether our lives have the ability to be satisfying and productive, or not. The WHO's definition is very telling, as it seems apparent that only a precious few have the means of securing that particular state of well-being. Is it most people that realize their own potential? Who can cope with what we consider as normal stresses of life, when that list is inclusive of social unrest, radical economic turbulence, and the escalating number of traumatic incident? To participate with such variables seems to be insanity. Consider what Nietzsche offered regarding the void. How can well-being result in such an environment with such conditions?

Who obtains meaningful and significant employment at a reasonable wage? In the United States, the real unemployment rate hovers near five percent, according to official standards, but that rate does not address whether the work is meaningful, or if the employed are productive, nor if the benefit of the job is fruitful, or even sufficient to address basic necessities. As far as making a contribution to society, it also seems to be the case that people can not look beyond their own needs in order to address the larger community. Or, as a lesser component of our times, people will not even look to the condition of their community and they refuse to contribute to its vitality, or longevity.

Do people believe that their contribution is necessary or of value? The idea of community might be considered lost upon the folks comprising them. By this, I mean that there is no real community, but merely a society of isolated individuals. Can we plausibly maintain that our culture/greater society has mental or psychological health, and provides the means of the production and maintenance of it? It seems more likely that conditions comprising the social, political, economic and environmental realms contribute to the very opposite. Kurt Vonnegut once wrote, "A sane person to an insane society must appear insane." Imagine the individual who belongs in a depraved society. They would be defined as sane as their peers, though a distanced, objective perspective would consider them differently altogether.

The condition of optimal well-being is physical health. A proper diet, a routine of exercise, rest, and meditation help keep our bodies functioning optimally. But, as pertaining to the aforementioned realms of the mental and emotional sectors of a community: what good is a healthy body when the head and the heart are in sorry states of disrepair or of a woefully degraded condition? It is almost as if, were it to actually be the case that optimal physical health has been achieved by a significant portion of the population, we are not operating as actors with bodies, but as automatons - husks devoid of substantial thoughts, lacking the vivacity provided by passion, if not disciplined, rational emotions. Prior cultures needed healthy slave populations to (perhaps) erect the pyramids or work plantations. Masters did not need or want mentally or spiritually healthy servants. All they needed was the bodies to labor and perform assigned tasks deemed below the position of the leadership or ruling class. This portion of the discussion assumes that the United States population is physically healthy, though. Our food system is in a wretched state. Joel Salatin's text, *Folks, this Ain't Normal*, depicts how far we have strayed from a previous standard of healthy, inclusive, communal local food system, and the consequences for our greater society. His conclusions demonstrate unnerving consequences. Given the increasing rate of obesity in the country, there is no real standard of exercise and, in this harried culture, it would be difficult to imagine that a real standard or routine of sufficient rest is in place, as well. Consider the percentage of folks who need keep several jobs in order to provide for basic necessities. The majority of folks have no real chance to rest.

In the section regarding energy, we discussed frequency or vibrations. For the purposes of this concept of health, we reiterate the fact that *everything is energy*. The thoughts or words we use have an energy component, as does food, music, or media, emotions, etc. The frequencies of the substances we eat, breathe, and otherwise absorb or encounter can heal or degrade us. One need welcome or participate with those frequencies that heal and build a comprehensively healthy person. What is our society doing to us, energetically? It seems quite obvious that it is a difficult task to be healthy mentally, physically, or spiritually, when greater social contexts are in extreme states of flux and disarray.

Heart

The heart is a physical organ responsible for pumping blood through the body. The term also refers to the emotional or moral natures as opposed to the intellectual nature or capacities. The term also refers to the central, innermost, essential or vital components of a system or construct (as in: the heart of the matter). The heart is a distinguishing characteristic and is most significant within the dynamics of most cultures.

The heart as a physical component is most important. I entrust science and biology classes to provide the fullest explication of the workings of the circulatory system. In this section, though, we focus on the heart chakra within the physical body. While the third eye chakra, or the pineal and pituitary glands bring about insight or spiritual connection, the heart chakra is absolutely central as to spiritual well-being and the energetic development of the individual. The heart is the point of balance within the energetic system. Physically, the heart is a huge center of electrical energy, just like the brain. The electrical signals that are carried through the cells and the muscles of the heart control the complex processes of the timing of the contractions of the chambers of the heart and the speed of heart rate, adjusting for activity levels. But the heart does much more.

According to the HeartMath Institute, "The heart generates the largest electromagnetic field of the body. The electrical field as measured in an electrocardiogram (ECG) is about 60 times greater in amplitude that the brain waves recorded by an electroencephalogram (EEG)."[13] The signal from one's heart is picked up, or registers in the brain of another person who is nearby. The field of our heart is so powerfully active and it is what influences our surroundings strongly. The heart is the center of connectivity with the rest of the world. Feelings emanate and pertain to the rest of the outside world, while thoughts can separate if not isolate us from our immediate surroundings. Imagine the individual who is lost in thought and walks into a pond or gets hit by a vehicle as they cross the street. It is not feelings that make an individual aloof, as thoughts do. When we apply our heart and connect to anything, be it nature, a loved one, the divine, or even a memory, that sense of connection is felt in the chest or heart region. It is of utmost importance then, to care for the physical heart and, specifically, its corresponding chakra. The more we clear blockages and facilitate that flow of energy, the more we are open to connect meaningfully, with whatever we have as our object or goal. And this means being responsible for the energies we put out to the surrounding area - outside of ourselves - as well. Energy permeates everything and its best to manage our participation responsibly and respectfully.

As an interesting aside, it is very interesting to understand the influence rest and dental hygiene have on the heart. A lack of sufficient rest or sleep and poor dental hygiene affects the well-being of the heart. Generally, a healthy mouth means a healthy heart and proper rest protects against heart disease and a host of other ills, too.

An examination of the emotional and moral component of the individual is most instructive. As stated previously, the energies of the heart are powerful; by extension, feelings are more powerful than thoughts. It is the emotional capacities that give strength and deeper character to our thoughts, and they are an integral, central aspect of our personhood. Emotional maturity refers to the ability to understand and manage emotions. An emotionally mature person has experienced the spectrum of emotions, understands the consequences of each, and knows the benefits of living in control of them. They know how to identify each emotion clearly. They know when and how to properly apply them. They manage themselves accordingly. An emotionally mature person is empathetic, accountable, self-aware, flexible, and confident. This list of characteristics is but a portion of greater self-mastery. Another part of self-mastery is the knowledge and inclusion of and the respect for others. This is the moral aspect of having and making good proper use of the heart.

We need be cognizant and respectful of the needs of others. And that does not mean that one need capitulate to the caprices of others or bend over backwards to satisfy the wants, whims, and fancies of all. Morality speaks to realizing the principles concerning the distinction between right and wrong. But, as we are not the sole humans living in this realm, we need be aware of the spectrum of human behavior and work with one another to implement and protect inclusive, moral principles. A study of cultures, history, philosophy, ethics, combines with the experience of coordinating or interacting with people informs us as to how we can behave. The moral element: applying our heart (!) is of critical importance. We recognize how everyone will experience the spectrum of emotions: happiness, sadness, anger, grief, joy, etc. We need make room for contrasting perspectives and experiences, while maintaining a mediated standard of morality. That someone believes in the merit of female genital mutilation does not mean that it is acceptable, only because someone believes it or it is a part of a culture. Genocide, similarly, is wrong, regardless of cultural, institutional, or historical precedence and implemented practice.

That one holds a belief does not absolve them of its moral component or consequence.

We will review the concept of moral relativism later. Simply: the moral component - the extension of the heart to include and connect with others - also need make use of critical engagement as to the righteousness of actions and behaviors. Apply your heart wisely, for not all people or behaviors deserve your care and greater love. The heart and its energies play essential roles for all of us. A vital portion of heart is how it composes a larger part of our character. Our heart and our emotions allow us to be of a generous disposition. We are bettered by feeling love and exchanging affection. Heart affords us the strength to be courageous, and passionate as the context or scene demands. This world is a beautiful place, albeit fraught with difficulties. TAKE HEART! You are up to the task of rising to the challenges of life. Open your heart and connect meaningfully with the greater world.

Help

To make it easier for someone to do something by offering services or resources is help. One can experience feeling helpless: unable to defend oneself or to act without help. The purpose of this section is to reiterate how everyone is in need. Nearly everyone could benefit from some form of help. The form that help takes depends on what is available as a resource to be applied or offered. Be mindful of how you can contribute to help a situation or a person in need. Help can consist of eye contact, or the sharing of time, enjoying conversation. Help can be in the form of money, a life-saving procedure, a ride to the grocery store, or a hug.

Be aware that help is a limited, or finite resource. While others can lend or apply resources to a cause, the individual in need is responsible for allaying concerns or reducing their own difficulties. The exceptions to this are the infirm, the elderly, the disabled: they require the defense, aid, and coordination of the community to safeguard them and ensure their well-being because they are unable to care or help themselves. This connects to a previous section regarding charity. You need live your own life, and it is most admirable - and in some cases necessary - to help others. Recognize, though, the need for balance. Apply resources to your own realm while being vigilant to the plight or condition of others. An important aspect of parenting (if not the central duty) is to provide the means by which the young can live a self-sufficient life. Part of the education a parent need instill or provide concerns the care of self, as well as the care of others. There is no fixed rule of care or help. Be aware as to how you can apply your self and the resources at your disposal. Look out for innocents, the elderly, or disabled people. Be mindful of variables that could affect others and help them to avoid ills or injuries. Treat others with concern; help as you are able. Sometimes aiding someone might entail your own inconvenience, pain, or death. A general rule might entail not allowing your own provision of aid to malign your own circumstance. But specific contexts require sacrifice. People give their own lives to save others. People rush into fires to save others and lose their own lives in the process. Lifeguards drown while trying to save others. There are many instances where death might serve a greater purpose. This is a very complex and particular context. Suffice it to say that the intricate relationship of providing aid or help is a greater human good and serves the recipient as well as the provider. One can help him or her self by helping others. The converse is true: one can help his or her own self, and in doing so, still serve others.

History

The study of past events in human affairs is history. Historiography is the study of how history is written. Generally, the victors of conquest, or those that maintain power or control, write history. History is a narrative that serves the interests of those in power, or those in positions of leadership or authority. History is never complete (See Fukuyama) and, importantly: it is also never objective. History demonstrates the values and perspective of the writer. It is never free of the encumbrances of character and subjective ethos.

Due to the innovation of the internet, the entire scope of human history is accessible nearly anywhere on the world, owing to its transit across fiber optic cables $1/8^{th}$ the diameter of a human hair (if not less, via cloud tech). That an awe-inspiring amount of data and information is available means we have access to contrasting perspectives that challenge the orthodoxy of established traditions and entrenched power structures. We have the capability, if not the responsibility, too, of investigating the veracity of claims, the authenticity of documents and sources, and the merit of much - if not all - of what we have been taught. In a previous section, we discussed objective beliefs. They are beliefs that are not influenced by personal feelings, interpretations, or prejudice. They contrast with subjective beliefs, which bear the mark of perspective; it is an expression of belief, opinion, or personal preference. They can not be proven right or wrong by any generally accepted criteria. An objective claim may be true or false; just because something is objective, though, does not mean that it is true.

That history is subjective means that *all of it* is in need of exploration, analysis, and review to ascertain bias, or even outright untruth. When something is true, it needs no protection. It stands on its own merit. The strength of truth will be recognized, and it neither deserves, nor needs insulation or distance from inquiry or investigation. Some elements and accounts of history are now illegal to question or critique. This is most problematic, and should give pause to consider why it is the case. Truth is not being verified; it is merely demarcated as the truth by authorities or people in power. Some countries imprison those who dare to contest the narrative of specific historical orthodoxies. This, again, serves the powerful, or those that stand to gain by such protectionism. Imprisoning those who take the initiative to research and inquire in an effort to understand their world is the hallmark of those who are threatened of a loss of power or resources. Consider what is deemed 'untouchable' or off-limits as far as investigation and critique.

Kevin Alfred Strom wrote, "To learn who rules over you, simply find out who you are not allowed to criticize." Those who restrict the possibility of critical engagement are often those who are hiding information that is pertinent to debate and greater development of individuals or groups. Matters that are forbidden could serve as the means of greater individual or group development. What if our human development and progress is impeded by the lack of access to data or the forbidden nature of some realms of study? The subjectivity of history demands that all of it need be carefully examined and reviewed, in the interests of greater humanity.

Honor

Honor is the state of being morally upright, honest, noble, and virtuous. It is a concept that is present in the works of Homer, in Shakespeare, and appears as a recurring theme from the 17th through the 20th century. It has an important role in the United States' Declaration of Independence, as the founding fathers pledged their own sacred honor. But, beside a distinct set of people who serve in the military, in fire departments, or in criminal gangs, the concept is nearly lost on people in the west.

Honor can be known as either horizontal (honor shared or exchanged between equals) or vertical (honor applied to superior values, behaviors, or people). The notion of honor has a public element. It depends on the opinion of others; others must recognize your honor for it to exist. That a person considers himself or herself to be honorable is not enough. It is the acknowledgement of that claim that realizes the presence of real honor. Honor is a reputation of respect and admiration. The reputation is earned by allegiance to an honor code. Standards of honor have been gender specific. It is universal to both men and women, but the standards per gender vary. Honor motivates people to fulfill societal obligation and expectations. It concerns the fulfillment of a social responsibility. If men were courageous, and demonstrated a mastery of skills, they were welcomed as a member of the tribe. If they excelled at the honor code, they were granted a fuller status, and often received privileges, as well. This has remained true, at least in part, in the United States. One's reputation and honor are (somewhat) dutifully protected so that privileges and gains are obtained. Jobs, marriage, and status are the result of seemingly honorable pursuits or an honorable lifestyle. What made one worthy of honor were appropriate/righteous deeds and the protection of that reputation.

That rewards and privilege are afforded to corrupt politicians, or motivated criminals calls into question the standard of honor and what our own society values as far as behavior.

An injury or insult to reputation once required immediate remedy. Saving face was important, and engagement or confrontation of the perceived slight demonstrated that one retained an honorable status by being willing to protect that code and standing. Self-defense had an honored place in the culture. The practice of protecting that honor could tear a group setting apart, whether it was a tribe, a community, or even in the workplace. Values including mercy and magnanimity insulated honor and reduced the occurrences of duels or 'pissing contests.' Chivalry and gentlemanliness alleviated the concern of outbursts of reflexive honor taken to extremes.

That establishment and protection of honor benefits the individual and the group.

The individual demonstrates worthiness and others benefit from the inclusion of good, virtuous, worthwhile members within a group. The group shames those who do not maintain their honor; the application of lesser behaviors is disloyal or destructive to the bonds of a tribe or group setting.

Honor means being true to a personal set of beliefs and being a broader person of integrity. John Wooden wrote, "Be more concerned with your character than your reputation; because your character is what you really are, while your reputation is what others think you are." Your opinion and knowledge of yourself will guide all of your actions. Your actions will demonstrate your values to the public and people will perceive your reputation based on consistent behaviors. Be ever mindful of propriety and how standards of virtue are applied per context. You need be confident in yourself, proud of good deeds. Be aware how the public perception of you makes a meaningful difference, especially today with the Internet, social media, and the remarkable public exposure provided by technology.

House vs. Home

The distinction between a house and a home is a meaningful one. A house is a structure that provides shelter while a home provides greater comforts. A home soothes the soul and allows for more than simple material protection. A home affords one the opportunity of expression, for the presentation of one's values and subjectivity. A house is a building, whereas a home can be made of a tent, a cave, in a house or apartment, or even in a automobile or a boat. The term 'home' connotes more than the presence of walls and a roof. American poet Edgar A. Guest wrote, "It takes a heap o' livin' in a house to make a home." Memories, possessions, and experience work transformational wonders to create a home from a simple structure.

Humility

A modest view of one's importance, or modesty, is synonymous with humility. Humility stands opposed to arrogance or conceit. It is an awareness of self within the greater scope or context of greatness. In religions and philosophies, humility is a contrast of self with others. The form of the contrasted object is the issue; a humble individual contrasts their self with nature's grandeur, God, or cosmic scope, as in the immensity of the stars in the night sky, for example. Humility is an understanding of place in the greater universe. It is not necessarily an acceptance of a lesser status to that of others. More so, it is a grasp of man/self on a scale that features greatness on a truly awe-inspiring spectrum. Those who commit to arrogance and conceit may be ignorant of that reality or truly lost or absorbed within their own narcissistic perception of self worth. Socrates offered a paradox: the only wisdom is in knowing one knows nothing.[14] Knowledge of self among the greatest of size, scale, scope or merit, etc. delivers the important characteristic of humility. Develop this character by educating yourself thoroughly. As humans, we are an amazing race, but we are but a minute particle as compared to the vast totality of life. We still have much to learn and there are many ways we could still develop and grow as a race. We are not the pinnacle achievement of biological reality and, in fact, we are *far* from it. A humble attitude imparts our understanding of that fact while we should also be encouraged as to our amazing capacity for good and personal growth.

Humor

Humor is the quality of being amusing or comical, especially as expressed in literature or speech. There is a time and place for humor; it is very contextualized. It can range from being poignant and classy to base and vulgar. It is either inclusive (the humor is understood by all) or exclusive (the humor is at someone's expense, or only a portion of the audience understands the meaning). Humor has no specific theory but is comprised of wit, mirth, and laughter. The first is the cognitive experience. Mirth is the emotional experience, and laughter is the physical experience. Humor allows us to experience joy even in the midst of adversity. Just as beauty is subjective, so too is humor: it is remarkably relative.

Humor is applied when someone perceives his or her self as superior to another, or above the confines of a particular structure or context. Humor can serve as a relief from conventional social requirements. It affords relief from the restraint of conforming. Some people burst into laughter when a strain is removed. It can serve as a defense mechanism. It protects the individual against anxiety and from the awareness of internal or external dangers or stress. Individuals can be unaware of this process; it may be a reflexive response. Defense mechanisms color the reaction to emotional stimuli and to perceived stress. Humor can also demonstrate a high adaptive level, transforming adversity or challenges into a lighter condition or state.

Humor is a benefit. It facilitates emotional processing, adjusts meaning such that events do not overwhelm or overpower us. Humor shifts the way we think and alleviates distress: a result of how we think. Stress is not a product of situations but a result of the meaning we place on the situations. Horace Walpole said, "Life is a tragedy for those who feel, and a comedy for those who think." Build for yourself a quick and able mind, and a humorous disposition by studying and being aware of your greater world. Life is a joy to experience; play a good part by bringing appropriate humor to situations or moments that deserve or require some levity.

Hygiene

Hygiene consists of conditions or practices conducive to maintaining health or preventing disease, especially through cleanliness, sanitation, and purity. Hygiene is important for your health and for your reputation. While staving off disease by being clean is a good in itself, your reputation benefits when people see that you care for yourself diligently.

Suggested Steps for Proper Hygiene

- Shower regularly. Use a gentle soap or bath gel. Washing your hair too often can dry your hair and cause it to be brittle.
- Use a deodorant, but avoid antiperspirants.
- Wear clean clothes.
- Care for your hair. Comb it. Unkempt hair is harder to manage or clean.
- Use shampoo often and conditioner only when you need it.
- Care for your nails.
- Have good dental hygiene. Brush and floss regularly.
- Brush your tongue. Replace your toothbrush every 3 months, or after you are ill.
- Wash your face twice a day.
- Apply lotion to skin that is rough, or to those areas you want to be smooth.

Chapter 9

Id

The part of the mind in which innate, instinctive impulses and primary processes are manifest is the id. It is the animal brain where antisocial desires and base drives are situated. It is the source of bodily wants, desires and impulses, and particularly our sexual and aggressive drives. The id acts according to the pleasure principle - the force that motivates a tendency to seek immediate gratification. The id, along with the ego and super-ego are components of a theory advanced by psychologist Sigmund Freud. They are not physical portions of the brain; they are only conceptual, theoretical apparatus.

The id is an unconscious force. It contains everything we are born with; therefore, it is a primary and innate part. It is instinctual and it lacks morality of any sort. The id demands immediate satisfaction. We all have the id. As we develop and become conditioned as to appropriate behaviors and social values, we grasp that this base drive is to be controlled and mastered. The benefit of discipline and focus is that we can grasp more complex and refined ideas. As we develop, we should be pursuing more elevated and sophisticated endeavors. Strive to be cultured, to entertain a bearing or demeanor that speaks to refinement, higher values, and a discriminating perspective. It would be a tremendous waste to forever be stuck on base drives or to maintain a vulgar disposition. Seek to refine your person by improving upon your character and condition through education and training.

Imagination

The faculty or action of forming new ideas, images, or concepts of external objects not present to the senses is the imagination. The imagination is present in various degrees in various people. In some it is highly developed; in others, it may be weaker. An imagination allows us to engage the world from a different perspective, helps us to solve problems, and even serves to connect us with both the past and the future. The imagination provides the greatest sense of freedom. That it is a component or activity of the mind means that we are in complete control of it. It can deliver us from reality when it is overly difficult, or unpleasant - at least temporarily.

Imagination is a creative power. You can apply it for all five senses. It has an important role in all fields as far as the achievement of goals and dreams, for it aids visualization and the creation of opportunities. Hence, it is vital to maintain control of its power. An imagination that runs wild owns its master. It can lead to psychosis, or even paralysis through analysis. The proper, measured application of the faculty delivers significant results. Once an individual harnesses a positive mindset and begins to direct the imagination appropriately, successes follow that creative force. Consider how the fullest realization of the mind is, as yet, unheralded or achieved.

You are responsible for establishing imaginative thresholds.

Steps to Build Improve The Imagination
-Avoid passive media like television and video games.
-Meditate.
-Read fiction and history: creative literature stimulates the mind. The more one studies and becomes aware of the world, the more tools the imagination can utilize.
-Listen to music without lyrics.
-Write for fun.
-Engage visual arts.
-Learn a musical instrument.

Imagination

-Participate in dress-up activities, like costume parties or Halloween events.
-Reorganize or decorate your room.
-Create a narrative for people, places, and things. Make a story about what you encounter: people you see, planes in the sky, squirrels playing at the park.
-Plan your ideal trip or vacation.
-Share time with interesting people.
-Do something boring. The imagination will make dull tasks more interesting.

"Logic will get you from A to B. Imagination will take you everywhere." - **Albert Einstein**

"If you can imagine it, you can achieve it. If you can dream it, you can become it." - **William Arthur Ward**

"You can't depend on your eyes when your imagination is out of focus." - **Mark Twain**

"The man who has no imagination has no wings." - **Muhammad Ali**

"Imagination will often carry us to worlds that never were. But without it we go nowhere." - **Carl Sagan**

"Reality leaves a lot to the imagination." - **John Lennon**

"Imagination and fiction make up more than three quarters of our real life." - **Simone Weil**

"I believed in myself. I never imagined myself as just an ordinary player."
Imran Khan

"When you can imagine you begin to create and when you begin to create you realize that you can create a world that you prefer to live in, rather than a world that you're suffering in." - **Ben Okri**

"Nobody is bored when he is trying to make something that is beautiful, or to discover something that is true." – **William Ralph Inge**

Inclusion

Inclusion is the act or the state of including or being included with a group or structure. Inclusion is the opposite of exclusion. Generally, everyone wants to be included in some way or another. While we have different preferences and tastes, we all desire company, or to belong. It is important to include entities in order to coordinate, but full inclusion is unnecessary in some situations. Some people need not be welcomed in all contexts. Our dog gets excluded from restaurants and from the couch on certain occasions. In a similar fashion, people get either excluded or included based on contextual matters. Meditation, bathroom breaks, and sexual activities are examples of exclusive activities. Inclusion and exclusion are not positive and negative constructs in and of themselves. They are based on contextual concerns. The unnecessary exclusion of a peer who wants to play on the playground is one matter, while excluding a particular person from a wedding may be a necessary initiative. One does not present all of their cards while playing poker, for example. One need not invite another's presence while coordinating with a teller at the bank counter. Company is welcome if and when it can make a situation pleasant and more enjoyable. Others can participate when their presence is appropriate and worthy. We do not refer to cartoons as we discuss complex math equations. We can exclude people whose company does not contribute to the general scene. Be mindful of when inclusion is necessary, desired, or even inappropriate.

We all have realms of our lives that are private and not for greater publication or even sharing. You need not include others or share elements that you want to keep to your own self. Examples might include the entries of your journal, your personal health issues, your sexuality, or personal feelings. Consider those aspects of your personal life that are better - secured and maintained away from public participation or coordination.

Inferior

To be inferior is to be lower in status or quality. There are inferior products on the market. A particular item may outperform or last longer than another. Sometimes people are designated as inferiors. They could be referred to as at a lower level of an established (or even informal) hierarchy, of lesser intelligence, or value. In the section concerning beliefs, we discussed limiting beliefs and how the projection of negative, limiting beliefs hinders the object/recipient of the judgment as well as the one who judges.

Every person has many different characteristics that must be evaluated separately. There are no people who are inferior at everything. Some individuals might have worse eyesight than others but are better at performing intricate dance moves. My martial arts abilities are efficient and refined, but they still pale in comparison to skill sets of others. People are not simple beings that can be evaluated in just one dimension. You can not express the value or ability of a person with just a number, nor evaluate people along a simplistic, objective scale.

Different items, or people, demonstrate their range of abilities or qualities. The influential essay, *An Educational Allegory* was published in the Journal of

Education in 1898. Prominent physicist and inventor Amos E. Dolbear emphasized the absurdity of using a single, inflexible standard for assessing the achievements of each individual student. A product, a person, or any object will present its quality. Avoid the mistake of judging a fish by its ability to climb a tree. People have different skill sets, different characters comprising an amazing spectrum of morality and values.

Associate with those individuals that demonstrate quality but remain open to the possibility that everyone has something to offer or teach. When you allow yourself to be teachable and receptive, you will encounter tremendous surprises, untold gifts and treasures.

Information

Facts learned or provided about something or someone, or data that is conveyed or represented is information. An astounding barrage of many different forms of data, and facts bombards us. Our phones relay not only the time, but facilitate many communicative transactions that convey information. TV imparts lots of data, as does every other form of media. Streams of information engulf us. It is of vital importance that we discern between good and bad information in order to make the best decisions in an effort to live a good, full life.

Information is a component of a process. We first receive data in the form of facts and statistics collected together for reference and analysis. Data is refined or synthesized into information. We process information into structures or groups that facilitate decision-making.

If information does not contribute to a greater effort, it fails to be processed into knowledge - information acquired by a person through experience or education. If information can not be used, it remains trivial or unimportant. Education and experience are meant to lead us out of ignorance. When we can not structure or apply information, it is not the fault of a lack of education or experience. Some material is simply trivial. An old saying contends, "All knowledge is worth having." A second, necessary part of that might be, "All knowledge is worth having, but *not all knowledge is useful*." Perhaps the best uses for simple information that is not knowledge, per se, is for use in trivia games, or as conversation starters.

The substance or amount of information sometimes hinders processing or application. A stream of information need be analyzed and elements harvested or culled. When too much information is received, one need be critical and separate those items or portions of value. All too often, a lot of information is relayed, but not much as far as worthy, substantive material. Be keen to discern valuable information and discard what is extraneous.

Information can be subjective or objective. It can pertain to a person's perspective and preferences or it can be objective, lacking that personal element of opinion, emotion, or personal feelings. Whether it is subjective or objective, the information can be utilized. That someone conveys that they are cold remains useful information. It does not lose its value merely because it is a subjective statement. When someone relays that there are sixty seconds remaining in a cooking process is valuable, as well. The merit of information lies in its utility. Be aware of the presence of both misinformation - false or inaccurate information, and disinformation - false information meant to mislead. Disinformation is always deliberately intended to deceive. Misinformation is simply incorrect material that is conveyed. A good way to critically engage information and media is to answer the following questions:

-Who is presenting the information? Why are they offering this information? (Is it their job?) Do they have sole access to, or knowledge of this information? How will this person, or others, benefit by conveying this information? Who is involved?

-What is happening, or what has occurred? Precisely what is occurring? What are the ramifications or consequences of this information? What do we do with this information? What is being excluded?

-When is this information pertinent? When will this information be of value, if not now? Is there a time at which this information becomes irrelevant? Is this information time-sensitive?

-Where did the information come from, or: what is the source of this information? Is the information pertinent to one sole/specific region, or realm? Where is this information applied?

-Why is this information conveyed – to educate, to entertain, to indoctrinate, to deceive, or mislead? Why is this information important? Why is the speaker disseminating this information?

-How is this information important, or pertinent? How is it being conveyed or presented? How does one make use of this information? How does one benefit from the spreading of this information?

"Knowledge is power. Information is liberating. Education is the premise of progress, in every society, in every family." - **Kofi Annan**

"The number one benefit of information technology is that it empowers people to do what they want to do. It lets people be creative. It lets people be productive. It lets people learn things they didn't think they could learn before, and so in a sense it is all about potential." - **Steve Ballmer**

"Democracy must be built through open societies that share information. When there is information, there is enlightenment. When there is debate, there are solutions. When there is no sharing of power, no rule of law, no accountability, there is abuse, corruption, subjugation and indignation." - **Atifete Jahjaga**

"Smart phones and social media expand our universe. We can connect with others or collect information easier and faster than ever." - **Daniel Goleman**

"The mere imparting of information is not education." - **Carter G. Woodson**

"While weight loss is important, what's more important is the quality of food you put in your body - food is information that quickly changes your metabolism and genes." - **Mark Hyman**

"You can have data without information, but you cannot have information without data." - **Daniel Keys Moran**

"True genius resides in the capacity for evaluation of uncertain, hazardous, and conflicting information." - **Winston Churchill**

Initiate

To cause to begin, or to admit someone into a secret or obscure society or group is to initiate. In this section, we address taking initiative, primarily. We do not await instructions for all endeavors. We need not be directed to do something. It is a parent's duty to facilitate the development of the young and to guide them as to how to be self-sufficient and independent. Your mom and I are teaching you a range of skills, imparting abilities such that you can make good decisions in your own life. Already you do not need us to guide you as far as many activities are concerned. We welcome and encourage you to take initiative within different contexts. For example, you have been taught to apply your own agency - the capacity of acting or exerting power to influence - when you recognize a need. You do not need to be told to clean up a mess, or to make sure that your pet is fed, and always has access to water. As you get more experience, you will encounter much more complex situations. Life gets more complicated as we age, for we become more familiar with an ever-increasing, amazing array of variables and concepts at play. So, as another example: as a younger child, you held our hand as we crossed a street. Later, you were allowed to travel across the neighborhood and you waited for the crosswalk sign to signal your turn to cross the street. But what if the signal tells you to cross, despite the approach of a speeding vehicle?

Following instructions in this case could prove to be fatal. Oftentimes, it is important to take your own initiative in the face of an authority's instruction. Teachers, firemen, and various other roles of authority, generally care for your health and well-being. But sometimes information is wrong and instructions could lead to harm. Likewise, unfortunately, folks that we are supposed to trust can prove fallible, and even malicious. You need apply your own experience, judgment, and values in order to take initiative that will serve your own person. Returning to our analogy: what if no cars are coming, or no one is waiting at a light? The key is to be able to think for oneself in each situation, and of great consequence: one need shoulder the responsibility of those actions and behaviors.

As an important segment of this discussion, we need include the obligation of opposing or contrasting with authority, or even your peers. You will experience occasions in which we need oppose or counter someone, or a group of people. Perhaps your team at work is operating under mistaken assumptions, and you need correct that error or confront a lapse in judgment. Taking initiative to voice a contrary viewpoint or perspective takes courage. You might have the occasion to help someone by providing resources. Should someone be attacked or victimized, it serves a good purpose to initiate violence in order to protect the defenseless. You need not wait for instruction to protect or safeguard yourself, or others. It is of consequential importance that you have a firm grasp of the facts of the matter. 'The road to hell is paved with good intentions' is an old phrase. One meaning of the statement is that individuals may have the intent to take good actions, but fail to take action. The inaction may be due to procrastination, laziness, or vice. Hence good intention is meaningless unless followed through with action. Also, wrongdoing, or evil actions are often masked by good intentions and occasionally, good intentions, when acted upon, may have bad, unforeseen consequences. Should you act, there are consequences; a mature individual accepts the responsibility of their behavior. Take initiative wisely. Identify the variables at play and apply your resources appropriately.

Innate

Innate refers to inborn, natural characteristics or that which originates in the mind. Innate traits are contrasted with those elements that are born of or elicited by experience. People have the innate ability to speak whereas animals do not. It is used figuratively or, in philosophical discussions, to refer to those things that come from the mind. An individual may demonstrate an innate sense of style. Some folks have an innate grasp of fairness, or ethics, while others seem to be natural bullies or cheaters. Innate behavior comes from genes, typically, while the behavior is learned, either from interacting with the world or by being taught.

The discussion of innate traits or ideas concerns the idea of human nature. Human nature refers to the distinguishing characteristics - ways of thinking, feeling, and acting - which humans tend to have naturally, independently of the influence of culture. The questions of what these characteristics are, how fixed or determined they are, and what causes them have important precedent in science and philosophy. The answers have implications in the realms of ethics, politics, and theology. Is man innately good or evil? The answer to that question says a lot about the perspective and values of the person offering the response.

IQ

IQ stands for intelligence quotient. It is a number used to apply a rank among others for a standardized test. An IQ test is a measure of what psychologists call our 'fluid and crystallized' intelligence. It measures reasoning and problem solving abilities. A very high IQ signifies that an individual has the ability to manipulate, process, and interpret information at a deeper level and at a higher speed than the average person.

The critique of an IQ test is that the results are not comprehensive, nor cumulative. The results are based on the performance of one child, on one particular test, on one particular day, with one particular tester applying the examination. It does not measure practical intelligence - how things work. It does not measure creativity, or curiosity. IQ does not measure emotional maturity. In short, IQ is a ranking that objectifies people through the application of a standardized test. The IQ does not represent subjective traits that demonstrate morality, or the appreciation of art or the ability to express oneself, nor are the tests meant to assess those abilities.

Standardized tests do not measure educational quality. They are a fair and objective measure of student achievement. They ensure teachers and schools are accountable to taxpayers. That IQ is not representative of significant human elements and abilities does not mean that the results are moot. Institutions use IQ results to identify students or candidates for roles and positions. That many institutions gauge an individual primarily on the IQ means much, if not the greater character of the individual is not represented, and hence not taken into consideration. Standardized testing demarcates rank based on similar material. What sets us apart is our sole subjective experience and the traits and abilities we refine as we grow and develop. IQ is but a snapshot of a person while there is so much more of the character presented via numerous other formats and occasions.

Intellect

Intellect refers to the cognition and rational mental processes gained through external input rather than internal. A distinction is sometimes made whereby intellect is related to facts, in contrast to intelligence, (which concerns emotions). Intellect denotes cognition - the rational, mental processes that constitute knowing. Intelligence is another, separate mental faculty that takes one beyond facts to suggest meaning, or purpose and determine a course of action. Intellect perceives facts while the intelligence uses feelings and meaning to motivate the actions we take after receiving the sensory input or information. An analogy: when you cross a street, you note a car coming at a fast rate - you can see its color, size, shape. You perceive these facts using your intellect. Your intelligence makes use of your feelings surrounding the event; is fear, confidence, or apprehension informing the moment? The combination of the two faculties motivates a range of possible choices of action. Will you stay at the side of the street, walk slowly across, run, or even yell at the speeding vehicle? Living by the intellect and facts alone makes for a boring experience, but a life guided by feelings alone makes for a wandering jaunt with no greater purpose. Balance your intellect with your intelligence.

Intent

Intent is purpose. It signifies the resolve or determination to do something. The intent look shows earnestness or eager attention. Every act has intent. Can you identify an act that is unintentional? Acting requires agency, initiative, or purpose. A baby may not intend to move and thrash about, if only because its mental faculties are only perceiving - taking everything in via the senses. A mentally disabled person might act similarly. Mental faculties might be lacking, or a nervous system is frenzied, or in a chaotic state, or even in disrepair, may lash out, or wrest control of limbs. There is no intent to lash out and use their limbs or body in such a manner.

Rationally cognizant, able people make use of intent. They formulate plans of actions and implement those plans in order to achieve a goal or realize an aim. What do you intend with your actions? What do you intend to achieve with your greater life? Be aware of the possibility of unintended consequences. We have discussed this concept earlier. Unforeseen or unanticipated results can, and do occur. Have a plan to achieve viable goals. Intent guides our lives instead of living aimlessly, adrift, as wood upon the sea.

Intimacy

Intimacy is close friendship or familiarity. The term implies closeness. When you are close to someone, you are near in proximity or location. You can also have close ties or be close knit - as in the relationship between people who are good friends, loving siblings, or affectionate and amorous lovers. An intimate relationship is an interpersonal relationship that involves physical and/or emotional intimacy. Physical intimacy is characterized by friendship, platonic and romantic love, and sexual activity.

Intimacy is not shared with everyone, and for good reason. Not everyone shares the same quality, or is worth having that special level of relationship. Not everyone is compatible with everyone else. Preferences and opinions shape relationships and the process of building or structuring intimacy is akin to that of an art. It is a process that requires focus, dedication, investment, if not sacrifice, too. Truly, not all relationships deserve the amount of effort involved in such a dynamic. One does not put equal energy into relating with a neighbor, the postal clerk, or the grocer as one does with a significant other or intimate partner.

Intimacy makes life worth living. The presence of someone who can be trusted with the responsibility of protecting one's feelings, thoughts, and body is an immense relief and pleasure. The intimate relationship need serve as a tremendous joy. If it is too much a chore, or worse: a burden, the dynamic needs attention, revision, or termination. Such a relationship is meant to console and aid the people involved. Relationships are worth time, effort, energy and investment. An intimate relationship exposes tremendously significant degree of depth, vivacity, meaning, and significance to life. Because of that, it deserves all the more diligent attention and careful application of the self and the resources at your disposal.

If it is worth doing, it is worth doing well.

When we put forth the best effort, and the best portion of ourselves in an intimate relationship, we should receive the same of our partner. Make certain you share intimacy with people who are of similar standards and qualities. Do not invest in that level of dynamic unless you and your partner are able and willing to invest to that degree.

Intuition

The ability to understand something immediately, without the need for conscious reasoning is intuition. Intuition gives us the ability to know something directly, without engaging in analysis. It bridges instinct and reason. Animals have basic instincts while humans are able to make use of reason and analytics. But we can also make use of intuition. While we *are* animals, we can utilize them both as needs dictate. About a hundred years ago, scientists did not give proper attention to the role of the unconscious. Today, we find that only about twenty percent of our grey matter is dedicated to conscious thought. We need pay heed to out faculties and also make proper use of our natural abilities and skills. The intuition works as an inner voice, and naturally, the best way to make proper use of it is to engage it in dialogue. Whereas the conscious mind makes use of logic, the unconscious, intuitive voice makes use of nonlinear thought. It weaves the past, present and future, creativity, hunches and feelings to contribute as it can. Einstein remarked how imagination is more important than knowledge. In a parallel sense, intuition has a similar priority as imagination. It can serve us as long as we develop and listen to that voice.

Develop your Intuition by:

-Keeping a journal
-Allowing for inner dialogue.
-Finding solitude.
-Meditating.

As a side note: is it possible to have different voices? Do voices have different tones, or characteristics? Are all of those voices YOU? Why or why not? Could they belong to others, perhaps?

"What we achieve inwardly will change outer reality." – **Plutarch**

Chapter 10

Jealous

To be jealous is to feel envy of someone for his or her achievements, advantages, or material belongings. Jealousy is a complex emotion that encompasses many different kinds of feelings which range from fear of abandonment to rage and even humiliation. Jealousy can pertain to social relations, as in the case of when either a male or a female perceives a third party as a threat to a valued relationship. Children get jealous of siblings competing for parental attention and affection. Peers get jealous of others' successes or the components of others' lives. While jealousy may preserve some social bonds, it can also cause more harm than good.

It is very important to grasp the need for self-control. The only thing that we have control over is our self. Through diligent, continual introspection the examination or observation of one's own mental and emotional processes - we can readily grasp the whole of our self. We need this self-knowledge else we encounter some painful lessons as we act impetuously, unconsciously. That inner dialogue, or the analysis of the self, yields meaningful results. As we delve into our own selves, we can identify significant thoughts, feelings, values, and beliefs that warrant attention and/or revision. We all have 'something' that requires maintenance. Human history bears no account of the individual that has attained complete self-mastery. Even those deemed ascended masters, or those who have obtained enlightenment, are never done with the process. We are meant to continually grow and develop.

Jealousy is concern for matters outside our immediate control; the sentiment need not be entertained. Keep in mind only those things you can control or address, and those items are few in number. You can only control your own thoughts, feelings, values and behavior. Preoccupying yourself with the material goods of others is a waste of time and energies. Spend your time instead addressing your own realm: material, or otherwise. Consider why you envy the possessions or the status/achievement of others. As you review the components of your own life, entertain the sentiment of gratitude in lieu of entertaining base jealousy. Examine the values that underlie your jealousy. Reviewing and possibly adjusting your feelings and behaviors will most likely reveal that the envy is unwarranted. Instead, given a maintained desire of obtaining a material item, you can formulate a plan and implement steps to achieve a goal. Waste no time being jealous; move on earning/retrieving an item instead of pining for the goods of another.

The same goes as far as jealousy of others. We need not ever view someone as a threat until they demonstrate those values or behaviors explicitly. A relationship is strong when both parties are committed and loyal. Jealousy can rend asunder ties of a relationship. It is most wise to put forth your best effort in a relationship - or any activity, for that matter. If a partner betrays you, you will recognize their values and hopefully understand that those values are beneath you. A partner that betrays your loyalty and trust - your best offering - is not worth your continued involvement and presence. Do not consider others a threat to a worthwhile relationship. A solid dynamic will be able to weather challenges, even those posed by third parties. Control those elements at your disposal - contribute to a strong, healthy, communicative, and loving relationship. Communicate your thoughts and feelings with your partner. A good partner will respect you, the relationship and protect your presence by negating any chance of jealousy or the presence of another. Jealousy is an ugly emotion; direct your attention and emotions toward better, worthy sentiments and behaviors.

"Life is one big road with lots of signs. So when you riding through the ruts, don't complicate your mind. Flee from hate, mischief and jealousy. Don't bury your thoughts, put your vision to reality. Wake Up and Live!" - **Bob Marley**

"The jealous are troublesome to others, but a torment to themselves." - **William Penn**

"You can be the moon and still be jealous of the stars." - **Gary Allan**

"A competent and self-confident person is incapable of jealousy in anything. Jealousy is invariably a symptom of neurotic insecurity." - **Robert A. Heinlein**

"Those who enjoy their own emotionally bad health and who habitually fill their own minds with the rank poisons of suspicion, jealousy and hatred, as a rule take umbrage at those who refuse to do likewise, and they find a perverted relief in trying to denigrate them." - **Johannes Brahms**

"Jealousy - that jumble of secret worship and ostensible aversion." - **Emile M. Cioran**

"Jealousy is the jaundice of the soul." - **John Dryden**

"As iron is eaten away by rust, so the envious are consumed by their own passion." - **Antisthenes**

"Jealousy, that dragon which slays love under the pretense of keeping it alive." - **Havelock Ellis**

Job

A paid position of regular employment, or a task/piece of work that is paid is a job. A job, or employment - being in the service of another for pay - is a means to an end. A job provides pay to afford goods and necessities. These roles require an applicable skill set that is rewarded on an hourly or salaried basis. A salary is a fixed, regular payment, often expressed as an annual sum. Individuals in this society progress through school and either university or trade schools in order to build a skill set, or range of abilities that will secure for them gainful employment. A job position lasts for as long as an employer has need of the particular worker, or the role itself. Any number of factors can influence that need. Technology could render the role unnecessary; a new machine might make the position extraneous. A changing economy could drastically affect a larger realm and cost an entire community potentially thousands of jobs.

Instead of pursuing a skill set that an employer can make use of, consider developing a range of abilities that will serve you over the course of your entire life. Rather than identifying a role or a job position you desire, identify a problem you want to address. Then develop or acquire the skills necessary to address that issue meaningfully. On another note, seeking a job and being employable involves giving your self to the dictates, or the caprice, of an employer. Having a job means that others govern you, or that you serve as someone else requires. I suggest structuring a skill set that serves you and affords you the means of your own employment. Working for yourself, being self-employed, is very challenging. An old phrase states, "Choose a job that you love, and you will never have to work a day in your life." This does not necessarily mean to pursue entrepreneurship. But working for someone else entails performing per his or her schedule and requirements. A worker is but a means to an end for a boss or a company. It is most rare to have an organization invest in a worker and more: to treat them as an end in themselves.

Prioritization of the employee, or care of the particular worker, is not cost effective. Typically, a company does not concern itself with the comprehensive development of its workforce. Organizations do not bother with the emotional, spiritual, or social health and development of their help. They require only that an employee can perform a particular set of tasks and achieve a standard of success, or completion of responsibilities. In addition to that, employees surrender certain rights and elements of their character once employment is obtained. They are not free to share portions of their personal values, as some ideas or conversations may not be welcome in the workplace. Self-employment serves as a trying, though superior, alternative to those who are willing and motivated to serve as their own boss. Working for him or her self, the individual is still tasked with responsibilities, but the cause or activity is something the entrepreneur - a person who organizes and operates a business or businesses - believes in or is passionate about. By working for themselves, they are still accountable to clients, but they answer to their own schedule and values. Not that they need shirk all established routines of hours and the like, but the entrepreneur performs per their own values, and greater self. They structure their life around their work and make the space for an inclusive character that is largely lost when someone acts as an employee for another. Provided their value is worthy, and their wares and service benefit others, they will be successful. Given maintenance of that applicable skill set, a knowledgeable perspective, an awareness of their industry, and a keen business sense, the focused and motivated individual can alleviate him or herself of the burden of employment and, instead, create the means of their own sustenance.

An entrepreneur has a very rare personality and drive. The responsibility of self-employment is a very consequential undertaking. I contend that most avoid the opportunity because they do not have the passion underlying their own skill set or even greater goals in life. Most folks are cultured/indoctrinated to the prospects of enduring schooling for the sole purpose of securing a job, earning a living by serving someone else's needs and dreams as an employee. Consider instead the prospects of structuring your life and employment as a means of complementing or strengthening your own values and abilities. A job need not be an onerous, one-sided transaction, or donation to an organization or company. Compensation provided can never truly reward an individual for the time spent in service. That is the opportunity cost one pays with their employment. By serving as an employee, they are forgoing other opportunities that might manifest over the same course of time. Time spent at a job is generally exclusive of the pursuit of subjective goals and greater ambitions. *Do what you love* and you will enjoy the moments spent serving the best portions of your own person.

Journey

The act of traveling from one place to another is a journey. For the purposes of this concept, we address the subjective journey of an individual in life, as well as American scholar Joseph Campbell's approach of a hero's journey in his piece, *Hero with a Thousand Faces*. Everyone is walking their own path, from birth until their eventual demise. All individuals will experience a spectrum of emotions and be responsible for the creation of meaning and significance with the moments of their lives. Our lives are a journey of radical subjectivity. While we may have guidance and counsel pertaining to objective reality, the application of the individual's values, thoughts, and experiences distinguish one's journey from another. As advised earlier, it is recommended that one keep in mind how folks are treading their own path and are grappling with the complicated concepts and variables of their own unique realm. Wendy Mass wrote, "Be kind, for everyone is fighting a battle you know nothing about." Strive to be humane, humble, and gentle towards those you encounter in your life. Our journeys are made ever so much easier as others lend support and encouragement to our path. Sometimes, harsh words, and critique can compose care and concern. Generally, though: allow folks proper civil respect and acknowledge that they are making their own way as best they can.

Joseph Campbell contributed meaningfully to the realms of history, culture, and the arts by examining the concept of the hero's journey in different societies. The hero's journey is the basic template of all great stories and is the tale that every culture tells. It is present in drama, stories, myths and religious rituals. An archetype of the hero goes and achieves great things on behalf of their group, tribe or civilization. As the hero progresses, they encounter significant stages. They face challenges, encounter others that contribute to their quest, and receive those gifts or skills that help them develop. The hero's journey is a simple formula, consisting on one level as overt drama and action, but an underlying psychological portion girds it. For the hero's journey is in no way a trite story of topical development; the hero need do a whole hell of a lot more than build musculature to win the day. The point of the struggle is that in order to do great, *truly meaningful* actions for the greater self and community means shouldering the consequences of an arduous, trying process. Significant rewards are the product of success in the face of daunting, nearly insurmountable odds, and tremendous adversity. The hero's journey is also composed of a hero's death, though it is also paired with elements of renewal, rebirth, and rejuvenation. It is the narrative that guides Star Wars, the Harry Potter series, and the Wizard of Oz, too.

Consider your own journey. How are you living a life less ordinary? Are you proceeding down a mundane path of routine and pattern? Seek to develop as you contribute your energies and resources to life. Shed those elements or characteristics that tether you unnecessarily. Reform your character and be rejuvenated by striving towards great deeds. Serve your soul and your greatest self by striving to be good, facilitating the highest and best good for all involved.

Make use of, and *enjoy your journey*.

Joy

A feeling of great pleasure or extreme happiness is joy. Joy is a feeling; hence, it is under your own control. No one external to you has any control or power over your emotions. You alone are their master. Eleanor Roosevelt once said, "No one can make you feel inferior without your consent." No one can make you feel ANYTHING unless you consent. While others may try to influence or affect you, it is always up to you as to how you respond or react.

> *No one can make you feel anything; it is your decision, and responsibility to act and feel as appropriate.*
> Maintain control of your emotional self.

Joy is entirely up to your own discretion, but I encourage you to live joyfully. Generate joy by feeling grateful, happy, and blessed: regardless of external conditions or events! Your emotions are always under your control, despite externalities. Connect joy with the achievement of important goals, with the association and company of worthy friends, with the day's sunrise and/or sunset. Attach joy to lofty concepts or simple events. Encountering fine art, or beholding the jubilant cries of a newborn baby can elicit joy, though of different sorts. Given the option, elect to experience and generate joy. Of nearly all emotions, it is one of the most meaningful and powerful.

Jubilee

A jubilee is a special anniversary, or celebration of an event. In ancient times, the Greeks, and Romans enjoyed festivals that coincided with agricultural events, like the sewing of the field, or the harvest of the crop. Greeks celebrated Cronus and the Romans, their equivalent: Saturn. The merrymaking lasted for varying amounts of time. The *Kronia* of the Greeks could last for two weeks while the Saturnalia of the Romans lasted for a week, in December. Jubilees could pertain to roles, financial matters, and land. Roles were often reversed for the festivals. Women and men exchanged roles, as did masters and their slaves. A debt jubilee pertained to land, property, and property rights. Slaves and prisoners were freed, debts were forgiven, and the mercies of their god were purportedly manifest. Obviously, such a specific type of jubilee has not been observed in quite some time.

Such a modern jubilee would serve the broadest group of people. That so many could enjoy freedom of movement, and shed debt speaks to the potential of a great number of social constructs and practices being revised. For the jubilee to equate to something even significant requires a re-ordering, or revising of social/cultural practices. It is insufficient should prisoners be released without a concomitant redress of morality or the revision of our institutions of law. The same concept applies to debt. If greater realms of finance and economics are not restructured, the same ills and woe entrap people until the next round of jubilee can occur.

That such a systematic event has not occurred in many centuries alludes to the parties involved. The banking, or larger financial sector would certainly not benefit. Consider that potential loss of revenue or that incredibly immense 'stoppage' of resources. That humanity would stand to gain and benefit overwhelmingly speaks to the presence and application of power. The same holds for the liberation of prisoners. The privatization of prisons has equated to huge profits for those that run them as well as the emergence of an entire industry. Those who benefit from the current implemented standards and institutions will not address morality and law; they enjoy the rewards of the status quo. These prisons contribute to increased recidivism, a person's relapse into criminal behavior, after the person receives sanctions or undergoes intervention for a previous crime.

Concepts such as that of the jubilee inform us as to precedent and possibilities along a general spectrum of experience. They demarcate that tools exist, and are available to contribute to remarkably changed circumstances. Be aware of how power is applied and who benefits by its different applications. That conceptual tools can be envisioned means we may do well to research and apply them whenever possible.

Chapter 11

Karma

The Sanskrit word karma means action, word, or deed. It is also a spiritual principle in Hinduism and Buddhism - among other religions, or sects - referring to the sum of a person's actions in this and previous states of existence. That sum is sometimes viewed as deciding their fate in future existences. If one behaves badly, they are given an opportunity to atone for their transgressions and trespasses in the next life. Should an individual live a good life, or transform to be overwhelmingly good through multiple lives, they can free themselves from the cycle of rebirths and proceed to another level of reality.

Generally, karma may have a causal element that may be ethical or non-ethical. It can mean that good or bad actions have consequences, and it may refer to rebirth among existences and different planes of existence. Earlier we discussed how every act has an energetic component. Some spiritual groups attribute causal properties to action. So whether you are good or bad, your behaviors influence your present life, and your future existence. I can not instruct as to the objective validity of that relationship or influence. It is an important concept to become familiar with as a significant portion of the people of the world make practical use of it.

Knowledge

Knowledge is theoretical or practical understanding of a subject. It is an awareness or familiarity gained by experience of a fact or situation. It involves complex cognitive processes, including perception, communication, and reasoning. Philosophers have studied and examined knowledge within the arena of epistemology. This realm underlies every aspect of knowledge and, interestingly enough, there is no set definition of knowledge - even today. The question of, "How do we come to knowledge, or to know $\underline{X}$?" is timeless, and remains a lively debate.

In 1936, James T. Mangan published, *You Can Do Anything*. A section titled '14 Ways to Acquire Knowledge' is paraphrased here:
- Practice Skills
- Ask questions
- Want and desire to learn
- Work on yourself to uncover the treasure within
- Walk around it: look at issues from all angles
- Experiment
- Teach
- Read
- Write
- Listen
- Observe
- Organize your knowledge
- Structure precise definitions
- Reason, and apply logic

It is important to address the realm of self-knowledge - the understanding of oneself or one's own motives or character. Above the threshold of the Delphic Oracle was written the words: *Know thyself*. The philosopher Plato maintained that all other matters are trivial, in contrast. How can we know other matters if we remain ignorant of the essential, primary *stuff*? Knowledge of the self is of vital importance. The better one grasps the intimate details and processes of their own self, the better equipped they are to engage maturely, appropriately, and respectfully with others.

Steps to Facilitate Self-Knowledge
-Meditate
-Write down key goals and priorities
-Take psychometric tests
-Ask trusted friends
-Get feedback at work
-Seek new experiences and people.

Chapter 12

Labor

Labor is work, especially hard, physical work. It can also be an expenditure of physical or mental effort, especially when difficult or compulsory. Labor is present as we toil, or as we put forth the initiative to create. One can labor as they create a piece of art, or even engage in sport. Mothers labor during childbirth. That specific activity is the definitive standard of labor. Labor is personal effort directed towards any number of activities, and is depicted in the following three general areas.

White-collar labor pertains to work that is performed in an office or a professional setting. Doctors, lawyers, and financial sector employees are all roles categorized as white collar. It is an educated, cultured, and clean profession that has the white collar. Green collar work is a relatively recent designation. It pertains to professions or roles whose products or services are used to improve the quality of the environment. Solar power, or clean energy, some public transportation, or recycling industry professionals are green collared. While I am heavily involved in the agriculture industry, my position would still be deemed as green collar, as our company addresses agricultural stewardship and local food system sustainability. Tradesmen, laborers on farms, and industry professionals are known as blue-collar workers. They toil physically, as a primary portion of their labor.

These collars reflect the shirts the workers may have utilized. White dress shirts reflect dignified, mentally intensive professions. Green shirts signify green methodologies, or the 'go green' sustainability trend.

Blue shirts are denim work shirts and are heartier, thicker – used specifically for heavy, physical labor. One can not differentiate individuals solely on the basis of clothing. While clothing does, to a certain extent, reflect the realm engaged, it is an insufficient factor to gauge or estimate someone's profession, or general worth or value, for that matter. Lawyers wear blue shirts, and laborers might also wear white. Regardless of the work, an individual will dedicate a significant portion of their self - their ethos - towards the satisfaction of responsibilities. They exert a meaningful amount of mental or physical effort whether they are laboring in an office or under the sun. A person should not be judged by the work they perform. So long as an individual applies themselves dutifully to their task or role, they are behaving well and honorably. A construction worker is worth the same treatment as a lawyer, a janitor, a scientist, a garbage collector, or the President of the United States, by virtue of the fact that they are a person, first and foremost. You will experience how people behave well or badly regardless of their job. Demonstrate that you some class by refusing to disparage a particular labor class.

Most roles or professions are necessary in a society. How can a community exist without bus or truck drivers, construction workers, or mechanics? We need doctors, lawyers, tradesmen just the same. You may encounter negative judgment concerning blue-collar labor from some perspectives. It is often the case that people look down on these roles because of the rate of pay, the financial reward of the position, its physical character, or the presence of dirt or sweat. Perhaps someone who earns a tremendous amount in a field that requires little physical effort casts aspersions on the mental abilities of a laborer. Consider that all realms require a level of specialization. A doctor or lawyer has their own field of expertise just as a mechanic, a gardener, or a farmer makes use of a specific skill set that utilizes their mental and physical faculties. A community can neither exist with only a white-collar group nor the sole presence of a blue or green labor pool. A society requires contributions from all abilities to survive and thrive.

A friend of mine, Bill, is a psychologist. Bill put himself through an immense amount of schooling and spent nearly twenty years as a health care professional. He wearied of the emotional toll of the work. He then transitioned to a job where he contracts to clean windows. He now spends time outside: enjoying a routine in the sunshine, making friends, and doing a job he enjoys more. Bill still counsels people, but he washes windows for the simple joys it provides. What he earns from doing it is a secondary consideration, at that. He receives repeat business because he does a good job; Bill does a good job because he puts forth significant effort and energy towards the activity. It would be a definite error in judgment if I gauged Bill's entire character upon the role of window washer. Instead, he demonstrates himself to be knowledgeable, kind, a world-traveler, too. Refrain from judging a 'book by its cover' when the real value of the text is offered within the actual pages - oftentimes between the lines, too. Be open to the possibility of every individual shining, as only *they* can. You will encounter many a good person if you are but receptive to possibilities.

Laughter

Laughter is a physical reaction in primates. It is due to the rhythmical, often audible contractions of the diaphragm and other parts of the respiratory system. Laughter is a response to external or internal stimuli. Humor and/or tickles can elicit it, but so, too, could nervousness or a feeling of courtesy. Age, gender, education, language, and culture play a role as to how laughter is performed or offered. A child might not laugh when adult humor is at play, though that same child might laugh at something an adult might perceive as childish or immature. Boys might be prone to laugh at things that make some girls blush, but women might react with laughter to some interactions to which men pay the slightest attention. It is a remarkably subjective phenomenon as to *who* laughs at *what, when, where, why,* and even *how.*

Laughter is a part of human behavior that is regulated by the brain. It clarifies intentions of social interaction by providing emotional context. Laughter denotes positive interactions of acceptance within a group. Consider how laughter is present in the company of friends and allies. Enemies laugh at each other rather than with each other.

In addition:
-Laughter can be contagious
-The study of laughter is called gelotology
-You can die from laughter
-Consider how antagonists in stories or drama utilize an 'evil' laugh
-Rats, dogs, and some birds can laugh, too
-Paradoxical laughter is misplaced laughter - it happens at the wrong time, sometimes when the fight or flight response is queued
-Involuntary or uncontrollable laughter (also occurs with crying, too) is known or perceived as a neurological disorder, or as a result of a brain injury
-Doctors have utilized psilocybin to treat people with depression as it elicits amazing fits of laughter

Law

The system of rules that a particular country or community recognizes as regulating the actions of its members and may enforce by the imposition of penalties is law. Law entails addressing the trespass by an individual or a group. The wrong, or crime (an offense that may be prosecuted by the state, punishable by law), committed can be against the self, another person, or the state; morality is almost always at play. For if abuses, trespasses, wrongs or perhaps even evil acts are not addressed and corrected, there runs a risk of validating that behavior via passive acceptance. Law pertains to justice within a community. In ancient terms, justice was a correction or balance of elements. Justice is personified in law by the figure of a blindfolded woman holding scales. The scales are a measure of a case's support and its opposition. Justice typically pertains to fairness but the concept of justice differs in every culture. Hence, law will be multi-faceted and sometimes very distinct in different countries, states, and communities.

Those who hold power, wield authority or serve in positions of leadership establish and implement law. The head of a tribe (the strong man, medicine man, or the magician) implemented rules to maintain or ensure the health and well-being of the greater group. Later, kings and rulers formulated and applied their dictates to govern larger groups of people over greater portions of land. Religions made and make use of their influence and power in the form of sacred texts and the Pope - among other notable figures/roles. Their laws governed entire groups, too. Laws were applied across populations but no set of laws held the powers that be to a standard of morality or proper justice. Rulers tended to be above the law. It was not until 1215 AD when citizens made King John sign the Magna Carta, or 'great document' - a text that subjected him to the rule of law. The rule of law is a concept that implies that every citizen is subject to the law - even the lawmakers themselves. It stands in contrast to an autocracy – (rule by one person), dictatorship (government by dictator), or oligarchy (rule by the few), where the rulers are held above the law. From among sixty-three clauses, the Magna Carta implemented *habeas corpus* - used to review the legality of the party's arrest, imprisonment, or detention. The United States' own 5th Amendment of The US Constitution is nearly identical to the original wording of the document, which is now 800 years old.

Historically, power structures vie for control. The secular contests the religious platforms for primary influence and power. Religious initiatives govern based on spiritual authority while secular authority wields temporal power. Religious authority rules via the spiritual element. Their authority is based on divine decree. A deity is the source from which their authority derives; God is the recognized king or ruler, His/Her laws are taken as the statute book of the kingdom. The laws are administered by a priestly order. In some cases, these clerics have power and their supreme leader could not be questioned in action. In contrast, secular authority rules via carceral means; they impose jail or prison as punishments. This form is more base - predicated on force, and the imposition of material punishment. They wield control of the body while religious authority addressed the soul and spirit (*they would also exert control on the body; see the Inquisition, the Crusades, and other examples of material play exercised by the Church, among other religions.* See also: Foucault!). Secular punishment could take the form of fines, incarceration, or even the death penalty. The secular authority need not address one's spiritual components or their worshipped deity. The only power that need be acknowledged was that of the ruler, or the broader state, or government in power.

There are many types of law.
-Administrative: regulates the operation and procedures of government agencies.
-Admiralty: Pertains to maritime questions, offenses; concerns domestic maritime operations and international relationships. It also concerns private entities that operate vessels on oceans.
-Blue: Enforces old, if not outdated religious standards.
-Civil: Concerns private relations between members of a community.
-Common: Derived from custom and judicial precedent rather than statutes. Concerns issues of mutual agreements, public behavior, and case law.
-Criminal: Concerns punishment of those who commit crimes.
-Constitutional: Defines the relationship of different entities within a state: executive, judicial and legislative.

-Contract: Pertains to agreements that create obligations enforceable by law.
-Family: Addresses marriage, civil unions, domestic partnerships, adoption, child abuse/abductions, divorce, property, child support, juvenile adjudication, and paternity, as well.
-Higher: The moral or religious principle believed to overrule secular constitutions and laws.
-Martial: The suspension of ordinary law.
-Public: Concerns the relationships between individuals and government.
-Trust: Pertains to property held by one entity for the benefit of another.

"The more corrupt the state, the more numerous the laws." - **Tacitus**

Terms and definitions are of the utmost importance and specifically pertinent in the realm of law. Some important terms include:
-Rights: a moral or legal entitlement to have or obtain something or to act in a certain way.
-Civil rights: the rights of citizens to political and social freedom and equality.
-Human Rights: a right that is believed to belong justifiably to every person - society, state, or government aside. A government can not abridge the human rights of a person.

It is interesting to note how the definitions involved in law - those listed in legal dictionaries - differ vastly in meaning from common usage. The legal definition of terms, including: 'property,' 'man,' 'beast,' 'appearance,' 'visit,' among others, are very distinct. That should give an individual reason to pause before engaging the legal realm, considering the gravity of court and legal proceedings. Consider how there exists a professional class of legal associates serving a populace that is woefully ignorant of the law; they are woefully dependent upon the legal class. It is apparent that the profitability and maintenance of the industry is prioritized over the knowledge base and well-being of the citizens. If we cared about rearing a citizenry comprised of honorable, law-abiding people, we would invest in that education and structure other aspects of culture that support that result.

Culture is always in a state of flux; it grows, shifts, and changes very dramatically. Its institutions, though, are slower to transform. This is intentional, for the realms of governance and infrastructure need be stable, consistent and reliable. The standards by which they operate need be firm and sound. But they, too, change and shift. The structure may remain rather static, but the personnel responsible for policy implementation and enforcement changes dynamically. Corruption is fraudulent or dishonest conduct by those in power, typically involving bribery. It is the abuse of entrusted power for private gain. It can be classified as grand, petty, or political, depending on the amount of money lost and the sector where it occurs.

Lately, behaviors of significant officials at all levels of public office have been identified as corrupt. A judge in Pennsylvania was sentenced to jail for 28 years for taking a $1 million kickback from the builder of for-profit prisons for juveniles. He and another judge used their role and power to sentence youngsters to prison they had a hand in building. Some of those sentenced were as young as 10 years old.[15] Their crimes received punishments that could color and affect their prospects and opportunities for the rest of their lives. A state crime lab analyst used her position for analyzing chemical evidence to intentionally forge results in order to get convictions for prosecutors with whom she had friendly ties. After years of tampering with evidence her actions may have tainted more than 40 thousand drug samples, involving thousands of defendants. She had forged signatures, tampered with evidence, and lied in court about her credentials to enhance her standing as an expert witness.[16] She received a light sentence for these remarkable transgressions.

"In a year-long investigation of sexual misconduct by U.S. law enforcement, the Associated Press uncovered about a thousand officers who lost their badges in a six year period for rape, sodomy, and other sexual assault; sex crimes that included possession of child pornography; or sexual misconduct such as propositioning citizens or having consensual but prohibited on-duty intercourse. The number is unquestionably an undercount because it represents only those officers whose licenses to work in law enforcement were revoked and not all states take such actions. California and New York – with several of the nation's largest law enforcement agencies – offered no records because they have no statewide system to decertify officers for misconduct."[17]

It is interesting to note how common individuals can be prosecuted for seemingly harmless actions: for living off-grid, for collecting rainwater, for studying certain subjects. A 19-year-old was arrested for cracking a joke. An 8th grader was recently arrested for refusing to remove his NRA T-shirt. In contrast, lots of notable celebrities and officials receive no prosecution or punishment for engaging in most questionable behavior. Singer Justin Bieber was charged with vandalism and assault but escaped punishment. Model and actress Paris Hilton backed her car into another vehicle and left the scene without leaving a note. She received no punishment for her transgression. Singer and actress Britney Spears was caught driving with her 4-month-old son in her lap without a child restraint. She paid no fine. In 2007, she was charged with a hit and run accident, and received no fine or punishment. In 1969, Ted Kennedy drove his car off a bridge. He escaped the car and left the scene, leaving a passenger to die. He did not admit to the crime until fishermen found the car the next day. He was only convicted of leaving the scene and got a two month suspended sentence. He ended up being a senator. Those that are famous, powerful, or particularly affluent escape accountability and justice - aided by a system that enables the perpetuation of very questionable behavior.

Invariably, you will need to interact with law enforcement personnel. Your interaction may have nothing to do with a crime or a wrong on your part - but that does not matter. An interaction with police can have serious consequences, up to and including death.

Some Suggestions for Engaging Police Officers:
-Use the buddy system. Travel with friends, so you can rely on another, and have a witness as to the encounter.
-Be calm. Breathe and keep your attitude in check. Be polite and diffuse the situation by behaving respectfully.
-Keep your hands visible. Keep them normally at your side or on the steering wheel if you are pulled over while driving. Do not make them think you are a physical threat by moving them quickly, menacingly, or threateningly.
-Be silent. Identify yourself. Do not argue. You do not have to speak and it is better not to.

The only things you should say are: "I wish to invoke my 5th Amendment rights and remain silent," and "I would like to speak with a lawyer."
-Have your Identification handy and accessible. When moving to get it from your pocket or purse, announce that intention, loudly, clearly. Move slowly.
-Find out if you are being detained. That is as simple as asking, "Officer, am I being detained, or am I free to go?" Check your attitude and ask the question. If they tell you are not being detained, leave immediately. If you are being detained, they assume a crime has been committed, or will be. Accept their ticket and comply with their instructions as to their investigation. Take the encounter in stride and leave the situation alive.

-Do not consent to illegal searches. If no evidence of a crime is apparent, if there is no reasonable suspicion or probable cause, or no search warrant, an officer can not go through your car or home. They can pat you down or frisk you, but that is it. Simply say, "Officer, I do not consent to any searches." Do not allow them to violate you or your 4th Amendment rights.

-Do not resist arrest or give the impression that you will. Simply comply if and when you are under arrest.

-Do not engage in violence. The police will make use of their years of training to subdue you. They might hurt or even kill you. Keep in mind: you are ALWAYS allowed to defend yourself against improper application of control or power upon your person. Importantly: you are allowed to kill ONLY in self-defense. This is a very particular discussion. You need not suffer rape, torture, or the threat to your well-being and life.

-Tell your friends to follow these rules as well. If they do not, you run the risk of suffering consequences they elicit.

-Use your eyes, ears, memory, and mobile device. Take mental notes. Be sober and cognizant. Remember what officers said, what they asked you, reasons for stopping you. Instruct witnesses to record the interaction. Be aware of laws pertaining to cell phone laws in your own local area. After the event, write down or record what happened and omit that which might be inaccurate. Get the names and badge numbers of responding officers, if possible.

The best way to keep out of trouble with the law is to behave, have a working knowledge of your rights, and know how to act if and when you encounter the police.

Law is a powerful social construct. Courts and authorities wield tremendous influence and we are at their mercy, sometimes. While legal professionals facilitate the greater legal process, we have the responsibility of ensuring a just system, and greater: our own well-being.

Morality, ethics, and fairness all need remain active and integral components of a responsive system. Behave such that you need not suffer the application of its resources upon your person and life. Consider whether you want to play a part in the system, as a professional. Strong, ethical players can make a meaningful difference for those who are facing legal action or those who need help in the system.

"Change is the law of life. And those who look only to the past or present are certain to miss the future." - **John F. Kennedy**

"Music is a moral law. It gives soul to the universe, wings to the mind, flight to the imagination, and charm and gaiety to life and to everything." - **Plato**

"Rightful liberty is unobstructed action according to our will within limits drawn around us by the equal rights of others. I do not add 'within the limits of the law' because law is often but the tyrant's will, and always so when it violates the rights of the individual." - **Thomas Jefferson**

"If the machine of government is of such a nature that it requires you to be the agent of injustice to another, then, I say, break the law." - **Henry David Thoreau**

"God and Nature first made us what we are, and then out of our own created genius we make ourselves what we want to be. Follow always that great law. Let the sky and God be our limit and Eternity our measurement." - **Marcus Garvey**

"Be peaceful, be courteous, obey the law, respect everyone; but if someone puts his hand on you, send him to the cemetery." - **Malcolm X**

"At his best, man is the noblest of all animals; separated from law and justice he is the worst." - **Aristotle**

"Justice that love gives is a surrender, justice that law gives is a punishment." - **Mahatma Gandhi**

"Democracy must be built through open societies that share information. When there is information, there is enlightenment. When there is debate, there are solutions. When there is no sharing of power, no rule of law, no accountability, there is abuse, corruption, subjugation and indignation." - **Atifete Jahjaga**

"In law a man is guilty when he violates the rights of others. In ethics he is guilty if he only thinks of doing so." - **Immanuel Kant**

"We must all obey the great law of change. It is the most powerful law of nature." - **Edmund Burke**

"It seems to be a law of nature, inflexible and inexorable, that those who will not risk cannot win." - **John Paul Jones**

"That old law about 'an eye for an eye' leaves everybody blind. The time is always right to do the right thing." - **Martin Luther King, Jr.**

Learning

The acquisition of knowledge or skills through experience, study, or by being taught is learning. The ability to learn is possessed by humans, animals, plants, and even some machines. Progress tends to follow a learning curve. It builds up and is shaped by previous knowledge. Learning is a process. Learning changes an individual, and those changes are generally permanent. Learning may be conscious, or occur without conscious awareness.

There are many different types of learning:

<u>Non-Associative</u>
-habituation
-sensitization

<u>Active Learning</u>

<u>Associative</u>

-Operant conditioning
-Classical conditioning
-reprinting

Learning concerns the head, the heart, and the hands (body). In terms of learning, knowledge gets categorized as cognitive, affective, or psychomotor. Learning can occur as play, as enculturation via multimedia, or rote means. It can be meaningful, whether it is informal, formal, or even non-formal, with combinations. Learning can be dialogic, incidental, or tangential. It can occur everywhere in all occasions. The list above is not complete, nor exhaustive, either.

External Factors Affecting Learning:

Heredity: governs or conditions our ability to learn and the rate of learning. Intelligent learners can establish and see relationship very easily and more quickly than others.
Status of Students: physical home conditions matter. Malnutrition, fatigue, and bad health obstruct learning. If the home is chaotic, violent, unsafe, unhygienic, poorly lit, learning is affected.
Physical: design, quality, setting of a learning space can be critical.

Comfort, size, air, and temperature: these all affect a student's learning. Technology, the arrangements of furniture, the classroom size, or the amount of students present are all conditions contributing to the ability to learn in a specific environment.

Internal Factors Affecting Learning Include:
- goals or purposes
- learning activities
- motivational behavior
- interest
- testing
- aptitude
- attention
- drill or practice
- speed re accuracy & retention
- guidance
- fatigue
- attitude

A person or animal need learn and evolve in order to survive. Learning increases the chances of success. Being open to the possibility of learning provides that opportunity in any, if not all, situations. That information is constantly available or offered means that we nearly always have the possibility of learning - consciously or unconsciously. Remain open and have a teachable disposition. While you may not have the means of making use of specific forms of information now does not mean that you will not be able to eventually, finally, make use of it. Using this text as an example: presently you may not have a reason to study many of these concepts. Yet the information may still prove applicable and worthwhile as you gain experience and develop your vocabulary, your skill set(s) and abilities. Generally, in my own experience, information stays with me and I later discover its pertinence or application. *The more you can integrate, the more you will be able to apply.*

Being aware of how the greater process of learning works will facilitate your growth and development. When you recognize how factors influence your own subjective process, you can then engage different forms of learning and that will help you actively and dynamically shape your character and broaden your greater horizons.

Level

A position on a real or imaginary scale of amount, quality, quantity or extent is a level. Level can be applied to effort, intelligence, awareness, culture, role/status, and power, among a great many other concepts and characteristics. The term has very broad pertinence, hence its inclusion - albeit via a brief section. Levels apply to different qualities and notions. I suggest making use of or associating with proper levels. Apply appropriate levels of emotion, intelligence, effort, or energies to different activities. One need adapt in the moment per the specific context. Associate with those whose levels of character, consideration, intelligence, and general worthiness align with your own. You are influenced and affected by those with whom you identify or associate. As you develop and shape your character, align with those whose level matches your own. Those who elect to be base, superficial, lazy, or unmotivated will slow your progress and growth. Associate with those who serve as positive influences, who care about themselves AND others.

You will encounter those with whom you sync well with in certain areas, though some notable differences will still remain. You need not be remarkably similar to all of your acquaintances, friends, family or coworkers. Oftentimes, a minute element serves as sufficient common ground to create a significant rapport or relationship. Generally, align and associate with those who share that element of similarity, and make sure that those elements, characteristics, and levels match your own. The breadth of your experience and learning will shape a greater character, an amalgam or composite of different characteristics and traits. A person is a radical combination of so many things: feelings, thoughts, actions, experience, etc. Apply a broad, comprehensive perspective in order to ascertain the broader, general level of a person. Utilize discernment in order to identify if and how you want someone to play a role in your own life. Be slow to make those decisions regarding the exclusion or inclusion of others, save for those circumstances that clearly depict the need of immediate acceptance, restriction, or termination of presence.

Liberty

Liberty is the state of being free within society from oppressive restrictions imposed by authority on one's way of life, behavior, or political views. It is the power or scope to act as one pleases. Liberty concerns self-ownership. It is contrary to the idea that someone else has a higher claim to you. No other person or group owns you, nor do you own others. Here we address how liberty is situated historically, and we include the work of John Stuart Mill's *On Liberty* as most pertinent. We contrast his work with how liberty is considered in our contemporary United States community.

Memorable phrases from Benjamin Franklin, Thomas Jefferson, or even Patrick Henry's utterance of the famous, "Give me Liberty, or give me death!" showcase a fervent belief in liberty. Founding Fathers of the United States spoke of liberty often and discussed what it would take to keep liberty strong, how liberty could be taken away, and how freedoms could be lost. These men, and others in modern times, have acknowledged liberty's place in a free society. It is a concept important enough that signers of the Declaration of Independence pledged their lives, fortune, and sacred honor in its defense.

"It was no idle pledge - nine signers died of wounds during the Revolutionary War. Five were captured or imprisoned. Wives and children were killed, jailed, mistreated, or left penniless. Twelve signers' houses were burned to the ground. Seventeen lost everything they owned. No signer defected - their honor, like their nation, remained intact." – **Engraved stone at the Declaration of Independence Memorial, Virginia**

The French applied the same vigor and enthusiasm in their endeavors. Liberty maintained a presence when they revolted. They went as far to enshrine it in their national motto and gift the Statue of Liberty - Lady Liberty - to the United States in 1886. What these Patriots voiced more than 200 years ago remains just as valid and consequential today, though perhaps even more so. Individual liberty is important to any society that wants to advance, generally.

It is a precious resource: never guaranteed and always threatened.

It allows for the flourishing of the individual, and the emergence of a just community. Liberty demands cooperation and invites innovation complemented by wealth creation. It *does* require that we conduct ourselves ably and well. We are rewarded as we do so. The alternative is slavery. Those who champion the cause of liberty are those who advocate for communal and individual transcendence. Only those who seek to advance exclusive aims and initiatives at the expense of others contend otherwise.

In 1958 liberal Philosopher Isaiah Berlin delivered a lecture before Oxford University entitled, *Two Concepts of Liberty*. Berlin identified positive and negative liberty. These two concepts were addressed in our discussion about freedom. Positive liberty equates to self-mastery but pertains also to one having a role in choosing who governs the society of which one is a part. Negative liberty is the absence of coercion or interference with possible private actions by an external institution (comprised of a plurality, or several people), or any singular entity. These two concepts of liberty help connect with that previous discussion of freedom; we are able to discern and distinguish the vital difference between liberty and freedom. Freedom applies to *all* living, sentient things. A bird, a fly, or a tapir can be considered free. When we refer to freedom, we mean acting without hindrance or restraint. Liberty is a concept that pertains specifically and exclusively to human affairs and initiative. Liberty is freedom from restrictions imposed by authority. A bird will not contend with authority, nor the fly or tapir. Though the three will also not shoulder the burdens of a conceptual array, consciousness, or the idea of self-ownership (as far as we know). So liberty is particular *human* freedom, one that renders an individual unlike a slave.

Ken Schoolland scripted *The Philosophy of Liberty*, a clear address of the concept:
Liberty has an esteemed position next to life, and property. Life and liberty make property available, or possible. Property is the fruit of one's labor or talent. It is that part of nature which is put to valuable use. In a society, property can be conveyed via voluntary exchanges involving mutual consent. Exchangers are better for the exchange; else they would not commit to the transaction. Liberty contends that only actors can make decisions for themselves. Force and fraud are the means by which liberty is impinged. A trespass of life is murder. The usurpation of liberty is slavery, and the taking of property is theft. One person may commit ills, just as a collective, or an organization can. Officials, or politicians are a special entity that moves to limit liberty as a routine.

One has the right to protect life, liberty, and property from aggression. One may ask others to help defend. One does not have the right to initiate force against the life, liberty, and property of others. One can not designate agents to do the same. Liberty delivers the right to seek leaders, but there is no right to impose leaders on others. Officials have no higher rights, regardless of labels or the amount of support they curry from their constituents or supporters. There is no right to murder, to enslave, or to steal. One can not give away rights that they do not have themselves. *We are responsible for our own life.* We do not rent life from others who demand obedience, nor are we slaves for those who demand sacrifice.

Our goals are based on values. Success and failure are incentives. One's action on behalf of others, or their action on behalf of one is virtuous only when it is derived from voluntary mutual consent. Virtue exists only where there is choice. Liberty is the means of a truly free society. It is the most practical and humanitarian arrangement. It stands as a very ethical social construct. It restricts government initiation of force. It identifies how evil arises not only from evil people, but also from good people who tolerate the initiation of force as a means to their own ends. Good people empower evil people through history! Having confidence in a free society means to focus on the process of discovery in the marketplace of values, rather than to focus on an imposed vision or goal. The protection of liberty is courage. For it takes an incredible amount of courage to think, talk, and act, especially when it is easier to do nothing.[18]

"But the chief penalty is to be governed by someone worse if a man will not himself hold office and rule. It is from fear of this, as it appears to me, that the better sort hold office when they do, and then they go to it not in the expectation of enjoyment nor as to a good thing, but as to a necessary evil and because they are unable to turn it over to better men than themselves..." – **Plato, The Republic: Book 1, 347c**

John Stuart Mill contributed meaningfully with his approach to liberty. He offered two maxims concerning the relationship of the individual to society, three basic liberties, and three legitimate objections to government, as well as a very thorough approach in his work, *On Liberty*. He addressed government, education, the market, and culture. His work is important because of the detail and scope of his work. Liberty plays an amazingly consequential part in a free society; Mill's address is noteworthy, if not most instructive.

In a society, individuals advance subjective claims, aims, and beliefs. Invariably, conflict occurs. Values and behaviors are a point of contention. Mill identifies how the majority opinion wields the capacity to effectively negate individual liberties. He identifies how the tyranny of the majority is worse than political tyranny (as there is no safeguard against it). Prevailing opinions are the basis of all rules of conduct in a society. Individuality plays a large role in Mill's project. It is a pre-requisite to the higher intellectual pleasures - in contrast to sensual/base or lower pleasures.[19] In order to provide for the protection of individualism, government need be controlled by the liberty of citizens.

Necessary rights of citizens need support, and constitutional checks applied via representative governance are the means of limiting trespass or intrusion upon individual liberty.

Mill's two maxims of liberalism are:
1.) the individual is not accountable to society for his actions, insofar as these concern the interests of no person but himself; and,
2.) that for such actions as are prejudicial to the interests of others, the individual is accountable and may be subjected either to social or legal punishment.

For Mill, liberty amounts to doing what one wants as long as others are not hurt in the process. Liberty can be limited only if it prevents harm to others. The physical and moral good is not a sufficient cause for interference. Mill states,"Over himself, over his body and mind, the individual is sovereign. The three basic liberties of an individual are:
1.) the freedoms of thought and action and the freedom to act on such freedom;
2.) the freedom to pursue tastes, even if they are deemed 'immoral.' So long as activity does not harm others, it need be left alone; and
3.) the freedom to unite, provided the constituents are of age, not forced, and no harm will befall others as a result of the association, or unity.

Free speech is of significant consequence for Mill. He discusses benefits of opinions that are wholly false, partly true, and wholly true. He identifies how all opinions benefit the public. Diversity is healthy, and should be encouraged.

Truth will necessarily survive persecution, and society need teach the grounds for truth, not the objections to it.

Hence society should promote individuality. As a prerequisite of creativity and diversity, conformity is dangerous. Mill addresses how a government operates with liberty in mind. Mill prefers a state that minds its own business. He contends that government should only punish an individual for neglecting to fulfill a duty to others (or causing harm to others), not the vice that brought about the neglect, which remains a personal matter. He maintains that harmful consequences, and not irrational conduct, itself, should be punished. He *does* contend that public indecency is condemnable, though. Where he draws the distinction between personal vices and public concern is unclear, however. Should consequences be delayed, distant, or unforeseen, Mill's conception of the restrained government encounters possible opposition.

Three legitimate objections to government interference include:
1.) if agents do action better than the government;
2.) if it benefits agents though government might be more qualified; and,
3.) if the interference increases governmental power so onerously,   that individual ambition would be turned into dependency.

Regarding taxes, Mill states that taxes should be applied only to what is deemed most dangerous. Mill's liberal approach to markets is of interest. Markets are best left alone to operate as free markets. Government interference is counter - productive. If government ran the economy - or even significant sectors, institutions, etc. - *everyone* would strive to be a part of the bureaucracy. Consider employment numbers for the NSA!

As far as education is concerned, society has the opportunity and duty to ensure that a generation, as a whole, is generally moral. Having individuals unaccountable to society for his actions enables that process. Society *can* advise, instruct, persuade, or avoid, and these are the *only* measures a society can apply its taste or preference, dislike, or disapprobation. Mill states that government-run education ruins diversity. Government ought to require and fund private education, because a diverse education, comprising opposing views, is only a benefit in a liberal society.

In short, the individual is accountable when actions affect others. This makes for a remarkably different standard than what is currently implemented. Mill adds some caveats to this perspective. People should not wait for harm to occur when they can take initiative to prevent it. Sometimes, something dangerous is not a bad by itself. Think about motor vehicles, alcohol, or firearms, as examples. Exclusive injuries can occur, though warning labels and advisories perform sufficient good. But the tools or activities need not be limited or prohibited outright. People can also be impeded when they are not in possession of all facts in a given scenario. It is best to warn, instead of serving an impediment, however. Consider if a driver does not know a road ends prematurely. He might want to be impeded, or perhaps he would not mind the temporary restriction of his liberty because it might save him his life. As another example, recently divulged, exclusive news, or material might provide the means of a radically different conclusion to a chain of events. Interfering with someone in order to educate and inform might amount to a positive result. Taking initiative to restrict the ability of others is a complex matter, indeed.

Our present society differs considerably from Mill's structure. By his estimate, our society would be opposed to his idea of liberty. The diminishment of civil liberties and the intrusive interference of government in education, the market, and morality, depict a ruling authority that is more concerned with protecting its position and insulating its power than with encouraging diversity of ideas, and the development, if not the flourishing, of its constituency. This present state of affairs is understandable, though, given the relative engagement of the citizenry. The powers that be do not emphasize or prioritize liberty. Personal matters and a perspective influenced by fear and laziness leave but a small percentage of people committed to the self-mastery necessary to maintain liberty in our community. We can make proper use of and enjoy liberty for as long as we are focused on its perpetuation. Liberty can be lessened - if not lost - within a generation. It is our responsibility, and the responsibility of every free person, to engage with liberty in mind, else slavery and assorted fetters result.

"They who can give up essential liberty to obtain a little temporary safety deserve neither liberty nor safety." - **Benjamin Franklin**

"We have all one common cause; let it, therefore, be our only contest, who shall most contribute to the security of the liberties of America." - **John Hancock**

"Our liberty can never be safe but in the hands of the people themselves."
Thomas Jefferson

"The liberties of our country, the freedom of our civil constitution, are worth defending against all hazards: And it is our duty to defend them against all attacks." - **Samuel   Adams**

"Is life so dear, or peace so sweet, as to be purchased at the price of chains and slavery? Forbid it, Almighty God! I know not what course others may take; but as for me, give me liberty or give me death!" - **Patrick Henry**

Life

Life is that which distinguishes living from inorganic matter. It is that which has the capacity for growth, reproduction, functional activity, and continual change preceding death. Life has been called existence but that a rock exists does not mean that is has life, either (as far as *this* writer is concerned, anyway). For the purposes of this section, we discuss the human condition as opposed to a comprehensive approach of life at the cellular, aquatic, or even cosmic levels. We approach the characteristics, key events, and situations that comprise the essentials of human existence such as birth, growth, emotionality, conflict, and mortality. This particular discussion will, of course, be shorter than the analysis provided by religion, philosophy, history, art, literature, anthropology, and biology.

The Sphinx challenged Oedipus with a riddle: "What has 4 legs, then 2, then 3?" The answer that Oedipus offered correctly was man: four as he crawls like a baby, two as he walks like a man, and three as he uses a cane for support in his later years. Some of us never get to utilize the fullness of a long life. Some individuals do not survive childbirth. We have discussed how death comes at its own time. Life, then, is about making use of the time available to us. More than engaging at just a base, biological level, we are fortunate to be able to do so much more. Certainly, the enjoyment of food, procreation, and recreation can be awesome activities, but there is so much more to life.

We have a remarkable array of faculties that imparts the means of applying significance to our moments. So on a momentary, or moment-to-moment, or even momentous basis, we have the privilege of engaging with our head, heart, and hands to create meaning. At this point of your life, you already have significant memories. Plato said that life is all about remembering - for we always have access to our previous experience per the application of memory. Some people can remember occasions when they were infants and toddlers, while others do not recall much until their early childhood. In the moments you have, punctuate them with an engaged perspective. Meaning: engage fully. Use your senses: see, feel, smell, taste, and hear the variables of the context. Make use of your intuitive faculties. Discern elements that are not so obvious and apparent. Investigate life and see what lies beyond the readily available. Seek to discover what else exists in the scene or in the equation, if even only marginally or tangentially.

We have discussed being open to what is offered, or maintaining a teachable disposition. As you proceed through life's events, occurrences, and experience, tend to the barrage of variables. You can catalogue any number of situational sights, sounds, scents, textures, and tastes. But more than just making use of your sensory perceptions, grasp and explore how they make you *feel*. Their inter-connected play will touch you - affect you emotionally - if and when you allow it. Since the beginning of culture, man has attempted to encapsulate that sense of wonder elicited by wondrous beauty, amazing occurrences, or the unnerving sublime. While you may or may not be moved to depict them for the public, you will create meaning based on the personal value of these events. Just as there are many forms of learning, there are many variables that signify things to different people. In fact, an object can mean several things to the same person. The writer Proust wrote 132 volumes about his childhood when he happened to encounter roses one day while he was walking! In a parallel circumstance, I walked by our friend Sarah one day as she sat with her friend. The latter was smoking a pipe, and as I perceived the particular odor of flavored tobacco, I recollected my own grandpa - my Mom's father - as he worked in his garage. I recalled the scene: his smile, how his pipe colored the entire moment. That scent moved me to tears, as I was transported to a meaningful scene of my childhood. I would have had trouble identifying the scene as significant, were it not for the scent and the specific recollection.

We are fortunate to have the ability of formulating connections and applying significance. It is no chore or responsibility but one of the means by which we grow and shape our own character and identity. We are our memories, thoughts, emotions, and behavior. What we value and hold as important influences and informs our actions as we progress through life. Hence, the necessity of holding onto the good stuff, learning lessons from what we are given, and releasing the bad, or lesser stuff. We can be utterly awesome as we develop from learning and take responsibility for what we carry as meaningful and significant. Conversely, we can be depressed, deflated, defeated, or simply unnecessarily encumbered or burdened should we elect to carry negativity, limited beliefs, and that which does not contribute to our greater health, well-being, and continued development.

This text has been structured to help you distinguish between options, elements, variables, and complex concepts. It is *your* life - your gift to enjoy. The provision of this extended list of concepts is meant to facilitate your path by guiding as to possible encounters, lessons, and possibilities. It is my hope that you make use of your time in the best possible way, and in imparting that, I do not need you to measure your choices or life's activities by my perspective. QUITE THE OPPOSITE, truly! A life is one's own and no one else is in your skin, or makes use of your filters, lenses, ethos and subjectivity. Heaven knows that my standard or perspective is in need of work, too - I am no sort of an expert as to the life choices of others. I can only make use of the information at my disposal to make my own best choices. Judging others as to their own selections is entirely outside of my realm.

There is no secret to life; there is no underlying objective meaning to life. While answers are to be found in books, discovered by interacting with others, or via the tranquility of meditation or introspection: *life is what you make of it.* Your mother and I have raised a bright, beautiful, and creative child, and you make us very proud. Make use of that good stuff, and continue to be aware, bubbly, confident, daring, effusive, fervent, glowing, happy, intelligent, joyful, keen, loving, memorable, nonconforming, occupied, (but not) preoccupied, qualified, rhythmic, skilled, teachable, understanding, versed, well, xenial, yearning (for more), and zippy.

"The only way that we can live, is if we grow. The only way that we can grow is if we change. The only way that we can change is if we learn. The only way we can learn is if we are exposed. And the only way that we can become exposed is if we throw ourselves out into the open. Do it. Throw yourself." — **C. JoyBell C.**

"People tend to complicate their own lives, as if living weren't already complicated enough." — **Carlos Ruiz Zafón, The Shadow of the Wind**

"There will be a few times in your life when all your instincts will tell you to do something, something that defies logic, upsets your plans, and may seem crazy to others. When that happens, you do it. Listen to your instincts and ignore everything else. Ignore logic, ignore the odds, ignore the complications, and just go for it." — **Judith McNaught, Remember When**

"This is an important lesson to remember when you're having a bad day, a bad month, or a shitty year. Things will change: you won't feel this way forever. And anyway, sometimes the hardest lessons to learn are the ones your soul needs most. I believe you can't feel real joy unless you've felt heartache. You can't have a sense of victory unless you know what it means to fail. You can't know what it's like to feel holy until you know what it's like to feel really fucking evil. And you can't be birthed again until you've died." — **Kelly Cutrone, If You Have to Cry, Go Outside: And Other Things Your Mother Never Told You**

"Instructions for living a life.
Pay attention.
Be astonished.
Tell about it." — **Mary Oliver**

"It is better to live your own destiny imperfectly than to live an imitation of somebody else's life with perfection."
— **Anonymous, The Bhagavad Gita**

"Make a pact with yourself today to not be defined by your past. Sometimes the greatest thing to come out of all your hard work isn't what you get for it, but what you become for it. Shake things up today! Be You...Be Free...Share." — **Steve Maraboli, Life, the Truth, and Being Free**

"First, let no one rule your mind or body. Take special care that your thoughts remain unfettered ...Give men your ear, but not your heart. Show respect for those in power, but don't follow them blindly. Judge with logic and reason, but comment not. Consider none your superior whatever their rank or station in life. Treat all fairly, or they will seek revenge. Be careful with your money. Hold fast to your beliefs and others will listen."
— **Christopher Paolini, Eragon**

"The idea that our society is best served when all family members separate in the morning, to do things they generally don't enjoy, could be the biggest fallacy ever imprinted upon humanity." - **Jason Christoff**

"The only people who see the whole picture are the ones who step outside the frame. Your agreement with reality defines your life." – **Unknown**

50 Life Lessons.[20] While some of these lessons might be experienced later in your life, some provisions will save you some concern and trouble. I hope the list guides you well. And when you have any questions, ask your Mother, or myself, or the great many others that love and care for you.

1. Life is now
2. Fear is an illusion (mostly)
3. Relationships rule
4. Debt isn't worth it
5. Your kids aren't you
6. Things gather dust
7. Fun is underrated
8. Failure is good
9. Friendships need care
10. Experiences first
11. Anger isn't worth it
12. Kindness matters
13. Age is a number
14. Vulnerability heals
15. Posturing builds walls
16. Exercise is power
17. Grudges cause pain
18. Passion upgrades life
19. Travel expands you
20. You aren't always right
21. It will pass
22. You define meaning
23. Risk expands you
24. Change is good
25. Thoughts aren't real
26. You can't control others
27. Your body is a temple
28. Touch heals

29. You can handle it
30. Gratitude multiplies happiness
31. Intuition counts
32. Please yourself first
33. Self-honesty is freedom
34. Perfection is boring
35. Serving creates meaning
36. Little things matter
37. Learning is forever
38. Aging happens
39. Marriages change
40. Worry is worthless
41. Heal your wounds
42. Simple is better
43. Do the work
44. It is never too late
45. Action beats angst
46. Creation beats reaction
47. Release attachments
48. Your words matter
49. Make every day count
50. Love is the answer.

Literature

Written works, especially those considered of superior and lasting, artistic or intellectual merit, are designated as literature. Literature can be designated as fiction or non-fiction, but generally, it encompasses a wide spectrum of works. For example, while it includes written pieces, literature is also comprised of spoken, or sung works – oral literature – as in the case of ancient epics, like Homer's *Iliad* or *The Odyssey*. Literature has a fluid definition. It has changed over time and varies according to culture as well. It includes poetry, prose, drama, history, journalism, law, philosophy, and scientific works, too.

Make use of the literary resources at your disposal. Literature through time and cultures has enriched,

Literature

enlightened, and entertained the world since people first structured myths, lore, and legends and disseminated them for groups, in community. Literature can educate, and it can also serve as a distraction. I recommend making use of those works that refine, improve, and even challenge your character. History, Philosophy, and poetry have conveyed meaning and significance to my life, and have shaped my person immensely. I have also indulged a great many titles that have humored me, diverted me from more serious endeavors and considerations. Seek those works that interest you, and be open to new genres, authors, and thoughts that broaden your horizon and challenge your perceptions of people, the world, and greater reality.

Some titles, and authors I recommend:
-Anything written by Plato, and nearly any other philosopher.
-*The Bible*
-*The Upanishads/Vedas*
-Thucydides
-Cicero
-*Tao Te Ching*
-All forms of mythology across cultures
-Ancient Plays (including Sophocles' *Oedipus Rex*, and then, later: Deleuze and Guattari's *Anti-Oedipus*, at that)
-Don Quixote, *Cervantes*
-Hesiod, *Theogony*, and *Works & Days*
-*The Epic of Gilgamesh*, and other Mesopotamian myths
-Virgil's *Aeneid*
-Ovid's *Metamorphoses*
-Chaucer's *Canterbury Tales*
-Dante's *Divine Comedy*
-Montaigne's Essays
-Anything by Shakespeare, though after diligent study of myth
-*1,001 Nights*
-Swift, *Gulliver's Travels*
-Goethe's *Faust*
-Hans Christian Anderson's *FairyTales*
-*Book of 5 Rings*

-J.R.R. Tolkien

This list is but a start. Be teachable, have an open mind, and recognize that the more you read, the more you know. The more you read, the more you grasp conceptually and figuratively.

Keep in mind that when you have a background in different cultural lore, legends, myths, history, and philosophy, the more you will be able to relate with a greater amount of people. Connect with different people by exploring the values at play in their literature. Truly, literature is a gateway to the people of the world.

Longing

A yearning desire is often characterized as longing. It is also referred to as a craving, an ache, a burning, a hunger, a thirst, or a hankering. The sentiment is a characterization of a form of motivation. What strikes this writer is how these forms of longing have a physical element. But longing need not be so base, or centered so physically. There are emotional and intellectual forms of longing. Longing can be emotional, as in the case of longing for the return of a long-distant lover. Longing is intellectual when one pines for the conditions of a bygone era.

People can long for a disparate spectrum of concepts or things including happiness, money, peace, love, security, companionship, balance, freedom, joy, or passion, among many others. Longing need serve a purpose, else it detracts from obtaining viable ends. It can equate to hope. People can long for both realistic and unrealistic aims. Both are acceptable, as even unrealistic events sometimes come to pass. However, longing needs be complemented, encouraged, and furthered by substantial action. Otherwise, longing remains a passive fancy of the mind and heart. The hands - the body - need take action to elicit or bring about meaningful results.

Consider the object of your longing. Is it an internal or external goal? From the list above: happiness, love, passion, and joy might all be internally available; you might generate all of these concepts by your own state of mind, or by centering yourself emotionally. Meditation, focus, awareness may bring about their realized presence. Money, love, security, companionship, and balance may require the cooperation or coordination of external variables. While you may conceptualize and long for money, for example, thinking and/or feeling alone will not manifest its presence. Work is required to generate or invite its presence. Self-love *can* be generated internally, but the meaningful love shared with others requires work and effort put forth by all parties involved. Similarly, security, companionship, and balance require significant action in the extended, external world in order to bring about their achievement.

Longing for viable goals amounts to wasted time and energy if the requisite actions are not applied or put forth. Longing for the impossible to occur amounts to watching grass grow - the world continues apace unheeding the solitary act of longing.

Loss

The fact or process of losing someone or something is what is known as loss. We can lose other people or things, and we can also lose our own selves. Consider being enthralled by any number of factors. We can lose our selves when in the throes of powerful rhetoric, amazing music, or even as we are influenced by an unworthy or unhealthy relationship. One can be at a loss when they are puzzled or uncertain as to what to think, say, or do. Grieving is a state, or a process of loss when deprived of something or someone of value. There is economic loss, which may be limited to a financial consequence as a balance sheet variable. An intellectual or informational loss might perhaps refer to a forgotten bit of information or data. An emotional loss, as mentioned previously, refers to the deprivation of someone or something of value. The reality of loss is a certain one in this existence. Because of the dynamism of life - life transforms, never stagnates - variables will shift and contexts will change. We must adapt to circumstances and prepare ourselves for the eventual occurrence of loss. Barring a total, catastrophic loss - in which one loses life, liberty, resources, wherewithal - we need structure plans and live life adapting to both incremental or radical change, or loss.

Life is about adaptation to both. We lose innocence, parents, friends, even track of time. We succeed by being considerate of the weight and consequence of our attachments to people, places, and things. Being overly concerned with, or attached to outcomes or the continuation of variables sets us up for loss as change occurs. A balanced plan that takes into consideration the reality and necessity of change and loss prepares us for dynamic shifts and developments in context.

"Death is not the greatest loss in life. The greatest loss is what dies inside us while we live." – **Norman Cousins**

"Success consists of going from failure to failure without loss of enthusiasm." – **Winston Churchill**

"Bad things do happen; how I respond to them defines my character and the quality of my life. I can choose to sit in perpetual sadness, immobilized by the gravity of my loss, or I can choose to rise from the pain and treasure the most precious gift I have - life itself." – **Walter Anderson**

"Do not measure your loss by itself; if you do, it will seem intolerable; but if you will take all human affairs into account you will find that some comfort is to be derived from them." – **Saint Basil**

"The most beautiful people we have known are those who have known defeat, known suffering, known struggle, known loss, and have found their way out of those depths." – **Elizabeth Kubler Ross**

"I never said I wanted a 'happy' life but an interesting one. From separation and loss, I have learned a lot. I have become strong and resilient, as is the case of almost every human being exposed to life and to the world. We don't even know how strong we are until we are forced to bring that hidden strength forward." – **Isabel Allende**

"It is wisest to be impartial. If you have health, but are attached to it, you will always be afraid of losing it. And if you fear that loss, but become ill, you will suffer. Why not remain forever joyful in the Self?" –
Paramahansa Yogananda

"Just as the body goes into shock after a physical trauma, so does the human psyche go into shock after the impact of a major loss." – **Anne Grant**

"One of the key elements of human behavior is, humans have a greater fear of loss than enjoyment of success. All the academic studies will show you that the fear of loss of capital is far greater than the enjoyment of gains." –
Laurence   D.   Fink

Love

An intense feeling of deep affection, or deep romantic, or sexual attraction is known as love. Few concepts have elicited as much conflict, creativity, or even craziness that love has, or does - even today. It is approached differently across cultures and has notable different approaches by both eastern/western perspectives.

Ancient Greeks approached love as:

"Agape (white) is unconditional love, used to describe the love of God and our love for Him. It allows self-sacrifice and the unwillingness to abandon. It shows affection to the soul, the reason for 'namaste', and generates mutual respect for everyone. It is universal, including nature and animals, unlimited.

Pragma (red) lovers feel the need to be of service and find value in practicality. It is expressed by working together for a common goal, aiding in the longevity of relationships. It forms a tendency to select or reject partners based on compatible traits and desirable attributes. It can lead to having expectations or seeing relationships as an exchange of utility rather than a mutual, loving bond, using relationships merely for survival and to avoid loneliness.

Eros (orange) is seen most often between husband and wife but can be Platonic. It is more physical, honoring romantic beauty, and is often mistaken for lust and animalistic urges. This carnal perspective often leads to broken families or a controlling partner. Proper eros is founded on trust and sanctity of the mind. A partnership with its foundation on eros does not last long, fading with the 'honeymoon phase'.

Philia (yellow) is more conditional, based on friendship and extends to those with the same core beliefs. It comes from having a special interest in someone, more than just an acquaintance. To not feel lonely in the world, friends who can understand you and share deep thoughts are necessary. With a discordant ego, it leads to seeing any friend as a potential sexual partner.

Storge (green) creates a bond with family members and the community. It is natural, almost like it's obligatory. As it ties us to our respective culture, it can be a hindrance to spiritual growth but can be expressed through charity and mutual support. This love includes the implied relationship between members of the body of Christ and those who seek Truth.

Ludus (blue) is playful, literally meaning "game". It is shown as wanting to have indoor/outdoor fun, pulling harmless pranks, etc. It is uncommitted, being more focused on experiences and activities than the individual but includes Philia as it develops friendships from acquaintances. It includes eros as it develops partnerships from friendships, being coy and flirtatious.

Philautia (indigo) is self-love, of which there are two types. It can become narcissism or prideful arrogance, being focused on personal fame or fortune or overindulgence in sensual desires of the flesh. However, it should promote self-confidence, self-worth, self-security, and includes self-sacrifice, or doing things for your health (mental or physical) that you don't really want to do. In it is found our purpose and through it is self-gnosis and its intrinsic intuition.

Mania (violet) is about esteem, speaking highly of one's partner, and includes ludus and eros. It gives the apparent need of someone in your life and, in excess, leads to codependency and obsessive jealousy which cause impulsiveness and delusions (often stemming from an unhappy childhood or anxious loneliness). It can be overwhelming and those focused in mania are easily manipulated by those in ludus.

The search for a soulmate to reciprocate all types of love in healthy balance can lead to depression if focus is external. Though it is possible to find in the physical/social environment, it is more important to develop one's psyche as its own soulmate, unifying the divine masculine and feminine principles with that from which they come." – **Ryan Archer, What About Reality**

In an abstract sense, love connotes care. One can love the self as well as another. Because of the remarkable complexity of love, and its different significance across time and cultures, love is extraordinarily difficult to define sans context. While romantic love is a modern concept, ancient love poetry is testament to similar sentiments predating courtly love of the middle ages.

The Greeks emphasized a sense or focus on balance and harmony. Love was a higher concept, and placed on a spectrum of behavior that valued discipline, restraint, and self-control. So platonic love - love between friends - was a contrast to the lustful, physical engagement. The former made use of higher goods including a refined sense of pleasure. For example, individuals engaged in platonic love could create and exchange meaning aside from copulation (sexual intercourse). They would not pursue forms of physical intimacy, as the relationship was significant despite lacking that particular element. The same holds true today: some relationships need not involve physicality.

A modern perspective of love emphasizes a lack of control - the 'falling in love' that is depicted in song, dramas, and art. It involves a lack of control, an assault on the head, heart, and hands/body by sentiments, thoughts, drives that render those experiencing such a barrage to be sometimes incapable of sleeping, eating, much less thinking in a clear, linear connected manner. And this form of love *can be* remarkably exciting, motivational, and even awe-inspiring. It has elicited tremendous products of creativity. It has served as an amazing source of motivation since even ancient times. Perhaps Menelaus and his allies began The Trojan War because of this type of love for Helen. But love need not include a loss of self-control, a lack of inhibition, or even an externality, meaning love need not be exclusively external, to/from an outside source, or entity.

In fact, an Aristotelian notion contends that one can neither care nor love another before one's own self is loved or cared for. One's own home/life need be in order before care is extended to another. Love is a tremendous pleasure, and offers a great many meaningful rewards. It is also a tremendous responsibility. It is important to keep in mind the priority of loving oneself. Taken to extremes, this self-love becomes narcissism, an exclusion of all else. Narcissists are fixated on themselves; they exclude all else save for their own person. This is unwarranted and, as mentioned many times before in this text, actions taken to extremes are very dangerous. But, in moderation, self-love is so very important. A meaningful, balanced love for another need be predicated on a weighted, considerate love of the self!

This self-love is elicited by a thorough knowledge of the self. This is achieved by living a conscious, respectful life. By knowing oneself, and living according to significant principles like honor, compassion, loyalty, an aware individual can extend that care to another person, or thing. For those that are unwilling to live with self-respect or examine their values and mores are also unable to extend that same consideration to others. And we can not expect of others what we, ourselves, are unwilling, or unable to do.

Erich Fromm's book, *The Art of Loving* denotes that true loving requires the reflection and perseverance of an art. An art requires constant attention, commitment, and effort. In order to love *any* other, an individual need put their entire person into the dynamic; that requires engaging in serious introspection, establishing principles and practices of respect for self and others. Until someone invests in their person and works on their self, they will not be able to love their own person, nor any other. Unless one loves their self, they can NOT love another.

In the Bible, The Apostle Paul wrote an oft-quoted passage about love in 1 Corinthians 13. Verses 4-8; 13 from the KJV are presented below. It is very important to note how the passage/quote is a translation. If I do not offer the following bit of advice anywhere else:

SEEK ORIGINAL SOURCES.

Translate from original texts, as nearly all translations demonstrate the ethos or the bias of the translator.

While I have a background with the Christian religion, and still both refer to, and study its text(s), I am not advancing that particular dogma as Truth. The information contained within the Bible and numerous extra-biblical sources of the same tradition serve many purposes and I hope you entertain an open mind when you encounter its influence. Holy texts - regardless of the background or the institution offering it - offer profound insights for those who are teachable and receptive.

4 Love suffers long and is kind; love does not envy; love does not parade itself, is not puffed up; 5 does not behave rudely, does not seek its own, is not provoked, thinks no evil; 6 does not rejoice in iniquity, but rejoices in the truth; 7 bears all things, believes all things, hopes all things, endures all things.
8 Love never fails. …
13 And now abide faith, hope, love, these three; but the greatest of these is love.

As mentioned earlier, the ancients had a more disciplined approach to love. There is a lot to extrapolate from Paul's words.

Verse 4
One way to translate 'love suffers long' is: Love is patient. Be patient with yourself! We will all make mistakes, and we need grasp our fallible characters. NO ONE is above reproach - everyone makes mistakes. Be

patient with yourself as you stumble and fail on some occasions. Recognizing how you and others err builds a patient component of love.

Love is kind, generous. Love does not give in to jealousy, nor is it boastful or based on false pride.

Verse 5

Love is not rude. It does not insist upon its own way - it allows for the presence of change, and dynamic circumstances.It is not easily provoked - it does not give in to baiting or to antics. Love thinks no evil and is, instead, wholly a Good thing.

Verse 6

Iniquity is immorality, or impropriety – wrongdoing or misconduct. So love is composed of good deeds, moral behavior, and virtuous acts. It is dressed in Truth. Lies have no place in Love.

Verse 7

Love: never gives up, never loses faith, is always hopeful, and endures through all circumstances.

Verse 8

…needs no translation.

Verse 13

Three things will last forever: faith, hope, and love, and the greatest of these is love.

Love makes one powerful, provided one works considerably and remains dedicated to virtue and self-discipline. By Paul's words, loving oneself and then loving others is no easy feat and, per Fromm's perspective, requires an extended effort. Love is not realized and then set permanently. It requires constant maintenance, and it is work on the self as well as in relationship with others. But again: it is personal work as a priority that makes possible the meaningful love for others. The ancient perspective of love stands so remarkably disparate to the modern concept of romantic love.

In contrast, as we discussed earlier, romantic love is wild and passionate - an uncontrolled barrage of thoughts and feelings that sometimes lead to reckless actions with disastrous results. Some scientific perspectives see romantic love as a base mammalian instinct that seeks out a perfect mate via illusions and projections. Fantasies may fill the mind of someone who meets a potential mate. They attach their fantasies to this seemingly ideal person and a narrative of how the romance will proceed or unfold is projected. Goal-oriented behavior and intense motivation seek to retain the person. This is dangerous, in that the behavior can seek to grasp someone who is really anything BUT ideal and wholesome - worthy of meaningful love. Those who are caught up in romantic love have been shown to have impaired judgment and then make bad decisions. Our sense of individuality is lost and we over-identify with the other. Because our lives are so affected by media, our sense of romantic love is illusory and we attach to a narrative that is anything but reality. *This is remarkably consequential.* The projections and fantasies will finally be countered by reality and the romantic love will end, either slowly or abruptly.

Love can be a feeling or it can be a deliberate choice and a disciplined activity. The difference between the two is that feelings change. Choices may differ along a path, in time, but those who identify with romantic love as true love are in for a rude awakening when reality becomes apparent. The dedication to a more deliberate and conscious form of love prepares the dedicated lover for a more dignified experience, one colored by the presence of higher pleasures - not just simple, physical ones. While elements of romantic love are necessary in a committed, long-lasting relationship, they need not be the overriding motivators or serve as the sole catalysts of action. This culture does not intend to produce reflective, considerate individuals. It is far easier to control a population of folks that are divided by both internal and external factors. Our society uses the media - among many other instruments - to sew doubt and discord within our own hearts and minds. Many individuals find themselves unable to love their own person because of the tremendous effort required to:

-Know Thyself (the words carved over the doorway/threshold of the Oracle at Delphi); and

-Remain true to their own considered principles and values (Via Shakespeare's *Hamlet*; consider the words of Ophelia's Father Polonius, who says, "To thine own self be true.").

Love is a product of a considerable investment in the self. Many do not enjoin in such an endeavor due to its remarkable difficulty. But the reward is a blessed one. For as an individual comes to love their own self as a consequence of such an undertaking, they are only then open and available to the wonders and higher pleasures of love offered by other similarly worthy, considerate individuals.

Concepts to Explore re: Love

-Plato's *Symposium, Phaedrus, Phaedo*
-Aristotle's *Nicomachean Ethics*
-Virgil's *Love Conquers All*
-St Thomas Aquinas
-The Beatles

"Being deeply loved by someone gives you strength, while loving someone deeply gives you courage." - **Lao Tzu**

"Keep love in your heart. A life without it is like a sunless garden when the flowers are dead." - **Oscar Wilde**

"The best thing to hold onto in life is each other." - **Audrey Hepburn**

"If you have only one smile in you give it to the people you love." – **Maya Angelou**

"The course of true love never did run smooth." - **William Shakespeare**

"Let the beauty of what you love be what you do." - **Rumi**

"When you arise in the morning, think of what a precious privilege it is to be alive - to breathe, to think, to enjoy, to love." - **Marcus Aurelius**

"True love stories never have endings." - **Richard Bach**

"Go and love someone exactly as they are. And then watch how quickly they transform into the greatest, truest version of themselves. When one feels seen and appreciated in their own essence, one is instantly empowered." – **Wes Angelozzi**

"Most of us remain strangers ourselves, hiding who we are, and ask other strangers, hiding who they are, to love us." – **Leo Buscagli**

Lying

The practice of communicating lies is called lying; someone who communicates a lie may be termed a liar. While lying generally has a negative connotation, in some contexts, it is permitted or even encouraged. As is the case with many other concepts addressed here, lying has an exclusive principle in that a party is excluded from receiving truth. That exclusion may not be completely negative in all cases. Truly, lying can sometimes save lives. Consider a hypothetical instance of someone fleeing another individual that means to assault, if not kill, the former. Lying to the pursuant may well save or ensure the well-being of the fleeing individual. What of lying to someone who is suffering? Imagine someone who is hospitalized because of injury. Relaying truth in the form of bad news may well elicit more suffering and a reduction in health for that injured individual. In this case, withholding truth may be a viable course of action. Telling the truth about a surprise birthday party may well ruin the surprise for the individual who would benefit from the gathering. In this case, lying ensures the positive surprise.

Lying can help people in many situations. It can be used as humor. It allows folks to save face in certain situations. Lying is very context specific. The negative character of lying is apparent when one excludes truth when it may benefit themselves. Some people behave as if truth, or greater morality, is a fixed sum, or a limited commodity. They hoard it, and use it sparingly - such behavior is to the detriment of others. Lying in business is usually to the benefit of one party's profit. In a court of law, lying can mean the difference between liberty and death. It can equate to years lost in prison.

Lying is a betrayal. It can rend asunder the fabric of a relationship; it can destroy trust and loyalty. The presence of lying may protect an individual in some cases though it may damage or harm others in other contexts. The routine of lying gives the liar practice, though there are myriad better skills to hone and develop. When a liar is caught enough times, or even perceived as a liar, their reputation suffers a serious consequence. Reputation is very important in a society. How peers perceive a community member affects their standing - their place - in the community. Someone who is known to offer lies, or even partial truths, is regarded as either untrustworthy or as a source of questionable material.

Establish solid character by engaging good habits. While lying may sometimes serve a beneficial/good purpose, it is best to be mindful of how everyone benefits through truth in the long run. An innocent or 'white' lie may be innocuous or harmless in the short run, but offering truth is always good. Truth-telling is the routine of the honorable and brave. For just as it is difficult to confront ills, or to be accountable for personal errors or transgressions, offering the truth allows people to make decisions based on good information. It is very rare to make good decisions based on bad information or on lies. Offering truth allows for behavior that is based on concrete certainty. It is only good fortune, or luck, that allows for a favorable outcome when decisions are based on falsehoods or partial truths. It is but wishful thinking to expect the best possible result when anything less than truth is at play. Maintaining its presence and ensuring its continued role is a responsibility - one that can never be taken too lightly.

Lysistrata

The *Lysistrata* is a play by the ancient Greek playwright Aristophanes. I first encountered it as I was in college as an undergraduate. The lessons and concepts involved within the text forever changed my perspective of women, and of the unique power they can, and do, wield in our society. Lysistrata is the main character of the play. She invites the women of Thebes, Athens and Sparta together to discuss how they could coordinate an end to the Peloponnesian War. The old women take control of the Acropolis and the treasury of Athens. The young women refuse to have sex with their husbands until the war is ended.

The chorus of old men try to make fires, in order to smoke the women from the Acropolis, but the latter defeat their efforts. Policemen are scared away, run off. The commissioner is scolded, and assailed...he is even dressed as a woman and derided. Lysistrata explains how war affects women: their sons and husbands are sacrificed unnecessarily. It is also most difficult to find a good husband in such times! The sex strike starts to affect the men, and they are depicted in great pain due to their most evident erections. A Greek by the name of Myrrhine conveys to his wife how their child needs her and how they love her. His wife Kinesias delays taking him. A Spartan herald arrives, sporting a painful erection as well. He describes the plight of his countrymen, and pleads for peace. A delegation from both parties meet, and Lysistrata emerges from the Acropolis with her naked handmaiden, Peace. While the men are distracted by Peace's nudity, Lysistrata states that because they share a heritage and have previously helped one another, the two states should not be fighting. Using Peace as a map, the delegations decide upon land rights which ends the war. Lysistrata releases the women to their men and a great celebration ensues.

In ancient times, women were the responsible party of the household; they were the distributor of resources, or the economist, of the home (see *oikos nomos*). The same holds true for today, as it is the women/mothers who care for the household. Unfortunately, today's society and culture pits husband against wife in a farcical effort to obtain equality between the sexes. But equality as a goal is farcical, for men will never be on a par with women.

In certain respects, women are superior to men.

Females have more neural connectivity in their brains. They are able to think and perceive using an incredible amount of their brain. They are a fuller, more complete character by physiology alone. They are superior in such an amazing way that men can never compete because their own biology is merely brutish, their character: violent, and, consequently, inferior in contrast.

While men are physically stronger, they amount to simple brutes when compared with women. But because men now control resources, and positions of power, women are relegated to that of an inferior status.

It is your responsibility to second guess and subvert this particular woefully unjust characterization.

Women are the heartier half of the sexes. Women are the life-bringers, the keepers of the hearth and home. You, and considerate women like you, are responsible for changing this society and culture. Men will not, as they remain the primary beneficiaries. If society is to change, women must shoulder a leading role and provide such a worthwhile standard that men can not help but acknowledge the superior model and abide by its guidelines.

You can do great things. You are physically capable and both emotionally and mentally equipped to elicit new, worthy, inclusive standards for not only our society, but also the greater world, as well. Connect with good women and do something important with your life. With this text I am striving to provide resources that will foster and develop your total person.

Marshal your resources, apply your divine femininity, and help transform this world for the better. I believe in you, and the world is waiting for the application of your specific gifts and abilities. Get to it!

Chapter 13

Magic

The use of means, including charms or spells, believed to have supernatural powers over natural forces is called magic. It is an ancient practice but the methodologies employed by different cultures, indigenous people, warlock, or wizards of the British Isles, or a Kahuna of the Hawaiian Islands, all varied dramatically. As such, there is no concrete, and set definition for magic.

Magic has been considered as an opposite to both science and religion. Concerning science, magic does not rely on logic or the rational approach, utilizing reason. Regarding religion, magical use of supernatural forces (things that can not be explained by science or by the laws of nature), including ghosts, gods, and other supernatural creatures or things beyond nature that are opposed to established dogma, church authority, and institutional orthodoxy. Yet magic has an ancient presence. The word itself comes from Persia, and the *magu, or magi* have been noted in history long before even the New Testament of the Bible.

Magic remains unconventional and, to some, even dangerous - or, at best, fraudulent. However, these ancient practices remain firmly in place both in major religions and among subcultures all over the world. Essentially, individuals - either experienced practitioners, fledgling initiates, or entertaining performers - make use of a radically diverse spectrum of resources in order to elicit a result. Magicians are known to work their craft - for good or evil purposes - along what is known as the left-hand or right-hand path. Yet this distinction is not so cut and dry. Some think that magic can be ceremonial, following a strict morality or code of conduct within a group, while other magic might be seen as breaking from convention and abandoning an established morality.

Magic need not feature a set distinction between good and evil. Some magicians practice in order to elicit results for themselves. Practices of the kabbalah include healing spells and charms of protection for the self and the community. Magic is a marshaling of metaphysical elements. With the application of a focused, and attentive practitioner, diverse results can be achieved. People are suspicious and doubtful as to its relevance or merit because it remains an esoteric, or occult, practice. Such practices are outside of the mainstream culture and often intentionally distanced from popular consumption. The use of rituals, magical symbols, and language concern the wider laity because of its unfamiliar and complex uses.

Magic has a respected place in many of today's modern cultures and societies. This speaks to the merits of the practice, or, because of the rhetorical - persuasive - influence of the practice. Because those practices remain throughout the world means that *something* merits its continued engagement. As a general bit of advice, you will encounter both internal and external resources that will fuel if not empower you. You might have clothes that make you feel at least comfortable, if not also confident and powerful. You might designate something as a talisman or a magical token. Whether by a practice of meditation, or focused attention, yoga, or investigation into mystical arts, you will discover the means of your own personal power. Folks can make use of energies that are either sourced via internal or external faculties.

Everyone has energy, power, or magic to make use of and apply. How they marshal their resources and direct their intention is the difference between good and poor results. Investigate everything at your disposal in order to shape your own character and to learn about this world. You will discover a great many things remain as yet unknown. Magic is steeped in lore, and a great number of different cultures recognize the benefits of its sustained practice. When you focus and apply your energy, power, and magic, apply your resources in a positive way, in order to bring about the highest and best good for all involved.

Maker

A consumer is someone who purchases goods and services for personal use. They usually eat or use things. In contrast, a maker makes and creates things. The former is more of a passive entity while the maker is anything but passive. The maker stands as a disparate contrast because productivity is their primary characteristic. A maker can serve as an artist of traditional arts and crafts, but their palette can also bring forth products in engineering, woodwork, and metal work, among many arts.

A maker is driven to apply subjective resources. Most makers have an inclination or a curiosity to learn a practical skill and apply it. What serves as the catalyst, or the motivation, for such a drive might be a curiosity that demands satisfaction. Many engineers ask how something works and, after diligent analysis, investigation, if not also experimentation, they encounter a solution to the original inquiry. They may then recognize how the proffered solution remains obsolete, and hasten to create a superior alternative. Other makers, along the lines of poets and philosophers, ask why something is the way it is, and enjoin in their own form of investigation and creation. The end result is not a conceptual one but a created product - some tangible thing brought forth by the process. The poet offers their poem and the philosopher offers their own prose.

Makers are a rare variety of individual. They engage in an active process, and create meaningfully. We can not identify the products such as the 'flowbee' or the 'chia pet' as trivial or wasted enterprises. Those items are the products of makers utilizing their craft and birthing what they will. We might give more weight, however, to those individuals who apply themselves and make something of their own person. I respect and honor those who strive to make something of their 'selves.' All too often, though, consumption and a passive existence stand as casual norms. Their lives are fed to them: their parents provide them values, and their preferences about music, among so many other things, provided by mainstream media. A superficial understanding of pertinent, worldly concepts and affairs is provided by another source. Create - engage actively! Be a maker! Make something worthwhile of your own self by applying the resources and abilities at your disposal. Be teachable, have an open mind, and be curious about your world. Investigate, learn and create! Just like everyone else, you have a unique spark - energy, magic, life - to you. That 'thing' is demonstrated when you harness and utilize it as only you can, and that process is anything but passive and amounts to a tremendous improvement when contrasted with base consumption.

Market

A gathering of people for the purchase of exchange of commodities, ideas, or, an area or arena in which dealings are coordinated is known as the market. When parties engage in an exchange, they are participating in a market of some sort. An exchange may consist of tangible commodities like a farmers' market, or intangible ideas, such as when politicians debate prior to an election. While many rules serve to regulate different forms of markets, a general rule takes precedence, and that is how quality is key. Else, why would parties participate in an exchange of inferior goods, services, or ideas?

You are participating in markets - even if you do not realize them. School is a type of marketplace of ideas. As you watch different types of media, you are barraged by ideas, values, and concepts. It is your responsibility to filter, to sort, and critique the notions conveyed. Question them as to their source, their content, and their quality. It is a careful, discerning perspective that discovers treasures among so much chaff and garbage. Market your self - your abilities - such that people have no option but to recognize your good quality and worthy character. Insist on those behaviors and values that best showcase your own personhood. Leave little to chance or interpretation as you market or demonstrate yourself. Not that every bit of your character or every one of your values need be on display, either. Consider that your presence, your being is a marketing endeavor. Be very aware of what it is you are depicting - marketing - as you live your life.

Materialism

Materialism is the belief that matter is the fundamental substance. It is one position in an argument of metaphysics (a branch of philosophy that investigates the fundamental nature of reality). Contrasting perspectives include other forms of monism, dualism, and idealism. Materialism holds that absolutely everything is caused by material interactions. This means that love, and all emotions, for that matter, amount to mere physical chemical engagements inside your body. That there remain so many unknowns in the world means that we have no certain grasp that materialism is undoubtedly true. It remains a theory, albeit a thorough and cogent one. But as far as contrasts, what sense do we then make of energy, or spirit? What of the divine ideas, or the nature of the soul? There are many available possibilities to encounter and investigate. When we settle on 'stuff' in the 'stuff vs. non-stuff' conversation, by necessity we eliminate a large swath of the spectrum of possibility. For starters, I contend that emotions are far more than chemical interactions in the brain and body. I love you for more reasons than dopamine, serotonin, and a mixture of endorphins and chemicals. I can not fathom how the depths of my person can be reduced to quarks within an atomistic or subatomic reality.

That humans can only apply the terms with which they are familiar to uncommon or unfamiliar concepts and phenomena only makes sense. We apply human terms to events and occurrences that transcend the human experience. It is not a failure to do so; by our very nature we certainly *appear* corporeal and limited. But we need not remain intentionally limited by a fixation on the material, or even material goods. An unhealthy portion of people are enamored with goods, be they fashion accessories or the newest gadget, or the shiny object that enthralls the public eye. An emphasis on the physical, or the material realm detracts from meaningful pursuits. The development of character, the habituation of good behavior, the development of virtues, and the health of the spirit and soul are worthy pursuits, yet the importance of them is nearly lost on our society.

The standard of materialism in our community has precedent over a great deal of other issues, and concepts that deserve more attention. And these matters need not be excluded for the sole presence of a material perspective. The great Aristotle recognized how material goods contribute to the pursuit of a good life. Like so much else, balance is key. The possession of material, or even designer or brand-name goods need not be a negative act, except in the event that the possession, or the pursuit of possessions is of greater importance than virtuous behavior or of self development. The habit of materialists is to forego meaningful introspection and work on the self. Weigh your priorities and values; consider that there are more important possessions than baubles, vehicles, and shiny objects.

Meaning

What is meant by a word, text, concept, or action is meaning. Meaning actually means different things in the realms of philosophy, language, and art. While there is some overlap, there are remarkable distinct definitions among different schools. Consider existentialism's definition of meaning as "the worth of life." While it is an institutional definition, the depth of it is going to vary between a rich king and a paralyzed pauper, or between perspectives among peers at a local brewpub.

Meaning is significance. Anything can be significant, can signify different things, and even signify more than one thing to the perceiver. Everyone generates or applies meaning to the events and objects of their lives. In order to grasp how meaning is applied, defined, or utilized, you need only live. While I suggest investigating precedent across time and cultures, the suggestion is nearly superfluous. For already, even at a young age, things mean different things to individuals, and *you*. When you listen to music, when you share time with family, as you are alone, your character is making use of experience to inform the present with significance and meaning.

One can learn a lot should they elect to explore different symbols, signs, myths, language, history, etc., in an effort to grasp a fuller appreciation of meaning. This is a solid idea! Explore precedent to understand what has come before, and how it shaped today. But meaning need not entail a thorough investigation. Humans start making sense of the world in utero, and while some individual's sense of meaning is considerate, dense, and maybe academic, another's uneducated perspective can be every bit as profound, or...meaningful...to them. By examining what things mean we unlock hidden treasures. Experience or encounters with new information broaden our horizons. Consider new music, a new book, or even new friends: they can all convey more meaning to our lives due to what they impart. And because nearly every
single
thing
can be meaningful, we had best be open to the potential significance or meaning in any event or occasion - even the most mundane or trivial occurrence. More than looking for it as an external item, generate and create meaning as you live your life, moment to moment.

"To live in the world without becoming aware of the meaning of the world is like wandering about in a great library without touching the books." – **Manly P. Hall**

"When a person can't find a deep sense of meaning, they distract themselves with pleasure." – **Viktor Frankl**

Moderation

The avoidance of excess or extremes, especially in one's behavior or political opinions, is moderation. Moderation refers to balance, maintaining a middle point between inefficiency and excess, according to Aristotle's theory of the golden mean. This concept need not be a long address, but its importance can not be emphasized enough. Aristotle's conceptualization was taken from the Greek standard of the time. Moderation was a component of beauty and this had correlates in truth. The consistent presence of moderation afforded symmetry, proportion, and *harmony*, in all things. This is remarkably different when compared to our own society's emphasis on values and character.

It is most rare to encounter moderation presented as a larger cultural norm or standard in our daily lives. More often than not, self-help books or lifestyle magazines focus on balance or moderation and, even then, the concept is presented as a response to ills and woes. For example, the beneficial effects of yoga or of a proper, balanced diet are posited in response to established, bad habits. That moderation as a foundational concept is not a priority means that a lack of balance, disharmony, or immoderation: the very opposite (!) is, in fact, the standard, if not the priority. Our cultural institutions benefit from the absence of moderation. Should the people be exercising self-control and restraint, balancing the activities and emotions of their daily lives, they would be more difficult to limit and control. As it stands now, moderation is posed as an antithesis to pleasure, joy, and a happy life. Moderation is now equivocated with the strictest asceticism. This is a radical reversal. It is only very recently that such a time-honored concept has been relegated to such an inferior status or position within our own society. The ramifications of such a change are remarkable. Because people are not taught to be in control of their heads, hearts, and hands, there are institutions in place to shoulder the responsibility. But institutions can only ever be reactionary; they can never be responsive. The institutions either take the role of the arms of the police or nanny state. Enforcement arms of the law discipline and punish transgressions, while coddling arms comfort, and then insulate or distance individuals from accountability, or even a responsible, mature path of self-ownership, self-discipline, and self-control.

Are any elements: activities and opinions outside of the realm of moderation? I can only identify happiness and love as being awesome, sans moderation. But, as stated previously, the conditions that elicit meaningful happiness and love include balance, self-control, and significant parts of self-mastery. Moderation is central to a life well-lived, and its presence and importance should never be underestimated nor minimized.

Morality

Morality is the foundation of ethics. It involves the differentiation of intentions, decisions, and actions - between those that are distinguished as proper and those that are improper, and living according to that understanding. Ethics is the philosophy of how that morality guides individual or group behavior. Morality is either publicized as a code of conduct via a religion, philosophy, or a broader organizational or group association, or it is a personally, radically subjective standard by which one lives their life. Morality is synonymous with goodness or rightness. Morality identifies what is proper or what is improper and ethics is how morality is applied practically.

Moral values and moral behavior are modeled everywhere, for values underlie all behavior. Standards of values and behavior vary between cultures, households, institutions, and individuals. A central characteristic of moral behavior concerns altruism and egotism, or the question of how values are applied to others, or the public (altruism) or performed for the self (egoism). The first question of moral values or behavior concerns the goodness/rightness of the value or act. Are they good or bad? The next question concerning ethics is: how will these behaviors affect or benefit the self and others?

The consideration of virtue (behavior showing high moral standards) and virtue ethics (an ethical approach that emphasizes an individual's character as the key element of ethical thinking) has occurred several times in the course of this text. It is an important consideration to have a system of principles and values that is established after investigation and with experience. This personal system need make space for your behavior within the structure of a wider society. Personal responsibility and moral behaviors are always necessary, even in a woeful degraded state or society.

That others may not share your personal values, or hold in high esteem concepts like ethics, goodness, or virtues, does not mean that those values need be discarded, or eliminated, in order to belong to a group or community.

The maintained presence and priority of morality helps guide those who may not be so conscious of the consequences of their actions, much less constrained by the considerations of self and others. Unfortunately, you will encounter intentionally amoral people. Thankfully they are few in number, for communities generally address egregious trespasses of self-indulgence. Justice is involved in every context, and 'sooner or later' issues are corrected.

Morality, and the interaction with ethics, is but one component of a life well-lived. The consideration of morality needs color and influence every day, if not every activity; else we are likely to violate standards of rightness, decency, and the Good. Socrates said, "The unexamined life is not worth living." Only by striving to know ourselves and also establish moral principles do our lives have significant meaning or value.

Consider The Law of Freedom, which contends that freedom and morality are directly proportional. As morality increases, freedom increases, and as morality declines, freedom declines. Finally, the presence of truth and morality in the lives of the people of any given society is inversely proportional to the presence of tyranny and slavery in that society. This idea is worth consideration.

Motivation

The reasons one has for acting in a particular way is motivation. It provides the reasons for people's actions, desires, and needs. Motivation is differentiated between content and process - what motivates in contrast to how motivation takes place. In addition to it being a chemical process involving dopamine receptors, the basal ganglia and numerous other components, motivation includes natural forces such as drives, needs, and desires, and rationality components like instrumentality, meaningfulness, and identity.

The internal physical component known as the basal ganglia serves as an action selector. It decides which of several possible behaviors to execute at any given time. Generally, people select among rewards and incentives (on a positive basis) or along a spectrum of drives, which are needs deficiencies, or needs that activate behavior (on a negative basis). Rewards are aligned along internal values, or external behaviors. Internal values prompt initiatives for self-improvement or art for art's sake. These internal values have no external pressure. Conversely, externalities address desired outcomes, in the form of rewards, like a pay raise, or an improved physical condition, or the escape from punishment, threat, or scarcity.

Thoughts influence behaviors. Behaviors drive performance. Performance affects thoughts and the motivation cycle begins anew. Attitudes, beliefs, and intention color efforts and influence the performance results, and withdrawal of serenity or disgust informs next actions. Motivation is also described as a push/pull dynamic. People push themselves via will and their willpower is only as strong as their desire. The pull aspect is much stronger and it is on display when a goal pulls an individual.

Gold medals require Olympian effort. Worthwhile results are born of substantial effort, action, and initiative. In life, there will be moments, or extended periods of time, that will depict how change is easier than remaining the same. The inconvenience of change and of work applied will be easier than the maintenance of a static, undeveloped self. Winning, or success, is predicated on effort. While you will never fail if effort is not put forward, progress, growth, and development is elicited by agency - by acting towards worthy goals. Motivation influences the conceptualization and the achievement of these worthy pursuits. Teddy Roosevelt once said, "Far and away the best prize that life has to offer is the chance to work hard at something worth doing." Your responsibility is to format of your own life a structure that will work for those activities that are worth doing. Some activities will hold value for short-term gains while other endeavors will be enjoined for their long-term rewards. Your experiences will inform and affect all of your motivations. I encourage you to be very deliberate as to your values: entertain noble aspirations, and motivate yourself by utilizing good variables, concepts, and factors.

Music

Sound organized in time is music. The creation, performance, significance, and even the definition of music vary according to cultural and social context. It has a prominent role in significant events and occasions, such as in religious rituals, rites of passage, and social activities like weddings, or public events including parades and rallies. Music serves as a recreational or professional endeavor.

Music is a basic human activity, one that touches and affects all of us, in remarkably objective ways. Music touches our soul, and helps establish connections. It factors in the life of all humans, across cultures, regardless of content, genre, artist. It is academic, in that it trains the brain for higher forms of thinking. It permanently wires the brain for enhanced learning. The physical activity of music promotes coordination. Singing and establishing rhythm develops not only subjective coordination but also coordination with others. It also promotes a healthy body. Music as an emotional outlet serves as a refined vehicle of expression. As an activity, musical skill lasts a lifetime.

There is no escaping a presence of music. It highlights and influences most - if not everything - we do. From our earliest moments in the womb, to our final stages of life as we know it, music colors nearly our complete existence. Regardless of context, genre, or artist you will ascertain those musical selections that move you. While *EVERYONE* can provide guidance as to their own experience and preference, you will structure your own tastes. Seek out a diverse array of genres and artists; you will not be dissatisfied by the fantastic array of music that is available. It is rewarding to experience new musical offerings, so be bold, and seek different forms as you are able to do so.

Music

"One good thing about music, when it hits you, you feel no pain." - **Bob Marley**

"There is geometry in the humming of the strings, there is music in the spacing of the spheres." - **Pythagoras**

"Music is the greatest communication in the world. Even if people don't understand the language that you're singing in, they still know good music when they hear it." - **Lou Rawls**

"Music is a higher revelation than all wisdom and philosophy." - **Ludwig van Beethoven**

"Music is the movement of sound to reach the soul for the education of its virtue." - **Plato**

"Next to the Word of God, the noble art of music is the greatest treasure in the world." - **Martin Luther**

"Music doesn't lie. If there is something to be changed in this world, then it can only happen through music." - **Jimi Hendrix**

"As you begin to realize that every different type of music, everybody's individual music, has its own rhythm, life, language and heritage, you realize how life changes, and you learn how to be more open and adaptive to what is around us." - **Yo-Yo Ma**

"Music is powered by ideas. If you don't have clarity of ideas, you're just communicating sheer sound." - **Yo-Yo Ma**

Myth

There are few things as important to western civilization as myth. Myths are traditional stories, especially ones concerning the early history of a people. The stories are a unique cultural, communal perspective that imparts meaning. Myths explain events, and apply significant meanings to life events (everything experienced between life and death) and occurrences in the natural world. So the seasons have a mythos; heroes follow an established structure of behavior, and have a communal set of values and guidelines. The significance of relations: dating, for example, or of related concepts like honor, loyalty, commitment, piety, etc., are all provided for by myth. Different societies value remarkably different things, and employ vastly contrasting ways of life. Myths provide substantial insight as to why a people and why individuals behave as they do, either collectively or as an individual.

Myths instruct the subject or individual as to a foundational part of community. They serve to explain, to teach lessons or values, to unify, and to entertain. It is important to note that, while myths were meant as entertainment, they always had a poignant lesson or a meaningful insight. Should tales and narratives lack that critical element, they become anecdotes, and not the tales that stand the test of time due gravitas and pertinence.

Firm values are imparted by established, traditional stories. People are guided as to behavior involving coming of age, child rearing, death, mortality, and even spirit and the soul. Myths cooperate with other cultural/communal practices or institutions to guide and inform its denizens. A lack of fixed myth equates to a variable spectrum of values. When no firm guide for subjective behavior or community interaction is maintained, the distinction between the sacred and the profane is blurred, if not broken entirely.

Note how established myths: stable tales and narratives, are discarded, if not left unattended in the face of a daunting barrage of corporate media, as well as the ever-expanding corpus of independent media provided by individuals via social media platforms. What is allowed is what is valued and, so, if and when everything is allowed, everything is valued. This means that everything is of the same value; there are no elevated levels for specific qualities or values. That covers a great many things that are far from good in any cogent and rational society. Certainly, tales of virtuous heroes and different conceptions of the good vary radically between people, and peoples. There can be overlap but there can be exclusive portions, elements, and characters. Some elements of one myth or narrative are opposed to, or stand in strict and striking contrast to other models. Some myths accept slavery, minimize (if not terrorize) the role of women, and generally: make use of a profoundly exclusive character that informs and shapes the character and behavior of those that adhere to that specific narrative.

Exploring myth, and untangling the meanings and mysteries of different people via their own traditional stories facilitates understanding between people and can also contribute to a fuller comprehension of the self. The availability of options or having access to different selections of meanings is a tremendous benefit. In this day and age of the internet, we are not limited to the tales of one tradition. We can shape our character based on the myths of people around the world. By making use of positive and worthy elements of myth and the characters and lessons contained therein, we can create for ourselves a good character that takes of many sources.

A good example of a modern myth is Star Wars. The first of a 9-movie collection was released in 1977. The last of the series is now released. Note how the elements of myth are present: creation stories, the hero's journey, the battle between good and evil, etc. The series appropriates a great many parts from multiple mythological platforms. Additionally, it is a creation of the corporate media and has been the product of an evolving cast and production team. 40 years has eclipsed from first to last movie. We also note the dynamic spectrum of values at play between the first and most recent performances. The eighth installment featured a critique of the heroes; the ethos of the heroic Jedi came under scrutiny. Similarly, in the Transformers movie storyline, the honored and revered protagonist Optimus Prime was made to be a villain in a recent installment of that particular franchise.

I do not claim that all myths are good and worthy of perpetuation, or continuance. Nevertheless, society throws the proverbial baby out with the bathwater when they move to restrict their telling or eliminate their presence. The specific minimization of myth robs audiences of the benefits of one of the most important foundational concepts in all of western civilization. It is an important consideration to imagine where the peoples of the world would be, without heroes the likes of Odysseus, Perseus, or Thor. Where would women seek inspiration and guidance, if not from Hera, Pallas Athena, Penelope, and Lilith? Further, if the showcasing of these familiar characters as guides is discontinued, who are the next standards of hero and leadership? Who will advance *their* position and standing?

Chapter 14

Nature

Nature refers to the natural world, as it exists without human beings or civilization, as surrounding mankind and existing independently of human activities, or the personal character or human condition. In reference to the first portion of the definition, I argue that the natural world is, in fact, everywhere. Certainly it is in the fullest manifestation in nature: away from social conventions and the city, but I insist the natural world is apparent if a perceiver is actively engaged and discerning a scene's elements. For humanity, equipped with its buildings, pavement, and internet, amounts to dross when compared to nature's width and wonder. The natural world lines sidewalks and volunteers - pops its head through the smallest spaces - in order to make the attempt to live, grow, and thrive. Note how weeds, if not volunteer tomato plants, as an example, appear, even among concrete and asphalt.

Despite the seeming ubiquity of civilization's fetters and general presence, nature shines through as the underlying foundation upon which all else is based. Ozymandias suggested we look upon his works and despair while nature provided her own handiwork: wordlessly, tirelessly, and unceasingly. It is our obligation to connect with nature as much, and as often as possible. For the connection facilitates a great many other connections. An attachment, or maintained association with nature elicits an awareness of occurrences available only in nature. Witnessing the interaction, or the divine overlap of countless lives, can, and perhaps *should,* elicit wonder if not admiration and a profound, reverential joy. The scope of nature is unparalleled and its power and myriad components can be sources of meaning and inspiration should one be wise enough to savor particulars of experience.

"Learn character from trees, values from roots, and change from leaves." – **Tasneem Hameed**

Human nature comprises general psychological characteristics, feelings and behavioral traits of humankind, regarded as shared by all humans. We have wrestled with the specific question of whether human nature is good or evil. Two of the most applicable perspectives belong to Jean Rousseau and Thomas Hobbes. The former believed that man was good, though corrupted by society. Hobbes contended that man was inclined to pursue power, and violently. I consider a mix of the two to comprise a better formula for human nature. Both man AND cultural institutions can be *both* good and evil.

Religions, philosophies and astute thinkers have long addressed the concept and the discussion would be incomplete were we not to include other viewpoints. But insofar as the contributions of minds including Plato, Buddha, and Mo Tzu would benefit us, here we err on the side of brevity and leave a fuller investigation of human nature for those so inclined to delve deeper into the subject. In my opinion, we are shaped by factors that influence our will, values, and behavior. We are not born good nor evil - it is our own pursuits and activities that flesh out or contribute to a worthy nature, or a subjective character. The question of whether an individual or humanity, writ large, is good or evil is most contextualized. Individuals or groups rise to challenges and behave well and, at times, most honorably just as much as they perform at a lower standard. Situations will elicit a wide array of responses and reactions. But character, or human nature, is comprises or is compiled by an extended record or behavior and actions.

Designating humanity as evil is remarkably shortsighted. It is easy to make the claim, but consider the amount of good in the world. Much of the natural world features violence; even chimpanzees are spectacularly vicious in some cases. That war, bullying, significant corruption, and other ills are present speaks to how man entertains lesser drives at the expense of cohesion, peace, security, and inclusion. It is very easy to be discouraged by the behavior of humans. Yet human goodness is a component of our biological make-up. Some might argue that we are actually wired to be good. For example, we are naturally empathetic, social creatures. Were we wholly evil, society would be impossible. We are instinctually cooperative and act for the good of others before ourselves. Consider those who give their lives for others when faced with the challenge of confronting very real danger. At a simpler level, our bodies react to love, to physical acts of sexual intimacy, hugging or even just holding hands. We are programmed or conditioned to recover after challenges and pain. Our resilience is an evolutionary product of surviving evil and accidents over the course of human history. Human goodness facilitates our continued success - the perpetuation of the race - despite the presence of some very ugly examples of behavior.

The discussion of human nature is a most interesting one. It is pertinent, and so much more than an academic endeavor. It reminds us of the available spectrum of available options and informs us as to possibilities of social connection, and subjective development. No definitive statement is offered here. Perspective is formed by one's own experience. I encourage delayed judgment. For just as soon as evil is identified, good will arrive on the scene as proper balance in the equation. And, if you fail to note its presence, be that good you wish to see in the specific scene and in the greater world. Both good and evil will ever be present, though the likelihood of their presence is predicated on our mindfulness and engagement.

Night

While night is literally time without sun exposure, the symbolic or allegorical application is most profound. The contrast of light and darkness is an ancient dynamic far beyond the rotation of the earth and its revolution around the sun. Night has come to refer to many things just as darkness has myriad applications. It is analogous to an unknowable path, a period of confusion, or a collapse of meaning for an individual, but the nighttime can be extraordinarily wondrous. The night features events and elements of life that are unavailable during the day. Moonlight is amazing. The presence of fireflies can be a sublime occurrence. The stillness of the night has elicited works of art - both in print and in paintings.

As is the case with so many other concepts, night is what we make of it. Nights can be the ideal setting for romance, but it can just as easily refer to a lack of moral values or the 'dark night of the soul.' I advise making use of anytime, or the hours at your disposal – whether sun is included or not. Escaping the orthodoxy of daylight provides opportunities. With less people out, there is the pleasure of silence or, at least, the presence of sounds, routines, and systems that we typically miss as we sleep and rest. Allow the night to work its magic and apply your own during those dark hours.

Nirvana

Associated with Buddhism, nirvana refers to the ultimate release from the successive life/death cycle of samsara. It can be equated with perfect, pure freedom, quietude, and the highest happiness. Approaches to nirvana differ between Buddhism, Hinduism, and Jainism. The realization of such a state is exceedingly rare, the product of a most difficult and extraordinary path. The process of seeking nirvana - much like that of enlightenment - entails a diligent, disciplined approach not realized by the greater laity. Different religions and spiritual platforms demarcate a path towards release in disparate ways. While those institutions advise different approaches to the achievement of ultimate release, there is no confirmation as to the relative viability of their prescriptions. In the same way, there is no certainty as to what occurs at the moment of death, or afterwards, for that matter - if there exists an afterlife. So, any offered instructions are on a wait-and-see basis; we do not know if methodologies are successful until that time comes. But that does not mean that we need not adhere to principles or concepts offered by spiritual exhortation. Generally, nirvana is obtained after living a good life, coupled with a very disciplined, if not an ascetic, approach.

Such a path is tread by those who engage spirituality at a very significant level. These individuals believe in the soul, and are convinced of the existence of an afterlife - either as a cycle of rebirth or as the presence of either heaven or hell. Those who pursue enlightenment or nirvana are in pursuit of meaning or consequence that underlies or lies beyond the typical human experience. For that reason, those that experience 'real' results are few and far between. There's a saying by Zen Master Linji, "if you meet the Buddha, kill him!" The road, the Buddha, and the killing are not to be taken literally. The road is one's own remarkable subjective path. The Buddha, whether a real/tangible/extended/corporeal entity, *you* in extended form, or some idealized concept of perfection/enlightenment or nirvana is wrong (put very simply).
Destroy/kill that image.
The point? Whatever your take on enlightenment, your perception, or your 'correct' image of what it means to be enlightened is merely distraction.

Recall that the (primarily) eastern platforms that include concepts such as nirvana and enlightenment consider reality to be *maya,* or illusion. Kill that false image and put in the work that will result in something that defies preconceived notion, definition, and experience. But also realize that, as far as nirvana goes, specifically: we only encounter that experience at death. Popular culture depicts enlightenment or nirvana as events that occur as a part of life and the reality is anything but (save for the case of the Buddha, a very rare instance, indeed...and even then, is that story allegory, or a narrative of true events that actually occurred?). The Way is subjective and results are manifested upon death.

Nurture

We previously discussed the concept of human nature. The contrast between nature and nurture concerns whether a person's development is predisposed by DNA or whether it is influenced by their life's experiences and environment. Nature provides the pre-wiring while nurture consists of the externals which occur post-conception. It is now generally accepted as bi-conditionally reciprocated. For this discussion, though, we refer to nurture to be the process of caring for and encouraging the growth or development of someone or something. In most simple terms, if a person is going to thrive and be successful in their life's endeavors, they need be cared for, encouraged, and allowed to grow and develop.

There are both external and internal sources that nurture. Hopefully, a home is the primary source of external nurturing. A family is to nurture ethics, integrity, and self-worth, as well as provide for the physical sustenance that facilitates growth and development. After the individual leaves the security of the home, they need be equipped to nurture their own self. In line with much of what has preceded this particular entry, we need nurture our own head, hearts, and hands. We need care for ourselves by developing our mental, emotional and physical resources. We do that by studying, investigating, and being open to new information, events, and occurrences. We can care for our hearts by engaging in those activities that facilitate self-respect, balance, and internally generated/regulated happiness. Physical means of nurture are important, too. Food, shelter, human contact, and meaningful intimacy are all necessary components of a self that is cared for and encouraged to thrive.

Unfortunately, we live in a society that does little to nurture a radical spectrum of human health, development, or even wellness. But we have the option to nurture ourselves. We can care for ourselves, and others in order to elicit meaningful returns with our character and for the greater communities in which we participate.

Chapter 15

Obstacle

A thing that block's one's way, prevents or hinders progress is an obstacle. Complications, problems, and difficulties will often frustrate or thwart your best intentions and plans. In some cases, you will be absolutely flummoxed by an obstacle and perplexed as to how to proceed. In order to avoid 'paralysis by analysis,' or severe indecision, practice problem-solving methodologies:

-BREATHE
-Identify issues
-Understand everyone's interests
-List options
-Evaluate
-Select options
-Implement process with observational rubrics
-Review, with feedback
-Repeat until solved

Challenges, complications and obstacles are learning experiences that can help us grow. When we remain mindful and open as to what is occurring, we can identify variables and coordinate a way forward. Consider: seedlings get stronger as they push through the soil to reach sunlight. If the soil were moved away for them, they would not be strong enough to thrive. The obstacle of the soil gives them the strength and conditioning to survive life as a plant. In a similar sense, baby chicks need persevere when it is time to emerge from their shell. If the chick is aided in its emergence from the shell, it is robbed of the necessary exercise that makes it strong enough to thrive as a rooster/hen. Lacking these elements, the chick may be affected adversely in the longer run. Obstacles comprise a portion of life. They can be of our own making or not. They can occur as accidents or result from unknown sources, chains of events. We serve our best interests by making good decisions so as to avoid unnecessary obstacles. In the course of encountering them, deal with them and remember: you are both sufficiently strong and smart enough to surmount most if not all difficulties.

Occult

Those concepts or subjects involving, or relating to supernatural, mystical, or magical beliefs, practices, or phenomena are referred to as occult. Occult knowledge is "knowledge of the hidden." It is meant only for certain people, those who study or investigate a deeper (spiritual) reality. As noted previously in many other concepts, meaning is embedded in symbols. And symbols abound. This ubiquity denotes their importance. That a great many symbols exist means that much is occult, or hidden. For symbols denote meaning. If the meaning were meant for immediate public consumption, the correlation between the symbol and the actual concept would be slight; there would be little need for an intermediate filter in the form of a symbol. Meaning would be clear, accessible, and apparent.

Today, our holidays and significant communal events (Christmas, Easter, solstices, etc., to name but a few) are clothed in the occult. Symbols distance the public's immediate grasp of very pertinent meanings, history, and practices. That the occult is hidden, or kept from popular acceptance, means that there *is* something - something very pertinent. For those in control of the flow of information are wielders of tremendous power. For what is information, if not both knowledge and power in capable hands? It is most important to remain open and receptive to the symbols and meanings at play and, further: to investigate and discern what lies hidden as occult material. Much of what lies distant from public consumption and interaction could have profound public consequences. When occult terms, history and methods make an appearance in the public realm, significant events come to pass. For when individuals or a community uncover the pertinence of previously hidden truths or commodities, development, growth - or at the very least - a transformation occurs. For, as the great Oliver Wendell Holmes once stated, "As one's mind, once stretched by a new idea, never regains its original dimensions."

The knowledge of ancient civilizations, and many secret societies could benefit modern day humanity should their occult doctrines be investigated and then disseminated for the good of humanity. Should today's people be motivated to address this fantastic realm of information, there is little doubt that a great many subjective and objective/cultural practices would need revision, if not possible abandonment. Just as a baby takes their first steps, or a teenager embarks on their first drive in a car, once we have experienced the expansion of consciousness wrought by such immense amounts of information, life can be different, and better! ...though never the same. The wealth of information, knowledge and even power available via occult sources is immense given the considerable efforts taken to keep them hidden and distanced from the laity.

Opinion

An opinion is a judgment formed about something not necessarily based on facts or knowledge. While everyone has the right to an opinion, not all opinions are equal. Some perspectives are worth more than others. Consider the knowledgeable opinions offered by doctors and lawyers. Their opinions carry weight because they have studied and shaped a valuable perspective based on incredible amounts of hours of rigorous investigation.

Their opinions are shaped by facts and knowledge. It is important to be critical of opinions and perspectives – even those offered by knowledgeable opinion.

All people are liable to err. Everyone makes mistakes!

Consider how it is the norm for an opinion to be offered from ignorance. Most are content to offer something, even if it is worth little. Just because a celebrity is given the opportunity to serve as a mouthpiece or a speaker has amassed a large audience does not mean that the opinion offered is a worthwhile one. Do yourself the favor of investigating opinions and the source of those perspectives. Diversify your own sources of information, and substantiate your opinion by seeking and speaking truths. Be aware that someone will always follow an opinion. Strive to provide something that is worthwhile: good, right, and true.

Opportunity

An opportunity is a set of circumstances that makes it possible to do something. Every instance, context, and situation is an opportunity. Make use of your moments and opportunities. With every breath, step, or blink of an eye, you have a considerable array of options available to you. Exercise self-control and self-discipline in order to make the fullest use of opportunities at your disposal.

Consider the spectrum of behaviors and initiatives open to you. In the next moment, and all others that follow, you can make great decisions. You can be happy. You can help another and yourself. You can sing, dance, or simply breathe, and take in the moment. Opportunities will change as you proceed through life. They will involve or concern relationships, finances, health, and wellness. Consider the benefits and consequences of your options and actions. Make use of the moment-to-moment opportunities that abound, and live a meaningful, engaged life.

Ownership

Ownership refers to the act, state, or right of possessing something. While ownership can refer to objects, land and real estate, or even intellectual property, for this concept we address self-ownership. We previously discussed how debt could own you. The concept of being over-extended is pertinent across some remarkably different realms. As far as ownership of the self, we can approach it as being composed of accountability and responsibility.

Creating of/for one's self a worthy character entails shouldering responsibility. We will have duties to address, or people to care for. We are accountable for those responsibilities; we need justify actions or decisions. We are responsible for owning our complete selves and our actions. We have the responsibility of engaging mindfully, actively. When we do so, we establish a worthy character and earn a solid reputation among other similar worthy, valued people and perspectives.

Self-ownership entails self-discipline. It means standing as the sole answerable party for one's total life. It means that fetters and attachments: corporeal or conceptual - tangible or figurative - burdens are managed in such a way that they do not endanger or detract from your highest good and your worthy endeavors. Addictions and lesser distractions *can* over-ride someone. It is up to us to be strong - to live an intentional, mindful, and purposeful existence so that we are not misguided by caprice and lower drives. Self-ownership elicits liberty, but it is not a guarantee of it.

Chapter 16

Particle

In the physical sciences, a particle is a small, localized object that can be ascribed several physical or chemical properties such as volume or mass. They can vary greatly in size or quality; particles can be subatomic, micro- or macroscopic. The particles can be the smallest bit of existence, and they can also be used analogously; they can be used to model behaviors of larger objects in a study (bees in a hive, cars on a highway). Particles can be elements of a whole - minute parts of a great tapestry. In the realm of cognition, perception, and epistemology, particles are contrasted with waves. Upon the application of human perception, waves become particular - the background amalgam of waves differentiates to provide specific objects. Otherwise, sans human perception, or general applied perception, waves exist in a context void of cognitive interaction. But, with that presence of perception, waves differentiate to more specific particles. *They coordinate in the presence of consciousness* and then comprise what we generally refer to as reality.

It is our involvement with particles that creates reality. Our minds, and our mindfulness - or lack thereof - are primary contributors and creators of reality. We have addressed this previously, elsewhere. Investigating the concept at the quantum level demonstrates a vast rabbit hole. It is not so much the case that reality is waiting for a percipient. More so, the utilization of mind creates and shapes reality with particles. While they might be minute, at times even unknowable to the base human senses, our minds orchestrate their coalescence, synthesis, and composition in very significant ways. This means that our minds are responsible for much of what is accepted as reality. The ramifications of this are staggering. Investigating particles, be they subatomic or featured in scientific models, is a most interesting, if not even counter-intuitive, activity that elicits meaningful results in the 'real' world.

Patriarchy

Patriarchy is a social system in which males hold primary power. Given the recent prevalence and debate of the merits of patriarchal rule, an examination of pertinent elements yields a fuller, broader understanding of the term and its place in human history. Patriarchal roots extend as far back as Sumerian texts, with the myths of Enki and Enlil. These foundational tales involve creation myths that involve sky gods as pitted against chthonic/earth gods and a hierarchy is established among those participating. A patriarchy is a type of hierarchy (an arrangement of items in which some are represented as above, below, or at the same level as others). Hierarchies are common occurrences. They are most noticeable in the natural world, among plants, animals, and humans. Hierarchies result due to several reasons, including, but certainly not limited to, merit and power. Biological characteristics, and the passing of worthy traits are the result of biological hierarchies. Some traits were more important to the continuation of the species; hence, they were prioritized: organized higher on a hierarchal structure.

The patriarchy that we discuss for the purposes of this section is being derided and criticized in certain circles at present. Some contend that the current hierarchy is overdue for revision, if not elimination. What hinders or impedes the implementation of that suggested structure is the lack of an alternative that serves as a superior model or standard. Instead, what is posed is the abolishment of the patriarchy for a matriarchal (rule by women) society. These individuals contend that a.) men and masculinity must change, that b.) women need be considered exactly the same as men, and that c.) women must be given privileges over men. What is lost in this shortsighted contention is how the patriarchy is equivocated with the entire western tradition. Those pushing for the eradication of the patriarchy demonize most unfairly the hierarchy of which they are a part. Just like *all* social structures, criticism is warranted and necessary! But the elimination of the system is unnecessary, reactionary knee-jerk initiative. Lacking superior alternatives, we are confined to existing within implemented structures. We can do much to engage revise occurrences of social, economic, and environmental injustices. But to identify all components of the current organizational/cultural/social/patriarchal arrangement as fruits of the poisoned tree is a false argument, a logical fallacy. What is at play is a fallacious argument (whole to part/part to whole). These individuals erroneously equate all portions of the patriarchy as evil, or as contributing to greater injustices and structural/cultural/institutional oppression. What is left unsaid concerns the tremendous array of positive benefits offered by the system/patriarchy/western tradition. The incredible spectrum of freedoms offered by this system is still unparalleled in history. Further, men and women have no need to be seen nor treated as the same. Both have unique capabilities and characteristics that serve different social/biological/cultural functions. Eliminating those differences, or legislating the ignorance of their differences, their particular importance, and necessity is a profound disservice to/for the greater community.

The concept of patriarchy is ancient. It has a wealth of related concepts, equivocations, and positive associations, and negative elements, at that. It is recommended that one become very familiar with, or very well versed, in history, politics, and a wide array of other subject matters before confronting it on the grounds of oppression, injustice, or as the cause of the day. Patriarchy is western civilization, and the tremendous benefits, innovations, and norms that are part and parcel to its structure need be grasped thoroughly before we shoulder the task of supplanting it with a suggested alternative.

As stated many times previously, it is important to address significant concepts on a piecemeal basis to avoid eliminating structures dangerously, unnecessarily. Consider what happens when a leader is dethroned or deposed. Nature, and community abhor a vacuum. What takes the place of the dethroned leader could very well be much worse than the initial arrangement. Critiquing components and a larger system is a layered and complex practice that need be gradually applied. Being reckless serves no one and corrects no ills. Strive to address wrongs with a diligent and measured manner or risk the consequences of undisciplined approaches.

Perfection

The condition, state, or quality of being fre, or as free as possible from all flaws or defects is perfection. Perfection is an ideal, a bookend, of a spectrum of values. If someone was a perfect beauty, they would comprise the epitome or standard of beauty; their beauty would be the hallmark by which all other beauty is measured. The philosopher Plato contended that there existed a realm of forms - a world of absolute values that existed apart from the material world. The world took or made use of the forms, but the items of the world were but distant approximations or imitations of the perfect forms. So, perfect justice, beauty, and goodness all had forms, as did triangle, table, etc. The forms were eternal, in contrast to the materials that made use of representation or imitation, were always undergoing change and could never realize that fixed, perfect ideal.

As far as growth and development are concerned, perfection is an unobtainable, and therefore, unrealistic goal. That we are mortal and subject to decay and change means that we are, by nature, distanced or removed from the possibility of attaining absolute perfection. That it, as a specific goal, is unobtainable or even unrealistic, though, does not absolve us of the responsibility of improving ourselves. We can seek to develop and build our character and, in doing so, contribute meaningfully to the betterment of our self and our communities. The existence of forms, or even the idea of perfection, specifically, is what gives rise to tales of gods and heroes, heroines. We can identify ideals and then ascribe meaning to them. The practice shapes our behaviors and ethos and it is the pursuit of those valued ideals that gives many activities their lasting worth and significance.

Perseverance

Steadfastness in doing something despite difficulty or delay in achieving success is perseverance. It is maintained or continued activity in the face of challenges, obstacles, or adversity. It amounts to meaningful work or effort. Consider how satisfying it feels to accomplish a task or to achieve a goal. Perseverance in the face of opposition delivers a meaningful sentiment. For something worth obtaining or achieving is going to cost time, effort, and maybe other resources including perhaps blood, sweat, and tears. Invest yourself, and apply your resources to worthy pursuits and activities. Persevere to achieve worthy, real goals. The self-respect you earn as a result of such work will be absolutely invaluable in the long run.

Person

A person is a human being regarded as an individual. The adjectival form personal relates to, or comes from, a particular person or individual. You are a human being. You are an individual. While there might be 7.6 billion other individuals that are similar, or share certain characteristics with you, no one else is *You*. You are both the product and the creator of your experiences, values and perspective. You are unique; there is nobody like you. Some - maybe a great many individuals, even - may have the same values, or have shared some similar experiences. But your unique personhood is a very particular set of circumstances. You are a sole entity and your life has value. When the world loses your involvement there can be no replacement; for no one feels, thinks, or acts as you do.

For this, and innumerable other reasons, you are most important. Your life is a specific and finite valuable commodity that is solely yours to live and enjoy. A person is a private entity, by nature, but can be as public as that particular entity so desires. That privacy affords some insulation from the rest of the world. It allows for sacred space, time, moments to be utilized solely for the benefit of the individual. Maintaining that hallowed commodity of privacy is the responsibility of the person. Were they not to value self-respect, or not entertain much as far as self-esteem, their life would have more of a public and accessible character. As it goes now, a disturbing trend among people is that of engaging social media. People now want to divulge the most personal aspects of their lives on different platforms. The practice of allowing access to what has been protected and honored among individuals is a clear depiction of a lesser view of self-esteem and self-respect. Now, all too often, individuals commoditize their moments and character in an effort to connect and fit in. For who does not want to engage in a practice that nearly all else do, and *seem* to enjoy? Peer pressure is formidable across cultures. But the social media activity has been demonstrated to have an overwhelmingly negative toll on society. Even the management of platforms have noted their awareness of its insidious creep, and the toll on the psyche and larger communities across the globe.

A central aspect of personhood concerns the balance between very dynamic elements of rights and responsibilities. While people have the right to do certain things, these are balanced by the duties of individual people within a community. To understand this contrast, we first identify human rights. Human rights are rights all humans have, regardless of their religious or national affiliation.

-Marriage and Family
-The Right to Own Your Own things
-Freedom of Thought
-Freedom of Expression
-The Right to Public Assembly
-The Right to Democracy
-Social Security
-Workers' Rights
-The Right to Play
-Food and Shelter for All
-The Right to Education
-Copyright (intellectual Property)
-A Fair and Free World
-Responsibility (A duty to other people)
-Human Rights are inviolable; no one can take away your human rights.

We will examine a theory of rights and responsibilities later, but suffice it to say that while we can make use of rights, they are balanced by duty, obligation, and responsibility. Cicero said that duties come from four different sources: as a result of being human, as a result of one's place in life (family, country, job), as a result of one's character, and as a result of one's own moral expectations for oneself. Just as life is a balance of pleasure and pain, so too is life a balance between duty and rights. A life well-lived strikes a subjective balance between the two and it is most important - if not absolutely necessary - to recognize the need for this balance as soon as possible. Else, one is shirked for the other and different maladies result.

Your subjective person: YOU! are a miracle. You are a remarkable natural thing of intellectual, emotional, and physical beauty. You have the capacity to create, to experience all of the wonders of this amazing existence. Make use of you and apply yourself to be the best you can be. Make use of time such that the finished product is something that makes you proud. There is considerable pain involved with the regrets of a wasted life. Set a standard with your person. Be a dynamic, unique person for your own good, and for the benefit of all else, too.

"Wanting to be someone else is a waste of the person you are." - **Kurt Cobain**

Perspective

Perspective is a particular attitude or way of regarding something. It is a point of view. It is an ethos, a stance, an angle, or approach that is comprised of values and experience. So those with unique experiences and values will undoubtedly have contrasts of perspective from everyone else. Experience might be shared, yet no two people will view a situation or scene from the same perspective. We all apply our own ethos, faculties, and filters to comprise our own perspective.

Perspectives can be based on remarkably disparate foundations. They can be religious, cultural, historical, and strategic. A person's perspective can be based on one realm and adapt to make use of another that is wholly different.

In order to understand one's self and others, it is imperative to grasp this concept.

Opinions differ across time, space, and subjective ethos. We need be prepared to analyze a complex array of contributing factors. A person's background shapes their philosophical position. Be sure to remain open and aware of the overwhelming spectrum of participating factors involved in someone's perspectives. A complete grasp of that totality is *impossible*. It is nigh impossible to have a complete grasp of one's own self. Differences in perspective are not due solely to ignorance. Grasping another's perspective and formulating one's own necessitates patience, understanding, analysis, introspection, and a host of other important concepts. Again: to understand one's self and others, a grasp of how perspectives are formed is absolutely essential.

Philosophy

Philosophy, literally: love of wisdom, is the study of general and fundamental problems concerning existence, knowledge, values, reason, death, mind, and language – among so many other concepts, too. Philosophers ask questions that have perplexed and delighted man since even before ancient times.

Questions include: what happens after death? Is it possible to know anything and prove it? What is right and good? What is beautiful? Do humans have free will? While historically, Philosophy encompasses, includes, and pertains to *all* subjects of investigation, it has five major realms:

-metaphysics; investigations concern being - or ontology
-epistemology; investigations discuss theories of knowledge
-ethics; investigations address moral issues
-aesthetics; investigations focus on art and beauty
-logic; investigations center on inference.

Philosophy investigates issues that motivate, inform, and inspire humanity through time. While answers have transformed across time and contexts, specific answers are not the goal of the speculative endeavor. The pursuit of truth has been the hallmark of philosophers since even before the western Pre-Socratics, and it continues to guide thinkers today.

Philosophers focus more on speculation, not necessarily on rigid answers. But this does not mean that the practice is an empty pursuit. The sharpening of critical faculties is never a frivolous exercise. Those with an able, philosophical mind will always be able to find meaningful work, and, importantly, live significant and meaningful lives. The philosopher Socrates once said, "The unexamined life is not worth living." Living unconsciously, sans meaningful introspection, self-analysis, or rigorous inquiry of the external world leaves people stunted and undeveloped. An absence of philosophical endeavors produces ignorant consumers who are content to follow others because they have neither the means nor the interest in thinking for themselves and forging their own unique path. Those who embark on a philosophical path investigate the treasures of a rich and complex existence.

Those who do not engage the practice are not so driven to explore for myriad reasons. They may not be so curious as to the density of available concepts and variables. The questions may frighten them. They may be lazy, or merely disinclined to think or speculate with no final, definite goal. Philosophy facilitates an active, critically engaged mind. It elicits communication skills and a fuller awareness of how a society operates. Philosophy and philosophizing is a necessary skill, at least for those curious and interested in understanding the complexity of the world and its components. It renders many social controls and restrictions unnecessary and obsolete. It enables people to live in a freer state as their minds are not limited by inactivity nor the imposed restraints of a burgeoning society. For that is what any society and government desires and needs: acquiescence and obedience. An able thinker can identify onerous and unnecessary shackles and limitations and, instead: opt to tread a path that need not be controlled by inferior standards or trite belief systems.

Philosophy is not dogmatic; it is not stuck on opinions, as if they were true. The very opposite is the case. Philosophy explores possibilities without attaching to doctrines espoused by different perspectives. It stands opposed to religion and other forms of institutional authority. Whereas dogmatic belief systems instruct as to 'what' to think, philosophy guides as to 'how' to think. And as far as life skills are concerned, this is one of the most important to have and develop. For in every person's life, they will seek solace from notable, consequential concerns. Morality will weigh upon them. And while faith and religion - dogma, writ large - offer comfort to those who can not or will not think, Philosophy offers comfort to able minds that are willing to discern particular variables in order to coordinate a way forward. Being able to think is of much greater value than calling on a belief system that demands requires blind faith and adherence to dogmatic ideals and concepts - sans reason. So long as one's mind is trained and open, possibilities and hope are forever available.

But be aware of what Nietzsche says about hope, at that: "In reality, hope is the worst of all evils, because it prolongs man's torments."

Philosophical inquiries concern love, justice, truth, piety, communication, death and so many more pertinent and consequential concepts. Indeed, Philosophy pertains to *everything* that makes life worth living.

Politics

Politics concern the affairs of the cities/communities. They refer to the organized control of a human community. Politics involves making decisions that apply to members of a group and achieving and exercising positions of government. Those who are elected to represent their constituents and community perform politics. These elected officials are tasked with decisions for the good of their people because it is remarkably difficult to reach agreement between all members of the community as to what is best for all. Hence representatives are selected to make decisions that represent the will of the people. Important concepts within the realm of politics include accountability, corruption, representation, and transparency.

Political representatives are supposed to serve their constituents. And the constituency is tasked with holding them accountable. The initial step of that accountability process is to speak truth to power - speaking out to those in authority - in order to address abuses, trespasses or usurpations committed by those in office. Should officials fail to serve responsibly, or honorably, the constituents are then responsible for removing those politicians from office. That effort proves to be a most challenging endeavor, for few will cede power despite evidence of wrongdoing, or malfeasance.

Corruption is a form of dishonest or unethical conduct by a person entrusted with a position of authority, often to acquire personal benefit. Politicians will use their public role to gain for themselves. This is *always* at the expense of the public because the corrupt make use of the public's trust to gain for them. Public office is meant solely for service. When politicians abuse power, office, or resources for personal gain, they need be disabused of such practices and held accountable for their behavior. Corruption is a very common occurrence in the realm of politics. In fact, corruption occurs in a great many realms. Another definition of politics refers to business conducted amongst a plurality. Therefore, politics occurs whenever there is more than one person participating in a dynamic. Corruption can then occur in a great many settings: school boards, administration committees, and even church leadership roles are often corrupted by those who seek to make use of power and resources at their disposal. More and more we see corruption in politics among so many other realms. Eliminating it is a formidable task for all societies, across time and space.

Politicians are meant to act on behalf of the people in the community of which they are a part. It should be noted, however, that most politicians are of the upper class. They come from wealthy families, are educated in esteemed institutions, and are groomed for positions of authority and power. Those who rule, or serve as politicians, are generally not representative of the largest portion of people. They come from a very different background, and hence hold very disparate values from the largest body of constituents. Given that experience, the people would be very foolish to hope for politicians to behave or vote against their own class interests. Question as to whether this is within the realm of possibility. Representing people means voting in line with the constituents' will and best interests. How can politicians, who have been raised to rule as members of a wealthy elite, actually represent those whose values are incredibly different, or in some cases, opposed to their own? Why would politicians - or anyone for that matter - vote against their own class interests? How can politicians represent the majority when they belong to the elite minority?

Transparency implies openness, communication, and accountability. When something is transparent, it is apparent - it can be seen through, as if looking through a window. Politicians vow to be transparent and accountable, yet it is remarkably rare when this occurs, if ever! Politicians hide behind the veil of state secrets, or opt to cloak their maneuvers as a means of protecting the state, or their own position. When significant decisions and processes are kept from the public eye, suspicion and doubt ought to be elicited. When is secrecy and unclear, opaque stratagems *ever* for the benefit of all? Inclusion and openness serve the greatest good. Consider the transparency of actors serving as politicians. When their initiatives and deals are kept from the public, it is a safe assumption that they are deliberately masking their intent and, perhaps also, some less than honorable maneuvers.

Thomas Jefferson once said, "Justice should be the goal of any government or people." The results of political maneuverings demonstrate how other goals and values are esteemed and emphasized in our community. Should justice or any number of higher values be honored, we would enjoy a remarkably different economic, social, and environmental condition, structure, and culture. The realm of politics demonstrates the values of leadership and government. One would be most wise to discern the values of those in politics by critically engaging behaviors of individuals and the greater state.

As a people, we have allowed corruption, among other evils, to maintain too powerful a presence in our political realm. The people have refused to hold politicians accountable. We do not insist on adequate representation. We do not demand transparency. Should we desire an improvement in these regards, we need entertain better values and coordinate together a revised national ethos. We need only good people of impeccable quality to serve as statesmen.

Popular

As far as cultural activities or products, something is popular when it is intended for or suited to the taste, understanding, or means of the general public rather than for specialists or intellectuals. Popularity has to deal with base people, essentially - not those who are educated, or cultured. What passes for popular is predicated on time and place; popularity is contextualized via cultures and experience. What is popular now varies drastically from what popular in ancient Rome, in medieval England, and even what was cool a few years ago in your own community.

What is popular in today's rapidly evolving, mass media barraged society transforms and shifts at a remarkable pace. A new celebrity will emerge, a hit song will color the airwaves and new fads will become apparent in *very* short amounts of time. The succession of popular and cool commodities serves to keep people distracted and engaged in groupthink/herd behavior. The less individuals are tempted to better themselves with meaningful, positive activities that contribute to self-development, the more they pay attention to trite pastimes and superficial goods. But what is popular is not necessarily good at the subjective or larger, communal level and popular approaches have never had substantial good in mind. Why would leadership want to press consequential pursuits and meaningful activities when popular/cool people/things could instead occupy and distract? Imagine the consequence of diverting attention from worthy pursuits that include healthy social coordination intended to facilitate the improvement of the community. Advancing valuable practices for the betterment of people only endangers the status quo and those in power certainly do not want those critically engaged constituents questioning authority or speaking truth to power. Leadership prefers distraction in the form of the popular and cool because it distances people from that meaningful engagement with the self and the community.

It takes strength to break from groupthink, to separate from the crowd that engages superficial thoughts and practices. It is a small number of people who recognize the trivial nature of popular commodities and seek to engage elsewhere with more consequential activities. We need not eschew all that is popular in order to entertain meaningful pursuits. Pop songs *can* make us feel great! The newest Hollywood blockbuster *can* present significant ideas and a worthy demonstration of heroic activity and positive modeling, besides. As is the case with many concepts, striking a balance is imperative. Contrast what is popular with your own hierarchy of values. If there is little to no contrast, consider how your tastes and engagements might be diversified and improved. Gandhi once said, "It's better to walk alone than with a crowd going in the wrong direction." Consider: what was once cool and popular in Rome, England, and even in your own community has probably since fallen from style and practice. Adopt activities and perspectives that will endure.

Power

Aristotle defined rhetoric as the faculty of identifying, in any given case, the available means of persuasion. A slight change yields a workable definition for power: the faculty of observing, in any given case, the available means of *influence*. Power is always applied. It needs have an object as a recipient. Power is nearly meaningless if there is no thing upon which it can be exerted. There are many types of power, many associations. Collectives can exert power, as can individuals. There is organizational power, just as there is the power wielded by one lone entity. Whether a plural or a single subject exerts the power, the result is the same: influence is brought to bear on something else.

There is a spectrum of power: influence can either be hard, soft, or a combination of the two. Hard power is coercion, or violence, while soft power is negotiation, cooperation, and rhetoric. A combination can be understood via a quote by former President Theodore Roosevelt, who said, "speak softly, and carry a big stick." Diplomacy can work well but it is very much more effective when it is complemented by different resources. This foreign policy paid dividends for the leader and it remains a viable strategy. On a subjective basis, individuals make use of their own skill sets. A beautiful woman makes use of her looks while a chess player utilizes tactics and strategy. It is a safe assumption that the woman makes use of more than just her beauty, just as the chess player will influence people by offering more than his playing ability. They are both aided by an engaged demeanor and appropriate dress.

Power is a concept that has been examined, researched, and discussed since ancient times. Thucydides' Melian Debate, Machiavelli's *The Prince*, and Greene's *48 Laws of Power*, are but three notable texts that address power. A general theory of power includes concepts of awareness, adaptability, strength and/or confidence, and the presence of an audience or an object upon which the power/influence is exerted. The wielder of power need be aware of the variables of a context - in order to marshal resources sufficiently - and they also need be able to apply the correct and measured amounts of resources to elicit success. Consider how a hostile force may not respond well to certain forms of influence or power. The Greeks at the gates of Troy were not going to be assuaged by nice words and negotiation. Different situations necessitate different forms and applications of power. Success is predicated in part by awareness. By being aware of parties involved, intentions of different entities, and how best to cater to goals and aims, specific resources can be put into play. Power is not a blanket tool, nor a one-size-fits-all remedy. A discerning, or keen awareness identifies key elements of a situation, and aligns the form and amount of influence to be applied. Being adaptable elicits results. Things change and we need adapt to dynamic conditions. One strategy may not always work, in fact: you can count on needing several plans in order to realize success. A fluid mindset and a set of alternative tools and resources generally yield favorable results. Having a diversified set of plans and means facilitates the odds of success. Entertaining but one skill set *can* birth favorable returns but a diverse skill set, and being willing (and able) to change course, and adopt different methodologies is a most valuable characteristic. Some situations require a finite application of tools. But, given dynamic conditions, power's meaningful application lies in adapting to change and the proverbial curveballs that are certain to occur.

Power necessitates strength and confidence. Truly, every situation is facilitated by strength of character and confidence. Walking with a confident gait delivers a powerful message. A strong grasp of vocabulary, timing, and tone elicits understanding by an audience; powerful thinkers and speakers have changed the course of history! Interestingly enough, feigned weakness and a lack of confidence can pay dividends, as well. Boxer Muhammad Ali's rope-a-dope earned him victory in the ring. Situational awareness will - again - be instructional as to how much strength or confidence need be brought to bear on a situation. But they are two important components of power that need be applied in nearly all contexts.

Being aware of what or to whom you are applying power/influence is very consequential. We addressed audience awareness earlier. Recognizing the audience with whom you are interacting is invaluable! Consider how, with different objects/audiences, only certain resources need be utilized. A surgeon is best served when he is equipped with a scalpel, and not a shotgun.

Judiciously applying power is a considerable ability.

Varying between hard and soft power applications will make a significant difference for your reputation as well as in different contexts as you make your way.

Power has many associations. Force is a common concept that is associated with power. It can be referenced as an external, as in the case in the movie series, Star Wars. Power can also be an internal resource. Whether it's the result of mindfulness, intelligence, aligned chakras, or kundalini practice, power is something that can be called upon by a considerate individual. I utilize the term *considerate* intentionally. Someone who is considerate is aware, measured, and disciplined. They apply themselves in a balanced fashion. They are not overbearing or rash and aggressive. A powerful individual has self-control and applies resources evenly, succinctly, and efficiently. I contend that true power is elicited by a balanced development of head, heart, and hands. Thoughts and the mind are restrained. Emotional intelligence is highly developed. The body is honed, coordinated, and cared for as a valuable tool. You will be powerful when you come to treat your person with self-respect and dignity. True power is a result of self-care and self-discipline. You will not need power over others when you have power over yourself and, as far as abilities and life skills, this one is so very important. Seek to develop that particular trait and you will have a constant source of power, and influence.

Practical

Being practical refers to a person, idea, or project as being more concerned or relevant to practice than theory. It can be equivocated with viability or workability. Generally, something is practical, or demonstrates practicality, when that person, idea, or project has a real life application. The aforementioned contrast between practice and theory is an important one. Some mistakenly draw a distinction between thinking and doing. They note that thinking lacks the practical aspect while the doing is where the 'rubber meets the road.' Your mind can tax your energy, and your health. Thinking *is* doing, but there is a point that applicability need be demonstrated. Results need be borne of concrete actions taken in the real world. Speculation and exploratory thought have an important place, but practical measures birth tangible results, and rewards.

Practical things are activities that serve as means to other ends. This begs the question: are there activities that are impractical but still worth doing? Having fun and enjoying one's self *does* have a practical purpose but the doing of the activity is an end, in and of itself. Daydreaming is not necessarily practical, per se, but it does pay dividends, nonetheless. Practicality means that something has an intended purpose. If and when an individual lacks practicality, they lack purpose. It might be all well and good for them to live as an aloof individual, but our modern society generally disapproves of those who lack purpose, direction, and practical application. Again, build multiple skill sets and shape a character that has practical value. When the time comes for you to demonstrate and showcase your quality and character, it will immediately benefit you to have applicable qualities and a practical, diverse array of skills.

Prepared

It is best to be prepared: ready for use or consideration. Consider your plans and have options for radical change and dynamic conditions. Being unprepared could mean the difference between success and failure or even life and death. There is no way to be prepared for everything that comes your way. Surprises and challenges deliver both joy and necessary character development. But with some forethought and initiative, you can sidestep many unnecessary hassles and problems. Taking the time to plan and prepare makes life safer, easier, and even more enjoyable. Some surprises will delight you while others can leave you aghast and horrified. Solving challenges and surmounting obstacles deliver self-respect and pride while other types of challenges can leave you vulnerable, and with a limited amount of options and resources. Prepare for the worst and hope for the best in all situations.

"Prior planning prevents piss poor performance." – **U.S. Military adage**.
Many thanks to Kellen Durose for this gem.

Present

While you make your way through your years, remain in the present. It is wise to consider your past, for those prior experiences and behaviors delivered you to *this* moment. Considering the future has benefits, as well. A long-term plan only makes sense; we need believe there will be a tomorrow and beyond. For what else is life for but to plant seeds that will bear fruit in the future? But remaining present, and having a presence is a meaningful practice. Being engaged in the present - being in the moment - allows us to savor the characteristics, emotions, and variables of right now. When we are elsewhere: dwelling in the past or looking to the future, we are missing the gift of the present. When time is lost, it is gone forever. It is advisable to grasp that present, and engage fully. Feel the wind, smell the scent of that particular moment. Get present by breathing, and take the time to re-engage that much more dynamically within a given context or situation. Make a practice of eliminating distractions - put your phone away - and connect with the here and now.

Profane

Profane acts refer to activities that are not sacred or even religious. Durkheim maintained that they were anything that was not religious, though I contend differently. While profanity can pertain to an irrelevance of religious items, symbols, or practice, this term can pertain to the subject, rather than the institutional belief system. Individuals prize certain people, places, or things and value them as untouchably sacred. On the other side of the spectrum lies the profane: lower activities and behaviors that are typified, generally, by common if not base approaches. Simply, people will value things at a much higher level than other things. Not all things can be valued similarly, and for good reason. A sneeze can not hold the same weight as the birth of a child, for example. Consider and rank items based on your subjective value system. With no bookends established, everything is profane and held at the same base level. What is sacred, or held to be of the highest value for you? What is of the highest worth according to your subjective values? Some examples of the sacred might include life, family, self-respect, along with concepts like innocence, honesty, truth, and an idea of the divine, or God.

This last concept is an interesting one; though take note how all listed concepts can differ person to person. The idea of God, or a deity differs per religion and even per person. While a holy book may conceptualize and describe the aspects of a possible anthropomorphic deity, for example, other conceptualizations contrast radically. Even among adherents of the same faith, their own filters, ethos, and subjectivity color their grasp or understanding. This is the same for the other listed concepts. The idea of life, and different definitions is a significant realm of contention between people, cultures, and religions. As we discussed earlier, the idea of family varies per experience. Because these experiences are remarkably disparate, people value things very differently. The treatment of women across cultures is a remarkable spectrum. Consider the meat industry in the United States and contrast it with how cattle are treated with reverence in India. While profanity can refer to words, or expletives/cursing, it can also refer to irreverent behaviors. What is not due reverence? Some comedic presentations are most irreverent. Perhaps sneezes and trips to the bathroom fall into the same category; we need not honor or revere base, common activities, and every single step, breath, or blink of an eye.

Consider how an increased sense of reverence could influence and color our own lives, and the condition and standards of our own communities, if not the state of the greater world. How could we facilitate the emergence of a more reverent attitude and perspective in our lives? Values are comprised largely of cultural factors. What changes at the subjective, and institutional levels would be necessary to foster greater reverence for life, for ourselves, and for one another? Considering the circumstances of the social, economic, and environmental realms, this shift could be immensely beneficial.

Promise

A promise is a declaration or a guarantee that one will do a particular thing or that a particular thing will happen. It is a serious undertaking to promise something. Such an activity amounts to a pledge, a vow, a commitment, or even a contract. The concept of honor plays a prominent role in any promise. Honor is intimately connected with respect and high esteem. To engage a promise means to commit with a significant level of respect for self and the person receiving the vow or commitment. To engage significantly: to utter a promise or to commit and promise equates to putting one's honor and reputation forth in a most meaningful way. All said, promises are very important and broken promises affect your reputation because the breaking of the oath amounts to a serious trespass on someone's trust. Failing to meet one's obligations demonstrates the quality of a person. Should you offer a promise be certain that it is a vow you can satisfy. Do not make empty promises. Validate your commitment by following through with substantiated, meaningful action. Lastly, as a general guideline: strive to under-promise, and over-deliver.

Propriety

The state or quality of conforming to conventionally accepted standards of behavior or morals is propriety. Morals, decency, respectability, courtesy and civility are all components of propriety. It is behavior that is socially or morally correct and proper. The contrast of propriety would be demonstrated by misconduct, misbehavior, bad manners, lawlessness, or general inappropriate behavior. Every context or situation has a standard of propriety. Conduct will differ and depend on the specific scene and instance. As mentioned previously, proper conduct will vary depending on the audience and activity involved.

Every activity has a right and wrong standard of behavior. An increasing trend in our United States has been the growing prevalence of relativism, or radically subjective standards or mores and behavior. Meaning: because someone has different values and experience, they can act as they see fit - audience and context aside. That means that there is no proper decorum or propriety, but that an individual can behave and act as if they are free of convention, rules, or even laws. As an example, if someone had experience in a society that allowed for egregious trespasses against women and children, that standard of behavior might be allowed or sanctioned in our society, if only because they had a different upbringing. Because those kinds of behavior suited them, we would have to consent because that's their own value system and perspective. But shared conventions and the collective grasp of norms equate to cohesion and unity. Should a community devolve to adopt only subjective behaviors as standards, there is no community. Accepted modes of behavior pertain to *everything*: clothing, volume in conversation, driving habits - all social and many individual behaviors done with the absence of an immediate audience, for that matter - feature a standard of propriety. Consider if a community member decided to live in the nude. While this may be acceptable in the isolation of his/her own home, this practice would largely be discouraged in public.

Mores, and the standard of behavior insist on an established decorum that addresses the needs of the larger amount of community members. What if a person decided to discard the notion of an 'inside voice' and communicate instead with yelling? If a person decided to communicate in a church or in a library in the same way they interact at a lively sporting event, most would deem the behavior as inappropriate and unwelcome because propriety had been ignored. Displays of impropriety are largely addressed and curtailed. If an individual decided to drive their vehicle as they desired they could cause mishaps, if not disasters, and even death. Propriety dictates common behavior that facilitates cohesion, safety, and the means of greater social coordination. We need abide by standards if we want to exist within a community of like-minded people. Else we need expect and suffer correction. The community, or the commons, will tend to address improper deviations of norms.

Propriety is a form of power structure. Conducting oneself as society demands maintains established order and hierarchy. In some cases, the established system and the ruling hierarchy need be challenged, if not confronted and revised. This pertains to governments and political parties but can also refer to workplace behavior and interaction elsewhere in the public sphere. Some conventions or practices may give rise to standards that negatively affect individuals or groups. As an example, it was once appropriate to abide by institutional racism. That conduct was acceptable behavior, a standard of propriety. People outgrew the standard and confronted and changed those institutional policies. Jim Crow laws were nullified, segregation was addressed via Brown v. Board of Education, and our culture proceeded to adopt more inclusive, more humane modes of propriety. This challenge continues today. We need be vigilant as to the relative justice involved in different standards of conduct. Sometimes what is generally accepted as legal remains unjust. We need gauge and confront unfair, unethical, and inhumane behavior, even if such a challenge to the accepted norms and standards is thought to be impropriety at first glance.

Other standards of conduct in different settings deserve confrontation as well. The presence of harassment is all too often taken for granted as acceptable behavior - as unfortunate, but otherwise acceptable conduct. Such standards of propriety can equate to the loss of rights, and dignity for individuals in the workplace. Confronting such practices can make people very uncomfortable. Challenging established standards is oftentimes very political and most consequential. Questioning the standards of propriety in the workplace can affect livelihoods, reputations, health, and well-being. But should behavior result in the loss of respect, dignity, or safety of an individual, it need be curtailed, opposed, and confronted. This is a very particular discussion. Cultural standards, including condoned/accepted workplace conduct, are the result of power structures and perpetuated implementation over time. Challenging accepted standards can be a rigorous if not a dangerous activity. People do not like to be held accountable, or accused of impropriety. Be very certain of the variables at play when considering power structures, orthodoxy, and established standards of propriety.

Factors influencing propriety include the subject, the family, peers, media, religion, and other associations, as well as law and government. A person's background will shape their perceptions of propriety. Their family and friends contribute to that understanding. All forms of media influence an understanding of behavior by presenting what is allowed, accepted. Religious and secular associations guide and shape people's conduct profoundly. Authority in the form of laws and government figures also contribute to our experience and understanding of propriety. Should an individual's reckoning of the concept be far removed, off-kilter, or at odds with the communal standard, one can assume they would be corrected by one, if not several of the entities listed. Component parts of a community work together to protect and maintain the structure. The concept of propriety is an important one as it pertains to several notable ideas, including the self, the self among others in a community, social mores and standards, ethics, and conflict, as well. Propriety is a concept that is relevant everywhere, in myriad different forms and contexts.

Psyche

The concept of Psyche refers to the totality of the human mind: conscious and unconscious. The former is a quality of awareness of being aware of both external and internal objects while the latter concerns the processes of the mind that occur automatically and are not available to introspection. They include thought processes, memories, interests, and motivations. Psychology is the objective or scientific study of the psyche. Interestingly, the Greek root for psyche pertains to breath, and derivative terms include spirit, ghost, soul, and self. Even more interesting is how cultures that had little to no contact or overlap with the Greeks had similar meanings. Both the Hebrews and the Chinese used similar ties to the term breath, or the breath of life.

Since ancient times, numerous thinkers have addressed the psyche, or the mind/soul. It remains an idea that guides discussions today. Postmodernist thinker Michel Foucault once deemed psychology the laughing stock of the sciences, because there is no objective basis that can map the amazingly dynamic array, or the radical subjectivity of each person's own mind. Pre-Socratic thinkers began with the concept of *nous*. Socrates maintained that after death, the psyche can achieve wisdom and experience the Forms since it would be unhindered by the body. Plato joined the discussion and offered several arguments that would color the discussion for centuries. In the *Phaedo*, he offered four arguments as to the immortality of the soul, while he also posited that the soul would separate from the body and proceed to a different realm for a life after death.

The proliferation of names and terms continued as Aristotle participated in the discussion. Soon, mind would be defined differently than soul, and different thinkers in their native tongues would utilize distinctions that clearly identified which concepts they addressed. And with good reason! Ideas of spirit, soul, mind, and the personal self all have profound ramifications in the western tradition.

Aristotle's *De Aenima* (*On The Soul*) used animal, vegetal, and rational minds as portions of man. These distinctions lasted until the 19th century, when phenomenologist Franz Brentano offered a uniquely more subjective mind. Freud defined the psyche as forces in an individual that influence thought, behavior, and personality. He distinguished between the id, the super-ego, and the ego. The id was comprised of basic sexual and aggressive instinctual drives like for that of food and procreation, for example. The super-ego was a person's conscious internalization of societal norms and morality. The ego moderated between the drives of the id with the prohibitions of the super-ego. Freud contended that the ego is the cause of neurosis, or a class of functional mental disorders involving chronic distress. Carl Jung was a student of both Freud and the philosopher Nietzsche. He advanced his idea of individuation, a lifelong psychological process of differentiation of the self out of each individual's conscious and unconscious elements. Individuation, Jung contended, is the main task of human development. Other important Jungian ideas include synchronicity, archetypal phenomena, collective unconscious, psychological complex, and both extraversion and introversion. Jung was an extraordinarily brilliant mind, and his work addressed a very broad spectrum of thought, much of which pertains to the idea of the psyche, and soul. His work covered the self, religion, anthropology, spirituality, literature, and philosophy. In order to have a firm understanding of theories of the self, it is necessary to have experience with his profundity.

The intellectual history of the psyche is a most consequential one. Identifying and understanding what motivates man has an incalculable benefit for the human race, for both rulers, and individuals. The investigation of the psyche via psychology has intimate connections with, but also, significant consequences for, cultural practices and institutions.

The myth of Psyche and Cupid was written in the 2nd Century AD, and remains remarkably pertinent today.

Psyche

Psyche was a most beautiful mortal, one of three sisters. She was so beautiful that mortal men began to worship her instead of Venus. This stirred the goddess' ire, who then dispatched her son Cupid to take revenge on the mortal by shooting her with one of his arrows and making her fall in love with the most hideous creature. Cupid instead falls deeply, uncontrollably in love with her. Meanwhile, Psyche can not find love. The Oracle of Apollo is consulted by her parents, and they are told that the son-in-law would not be human, but winged, and a creature that renders Jupiter - King of the Gods, himself - powerless. Frightened by these words of the Oracle, the parents clothed Psyche in funeral garb and left her on a cliff: alone and isolated, exposed to the elements, awaiting her doom at the hands of the 'winged serpent.' Zephyr, the God of the West Wind (aka the Wind of Change), transports her away to a meadow, where she sleeps peacefully. She awakes in a cultivated grove.

Among the amazing scenery sits a lavishly decorated house. A feast serves itself, and a dismembered voice instructs Psyche to make herself comfortable. She eats and amuses herself by singing to an invisible lyre. Psyche goes to bed and Cupid, whose form is disguised by cover of darkness, visits her. They make love and this process of Cupid visiting at night, with hidden form, is repeated for some time. Psyche becomes pregnant. Cupid allows Psyche's sisters to visit. Zephyr carries them to the house, and where they become instantly, immediately jealous of their sister's fortune. They undermine her happiness by devising a plan meant to uncover Cupid's identity. After all, Psyche *could* be lying with a hideous winged serpent! One night Psyche visits Cupid as he is sleeping. She carries an oil lamp, and a knife in order to defend herself, if not slay the 'hideous' beast. Taken aback by his remarkable beauty, she accidentally drops hot oil on Cupid and burns his shoulder badly. Pained by her betrayal and his injury, Cupid flees, but not before depositing Psyche on the side of a river, where she is discovered by the wilderness God Pan. She acknowledges the latter's divinity and then proceeds to wander the earth looking for love.

Psyche visits her sisters, one at a time. Seeking to be her replacement, they climb the cliff and throw themselves to Zephyr, hoping he would transport them up to the amazing home Psyche shared with Cupid. Instead, Zephyr lets them fall to their deaths. Meanwhile, Psyche goes from temple to temple, beseeching different Goddesses for help. Because they will not challenge Venus, Psyche accepts that she must instead serve the Goddess. Psyche surrenders herself. Venus revels having Psyche in her power, and she hands her over to her handmaidens: Worry, and Sadness, who torture her. Venus assaults and ridicules Psyche for conceiving a child in a sham marriage. She throws before Psyche an assemblage of mixed seeds, and instructs her to separate it into separate piles. Venus returns to a party, when a kind ant takes pity on Psyche, and coordinates a fleet of insects to help separate the seeds. Venus returns drunk from the party, and throws Psyche a crust of bread before becoming furious that the task is completed. It is revealed that Cupid is in the house, healing.

For Psyche's next task, she is told to gather golden wool from sheep belonging to the sun. As Psyche approaches a river that separates her from the sheep, a reed offers advice and stops her from committing suicide. Psyche gathers wool from briars that line the riverbank, and completes the second task successfully. For the third task, Psyche is instructed to gather the black waters that issue from the source of both the Styx and Cocytus rivers. The foul air and dragons daunt her. Jupiter sends his eagle to battle the dragons, and Psyche is able to collect the waters, completing this task. For her final task, Psyche is instructed to go to the underworld and collect Beauty from the Goddess of the Underworld, Proserpina. Venus claims she needs it as she has lost some of her while caring for her son. At some point, Psyche is tempted to kill herself while in a high tower. The tower itself speaks to her and gives her advice. She is to bring cakes for

Cerberus, tokens for the ferryman of the dead, and she is to ignore temptations along the way. All comes to pass, just as the tower says, and Psyche is able to persuade Proserpina to offer some of her beauty. On the return journey, Psyche's curiosity again gets the best of her, and, as she peers into the box, seeing nothing, is overcome by a magical sleep just as she exits the underworld. By this time, Cupid has escaped his mother's home by flying out a window. He conveniently finds Psyche. He removes the sleep from her, and pricks her with an arrow, and carries her to Jupiter for an audience with the King of the Gods. Cupid makes a case to marry Psyche, and Jupiter agrees, in exchange for Cupid's future aid with Jupiter's pursuits of lovely maidens. Jupiter convenes the gods, gives assent to their marriage, and tells Venus to relent her antagonism. Psyche is given ambrosia, the nectar of the gods, and becomes immortal. The union absolves Cupid's role in previous entanglements that elicited adultery and other sordid liaisons. Their child is named 'Pleasure.' Numerous aspects of the myth warrant investigation.

-It's interesting how Psyche falls for erotic, or 'lustful' love, while the total story deals with Psyche's ascent and her union with divine love.
-Regarding when people worship Psyche: Are they engaging in self-love?
-Cupid intends to love Psyche. Love itself wants to fall for mind/soul/spirit.
-When Psyche is left alone on a cliff by her parents, this is her first exposure to the world.
-The winged serpent could be a veiled kundalini reference.
-Psyche literally burns Love.
-When she recognizes Pan's divinity, she comes to terms with how things are. (reference to the Greek term: *Noumena*)
-Zephyr is the God of Change. That Psyche's sisters will not change means that they are left to their own devices. They kill themselves by hurtling themselves at Zephyr. In fact, they are doomed because they refuse to change.

-Temples visited by Psyche include those of Ceres and Juno (agriculture and the home/motherhood). No Goddess dares impede Venus' wrath.
-Regarding the tasks. Love coordinates the lowest creatures (insects), the highest (gods), and even inanimate objects (the tower) to serve the interests and needs of Love.

Psyche debases herself for a lustful enterprise. But a sacred union is achieved after she strives to earn the favor of the gods through dangerous, challenging toil. Pleasure is the result of Psyche's journey and travails to realize the divine connection with Love. This is complementing much of what we have discussed about the need to develop the self, in order to enjoy the rewards of that investment. The ancients recognized how the soul's work elicits the most amazing reward: meaningful Love.

Publicity

An examination of public life, with a view to a current trend of publicity, focuses on today's social media practices. Whereas private life is comprised of the social life, family life, or personal relationships of an individual, the public life consists of those aspects of social life that are happening in public, out in the open. An individual's private life is generally valued and held in such esteem so as to be protected from public consumption. Yet today's social media websites and applications that enable us to create and share content or to participate in social networking, facilitate a consequential trend of publicity: the giving of information about a product, person, or company for advertising or promotional purposes. Social media platforms and applications are largely free of charge; their producers do not collect a fee for their use - they are not selling anything to the public. But because the services are free, individual participants - those that utilize the services - are the product. Privacy is the currency.

Those elements that are typically kept to the private realm are offered to social media and these producers monetize this content by selling it to advertisers. Companies are now making use of people's content because the platforms take ownership of anything that is posted online. What is posted on Instagram, Facebook, and Twitter becomes the companies' property. Using that content, they tailor marketing and advertising to individual users. Their participants are the product. Producers insidiously make use of the voluntary posts by users, and the results have profoundly negative consequences.

Negative effects of social media include:
-No emotional connection to content or to the activity itself.
-A license provided to be hurtful.
-Decreased face-to-face communication skills.
-Inauthentic expression of feelings; falsehoods increase.
-Diminished understanding and thoughtfulness.
-Disconnected face-to-face interactions.
-Increased laziness.

The issues are serious enough that former executives at Facebook have voiced their criticism of the platform's deleterious effect on society. Facebook founding President Sean Parker objected as to how the company, "exploits a vulnerability in human psychology" via a "social validation feedback loop" during a conversation at an *Axios* event. Generally, by participating on social media platforms, individuals' pursuit of 'likes' and attention has side effects that include delusion of acceptance by their peers, a diminished inclination and ability to socialize, inflated self-importance, and other sociopathic behaviors.

Chamath Palihapitiya was vice-president for user growth at Facebook, and said he feels "tremendous guilt" for his work that is "ripping apart the social fabric of how society works." In November 2017, at a Stanford Business School event, he said, "The short-term dopamine driven feedback loops that we have created are destroying how society works. No civil discourse, no cooperation, misinformation, mistruth."[21] The influences of social media on the larger society have been overwhelmingly negative, and the personnel responsible for the platforms have voiced their regret and chagrin for their contribution to the worsened condition of the state. How much longer will we feed an enterprise that elicits a serious cost and toll on the psyche of the participants and the larger community?

Our culture shapes its constituency, just as the constituency formats the culture via bi-conditional reciprocation. However, that our culture allows and encourages rampant narcissism demonstrates how we, as participants and co-creators of the culture, entertain a woeful sense of self-respect/esteem. We value ourselves so little as to seek external recognition and acceptance instead of cultivating an internal value system that could guide us via a strong set of morals, principles, and ethics. Until we come to regard our lives, and the greater community as sacred, and worth more than commodities or resources meant for corporate and/or government use and gain, we will continue to suffer. Our communities will continue to erode. The distinction between private and public lives and the connection with an increasing use of social media has lasting consequences for both the individuals and institutions that comprise our communities.

"Travel and tell no one, live a true story and tell no one, live happily and tell no one, people ruin beautiful things."

– **Kahlil Gibran**

Chapter 17

Quality vs. Quantity

An important contrast is that of quality and quantity. The former is the standard of something as measured against other things of a similar kind. It can also refer to the excellence of something. The latter refers to a multitude or a magnitude and is described in terms of more, less, or equal, or with numerical values. Quality can refer to a characteristic or feature of something while quantity refers to the number or amount of something. A key distinction is how quality is subjective while quantity is not.

Here I repeat the encouragement to develop a character of worthy quality. Different people will identify quality in vastly different ways. What is worthy to some will disgust others. Some would seek to grow, develop, and progress while others have no qualms about living a life free of critique, introspection, and self-development. The majority of individuals may not have the means of pursuing self-fulfillment as they strive to live and make basic ends meet. Success for an overwhelming number of people may be the mere payment of bills and the satisfaction of basic responsibilities. It is a small sum of people who can attend to the upper reaches of the hierarchy of needs, as presented by Maslow. Quality might be a term that is inapplicable, given the pressing concerns of daily travails. Economic concerns and the daily process of earning a living beset the majority of people. Indeed, keeping the lights on, and obtaining sustenance - nutritious or not - are priorities. Enjoining in the active pursuit or development of quality at a young age paves a route towards greater successes, fulfillment and the presence of more refined qualities later.

What occurs as individuals apply a disciplined perspective and approach to the active pursuit of goals is a realization of abilities, a proliferation of skills, and the enjoyment of greater opportunities. Different levels of quality will invite and encourage complementary people, places, and things. Should someone eschew, or disregard the endeavor, life responds in kind. People of similar base quality will be present. Life will provide a more closed or limited perspective, with the equally base or limited range of options. The spectrum of events and places to discover, explore, and enjoy will fit the narrative of subjective levels of quality. So there is a remarkable difference between those who refuse to pursue or develop refined quality, and those who can not, due to their material, educational, economic, social/cultural (etc.) circumstance.

Focusing on those who have the means and the wherewithal to address that activity, this writer encourages the persistent directed endeavor of refining the self and developing worthy quality and a refined, cultured character. Every instance of life, be it a challenge or not, is the means of demonstrating quality. Edify your life by seeking that better level. The level of quality obtained, developed, and put forth will be met by a similar standard; it, again, is a case of like with like, or of water finding its own level. Water seeks its own level based on pressure and depth. It means high quality finds high quality and vice versa. A similar sentiment would be, "birds of a feather flock together."

Connecting the two concepts of quality and quantity, we recognize different applications. As an example, consider a manager seeks to fulfill a quota of manufactured products. He might be more concerned with a greater number of products being made than a maintained standard of quality. The team might meet the quota, but the standard quality of products might be poor. Consider the ratio or standard between the two. While someone may want many relationships, years, thoughts, or memories, what of their respective quality? What good does many relationships elicit if they are of poor quality? The same question applies for years, thoughts, and memories. Structuring, emphasizing, or prioritizing quality over quantity yields a considerable benefit. Time, energy, and other resources could be saved, and directed towards more fulfilling pursuits when quality is maintained as the priority among concepts. Otherwise, more sub-standard experiences could become an unfortunate norm.

As an analogy, consider ice cream. Eliminating the idea of moderation for this discussion, imagine the consumption of ice cream. The enjoyment lies in its worthy quality - its pleasant flavor, cold temperature, and relative consistency - among flavors like rocky road, sherbet, and mint chocolate chip. But what if the ice cream is bad? What happens when the flavor is disappointing, if not disgusting? What if the ice cream is no longer cold, and just a puddle of warm cream? What if the components separate and never congeal to even become a composite? Instead, the marshmallows separate from the chocolate, the fruit never connects with the cream, or the chocolate chips do not adhere with the mint. What good is ice cream, or anything for that matter, when quality is compromised? It will amount to an unfortunate amount of regret should the quantity of thoughts, feelings, memories, and relationships be prioritized in lieu of the quality of those respective events and occurrences. Prioritizing quality produces a favorable if not a pleasant outcome. It is not the number of years that make a life well-lived, but the quality of those years. Develop qualities and seek a refined quality in people, places, things, events and activities in order to enjoy and savor the very best in life. Doing so will minimize regrets and impart both higher pleasure, and meaningful satisfaction.

Quanta

Mankind seeks definitive answers about the nature of reality. The investigation of the quanta, the minimum amount of any physical entity involved in an interaction, and that of quantum mechanics (QM) guides the most pertinent investigations, presently. It seems arrogant, or questionable, at best, that I could come close to providing a reasonable estimate of the depth of the discussion as it stands today. Addressing such a task -providing a basis for the laity - is beyond this mind, and a great many others. In fact, prominent physicist and lecturer Richard Feynman was at a loss to structure a freshman lecture about a specific topic in QM, and he recognized that since it was not possible, he probably did not understand it, either. I am no Feynman. I will instead provide but a brief synopsis of some pertinent ideas at play within the field in an effort to introduce the topic and pique the interest of select minds.

Previously we discussed waves and particles. A photon is a simple quantum of light. It is the smallest particle, essentially. It is smaller than atoms, smaller still than protons, neutrons, and electrons. It is the 'force carrier' of the electromagnetic force. The energy of a particle at the quantum level, or the quantization of the energy and its influences on how energy and matter interact is part of the fundamental framework for understanding and describing nature. Quantum theory is a fundamental theory in physics that describes nature at the smallest scales of energy levels of atoms and atomic particles. It differs from classical physics in that energy, momentum, and the qualities of a system may be restricted to discrete variables. Objects have characteristics of both waves and particles and there are limits to the precision with which qualities can be known.

Werner Heisenberg and Niels Bohr offered the Copenhagen Interpretation, which emphasized the role of observation and how experiments were established. These two great minds considered their theory to be the nail in the coffin of the idea of causality, an idea that held sway since ancient times. Einstein argued against this point, maintaining that a physical state need not depend on the experimental arrangement for its measurement. A state of nature occurs, regardless of whether, or how it might be observed.

This is a philosophical question addressed by the likes of Plato, Kant, and Berkeley. Is reality predicated by observation and participation or is it the thing-in-itself, regardless of experiment and involvement? The Bohr-Einstein debates were fascinating back and forth thought experiments. Einstein and his team posited the need for 'hidden variables' to measure the position and momentum of particles more accurately than Heisenberg's uncertainty principle. Yet it was Bohr's team that proved somewhat victorious with their quantum entanglement approach. In this arrangement, one 'entangled' particle knows what measurement has been performed on another entangled particle, and with what outcome, even though there is no known means for such information to be communicated between the particles. This writer grapples with the ramifications of this conclusion. Feynman remarked, "I think I can safely say that no one understands quantum mechanics." While QM has not provided a comprehensive or unified theory that connects everything else, it has shaped our investigations of reality in meaningful, tangible ways. Modern cryptography is a result of QM as is maybe the whole of modern telecommunications and electronics.

The investigations of reality at the level of quanta may not interest everyone, but the ramifications of its conceptualizations pertain to anyone who has used a handheld device or used the internet. We remain seeking satisfactory answers concerning metaphysical reality. Forever assailed by questions concerning our existence and place in the cosmos, investigating the realm of QM is a means of engaging the discussion of what it means to exist here and now as humans in this amazing universe…or multiverse…? Enjoy this rabbit hole!

Queen

A Queen is a female ruler, and they can hold power equivalent to that of a king and rule her own kingdom. She can be a queen consort - the wife of a king - or she can be a queen regent, one who holds power until a child comes of age to rule. This entry addresses the qualities that comprise the behaviors and activities of a successful Queen. Here, we discuss leadership again. We review particular queens in history, there is an amazing array of quality ladies that served with distinction by uniting their people, serving the greater good, and maneuvering with seeming ease and efficiency if not graceful strategy and ruthless, brazen cunning.

Some notable Queens include:

-Elizabeth, who served as Queen of England and Ireland from 1558 to 1603. She was such an important figure that they named an age after her. During her reign, the arts flourished. Stability, even in the face of surrounding kingdoms that were rife with conflict, was a key component of her rule. Elizabeth ruled with the help of good counsel, was most tolerant, and very cautious with foreign affairs.

-Isabella, Queen of Spain from 1833-1868. She came to the throne as an infant! While her rule was marked by palace intrigues, she opened the Philippines up to trade, made progress with public works - railways, specifically - and improved the realms of commerce and finance during her time as ruler.

-Nefertiti was an Eqyptian Queen, the wife of Akhenaten. During her time on the throne, a profound shift from polytheism to monotheism took place in the kingdom. Her rule is known as the wealthiest point of Ancient Egyptian history. She assumed the rule of pharaoh after her husband's death, and performed damage control in order to maintain her status and role.

-Victoria ruled England and Ireland from 1837 until 1876. She influenced government privately, emphasized personal morality, and expanded the Empire, bringing India into the fold. While she ruled, major changes in the political, industrial, cultural, scientific, and military occurred.

-Cleopatra was the last ruler of the Ptolemaic kingdom of Egypt. She represented herself as the reincarnation of the Egyptian goddess Isis! She was also extremely well educated by the greats at Alexandria. She married Caesar and consolidated, if not insured, her place on the throne. When he was murdered, she associated with Marc Antony and protected the kingdom with his aid and resources.

-Catherine the Great served as the Empress of Russia from 1762 until 1796. She helped Russia expand and grow stronger. This 'enlightened despot' supported the ideals of the enlightenment and, under her watch, the first state-sponsored institute of higher education for women, the Smolny Institute, opened.

Extrapolating skills and abilities from the biographies of these queens and notable others, we have a list of attributes with which to rule, or lead. Should you wish to lead, the following counsel would serve you well.

-Be decisive. Make decisions and lead. Do not be divisive. Unite your team, lift morale and spirits, and connect, or rally around common goals. Do not be derisive or disrespectful. Leaders encourage their team members; they do not break them down.

-Maintain a clear purpose. Identify goals and the steps necessary to achieve them. Do not change plans or goals in the midst of operating. Have the will to commit to a plan and see it through to the end. Adapt and make changes with methodologies, if necessary, but be certain as to purpose.

-Work hard, and work smart. Engaging with direction and motivation, while being efficient, will elicit favorable returns. Working hard is worthwhile if and only if work is done consciously, with consideration and mental engagement.

-Engage with others and communicate well. Leadership involves communication and a considerable amount of quality, clear communication produces rewards. As a leader, utilize the team and kingdom to reach goals. Be clear, respectful, and repetitive (!) in order to have everyone operating from the same page regarding projects and initiatives.

-Respect others while earning, if not commanding, the respect of others with worthy, if not peerless, behavior. We will address the consequential concept of respect in the next chapter but, suffice it to say here, that unless you hold yourself in high esteem, others will be reluctant to do the same. Similarly, if a leader wants a unified team - performing together to reach a shared goal - team members need be treated as valuable contributors.

Respecting the self, and others, is perhaps the single most important lesson of this entire text, if not all of life, itself.

-Delegate responsibility and do not interfere with team members/constituents as they perform. Everything can not be done by one person. "Teamwork makes the dream work," is a common phrase used by many a kitchen team. Designate responsibilities to individuals or groups, according to skill sets and abilities, and allow them to succeed or fail. Trusting your team is a mark of a good leader. Do not micromanage - allow tasks to be completed as assigned. Utilize the team so that you are not shouldering everything, alone.

-Be discrete. Share what is necessary and limit information flow to those who need to have that data in their possession. Greater information flow does not always equate to success, and "loose lips sink ships." Be mindful of the content that is shared and how much information is released to certain parties.

-Be disciplined. Be moderate with everything. Adopt a 'middle path' and avoid dwelling in or acting to/from extremes. Self-control, restraint, and poise will elicit worthy returns while anything else yields consequences and, in some cases, very ill will from others.

-Apply wisdom judiciously. As a leader, you are responsible for the kingdom. You are tasked with the maintenance and improvement of the realm. A leader need keep a large array of entities, variables, and concepts in mind and resources in hand. Develop the head, heart, and hands in order to apply them sagaciously. Sustain the kingdom with application of worthy behavior and leadership!

-Understand the contrast between fear and love. In the text, *The Prince*, Machiavelli asked whether it was better for a leader to be feared or loved. This text is invaluable for those who are considering entertaining a leadership role. Another necessary text regarding leadership is Sun Tzu's *The Art of War*.

Note that a Queen needs no King in order to have a kingdom, or a vast array of power, resources, and important responsibilities. Examining the precedent of leaders through time guides us in the present. My Queen! Make use of these lessons, and help your kingdom, and team thrive!

Quiet

Quiet is the absence of noise or bustle; it is silence or calmness/tranquility. For this concept, we address both external and internal quiet as well as the necessity and benefit of both. Quiet is remarkably rare. In our communities, it is difficult to escape the human influence of mechanical or technological noise and sounds, generally. Even during nighttime hours, a city will offer but a reduced amount of ambient noise. It is *more* quiet than day, yet that stillness is fleeting and rather temporary, at best. As you focus on quiet, discern the punctuated interruptions during extended moments of silence in your own town or community. It is remarkably difficult to escape the intrusion of man, or the civil arena. Stillness is far more pervasive and nearly complete in the natural world. A distant locale: a forest, a hike out of town, a beach, or a high mountaintop serve as ideal settings in which to experience, enjoy, and make beneficial use of overwhelming quiet.

Quiet is a powerful component of health and regeneration. Quiet can actually help heal the body. This is profound. Noise and ambient stimuli take a toll on our well-being; they amount to a contribution of stress. Quiet facilitates the emergence of new brain cells. Even during rest the brain internalizes and evaluates information. Silence provides our faculties with the opportunity to address the outrageous amount of data that is absorbed by us through the day. The brain is perpetually active. Eliminating just one type of stimuli in the form of sound allows our brains to heal, and digest all that it has backlogged. Providing silence and quiet allows the brain to figure itself out, catch up, and process/perform as it actually should. Quiet relieves stress and tension. Noise and sounds elicit stress hormones. It is even better than relaxing music, which – again - is only more stimuli to process and digest. Finally, silence facilitates our cognitive resources. Researchers investigated how subjects dealt with ambient noise, including airports, trains, and highways. Those near heavy traffic and noisy areas have lower reading scores, and are slower in their development of cognitive and language skills. Brains start to ignore the noise and stress but they also start to ignore important stimuli, too. It is important to recognize how silence allows our brains to decompress and relax its defenses.

External stimuli influence our well-being and internal 'noise' can be detrimental, as well. By internal noise, I mean an overactive brain, or that flow of inane chatter or excessive mental activity that drains our energy and detracts from meaningful endeavors. We have discussed how meditation works well to quiet that stream. Specific breathing techniques complement meditation by coordinating heart and brain waves. All the silence of a sensory deprivation chamber would not be sufficient should the brain/mind be out of control and undisciplined, suffering from a continual stream of 'stuff.' It is necessary to re-center, and master mental focus. Retaining control of ourselves means that we need not be controlled by other externals, either in the form of people/authorities or things like drugs and alcohol. We have at our disposal the means of quieting the mind as we want to and it requires but a few moments of conscious breathing and quiet focus. Numerous techniques are available to still the mind, and applying them on a regular basis facilitates health, balance, presence, and perspective. Utilize those techniques that benefit you and quiet your internal realm in order to remain healthy.

Chapter 18

Race

The concept of race: a category of humankind that shares distinctive physical traits is *the* most divisive aspect of today's United States culture. Race has served to influence cultural practice and mores, institutional methodologies, and domestic social relations, overwhelmingly for the worse. The use of race as a tool of power and hegemony has splintered and fractured this great nation. Racism - the prejudice, discrimination, or antagonism directed against someone of a different race based on the belief that one's own race is superior - is alive and unfortunately well in this country. Racists, those who engage and promote racism, are in nearly every social arena. It is the task, responsibility and *great* opportunity of the people of this great nation to confront, surmount, and eradicate racism, if not the perpetuation of the concept from the culture, should we meaningfully entertain the any hope of thriving as a unified country of self-respecting, dignified individuals.

Educator Jane Elliott conducted an experiment in her elementary school classroom the day after MLK Jr.'s assassination, on April 4, 1968. She separated the students according to the color of their eyes. On a rotating basis, the brown and blue eyed were designated as the superior group between the two. As soon as a group recognized its status, they performed to that level, and, conversely, they treated the other group at their level. Simply, those who were designated as superior and in power performed at a better rate and, what is more telling: they made use of their power to subjugate and demoralize the inferior group. Those who were deemed inferior performed at a lesser level and provided a lesser quality of work. They were so demoralized that they accepted the condition of their inferiority as fact. The lesson: people rise to the level at which they are placed or designated. Give people respect, encouragement, standing, and watch them flourish. The opposite is also true. Demoralize, antagonize, and remove resources from availability or implementation and we would invariably recognize the opposite patterns emerging. The consequences of this have played out at both the objective and subjective level.

This segues to an interesting aspect. Many do *not* grasp how the situation has played out for a variety of reasons. Some may not recognize the cultural/institutional practices that have victimized a significant swath of the people of this nation. Racism affects all people. Racism limits the victim and demonstrates the ignorance of the racist. The conditioning of racism and the posited superiority/inferiority dynamic limits our nation and reduces the prospects of social stability, growth and well-being. Racism uses arbitrary characteristics to distinguish between different classes of people. Skin color is the modus operandi of our nation's racism. Those with a darker hue of skin: anything other than white (!) have been demarcated as a color, instead of honored, revered and protected as meaningful, significant contributors to the United States cultural tapestry. Some 'thinkers' maintain how they are choosing the role of victim, and are perpetuating, if not contributing, to their own degradation willingly. The racist conditioning is pervasive, overwhelming, and nearly total. Elliott referred to it as prenatal. Studies and experiments show that toddlers apply racist methodologies, associating whiteness with goodness, while dark skinned dolls are perceived as bad or lesser beings. Until we recognize that this is intentional, a detriment to the state of the nation, and still in place due to our *own tacit consent*, the presence and consequence of racism will remain and be perpetuated over still more generations.

Racism is intentional. It was and *is* implemented to limit its victims. Its forms have been disguised, made less obvious as public awareness, mindfulness, and participation chased it from its woeful public pedestal. Regrettably, it persists. An unhealthy amount of individuals remain fixed to its disappointing practices. Furthermore, institutions facilitate its continuance. Media, education, and law all contribute to racist ideology. Elliott believes these practices need not be perpetuated and I am inclined to agree. Should we as a nation finally be inclined to coordinate the variables and conditions that elicit racial justice among institutions, we can all enjoy social peace.

Racism divides us. It structures an 'us vs. them' dynamic. This is akin to a rowboat with those applying the oars against one another. This boat is going around in circles and is in danger of capsizing. A house divided against itself can not stand,[22] and this one concept figures most prominently in our deplorable social condition. When we recognize how race, as commonly understood, stands as a divisive factor, and not as a positive, unifying one, we will progress and surmount many other ills. But this progress is a most formidable task. We would need to discard a misconception about race; that involves the mistaken concept of race as predicated by skin color. There is no black, brown, white, yellow race; there is only the human race on this spaceship Earth. We need alleviate the tension of the scene by dispelling the term's association with color.

Melanin is a dark brown to black pigment occurring in the hair, skin, and iris of the eye - both in people and animals. It is responsible for the tanning of the skin exposed to sunlight. It is absolutely ludicrous that we judge and create such consequential rifts based on a mere pigment of skin. This is certainly no rational basis for discrimination, and this is the central point: there is no justifiable basis for its continuation. Racism in the United States is predicated on a nonsensical concept and we are responsible for perpetuating horrendous, disgusting ills of astounding severity over generations. Clinging to such a weak practice demonstrates our pathetic national character. Confronting this issue means grasping this untenable foundation and disregarding it - disabusing its perpetuation - and then identifying the spectrum of similar traits and qualities that connect us as brothers and sisters. The one characteristic separates us when so many other traits could serve to connect us. Remaining attached to merely topical prejudice is most unbecoming, indeed. There is no place for racism in a society that poses much promise, still.

Shakespeare, in *The Merchant of Venice,* offered these words via his character Shylock:
"Hath not a Jew eyes? Hath not a Jew hands, organs, dimensions, senses, affections, passions? Fed with the same food, hurt with the same weapons, subject to the same diseases, healed by the same means, warmed and cooled by the same winter and summer as a Christian is? If you prick us, do we not bleed? If you tickle us, do we not laugh? If you poison us, do we not die? And if you wrong us, shall we not revenge?" We discard the opportunity to connect in lieu of maintaining trivial preferences and biases.

Skin color is but one arbitrary trait among a spectrum of others that effectively serves as an impediment to social wellness. It serves no other purpose but to keep people from uniting under the aegis of greater humanity. We need, in the words, of Elliott, to "get over the color." And that does not mean we need supplant or exchange one form of discrimination for another. The opportunity for growth and development is too great a benefit than to remain dwelling in a somewhat comfortable ignorance. That comfort enjoyed by the 'superior' group will always turn; the scene will be corrected and the conditions will shift. It is far better to revise this course now before even greater consequences are elicited by maintaining a status quo in such a disastrous equation.

What manager, team captain, or head of a household would consider it wise to handicap parts of a company, team, or family, and still cling to an empty hope of a positive, inclusive, and comprehensive, rewarding outcome? This situation can not end well and the context only serves those who gain by the separation of the people. A unified fraternity - a brotherhood of man - is a serious threat to those who wield power and it is the *only* effective means of this country's betterment and ultimate survival.

Elliott states, "Prejudice is an emotional commitment to ignorance." We cling to the prejudice of racism because we have all been conditioned to conform. We conform to evil. Racism is a plague on our country and among all nations. I repeat the term 'we' because it is our responsibility to adjust the situation. We need not rely on government for we *are* the government. We need revise media, for we are its masters. We need reform education, for we know what is best for our communities. We hold the reins, and we can behave wisely, and well, or we use those same reins to steer *all of us* off a steep cliff. That eventual fall will prove most painful and fatal to all. Elliott instructed her students to memorize the Sioux Indian Prayer:

"Oh great spirit, keep me from judging a man until I've walked a mile in his moccasins."

We have been taught to accept this pervasive script: that a group of people is inferior to another. That narrative has never served a valid, positive communal purpose. Conscious and persistent application of the golden rule is the only way forward. Simply, do to others what you would have them do to you, and conversely: do not do to others what you do not want them doing to you. We would be most hard pressed to agree to the terms and conditions that African Americans, or people of color, have to suffer and endure, so why are they burdened? They shoulder the consequences of a gross application of power. But that predicament is unnecessary and dynamic; this situation is not permanent - the scene, can, will, MUST change if we are to experience improved circumstances.

Ending racism starts with education. We are tasked with leading people out of ignorance. Elliott contends that we can eliminate racism in less than two generations. Persistence makes a genuine and marked difference. Elliott's experiment works and we need repeat its lessons and make them resound in the schools, in the media, and have them enshrined by law and government. The change needs begin at the individual level. We need recognize the potential good in every man, regardless of skin color. A white, black, brown, red or yellow: any person - can behave well, honorably, and with compassion and benevolence in his heart and mind, despite what a proffered narrative supposes. We need focus on the character of the individual, in lieu of topical approaches (i.e., skin color).

Color is no designation of quality.

We need rethink society, and sidestep, if not succinctly eliminate *any* limited racist narrative. We must not be constrained by something so ineffectual, negative, and divisive. We are at a juncture where we can structure and implement new, inclusive, positive norms. It is time to make a reasoned and passionate commitment to justice and peace. The way forward is based on self-respect and respect for others. Empathy, forgiveness, and unity need light the way should we be serious about surviving and thriving as a human race.

Rationality

The quality of being based on or in accordance with reason, or logic, is rationality. It is also synonymous with reasonableness. Different thinkers among different societies in time have conceptualized items in profoundly different terms. Rationality, like justice, is one of those concepts that have been addressed in a variety of ways. A great many disparate approaches have been utilized and, still, there is no set standard in place other than the one that is applied per specific realm. Concepts of rationality and justice are as fixed as the communities of which they are a part.

While people apply different structures of rationality, the subjective aspect of the concept (an individual's own rationality, or rational approach) is of particular significance. A personal model of rationality need take the public realm or the role/presence of others into consideration. An obvious exception to this would be if an individual elected to be a reclusive hermit, eschewing all forms of human interaction. Because this is a far extreme; it is highly unlikely to be the standard. We live in a remarkably small world, and human interaction is the norm, for better or worse. One's sense of reasonableness need afford others the opportunity of participation and coordination. In simple terms, in a public realm, one need be understood. A structure of rationality need be grasped by one another for matters of security, coordination, and acceptance. If others could not identify the rational nature of one's behavior, they would be ill at ease, if not suspicious and insecure. For cooperative endeavors to be enjoyed, much less realized, or achieved successfully, individuals must employ a publicized rationale that is comprehensible. When basic rationality is lost or missing, acceptance is very hard to come by. How can individuals accept one another, or an individual in a group, if the means by which they make sense of the world is unintelligible or nonsensical? We need a basic, shared sense of rationality in order to live amongst others in a community. We require rationality to engage in cooperative endeavors. Otherwise, the contrast is a reality akin to that of Alice in Wonderland, or the very worst of debauched existences. How can we live together sans significant portions of a shared rationality?

A consistent rationality is discerned or identified when elements of an activity, sentence, or scene overlap and interact as they so often do. Values underlie behavior. Values demand consistency, else we question and critique the model or presentation offered. As a quick example:

-Michael departs for the store, as he is hungry. He desires to obtain the means of making a meal upon his return home.

We have a subject, Michael. We note the reason for his departure to the store, his hunger. His devised goal is the procurement of ingredients so he can fix for himself a meal later, thereby satisfying his hunger. However much fun the following sentence was to write, it remains an irrational contrast to the preceding, concerning Michael's exciting trip to the store:

-Rogen flown to breadbasket he will, while she to the dome did knock.

There is no rationality to the preceding statement. At least one subject has been identified, but Rogen is a sticking point. Identified as something important by capitalization of the name, we do not know who or what they are, specifically. Pronouns and verb tense are skewed and meaning is lost to everyone save the writer (and even then, I outdid myself with this one).

Concepts of rationality, again: like that of justice, have been addressed by thinkers including Homer, Aristotle, Kant, and Hume. Their conceptualizations comprise intellectual, historical precedent for ideas that followed. While an objective standard has not been achieved nor agreed upon, the subjective sense of rationality is absolutely necessary for those desiring to live in a community of similar, rational individuals. A rationalization is the action or attempting to explain or justify behavior or an attitude with logical reasons, even if these are not appropriate. Rationalizations are generally subjectively offered, though quite often objectively denied, negated, or refused. While reasons offered by an individual may make sense for *them*, it remains to be seen whether those same reasons will be accepted as an external audience or community. Radically subjective rationalizations tend to alienate individuals from a group should they be exclusive, or pertinent only to the individual issuing them. By contrast, a rationale speaks to that wider community, is inclusive, and is more readily accepted because of its general pertinence and applicability. As you apply rationality and make use of rationales and or rationalizations, keep your external world and immediate community in mind. You are not a solipsist, living in your own world, alone. Your success and well-being are predicated on the involvement and presence of so many other individuals and entities. Make space for the considerate involvement by behaving rationally and inclusively…within reason.

Reading

The importance of the action or skill of reading written or printed matter silently or aloud can not be overemphasized. The activity is an overwhelmingly positive one for several reasons. An active brain, one stimulated by reading, creates and forms images. Mental stimulation produces the very behavior a brain is meant for: thinking. Thinking is exercise. So, essentially, reading builds the brain. Interestingly enough, it stimulates the same neurological regions as those piqued by actual 'lived' experience in the real world. Reading literature provides a workout for complex cognitive functions, while pleasure reading increases blood flow.

Foreign language reading *really* challenges the brain. Engaging stories encourage the brain to move linearly and proceed via a structure. White matter in the brain, the area that serves as relays - coordinating communication for different brain regions - grows with reading. Reading increases memory, with poetry being a powerful tool. It reduces stress more than drinking tea, or even listening to music! Reading increases empathy for characters, and also for characters in the real world.

This is the central importance of reading: it facilitates and contributes to a well-lived life. This is predicated by what one reads. Seek sources that convey concepts and ideas from 500 years ago, if not from ancient times. Structuring a broad based, multi-disciplinary education of the world's great basic ideas will allow you to identify a preferred realm of study for specialization. The more we experience, investigate and explore the lasting, time tested ideas offered by the greats, the more we benefit.

Trite expressions of popular notions and sentiments do not build valuable skills or poignant perspective.

We grow by grasping, understanding significant precedent and then building on that material with meaningful contributions of our own. These contributions are significant, largely, when structured upon the foundations of ideas that have demonstrated their merits and value by lasting the test of time. Original, standalone creation is a marvelous feat, and - of course! - encouraged.

Reading allows us to connect with people, places, and things. We can empathize when we grasp the spectrum of actions. A remarkable array of titles facilitates that understanding. Seek the greats! Explore ancient titles, and thinkers! Delve into the classics, which are categorized as such for a very particular reason. Plato and Aristotle, for example, have stood the test of time, and still impart significant concepts for discussion. The lessons imparted by Thucydides, Herodotus, and Cicero are as pertinent today as they were thousands of years ago. The texts belonging to the realms of Philosophy, religion, and certain elements of fiction all offer a remarkable array of concepts that facilitate our growth and development. Read and engage those works that have guided different people across ages and cultures. You will never be led wrong so long as you engage critically - with discernment and a keen eye. Read often and much, and explore the characters, plots, and writers that have provided humanity with inspiring titles. Add to that body of work by building on the back of precedent and offer something that is every bit as remarkable so as to make an important, positive difference that stands the test of time.

Real, Reality

The world, or the state of things as they actually exist, or: having existence or substance, is what is known as being real, or having/being reality. The question of what is real is the study of being: ontology. It pertains to metaphysics and the investigation of being, existence, and reality. These studies are elicited by the questions raised by prominent thinkers in ancient times. Pre-Socratic thinkers wrestled with ideas that have paved the way for dense, complex discussions that have yielded only more complex questions and investigation. Today, we still grapple with ideas concerning life and what exists, or what is real. Some thinkers contend that we are simulations in a software program, or in a reality of artificial intelligence. Others contend that we have no basis to assume that we are anything more than brains in a vat.

Various sources shape and influence how we view the 'real' world. Philosophy, religion, our families, friends, and the media all contribute to our understanding of how the world exists and operates. What is truly fascinating is how our knowledge base is expanding. We have completely revised our perspective on the brain over the course of the last ten years. Since our understanding of ourselves is not yet firmly in-hand, it stands to reason that there remains elements of perception that are also likely to be amended and revised. How can we grasp the external world when our own self - the internal world - is in a state of flux and uncertainty? That we change our minds and continue to learn new things does not mean that there can be no certainty about how things are or what can be known to exist in our lives. The lesson here is that an open mind facilitates the flow of ideas and variables and allows us to proceed with an engaged perspective - instead of one mired or anchored by static belief, dogma, or preconceived notions.

When we consider the electro-magnetic spectrum, we see less than *1/10 billionth* of what is actually there. That percentage is visible light. Everything else is invisible to us. Even if we accept what we perceive as true, there is more occurring than what meets our eye, or even the rest of our faculties. Returning to our discussion of the quanta and quantum mechanics, we perceive an energy exchange - quantification - and it creates an individual reference point unique to each observer. So how did observation exist or what kind of entity created a reality that can be shaped by different minds? The questions of reality are, as of yet far from answered concretely, with certainty. A particular joy in life lies in grappling with these notions and trying to come to our own terms as to what is occurring and real. Engage vivaciously and enjoy the investigation!

Receptive

Being willing to consider and/or accept new suggestions and ideas is being receptive. The opposite of being receptive is being close-minded, or rigidly dogmatic. When one closes their mind to new ideas, or experiences, they lose the opportunity to engage, learn and grow. Being receptive provides the opportunity for enrichment, for experience, for lessons! It is so very important to maintain an open mind, to be welcome to what is conveyed. That does not mean that every idea need be accepted. It means that it need be considered and weighed before judgment is passed. As an analogy, we consider the consumption of food. While we may have established preferences, we would be wise to expand our horizons and try new things. The same holds true of the arts, in the form of music or different genres of performance. Ideas need be considered and entertained in order to shape and develop character. Remain open to opportunities for growth and development. Do not exclude options in the name of fear, laziness, ignorance, or prejudice. Remain curious and be willing to engage the barrage of new information, people, and opportunities that are sure to come your way.

Relationship

Relationship is the state of being connected…and *everything* is connected. It is remarkable to grasp how things are related. We might focus on the pertinence of social relationships, be they family members, generations, or larger social groups among a community. But relationships can pertain to even broader concepts, including space/proximity, time, and ideas. We discover that even the most tangential occurrences can connect and be in relationship with radically disparate, seemingly unconnected matters. The discussion of how entities, or concepts and ideas overlap includes a review of some aspects of chaos theory, relativity, and some social 'science.'

I note how this concept could amount to volumes, indeed. We might start at one end of the spectrum to utilize Carl Sagan's consideration how we are all elements of the stars and contain a portion of the greater elemental reality among possible realities and dimensions. We might address another end of the spectrum and begin by listing mere terrestrial connections. Distilling that total conversation, we find out how chemistry, culture, and so many variables connect to provide the space/time contexts for instances of relationship. A young man in Indiana is in a relationship with an impoverished child in Thailand due to consumptive habits. A young woman worshipping Allah in Brazil is in a relationship of faith just as the individual on sojourn to Mecca is. An individual's preferences for food, style, and expression connect to myriad others in remarkably diverse ways. Those who share specific modes of thought bridge the divide of distance across eons. These relationships are remarkably fluid. Preferences change, affiliations develop, and habits turn with the winds. Relationships begin and end due to mortality and a persistent, dynamic flux of ever transforming variables. Relationships can be tenuous, or most significant, held most dear. The Indianan might have no consideration for his relationship with those who make his food, music, or clothing, while those who are in relationship with a pen-pal, a business supplier, or a lover might nurture and seek to maintain those dynamics.

The care and consideration of relationships involves elements of mindfulness and a diverse array of resources and variables. Mindfulness is most applicable. When we grasp how inter-connected and related we ALL are: animal, mineral, and vegetable, we can extend more consideration, care, and respect for self and others - sentient or not. The idea of the butterfly effect is pertinent here. This is a concept of chaos theory that posits how the absolute smallest change or general action can elicit monumental changes in the remarkably complex web of relationships across the world, if not multiverses, should we again take the contents of the quanta into consideration. The saying: "a butterfly in Brazil can cause a tornado in Texas" is certainly not literally true but the elements of relationship can be slight yet still prove most consequential. The significance of elements can be realized even after decades have passed. Consider the gravity of ideas. Perhaps a string of thought is grasped only after the singular, lone mind is able to grasp and run with it. It is interesting to note how this is *such* a rare, extreme analogy, given technological levels and the wherewithal of minds across the globe. But we still have yet to come to terms with *much* of what has been offered by mystics, philosophers, and sages we have still to recognize as pertinent or even poignant. Consider the work of Edward Leedskalnin and his notebook! The man inexplicably moved tonnage of rock in Florida, and his notebook that details his work and processes amounts to the level of, seemingly, an illiterate child.

In 1929, Frigyes Karinthy presented the idea of six degrees of separation. It holds that all living things, and *everything else in the world,* are six or fewer steps away from each other so that a chain of "a friend of a friend" statements can be made to connect any two people in a maximum of six steps. This means that your encounter with a postman can have relevance, perhaps, to a transaction in New Delhi in the not-too-distant future. Our actions - all actions, for that matter - amount to a consequence that affects the bonds of relationships across incredibly diverse continuums and contexts. Gauge your initiatives and think beyond the immediate present to offer lasting value. Also, that we have good intentions amounts to precious little, given the overlap of variables, from one side of a limited linear spectrum, as opposed to a multi-dimension model of even broader consequential concepts. Nurturing and maintaining relationships, like all other behaviors, has an opportunity cost. Something is always excluded at the expense of electing or prioritizing another activity, person, etc. Consider your values and principles, apply an inclusive, beneficial perspective, and strive to attend to a greater reality beyond the scope of the immediate behavior, or context at hand.

Relief

Relief is a feeling of reassurance, relaxation following release from anxiety or distress. It can be assistance in the form of food, clothing, or money given to those in special need or difficulty. It can be the release from bondage, or the intake of a large, deep and full breath. A good joke can spell relief from the flow of business, politics, and everyday routine. Relief can be the sight of a friend, the approach of an affectionate puppy, or the gentle caress of the summer wind. Relief takes many forms, according to the individual in need. What one offers as relief may not address the needs/wants of the person experiencing distress or shouldering a burden. This concept may amount to a short entry but its pertinence can not be minimized. You will mean relief to someone in need.

Strive to identify then seek the relief that addresses the cause of discomfort. Relief that addresses mere symptoms amounts to a superficial band-aid approach. Meaningful relief eliminates root cause of the underlying malady that elicits the tears, frustration, and hardship. Go deeper! Be critical enough to address the substantive issues at play. As for applying relief, you do not need to uncover the underlying reason for the woes of others. That is the responsibility of the sufferer. Your aid might be offered from a critical perspective and address their issue. However, it may not amount to the meaningful solution they need or want. Offer yourself in ways that are positive.

You make a difference by extending yourself with authentic care and concern.

Sometimes that succor will be in something as simple as eye contact, a quick touch, a text message, or even better: a phone call.

When you offer yourself, offer without the hope for reward. Engage authentically, openly, and with a view towards applying your own skills, person, and magic. When you engage with presence, your offering will spell relief because it is positive and well intentioned. Being your best self is a relief that others, and the wider world, can grasp and appreciate.

Renaissance

Between the 14th and 17th centuries, a rediscovery of ancient Greece and Rome led to the cultural rebirth of Europe. It was known as the Renaissance, which means rebirth or awakening. While an individual can be a renaissance man, for the purposes of this entry we focus principally on a broader renaissance, the need for a cultural rebirth in the United States. Briefly, then, concerning the subjective renaissance: Given the spectacular flow of information via the world wide web, we have access to the near totality of human history transmitted by fiber optic cables that are less than an eighth the diameter of a human hair. In light of the data available, the recurrence of whistle blowers, releases of previously unavailable, guarded, privileged information, and the discoveries of scientists and prominent thinkers, we are besieged by variables that are eliciting the motivation for a broader change of objective circumstances and subjective behaviors. Simply, the standards of behavior and activity are perceived to be in need of drastic revision. This applies equally at the subjective *and* objective levels. We touched on the work of Soren Kierkegaard earlier. He contended how an individual will reach a plateau and feel the pressing need to improve: immediately. This urge to increase/improve our level, our person is an important and dramatic one. For the time comes when the old customs and methodologies no longer offer sufficient rewards or meaningful benefits.

Ignoring that urge is a dangerous affair. For the void left by not implementing meaningful change can be filled by vacuous externals like drugs, alcohol, and sex. Or the individual retards growth and progress by living a life guided by cognitive dissonance, the state of having inconsistent thoughts, beliefs, or attitudes, especially as relating to behavioral decisions and attitude change. We are the only being that can elect to stagnate. Animals and vegetables grow and develop. Humans - all too often - elect to take the easy route of stagnation and escapism. Growth is a difficult path and maybe even a painful one. But what is more painful is not reaching potential, or ignoring the very best encouragement of one's head, heart, and hands.

We ***ALL*** receive the opportunity, encouragement, or the 'cosmic' invitation to develop, or pursue the challenging path of introspection. To be guided by the thought of improvement, changed circumstances, and a revitalized self is invigorating. Hence, when people recognize the merit of posited benefits, they engage new methodologies and behaviors meaningfully in order to realize that personal renaissance, or rebirth. We are meant to grow, to reach for the sun, in order to realize and fulfill amazing potential. I entreat and encourage you to pursue the personal calling that will elicit your personal renaissance. Be receptive as to information and heed the urge to grow! Listen to your inner voice and abide by that highest, best calling in order to develop and perform as only you can.

My friend Matt Piper posted a list of subjective shortcomings that he identified as remaining under the control or authority of the self. In light of a spate of recent school shootings, the list was the product of his investigation as to why people are taking such initiative against their peers. His inquiry produced the following list of qualities:

-lack of meaning
-pathological self-consciousness
-lack of presence
-lack of success or acknowledgement of success
-lack of authenticity   -repression of the shadow
-lack of perception of personal value
-lack of organization
-identification with negative personal narrative
-lack of physical strength/robustness
-lack of self confidence   -lack of connection

The subjects on the list are items for discussion in another text, perhaps. But what gives rise to such behavior is a combination of personal agency, or initiative and cultural/communal failings. The responsibility of individuals can not be diminished, but the importance of their culture is spectacularly important. An individual, and people, can not and WILL NOT behave well should positive behavior not be prioritized, modeled, and encouraged by the greater cultural community. Our culture is failing us and the world. Values underlie behavior, and the values we model are disappointing. How this culture - writ large, as the United States - behaves has significant consequences for both domestic people and the international community. In short, we adhere to standards and conditions that give rise to ignorant, close-minded people that are ill in the head, heart, and hands.

Just as individuals are recognizing the need to improve their own subjective condition, so, too, do they recognize that the present standard of culture is not keeping pace to serve the needs of its people. The people are on the verge of a new American renaissance. *We* are nearing the occasion/event/time where the fetters of the system will prove too onerous to bear. In order for an objective renaissance to occur, individuals need first awaken and engage a remarkably different path than the one provided by their culture and community. This is significantly difficult, were it not for the ability of the people to discern and coordinate to implement viable, meaningful alternatives. What the establishment offers pales in comparison to the vibrant and healthy array of available alternatives. This text is meant to counter the conditions that give rise to the concepts enumerated on my friend's list. By starting with terms, motivated individuals can work on personal application. The emergence of respect for self and others will gain momentum and petty tribalism can be eclipsed by a meaningful standard of care and consideration for one another. We will experience, benefit from, and enjoy an American renaissance when we care for ourselves. A component of self-care lies in inclusivity. It is only through caring for others that we can fully and completely care for our own selves.

We will elicit an American renaissance with a new ethos. When the people elect to cease trite squabbles, the pertinent sectors, or cultural institutions of education, media, government, law, economics, food and water, etc. can be rearranged to benefit and serve the highest and best good for all involved. Until *we* decide that we are worth that monumental effort and investment in our self, we will continue to shoulder the burdens of an ill culture and subject ourselves and our communities to unnecessary suffering.

Respect

Respect is the positive feeling or action shown towards someone or something considered important or held in high esteem or regard. It is a sense of admiration for good or valuable qualities and it is also the process of honoring someone or something by exhibiting care, concern, or consideration for their needs and feelings. It comes from the Latin *respectus,* which means to look back at or regard. Throughout this text, it is advised to have respect for self and other. But what does that mean, precisely? With respect, we note two linguistic roots, that of re-, and - spect. To apply that, then: respect involves looking at/inspecting self and others multiple times. It means applying a considerate and forgiving perspective, for the repeated inspection, or regarding of the subject/object, or the self and other will yield different results and a greater understanding. A crucial part of this discussion concerns the necessity and primacy of self-respect and how it makes respecting others and receiving the respect of others possible.

Self-respect has significant overlap with the concept of self-esteem. One has or builds self-esteem by caring for one's self and behaving appropriately. The concept of propriety is again (and always) at play. A self-respecting individual cares enough about their person to dress well, practice proper hygiene and grooming, and offer behavior and language that match the context, if not set the tone and standard for the situation! What an individual consumes is a demarcation of values, and how/if they respect their own person. For if an individual is immoderate, they could hardly be considered as disciplined or exercising self-control. Further, if they ate only fast food and unhealthy snacks, they would demonstrate a lack of regard for their greater well-being. Self-respect has connections with other items that are consumed. We devour and digest media, style, and other cultural preferences and components. How does one say they are self-respecting since/if they consume or engage practices that limit or degrade the greater intellectual, emotional, or physical condition? An overwhelming number of individuals take in stupefying amounts of mind-numbing television, hand-held device distractions, as well as entertainment that only delivers comfort and escape. Since we are what we digest (or even engage), how can these 'products' (us!) be of superior quality?

Self-respect is synonymous with self-ownership. It involves being in the world and living a life of implemented good practices. We note how individuals can not respect themselves if particularly bad behavior is offered, as in the case of a foul-mouthed drunk, perhaps. Self-respect is born of good habits. Aristotle noted how the virtuous individual was a creature of habit. Being honest, being accountable, and maintaining personal integrity builds self-respect. When this initiative is begun, and then structured to be a routine, both self-esteem and self-respect are elicited. Putting the self to work with diligence and dedication - having faith in the outcome, regardless of consequences - yields worthy rewards. Maintaining principles, doing what is right and good, even in the face of significant contrast or opposition: an individual who does not share the same values, or mores, delivers a significant sense of self-worth and positive development. This is most important. Paralleling the previous discussion of dignity, self-respect should never be satisfied for a temporary gain. Maintaining principles can be difficult; opposition to your developed sense of morality, ethics, and self-worth/image can be most severe.

Values underlie behavior. We demonstrate a significant disregard for our own self-respect. The seven pillars of influence within a society are recognized as government, the family, business, media, education, religion, and science. Together, these significant institutions comprise the bedrock of our culture. They coordinate, if not interact and overlap, to provide the rules and standards for society. Examining them piecemeal reveals how they act independently, much to the contrary of an idea of self-respect.

-A government is structured to limit and control its human resources. The state seeks to provide oversight of its wards while being powerful enough to commit egregious trespasses and overreach of its power against human rights and violate individual sovereignty.

-The family is not inviolable: it is liable to be broken, infringed or dishonored. The family, all too often, is a product of happenstance; it is not the product of careful planning or shared values. That the 'broken' family is the norm means that it is an accepted standard, or the desired form or level of relationship.

-Business is exclusive and predatory. The market system is structured for the few at the expense and exclusion of the greater portion of the audience, both objectively and subjectively. How can people respect themselves when their lives amount to common ingredients of an economic machination run by those who care little for the proper treatment or representation of human resources?

-Media offers a portrayal and representation of values. Consider what it models. The standards are comprised largely of strife, warfare, and scarcity. In the modeled spectrum of possibilities, we are provided limits instead of ideals, oppression instead of opportunities.

-Education is a farcical misnomer. It is anything but and, hence, should properly be identified as cultural or institutional indoctrination. Public education is a factory of ignorance and conformity instead of an honorable setting that elevates as it educates its people.

-Western Religion is faux spirituality by authority. Its power is based on submission and conformity to ideals and rules that are largely empty, false, and detractions from what is whole, holy, attainable, and good.

-Science is the benchmark by which numerous realms and settings are structured. It provides the facts by which specialized realms are arrayed. The paradigm of science guides living systems of water, food, biology, electricity, the quanta, and, importantly: the remarkable overlap and connections between seemingly unconnected disparate studies and areas. That science is under the direct supervision and control of government powers is problematic at best.

Taken singularly, the seven pillars operate in separate realms performing disparate operations and providing different functions. Together, they are our culture and society. They can *only* limit individuals because that is their intended goal. As discussed earlier, an active, engaged, critical populace can not and will not acquiesce to the constraints imposed upon them by an inferior ruling party, class, or structure. But there is but a slim representation of self-respect demonstrated by the constituency. Too distracted from priorities by crumbs and baubles, we settle on our present condition and state of affairs. A self-respecting audience would recognize the system (and its components) for what it is and strive to reform it, post-haste.

"Cages. Consider a birdcage. If you look very closely at just one wire in the cage, you cannot see the other wires. If your conception of what is before you is determined by this myopic focus, you could look at that one wire, up and down the length of it, and be unable to see why a bird would not just fly around the wire any time it wanted to go somewhere. Furthermore, even if, one day at a time, you myopically inspected each wire, you still could not see why a bird would have trouble going past the wires to get anywhere. There is no physical property of any one wire, nothing that the closest scrutiny could discover, that will reveal how a bird could be inhibited or harmed by it except in the most accidental way. It is only when you step back, stop looking at the wires one by one, microscopically, and take a macroscopic view of the whole cage, that you can see why the bird does not go anywhere; and then you will see it in a moment. It will require no great subtlety of mental powers. It is perfectly obvious that the bird is surrounded by a network of systematically related barriers, no one of which would be the least hindrance to its flight, but which, by their relations to each other, are as confining as the solid walls of a dungeon."

"Oppression", in *Politics Of Reality – Essays In Feminist Theory* (1983)

A crucial aspect or component of self-respect is the practice of treating one's self as a valued investment. The future 'you' will mature and pay dividends after investment and work is tended. When an individual believes in the promise of the improved, better self, they put forth the resources such that the return on the investment is sufficient if not awe-inspiring and overwhelming. The self-respecting individual views the future self as worth the work, and will view that product as a worthy endeavor. Self-respect affords the perspective of the long-view. Tomorrow can, and will be better if the resources are distributed, delegated, and applied. Another significant element of self-respect involves reciprocity. Someone who has self-respect will treat others the way they wish to be treated. That means that every other person, regardless of role, age, background, etc., is treated with dignity, civility, care and concern. Respect need be earned, but compassionate civility is the fundamental hallmark of a self-respecting adult. The respect of and for others is remarkably intertwined with the concept of self-respect. It is challenging to confront opposing standards, much less a social standard that seems structured against the realization of an individual's self-respect and greater comprehensive flourishing. So, too, is it very unsettling, or most disappointing, to betray your own values and worth. Build and develop self-respect by doing good in the world. Care for yourself; structure good habits and perform worthy actions that elicit a strong sense of virtue. When that sentiment is present, a meaningful confidence is formed. Respecting ourselves enables us to engage the world with our own powerful self-image. A sense of one's self worth - one not formed of arrogance or narcissism - elicits acknowledgement in the greater world.

People respond to individuals when they carry themselves with a dignified air. That is to say, they respond better to those with self-respect and a refined punctilio. Else, to the individual who is lacking in hygiene, scruples, bearing, and propriety, only a passing glance is usually all that is afforded. Why should an individual lacking self-respect receive anything more? It is enough to merely recognize poor form. It is, in some cases, too much to engage or encourage its continuance. Interestingly, respect is now commonly equivocated with the term 'recognition.' People demand respect when it is recognition they seek. People can certainly demand respect of others but it is a hollow demand. For, again, respect is not a given - it is earned.

Consider again the definition of the term. Not everything is due respect because not everything is held in high regard or recognized as of high quality. It is the same with art. If every creation is honored, there is no distinction between higher and lesser forms. So, only those people that exhibit good or valuable qualities deserve the honor of respect. Extending it to everything demeans and lessens its meaning. We should not - can not - respect everything or everyone. People are due recognition as human beings, and their civil and human rights need be protected, but their specific character and behaviors will deserve criticism, if not confrontation, upon certain encounters and interactions. Pertinent to the encounter with other individuals, only a person with self-respect can offer and supply the concept of respect meaningfully. For they recognize the demonstration of similar regard presented by general behavior and activities.

The converse is true of respect bestowed upon you by others. Again, respect is a commodity, earned by an especially hallowed regard for self and good/valuable qualities. To be respected means to be worthy, honorable, disciplined, and principled. It is neither because you simply exist nor because you demand it mistakenly. Receiving respect is an honor, for someone of similar regard and quality recognizes your distinctly dignified bearing and standard of behavior. When you are sufficiently worthy to receive respect, strive to continue if not improve upon the same standard of activity that earned it in the first place.

The incorrect and liberal use of the term has diminished the meaning of the word respect. Still, the presence of the concept is as pertinent and necessary as it ever was. Respect for the self is primary and is elicited by self-control and the ability to recognize worthy, good, and honorable behavior and presentation. Respect for others follows the same guidelines: people are worthy of respect by earning it, not for mere existence or presence. The respect paid to you from others means something if and only if they demonstrate a similar regard for themselves. As a standard, strive to be worthy of respect; and associate with those capable of self-respect. That aspect of respect as looking again pertains to judgment. Simply: do not rush judgment. Take the time to consider your own behaviors as well as the motivations, ethos, and behaviors of others. Taking time provides perspective and that allows for a more considerate opinion of self and others. Rushing to judgment is disrespectful. Instead form an opinion after a second (third, fourth, and fifth...) view of the concept or object at hand. A better estimation will almost always be the result; this is an invaluable aid.

Responsibility

A responsibility is a state or fact of having a duty to deal with something. Being responsible also means to be accountable or to blame. A duty is a moral or legal obligation. It refers to something that needs to be done and specifically: something you need do. We all have responsibilities. We need care for ourselves and maintain a healthy balance within our head, heart, and hands. We need structure a set of abilities that will help us make our way - by making a living, but more so: by living a meaningful and joyous life. While we aim for joy and significance, we will be tethered to responsibility. We will need to do certain activities we do not enjoy. Such is life: c'est la vie - though the satisfaction of responsibility is immensely positive. As we complete tasks or eliminate items from the ever-expanding list of things to do, we build character. We establish ourselves as mature, capable individuals. Through the barrage and balance of responsibilities, we present ourselves as those who have emerged as independent, self-sufficient adults. Responsibility provides the opportunity to shape character and to test our mettle and demonstrate quality, or who we are. Our priorities become clear by how we prioritize one task over another. The manner in which we address and/or surmount those obligations displays our sense of self-respect and other personal values.

Your acceptance and satisfaction of responsibility will feed, clothe, and house you. It will deliver self-esteem and prioritize preferences, as previously mentioned. A balance need be struck between those activities that you shoulder of your own accord and those tasks that are assigned, or put to you. Some responsibilities are given as a show of confidence in your person and abilities. Your Mother and I trust you, and recognize your ability to handle an increasing number of complex tasks in the house. A boss might note similar qualities and give you more authority, and responsibility. Still others might want to make opportunistic use of your abilities and present responsibilities as if they are uniquely and solely yours to address. One can imagine an association, club, or committee delegating and distributing responsibilities, activities, and tasks. As stated earlier, accept what you can handle and avoid becoming over-extended. Handle your responsibility. When you accept responsibility, carry it through until its final end. Finally, be accountable. Take the responsibility if you are at fault, or to blame for a mistake or transaction.

All too often people disregard responsibility. I am guilty of it, too. Some people rationalize how a task is for someone else, or that it is beneath them. The balance between rights and responsibilities, or play and work, is an important one. Addressing responsibility, or work, first, delivers rewards. Commit to the work. Shoulder the responsibility so that the play, or the enjoyment of the rights has more meaning, value, and consequence. From my own personal experience, sacrificing in the name of greater responsibility yields meaningful returns. Not owning up, or refusing to be accountable, elicits pain and hardship for self and others. Address your responsibilities so others need not be burdened by your failing to do so.

Consider when a doctor uses his medical hammer to strike the body to elicit a reaction. He is testing your physical reflexes by striking your knee, for example. Your body involuntarily reacts to the strike. It is a physical activity sans thought or planning. This action is the polar opposite of a response, which is intentionally considered, borne of balance, mindfulness. Only a slight portion of catalysts deserves an instinctual, base reaction. The greater percentage of events and occurrences in our lives require, instead, a response. It is our ability to respond well and ably that distinguishes us from the rest of the animal kingdom. We are biologically wired to offer rational, deliberate, and measured behavior. When we exercise responsibility, we are engaging a crucial aspect of ourselves. We know that we will be greeted with, challenged, and beset by numerous external occasions of *all* types. We need perform to the standard of willing and able, mature and balanced individuals. We ably respond, or demonstrate responsibility, by addressing whatever we encounter with fortitude, balance, and mindfulness. Such an approach will elicit better circumstances while you interact with the world.

Rest

Rest is repose, or sleep, but is also comprised by an amalgamation of any physical, spiritual, intellectual, or emotional practice that spells relief for an individual. Our adrenal system is responsible for our stress mitigation. It is located on top of the kidneys and is tied to both the sympathetic and parasympathetic nervous systems. Adrenals react via the flight or fight instinct. While stress can be born of a lack of conditioned processing measures, stress is also a very real external. Weather is one example. Hence, there will always be stress to address. In our society, our adrenals systems are burdened, and taxed unnecessarily, even overloaded. We do not have sufficient rest to recuperate and heal from the adverse affects and consequences of our culture. In short, our culture eats us alive. So, rest is absolutely essential in our lives.

Rest is a remarkably subjective practice. While we all need sufficient hours of sleep, what constitutes relief and the significant means of health vary per individual.

Knowing your own self, and your subjective needs is absolutely necessary.

Without integral self-knowledge, one lives as a buoy, ceaselessly barraged and battered by waves on the ocean. [23] Stress mitigation and balance are critical components of health. Healthy individuals will identify and implement methodologies that contribute to their recuperation and development. Physical, spiritual, intellectual, and emotional coping mechanisms facilitate rest and health. Individuals engage yoga, attend the gym, or address responsibility/work as rest. Some meditate or pray. Others read or complete crossword puzzles. Watching a movie or listening to music can also be soothing, and provide a rest. Should independent methodologies lack appeal, consider coordinating with someone. Sharing time, holding hands, snuggling/cuddling, and engaging intimately can heal and constitute more on that diverse spectrum of rest.

Rest is a necessary ingredient of health, and it amounts to much more than sleep, and a lack of activity. In our society, there is little time for rest. As we must attend to consequential economic and social concerns, all too often we minimize the importance of rest if not disregard this all too important activity, altogether. We live in what passes for a hummingbird society: we fly to eat and eat in order to fly. Yet this is not a necessary condition. We can – we *must* - prioritize personal health and balance in order to live productive and meaningful lives. Failing to do so equates to ignoring crucial, necessary aspects of self-maintenance and preservation. Rest allows our head, heart, and hands to digest the contents and events of our lives. It is absolutely necessary to rest and replenish our stores of energy and savor other precious resources, like time, thoughts, sentiments, and physical activities.

Repayment

Repayment is paying someone back, typically for a loan, but it can also refer to other forms of compensation. We can repay someone's kindness or their demonstration of care, consideration, or respect. It is important to address and satisfy one's financial responsibilities and obligations, and it is essential to recognize and return the favor of good, kind treatment. We are not due respect or even civility. But sometimes individuals will offer a standard that absolutely outstrips or exceeds the established paradigm or routine. It is just to acknowledge those rare occasions and, what is more: to repay that exemplification of the Good. Repaying someone for their initiative demonstrates not only recognition and respect for their original initiative - it demonstrates self-respect, as well, for taking kindness in stride, sans acknowledgement, is gross entitlement and poor form, indeed. A simple 'thank you' is sufficient in the moment. Returning the kindness, or performing a similar action to another is a good way of perpetuating care and concern in your immediate context or scene. Oftentimes we will receive rewards born of the actions of others, only we will not have the opportunity to personally recognize or thank them. 'Paying it forward' is when a beneficiary (someone receiving a good deed) repays it to others instead of the original benefactor. This can be implemented with loans as well as good deeds. A creditor can offer the debtor the option of paying the debt forward by lending it to a third person instead of paying it back to the original creditor. Debt and payments can be monetary or by good deeds. Repayment, regardless of form, needs fulfill the pertinent obligation. While you are under no obligation to be kind, it demonstrates self-respect and makes the community and larger world a better place.

Restraint

Restraint is a measure or condition that keeps something under control, or within limits. For the purpose of this discussion, here we address self-restraint. The idea of moderation and self-discipline are again at play. Restraint is balance, a control of self when exploring or offering extremes of behavior is a possible option. It is important, for serious consequences are elicited by a lack of control, immoderate behavior, and/or rash decisions. Restraint pertains to appetites - whether we eat, drink, or engage. Consequences elicited by a lack of restraint have far - reaching, long lasting, and damaging effects. What is said, or done with a lack of self-control can wound others as well as the self.

The temptation to act impulsively, to lash out, and offer vindictiveness, righteous indignation, and what seems to be personal truth of an ugly nature can have unintended consequences, and color time, place, and people significantly. Restraint requires that we acknowledge the spectrum of possible behaviors, and select the moderate, or most balanced of paths. It can be astoundingly difficult to quell the desire to act impulsively by exercising restraint and forbearance.

Chapter 19

Satiety

The idea of satiety: the state of being sated, has ties to different concepts. Its root comes from the Latin, for 'enough.' This entry has the fortune of being connected to several significant previous entries, so this particular concept is aided immensely by prior work. Appetite needs satisfaction, as do the general apparatus of the head, heart, and hands. Your need to feed an intellectual, emotional, or physical desire/drive should lead you to question and investigate the activities and solutions that will elicit satisfaction. Else, a drive owns you; one or several horses are driving the chariot in lieu of the balanced and centered charioteer. Lesser drives are physical. You will hunger, thirst, and want to engage sexually. I would be mistaken to construe mental/intellectual and emotional drives/desires as elevated, or of a higher order. Content of the activity references or establishes the relative quality of an act. Just because the head and heart engage does not mean that they have a privileged position when contrasted with physical urges and hankerings. In a biological, socio-economic, and cultural sense, they are all pulls or pushes that demand attention. You will need to recognize your standards, and values: your rubric for your behavior that identifies what and how much constitutes enough, or satiety. If you have self-control and minimal material attachments, perhaps satisfaction comes easily enough. Satiety is connected with ideas including moderation and self-respect. It is associated with relationships, psychology, and a theory of the self at subjective study and objective analysis.

Know your limits and your spectrums. You will interact and perform with many different people in very disparate functions and roles. Grasp how you are wired, how you are structured, and conditioned in order to behave within your character. The address of desires, urges, and appetites must include an idea of satiety, else the pursuit of solutions never relents. What is the point of activity were there *no* positive elicited, or realized goal? Format a value structure, or a conceptual apparatus to explore and establish your standard of satiety.

Secret

Something that is kept or meant to be kept unknown or unseen by others is a secret. Secrets involve concepts including confidentiality, trust, power, and that of resources, or being resourceful. Some secrets are personal. Some aspects of our lives are best kept as privileged and guarded material. Other matters might pertain to the work realm and concern employment. Some information or methodologies need not be divulged or made public. All information is not worth the same. Some bits of data can benefit and serve us while others are very damaging. When the latter remains private, that damage is limited, controlled, or even possibly negated. The release or public knowledge of privileged material could produce meaningful, positive returns.

Secrets exist for several reasons. They exist because of regard; a particular thought need be maintained, in some cases. As an example, an employer need be confident in the skills and/or reputation of their employees. Hence, negative information might best be kept from the employer's awareness. Secrets are resources. Divulging a secret can deliver a benefit. Releasing intellectual property can aid the competition in an industry. Those who divulge the data could benefit by being deemed a contributor of pertinent and privileged information. Secrets are oft times a necessity. For the truth can sometimes work ills, and an innocent falsehood might sometimes amount to a lesser wrong than the knowledge or awareness of a particular truth.

Keeping and maintaining a secret is a particular double-edged sword. By successfully holding confidence, and not releasing a secret, confidentiality is demonstrated and trust is earned. Conveying a secret does just the opposite. By betraying a trust, lesser values are demonstrated and the offended party will have reason to distrust, or refuse to engage similarly again. Be very certain as to the obligation of protecting and honoring one's trust in you when you commit to holding a secret. Some information may need to come to light if the release of a secret could end pain or save someone hardship or loss. Not every secret deserves protection and security. Whistleblowers - those who release privileged or secret information - have been responsible for divulging secrets and, in doing so, have brought to life nefarious activity, wrongdoing that was previously distanced from public awareness. Their releases aid a greater audience by exposing information, which, had it remained secret, could have elicited significant consequences. Trust *was* betrayed in these whistleblower cases, though the trust betrayed belonged to those who were engaging to the detriment of others. The betrayal served a greater good as the release of information helped affected parties and entities.

Holding or keeping a secret has interesting consequences. Secrets take a toll on both the physical and energy body of an individual. Recent studies have shown that secrets decrease people's overall sense of well-being. *Thinking* about secrets was also associated with poorer health. Keeping secrets decreased people's feelings that they were acting authentically. That decrease in authenticity led people to feel worse about their life. The stress caused by secrets arises because people think about the information they are keeping secret often - even when they are not around the person they are hiding information from. When people were thinking about their secrets, they behaved as if they were burdened by physical weight. Secrets detract from mental resources, and they take a toll on the body. Keeping a secret about a birthday surprise party may not injure or break your person, but it is hardly the most pressing concern when contrasted with extra-relational thoughts, romantic desire, sexual behavior, and lies. The power of a secret lies in the fact that the goal of keeping it can never fully be accomplished; it is a prolonged, persistent effort to protect a secret.

Secrets have consequences in the external and internal worlds. Information shapes the world itself, and also profoundly affects the well-being of those holding secrets. The mind and body are assailed by the activity of protecting certain forms of information. Though we might be able to think about the privileged data less, the presence of a secret has consequences that are inescapable. And for that matter, secrets are similar - they are a part of life. From birthday surprises to more pressing concerns, there are bits of information that are protected, and distanced from release and public awareness. It does no good to advise against holding secrets, as *everyone* will have personal things they want kept private. Others will ask individuals to protect information and be tasked with a secret. The best counsel would be to know your own self. If you do not wish to be burdened with a secret, make that clear to people. Carrying a secret has consequences that you will bear should you agree to be a confidant. Be certain that the privilege is worth the effort, and reward.

The Self

The self is an individual person as the object of his or her own reflective consciousness. The self is YOU. This labor of love has been meant as a supplementary guide as you live and navigate the spectrum of life's experiences. It is meant to instruct as to what lies between birth and death. The importance of subjectivity, authenticity, and the care of the self are of vital importance, and for everyone - whether individuals grasp their pertinence or not. This particular concept is an ode to You, and an amalgam of so many concepts addressed previously.

You are here because you are important. Your life has value! Those who want to enjoy your continued presence value you. You have been provided the opportunity and privilege to make something remarkable and special with your time here. By honing abilities and structuring a diverse skill set, you can care for your self. More than mere survival, you have the chance to thrive in this existence. In order to do that, you need discern among a great many concepts and variables in order to properly attend to the valuable resources of your head, heart, and hands. Care of the self can elicit mindfulness, balance, and vivacity should those be of interest to you.

While there are such remarkable similarities shared between human selves, there exist some striking differences. These differences distinguish our own unique self. We will all develop and come to terms with the idea of our self, individuated in the world, separated from 'the other,' making our way via values, mores, ethics, and with different elements of culture. How we care for our own person overlaps with how we engage the community, how we connect and interact with the outer world. Our practices of inclusion and exclusion will demarcate and structure our own path. One of the most consequential components of a healthy self is the presence of authenticity. Being authentic means to be true to one's own personality, spirit, or character. Your behaviors will showcase your values. If you are wise, you will explore, investigate and format your own subjective values, principles, and ethics. You will discover and then represent to the world that which makes you a unique entity. The authentic self lives consistently as that sole individual. They are not a collectivist, nor a sycophant playing to any audience, striving to curry favor or acknowledgement.

The healthy, authentic self is an individualist who knows their self (via Plato), who remains true to their own apparatus of values and principles (via Polonius, in Shakespeare's Hamlet). They recognize how they stand whole, apart from a greater cultural product line or platform. The realized self makes use of their person to showcase self-esteem, to demonstrate self-worth, to respect not only their own self, but others, as well, and to practice self-control and self-discipline. Striving to be healthy, stable, and secure requires paying particular attention to what influences, affects, and colors the condition of the self. Being self-sufficient, self-reliant means being a self-starter. This text is meant to facilitate *that* particular endeavor. The provision of these concepts is an invitation to life's great dining/mess hall. Engorge yourself on the good that life has to offer in order to structure a healthy, confident, competent self. Create something that you can be proud of, for the opportunity and experience is a once-in-a-lifetime privilege. Make the most of it, and do something important with yourself.

"No man is free who is not master of himself." - **Epictetus**

Service

The action of helping or doing work for someone is called service. We can be in service to self or we can be in service to others. Life offers both opportunities, and we need balance the activities. This is the discussion of egoism and altruism. The former is concern of or care for the self, while the latter: care for others, and people, in general. Remaining self-serving - excluding others, or the opportunity to serve others - only limits experience. The contrast holds true: if we are solely in service to others, we are not addressing our self and honing, structuring, or discovering those personal attributes and abilities that differentiate us and allow us to live meaningful lives. By being moderate and behaving in service to self, we develop. We build those skill sets and care for our own self. This needs be balanced with service to others. When we serve others, we apply our own unique strength and talents within the community. We demonstrate our self through interaction, engaging others with (hopefully) positive quality and meaningful initiatives.

Some thinkers contend how we need serve our soul, in this case referring to serving the best part or most essential, best component of us. A portion of that service of soul - a responsibility - lies in coordinating with and benefiting others. No man is an island, and we need operate with that in mind. We are improved and shaped by our dynamics and exchanges with others. Work on your self; serve your own interests but balance that approach with a welcome inclusion of the greater world, be being of service to others.

"To give real service you must add something which can not be bought or measured with money, and that is sincerity and integrity."
– Douglas Adams

Settling

To determine, or decide in a less than satisfactory standard is what known as settling. Generally, we can settle on a decision, a conclusion, or a course of action. With this entry we engage the negative connotation of settling. By this use, we refer to the event where we accept a less than ideal standard as the option, or course of action. In some situations, we have no resources from which to choose. Options are limited and alternatives are in very short supply. In these instances, we settle on the proverbial breadcrumbs that remain. We need make do in these circumstances; we need persevere and make the most of the situation. The point is to make the act of settling an exception - definitely NOT the standard or rule of things.

Settling on an option or route need not be the baseline methodology. Insist on self-worth and pursue goals, aims, and dreams with gusto, vivacity, strength, and determination. If success can not be achieved immediately: adapt and overcome. Do not allow circumstances to defeat you or cajole you into making decisions that consistently forego or eliminate the possibility or presence of your highest good. You are worth a life that is abundantly positive, one that is marked by plenty and the Good. Owning up to that likelihood means refusing to settle as a standard. Make due with what you have and always insist and pursue the best options as the rule. Life and its diverse array of variables and accidents will conspire to meet your level of mindfulness.

The Shadow

The concept of the Shadow is a very complex one, indeed. The Shadow refers to that part of the person whose secrets, repressed feelings, primitive impulses, parts deemed unacceptable, shameful, sinful, or even 'evil,' reside. It is a product of the unconscious mind, and social conditioning. It is a consequential component of the self, and been treated or addressed in myriad cultural forms. The Yin-Yang is a significant representation of it. It is what is referred to in Dr. Faustus, the story of Jekyl and Hyde, Peter Pan, and even the modern Star Wars narrative. An approach of the Shadow is important; it plays a significant role in every hero's journey. For this entry, we explore how the Shadow is created, how it plays a role in *everyone's* life, and how we can incorporate it in order to heal, develop, and thrive.

Over the course of this text, we have examined how we create our self by making use of both external and internal resources, cues, and tools. The Shadow is a product of the same process. Those elements that are discarded or rejected in favor of more acceptable, or more beneficial characteristics compose the Shadow. Everything that we are ashamed of feeling or thinking, impulses, repressed ideas, desires, and fears gives rise to the Shadow. We adopt certain traits as we progress from childhood. The rejected parts live on in the unconscious. These parts are what the individual rejects should they prioritize other character aspects or the larger society minimizes or forbids their presence. As we seek to fit in, be accepted, liked, and loved, we act in certain *acceptable* manners. This gives rise to a question about authenticity. As we accept/reject certain portions of character, we need be aware as to very real consequences of the activity. What aspects of our own very real, and true selves do we eliminate in order to play a role in a society, in a company, a family, or any relationship? The wild, unfettered aspects of our selves reside in the Shadow.

Carl Jung said, "Everyone carries a shadow, and the less it is embodied in the individual's conscious life, the blacker and denser it is." Everyone, without exception, has a Shadow. It is the reflection in the mirror, a product of our own making. But the Shadow and its parts are not entirely bad, per se. In fact, addressing it can elicit benefits if not amazing gifts. Simply: we *must* engage the Shadow as it is necessary in order to heal and grow. We have repeated many times about the importance of positive thinking and mindfulness. Incorporating 'love and light' only go so far. Shadow work, the exploration of the dark side of our selves, touches the very depths of our being. Ignoring, or refusing to administer to it amounts to a trite, superficial approach of life. The consequence of living as an idealized self is so very unhealthy and delusional. The Shadow is real - its effects powerful. How can we aim for oneness, or a whole self, if we disregard such a major part? When an individual refuses to investigate their Shadow, they remain burdened. Anger, grief, guilt, shame, disgust are a part of everyone's character. It is vital what we do with these elements. We can choose to adopt them as tools, or instruments to be used in our development and growth, or we can shoulder them as burdens, unnecessarily. The Shadow seeks to be known. The more it is ignored, the more it seeks opportunities to make itself known. It is responsible for low self-esteem, mental illness, chronic illness, addictions, and various neuroses.

Our lesser parts need be included on our path to a whole self. When the Shadow remains unexamined, it gives rise to behaviors and issues such as lies, self-deceit, hypocrisy, rage and anger, compulsions, anxiety, depression, self-loathing, self-absorption, and self-sabotage. The Shadow is a very real, and quite formidable entity to address, though the benefits of Shadow work are remarkable. Examining the Shadow can yield artistic competitive, innovative, intuitive, and even sexual potentials and capabilities.

We can improve, and be made whole, if not merely more complete, with the aid of a diligent approach. Despite the difficulty of the activity, alchemizing the Shadow can result in acceptance, and self-love, better relationships, mental and emotional clarity, creativity, the discovery of hidden talents, courage, passion, and wholeness. The investigation is necessary, for we are comprised in part by the Shadow and what is more: it is an essential component. Just as we need exercise all elements of our body for optimal health, so too, do we need explore and resolve the issues offered by the Shadow. The following list contains suggested methods of addressing the Shadow:

-Pay special attention to your emotional reactions to events and incidents. Note how and why you feel the way you do in specific, if not repeated occurrences.
-Engage art therapy. Be spontaneous while making use of a medium that sings, or calls to you.
-Start a project. Explore yourself as you put the best of you into a meaningful enterprise.
-Keep a journal.
-Explore Shadow archetypes. Just as there are positive archetypes, there are lesser. Among them: the dictator, the victim, the addict, the idiot, the slave, the

hag, and the hermit. This list is not comprehensive.
-Engage an inner dialogue. All parts of you respond when you interact with them and the Shadow is no different. Be mindful. Do not force the conversation. Be open and receptive.
-Be aware and beware of projecting. This occurs when we are upset at others for demonstrating behavior we loathe about our own selves. Mind your self - care for you and your side of the street - in order to engage self and others meaningfully, and well. This aspect is so very important.

Shadow work can be transformational. It is a necessary activity for those who seek health, wholeness, and peace. Life is full of pleasures, delights, love, and light, but these elements are but one half of the greater sum of life. A significant life entails grappling with some difficult, and even painful circumstances. Do not sidestep those opportunities for growth, else the lessons pursue with increased fortitude and consequence. You owe it to yourself, and to your community, to not only engage your Shadow, but also harness it, as well. Come to terms with it, and grasp your complete self by committing to the most meaningful of work.

Sharing

To have a portion of something with another is sharing. This concept deserves a bit more in addition to something about caring. We can share tangible and intangible items. Foods, fluids, space, and time are all available to be shared. The central aspect of sharing involves the who and what of the equation. Who is worth your time, energy, and resources? What activities are worthy of your participation? Life offers only so many opportunities. We would be wise to share experiences, love, and the very best that is within us with people who recognize the gravity and significance of the transaction. A word of caution: not everything need be shared. Decide how inclusive or exclusive you need be.

The Soul

Souls are essential parts of the human narrative. Pre-Socratics discussed them and, with Thales in the 4th century, and greats, including the likes of Socrates/Plato, Aristotle, the schoolmen and others, much has been contributed to what understanding we profess. The incorporeal essence of a living being is a soul. We discussed Psyche as soul, earlier. While myths, poems, and other cultural memes make use of the subject, upon investigation we find little that substantiates the belief in the soul. We review Plato as we examine the beginnings of the idea. We include brief aspects of Christianity and Theosophy before we conclude with a discussion about physicalists and materialism along with idealists and dualism.

Souls were originally referred to as the 'life' of a person. The anima was what animated living things. Rivers and mountains are sometimes considered to have souls. In the Bible, Genesis 2:7, God breathes life into man, and makes him a living soul. Over time, the soul took on mental abilities of a living being, like reason, character, feeling consciousness, memory, perception, etc. A soul came to hunger. A soul could ache. A soul could even die. With Socrates, Plato, and Aristotle, the definition of soul became more particular. The logical faculty differentiated man, hence its exercise and development was the most divine of human actions. Excellence for the soul was the improvement of the logos. Socrates considered his teachings to be an entreaty to excel in matters of the psyche, since all bodily goods were dependent on such excellence.

How did these most notable thinkers arrive at their conclusions and what questions did they utilize in their inquiry? How did the soul become so established as a concept? Those who believe in non-material, or non-stuff are idealists. They contend that all matter is mentally construed, if not immaterial. Those who believe in the soul, or immaterial things are idealists, while dualists hold that matter exists alongside non-corporeal stuff, i.e., minds. Because it is rare for someone to assert their idealism, most concerned with an idea of the soul are dualists and we focus on their approach. For them, a soul is viewed as separate from but integrated with the body. When the harmony of the body dissolves, the soul is released.

Plato considered the body to be the prison of the soul. Its limitations only inhibit the soul and an individual's grasp of the divine Forms. Because the body hinders wisdom, man's purest thoughts can only amount to mere approximation. So, the philosopher despises material, bodily pleasures, as they are distractions - only dressings of the prison. We would escape, be done with the deceptions elicited by the corporeal upon death, the soul's separation from the body. But what happens to the soul, post-body demise? The soul is immaterial and even posited to be immortal. Christian explanations about the soul are offered via creationism, traducianism, and pre-existence. Creationism maintains that God creates souls at conception. Traducianism holds that soul is transferred via parents and natural generation. Pre-existence theory states that souls existed before conception. In the Christian system, the souls are judged by God and sentenced to either Heaven or Hell. In contrast, Theosophists hold that the soul was the middle dominion between the body and the spirit. It was the battlefield of good and evil, the general field of psychological activity.

It is fascinating to witness how we emphasize the idea of a soul. We have precious little reason to hold such a belief, yet that is entirely the point. Belief is a powerful activity. Because we have a larger cultural fear and avoidance of death, we move to stifle mortality's blow. The presence of a soul delivers immortality, and the prospect of another reality: life after death. That the physicalists - those who believe in matter and all of life being explained by physical phenomena - can explain soul as a process of body and/or mind in the same way leads us to question ontology - the metaphysics of the concept. On what grounds do we insist on the presence of a soul? What does a soul provide for and address that materialism can not account for? Numerous aspects of reality have only recently come to the fore. Our knowledge bases regarding the brain and the quanta increase dramatically, even exponentially. A soul provides a structure by which we can address certain other concepts that are presented as divine, pure, unattainable items of reference, reflection, and speculation. But in the case that love, truth and peace *are* non-transcendent principles hallowed by man, but still entirely products of biological entities engaging in social constructs, we are not worsened for it. We are just that much more in control of tangible reins. The means of the successful realization of these concepts are available and, in fact, even material. No longer would such hallowed concepts be distant ideals when people grasped their immediate vicinity and material application. Consider the world that accepted peace, truth, and love as real, tangible, immediate concerns and tools, instead of vacuous Forms of a posited realm obtainable only after death.

Still, the discussion about soul is incomplete and this specific entry would indeed be lacking were we to review only Psyche and the opposing perspectives of materialists and idealists. Most discussions concerning the soul are academic. Religious or spiritual orthodoxy is offered, along with Socrates and the philosopher ilk. The idea of mind becomes involved, and we have quite a complex endeavor. Our culture is largely material and increasingly so. The presence of immaterial substances, much less a care of an immortal soul, does not lend themselves to a moneymaking industry, save perhaps for the Church. The self-help industry is lucrative for some but a care of the soul would separate the individual from cultural consumptive practices with a lessening of fear and lower sentiments, energy. The idea of an immortal and immaterial soul is a minor concern for those institutions that require a tangible body to discipline, limit, and control.

While the discussion of soul is an ancient one, recent explorations make the context that much more accessible. The International Academy of Consciousness delves into some remarkable subject matter. They explore out of body experiences (OBEs), after-death experiences, aliens, ghosts, and remote viewings, among a diverse array of other topics and ideas. There exists a plethora of things not yet accounted for by material substances or physical causes. A sampling of experiences across cultures speaks to the very real possibility for an existence that surpasses or eclipses the physical plane and third dimensional existence. Simply: we are left unable to explain *so much* of what life has to offer. Via knowledgeable opinion in the form of governments, spiritual and religious institutions, and academia, we are given the means of believing in things we should not - concepts including scarcity, the viability of central planning, and never-ending war. These same knowledgeable opinions are unable to convincingly disprove the overwhelming amount of evidence for these immaterial incidents and subjects. That DARPA (Defense Advanced Research Projects Agency) engages in research involving remote viewing, and internal energies means that there is definite substance to the idea. Those who refuse to believe in immaterial substances or supernatural events have their blinders up against an array of incredible subject matter that could prove most advantageous for the entire human race. The importance of the soul and other immaterial substances, for that matter, can not be minimized or understated in light of such evidence.

The soul provides insulation from the present realm, yet its maintained presence as a concept speaks to a larger, cultural approach to the larger thoughts of life and death. Your own approach to your subjectivity, your essence, character, etc. is on display with each activity. Investigate whether the idea of a soul has a place within you and examine your materialistic/dualistic/idealistic filters. It will influence a large swath of how you live your days and this particular portion of the personal investigative endeavor is worth all the while.

Spells

Spells are a form of words, or an arrangement of words which serve as a magical charm. Words are powerful instruments, whether written or in spoken form. Thoughts, being colored by feelings, and then uttered, or offered in text, provide the means of chaos or bliss, curses or blessings. It is precisely the reason why we practice spelling as you work on reading comprehension and vocabulary. The power of words is examined and applied in the Kabbalah. Other significant institutions make use of mantras, chants, Ki-ai, and even affirmations, demonstrating how man has acknowledged and made use of power via spells since ancient times. Should you engage the occult, you will undoubtedly explore the idea of spells and this specific realm of magic. Without that particular study, you still need pay mind to your words, even your thoughts. Frequencies and vibrations emanate and create! Be considerate of the resources at your command, and apply a mindful perspective to the best instruments in order to develop and be of service to your fellow man.

Standards

Standards refer to levels of quality or attainment used as a measure or model. Standards are closely equivocated with the idea of principles. Principles are propositions that serve as the foundations for a system of belief, behavior, or for a chain of reasoning. Buildings are built to standards in order to achieve success with their economic goals and larger aims. By structuring and applying worthy standards and principles to our own selves, we can survive, thrive, and succeed with our life's endeavors. Worthy standards are the foundations of success. I do not care to imagine the reality where gross, inferior standards rule the day. Shoddy standards and principles invite similar consequences. Goals and dreams need be amazing, thoughtful, and worthy of considerable investment and work. Otherwise, we settle on crass, immediate gains at the expense of quality. Principles and standards are in play with every activity and behavior: personal, professional, private, or public. We demonstrate values and greater guiding standards with each and every undertaking.

Demonstrate worthy standards and commit to having considerable principles. Carry yourself well by engaging standards that support and defend your well-being, your self-respect, and dignity. Behave with a view towards these essential concepts as guides. Structure your well-lived life by applying standards that will invite and include only the good in your life. Remember: exclusive standards are not wholly bad.

Sustenance

What is imbibed as a source of strength or nourishment - OR - the maintaining of someone or something in life or existence is sustenance. Physical and non-tangible goods can sustain us in different contexts. Food, drink, and touch will generally sustain man. Subjective preferences make for a broad spectrum of goods, or activities, that can support, offer succor or relief, though sustenance refers specifically to those items that enable one's continued existence. While arts and music may feed our souls, or nourish our beings, sustenance refers to the very real effects of tangible goods being imbibed or ingested.

Symptom

A symptom is a departure from normal function or feeling, which is noticed by a patient, reflecting the presence of an unusual state, or of a disease. Symptoms are subjective, and can not be measured objectively. While sometimes nonspecific, combinations of symptoms and signs are suggestive as to certain diagnoses. We will become aware of changed states with our own individual persons and at a larger cultural level. Being sufficiently self-aware allows us the ability to note conditions or events that are out of the norm. We should investigate these occurrences and include or make use of perception checking, if not knowledgeable opinion in order to properly diagnose the incident.

Symptoms are sometimes conflated and identified to be the cause of an issue or malady. Too often, though, we recognize how, after diligent investigation and inquiry, symptoms are only topical representations of underlying conditions. While it is easier to take a circumstance as a total context, many times we become aware of other deeper variables at play. This applies to individuals and greater incidents, too. What occurs is a manifestation that is taken as a standalone independent occurrence when, in reality, the incident is but one in a longer chain of events and variables.

So, with real variables: someone's mood is influenced by external factors; someone's momentary unhappiness is not their baseline status. A medical symptom usually has contributing, underlying factors. Wars, poverty, environmental degradation, if not collapse, have - at their root - other several consequential factors that give rise to demonstrative symptoms.

A proper diagnosis is born of a nearly comprehensive set of variables. Contributing factors and elements need be recognized in order to ascertain primary concerns and relevance. In short, only topical approaches can address symptoms. Band-aids merely mask an exposed wound. What proves meaningful and consequential is a response born of investigation, inquiry, and diligent inspection. Otherwise, we run the risk of settling for cosmetic approaches when extensive, complex addresses are what are required. There are significant differences between the diagnosis of ills pertinent to larger cultural institutions and the analysis of the self. As a start, an institution is comprised of peoples. Its ills will be the product of or caused by the actors who are coordinating and contributing. An analysis of institution requires an examination of the players involved in order to understand the scene. Without an investigation of the entities participating, nearly all else is moot. For an institution has no sovereignty or agency; an institution can not take initiative of its own accord. It needs be harnessed or applied by actors who have the means of acting independently or as a group. As far as the diagnosis of an individual is concerned, a wholly different analysis is required. It is similar in that an inventory, or a study of the subject/entity, is necessary. We need understand what moves or drives the individual and how their mental/cognitive emotional, and physical realms are aligned, or arrayed. Though, again, should we be investigating a self's medical symptoms, we might focus more on physical variables at play. *This* is the essential difference between institutional and subjective analysis. In contrast to the subject, the former will pale considerably as far as dynamic forces and organic factors play a role. The individual will be influenced by a far greater spectrum of 'lively' and dynamic contributors. The amount of elements affecting or assailing an individual is significantly greater than those facing an institution. And the elements are consequential, at that; factors including meaning, memory, and attachment are but only a few notable concepts that can influence or sway an individual. Contrast the variables pertinent to an institutional analysis and the majority of issues at play will consist of interpersonal dynamics and issues concerning personality conflicts or issues concerning communication.

Addressing an ill as symptomatic (serving as a symptom or sign, especially of something undesirable) is a distinct process for institutions and individuals. The former are the product of people involved while the latter's diagnosis warrants an approach that addresses very particular elements and variables. We are correct in noting how the extension of this thought yields an interesting conclusion. Our nation state is the product of its people playing a role within the cultural arena. Further, individuals who are sufficiently self-aware and critically engaged are a far easier study than the alternative. In short, these individuals provide a more direct study than those who are inclined to be entertaining chaos or disorder in the realms of head, heart, and hands. The diagnosis of ills facing our nation is facilitated by a study and knowledge of its people. Additionally, should the people understand the nature of the general self and their own person, they would be able to recognize and address symptoms directly, and even, perhaps, efficiently. We can revise our larger community by first caring for our own persons. That self-care elicits substantial returns for us, and our peers, and then for greater social realms and arenas. But until we work on the sundry symptoms that face us as individuals, we will remain unable to meaningfully address if not even fully comprehend issues of greater social consequence.

System

A set of connected things or parts forming a complex whole is a system. This text separates and approaches myriad concepts among different systems and structures. The reader can not help but acknowledge the incredible amount of overlap shared between many disparate concepts and ideas. Seemingly trivial or unconnected data and variables *somehow* play a role in life and this is the point: Life consists of relationships among many different systems. In fact, this particular concept has significance with the concept of relationship, for systems are structures of relationship. We note how elements as particular and minute as those belonging to the quanta or items as grand as the stardust of the greater celestial cosmos play a role in the life of an individual. From both realms we interact with a spectacular spectrum of systems.

A significant activity of life involves discerning how factors contribute to our lives. We need also recognize how our own conditions influence our own relationships and systems. So, what systems act as contributors to our lives? We previously mentioned the cosmic variety as well as the quanta. We are all made of star-stuff and, via quantum mechanics, we note how the space between 'anything' is negligible, given the uncertainty principle and the application of mind, among other concepts. As we proceed to smaller scale systems that affect or influence us more immediately, we recognize biological systems - those including water, food, and weather. Differentiating people across the globe are cultural systems, or those pertaining to education, media, religion and spirituality, economics, and law, among others. We then have systems of relationships within our communities. Discerning consequential factors and recognizing their places in systems allows us to make sense or order of the barrage of ideas, concepts, and variables at play. A systematic approach to pertinent items involves organization, discipline, and a routine. Understanding, and making proper, good use of systems involves a structured approach to an astounding array of concepts. The more we seek to understand life and this spectrum, the more we understand ourselves and our own remarkable place in the greater reality. I entreat you to seek information, knowledge, and wisdom. Systems order and connect the minutiae and the magnificent, and allow us to work what magic we can contextually, with our own talents and abilities. Be a systems thinker, and have access to even more of the world!

Chapter 20

Tact

Tact is adroitness or sensitivity in dealing with others or with sensitive issues. Tact is a result elicited by diplomacy, understanding, consideration, propriety, and delicacy, too. Its presence helps maintain good relations, and avoid offense. Ancient philosophers' approach to rhetoric overlaps with the idea of tact. Plato defined rhetoric as the art of enchanting the soul or the art of winning the soul via discourse. We utilized Aristotle's definition of rhetoric for use in our concept of power, namely: rhetoric is the faculty of discovering, in any particular case, all of the available means of persuasion. Plato recognized that an audience is won with a bit of tactical enchantment; Aristotle identified how we need identify tact as one of many resources needed in order to succeed in a persuasive enterprise.

Tact is a thoughtful, prudent route of communication. The imparted message soothes, rather than upbraids the audience. The receiver of the information is calmed and comforted by tact, rather than piqued, upset, or challenged unnecessarily by a harsher message. It delivers potentially difficult information gently. It is a tool applied by an able communicator that can discern variables and the consequences of significance and meaning. A caring individual applies tact because it is a considerate act. The presence of tact denotes how a speaker cares for their audience and for the relationship. Tact delivers results and the ability is elicited over the course of interactions and exchanges. Consider how unwieldy an untrained head, heart, and set of hands. A youth is less efficient at a great many things and it is only with practice and experience that skills are structured. The same applies for tact. Youth is generally loud, exuberant, and undisciplined. Communication demonstrates the mindfulness and ability of its wielder. Tact is elicited by experience and the knowledge that arises while gauging and interacting with different audiences. It is a tool worth developing, and applying respectfully.

Taste

For the purposes of this entry concerning taste, we focus on an individual's personal and cultural patterns of choice and preference. Taste consists of the subjective ability to judge what is beautiful, good, and proper. It is therefore a consequential concern as it pertains to metaphysical notions as well as aesthetical and ethical issues. Taste is a product of social relations, and dynamics between people. Family, friends, and institutions introduce us to a spectrum of possible values. The provision instructs as to the available range of acceptable preferences among behaviors and activities. Different socioeconomic groups have different tastes. This makes sense, for given different backgrounds and experience, disparate values are certain to exist. Social class is a very prominent factor of taste. Elites engage in far different activities than lower class individuals who struggle to survive and thrive, who have fewer opportunities to explore and experience a wider swath of possibility.

Your own taste will demonstrate your subjective values and preferences. Strive to refine them. Make certain that the best elements of taste are situated in realms other than the mouth. Meaning: some tastes are base and physical. Other tastes concern the emotions or intellect, as in the case of reviewing significant pieces of art. Differentiate and distinguish between these higher and lower pleasures and apply a broad perspective of taste that demonstrates wherewithal and development of a greater self.

Terror

A state of intense fear is terror. The presence of terror has set in motion a radical revision of our culture and society. Over the course of nearly two decades, the United States has adopted an approach that has fundamentally changed our way of life. As individuals we have changed, as have our institutions and communities. Underlying the change is terror, a particularly insidious form of fear that compromises good judgment and makes a mockery of representative democracy in this republic. We address how terror came to our country and how we might then restrain and limit its perpetuation.

Terror arrived in the form of attacks in New York and Washington DC in September of 2001. Nearly 3000 people died, and more than 6000 were injured as planes struck the Twin Towers of the World Trade Center in New York City. Official narrative identifies how a plane collided with the Pentagon and another airliner crashed into a field in rural Pennsylvania. Mainstream media and the government identified a culprit and addressed posited boogiemen, first in Afghanistan, and then in Iraq. As a consequence of a protracted War on Terror, estimated millions are dead or displaced. Villains and organizations are dispelled if not distributed to other lands that remain ripe for the seed of discord and aggression, chaos and strife. While we might be pleased that our government has taken notice of the disconnect between the realities of military force and nation building, we need remain vigilant and concerned that a revised approach addresses localities utilizing armed drones and special mercenary forces.

A focus on terror in our own American backyard is myopic and woefully shortsighted. Uniquely American exceptionalism blinds us to the realities that exist beyond our bubble. We would be wise to note how terror, and terrorism: the use of violence and intimidation, especially against civilians, in the pursuit of political aims - have been significant components of life overseas. Most troubling is the fact that our own nation contributes to if not foments the means of such extreme fear and terror in those lands. We can not wring our hands and behave as if we are the sole victims of terror. We have sewn dangerous seeds long before we outed the Shah of Iran in 1953. Our country is a particularly violent one, having engaged in war 93% of the time, or 222 out of 239 years, since 1976. Consider *that* standard. We can not expect a different harvest when what we sew is primarily discord via fear-based aggression. Our initiatives in other lands are not the work of stable, conscientious considerate leaders. Those who advance these schemes can only be concerned with their own gains at the expense of the well-being and security of the people of the world, not to mention the United States.

Yet I contend that terror came to America long before 9-11; its creep commenced the very first instance in which the people stopped holding their representatives accountable. The specific events of 9/11 left people utterly debilitated, gutted by extreme shock, and soon: less than virtuous figures provided misleadership. A coordinated media and political effort placated us: media sound-bytes depicted facts that served the administration and powers that be. Bad guys were identified and pursued across the globe, creating a worldwide stage for an approach to terror that is now grasped as farcical, at best. The prospect of future destruction is kept ever at hand by the same media and political partnership; we are conditioned to be fearful of shoes, rockets, vehicles, bombs, drones, and one another. A whitewashed investigation of 9/11 stymied and discouraged better, more substantial critical engagements. Witnesses died and eliminated the presence of many first person accounts and testimony. That *much* of the Official 9/11 Report remains redacted is evidence of how the protection of politicians and their activities is prioritized over truth and the health and security of the nation.

The events of September 11, 2001 ushered in profound changes and shifts among all sectors of United States policy, both foreign and domestic. The definition of terror itself changed, and continues to change, given dynamic variables of technology, cultures and people. We are relentlessly barraged with news concerning new boogiemen. If we are inclined to believe the media, a veritable merry-go-round of radicalized sects and associations grow in number, diversify and extend a reach across the globe. Terror cells and their operatives are rumored to be lurking around the corner, making people suspicious of neighbors and community members. In order to realize the aims of the strategists and power holders, a focus on combating terrorism utilizes new tools and methodologies, including secret prisons, torture, extraordinary rendition, and indefinite detention. This means that the world is on war footing, and *every* resource can be harnessed in order to combat amorphous terrorism. Terrorists can be anyone and everyone. Yet perhaps most dangerous of them are those that stand opposed to the ideology of another war that serves the thinly veiled interests of a precious few.

The oversimplified approach of inquiring, "are you with or against us?" is watered down still further to no longer even ask for a response. Instead, an individual is what the government or authority designates: enemy combatant or innocent civilian, perhaps in the wrong place at the wrong time. Judgment in the form of bombs or drones amounts to no sort of fair trial or due process. In this supposed land of the free, and home of the brave, terror has undermined once hallowed ideals. Freedom and bravery, as American adjectives, are in danger of becoming husks. The longer we haphazardly abandon the responsibility of reigning in our government, the more difficult it will be to enjoy a return to normalcy, sans terror. A significant portion of the world deals with the very real threat of terror and violence as a standard of daily life. In faraway theatres featuring repetitive drone strikes, children now fear the very sky. Our methodologies are conditioning people the world over. Understandably, the international community cringes at the idea of further nation building and anti-terror initiatives since the consequences are glaringly manifest.

The domestic realm of the United States is encountering the consequences of their foreign intrusions and entanglements. Not only are future dissidents, malcontents, and freedom fighters encouraged to harbor serious resentments towards the country, but a different, though maybe even more significant consequence has come home to roost. The continuation of a war effort has necessitated a rotation of personnel and soldiers. The increased presence of former military personnel in the local community law enforcement means a cultural shift has been underway there, too. Support apparatus for those returning from war have been substandard, at best, and has given rise to an extraordinarily high rate of suicide among former soldiers. Servicemen and women were used for less than noble aspirations, and then discarded by a support system that remains unable to take their greater well-being into account. Similarly, activity in distant lands has elicited the arrival of refugees. It remains to be seen how our depleted system can care for others, as we are financially (and morally?) bankrupt already. It will be interesting to witness how others are cared for when the present support network is unable (or unwilling?) to care for present constituents.

Our national character stagnates under the weight and burden of terror. Our own woes impact the condition of lives around the world. Should people desire better circumstances, it makes for a unique opportunity, and a uniquely American responsibility to address. Being that our culture is a product of the tools we apply in the domestic and international realms, we need implement different methodologies and apply new tools to transform this culture and eliminate a good portion of terror. A meaningful first step involves the cessation of its enablement. That means we need limit our own use of terror. We can not combat terror with terror. Continuing to do so risks making the entire world blind. Fighting terrorism amounts to herding cats if we continue to contribute to conditions that both foment and make possible terrorism's presence. We need grasp who benefits from the present arrangement, for it certainly is *not* the people.

It is largely those in power, and those who are connected to the military industrial complex who stand to gain from an extended approach to terrorism. Leadership need be restrained, or brought to heel, lest the greater portion of the civilized world be brought to ruin. The associations, affiliations, and alliances that are connected with that leadership need be restricted, for their contributions drive or elicit more of the same.

Methodologies need be revised at the international and domestic levels. The biggest question is: how do we structure, or format a cultural system that produces individuals that are not prone to the overriding influence of terror/fear? Prussian leadership pursued a similar inquiry as they witnessed their soldiers fleeing before Napoleon, hence the institution of the kindergarten and a completely new form of education.

A guarded and secretive approach to a sliding scale of amorphous enemies, causes, and fronts deserves pointed questions. What does victory mean? Can this war be won; can it end? For how much longer need we entertain these conditions? Would we recognize victory? These larger issues are of overwhelming concern, yet smaller initiatives creep and herald still more challenges. The global surveillance apparatus serves as both the sword and shield in this war on terror. Minute transactions and events are gathered for the sake of freedom. Surveillance is now oppressive and we are hard pressed to entertain freedom as a reality because such fear is present. We are beset by enough in life without the onerous presence of an intrusive police/nanny state.

Worse still, these conditions can not improve when such intense fear undergirds our national character and culture. We have been conditioned to fear. Our younger generations have been made numb to the transforming cultural condition. They know nothing else save for the conditions elicited by the war on terror. It is more difficult to change character the more it is entrenched. We need revise our practices, lest the state of fear remains unchallenged, and predominant in our society, and world.

I *do* believe in security. But we have rendered our cultural platform asunder with an approach to security via extreme fear. Methinks we are able instead to enjoy security by way of responsibility, knowledge, hope, love, and courage. We enjoin the endeavor because it is our responsibility to care for our families, our homes, our communities, and our globe! We need seek a dense and thorough education that makes use of the myriad variables involved within the context of terror. What factors have influenced or wrought such a despicable, fearful, terrified character? This is an interesting equation, to identify and address how cultural components produce a certain character, or type of individual. A critical eye trained on the realms of government, education, economics, media, religion/spirituality, leisure, and the family will discern an extraordinary amount of variables and plenty of food for thought.

Our new culture of terror is borne of years of intentional methodologies. That we entertain such a fearful state means that it, too, is intentional. Should we wish to experience better circumstances, we need apply a long view and act with a big picture in mind. Until the people unite upon a foundation of shared, inclusive principles, we need work on our subjective selves.

Investing in the self builds strong character, and only the strong are virtuous.

Investing in refining our thoughts, feelings, and behaviors will yield positive results if and only if we are strong enough to maintain a disciplined and rigorous course. We need get fit - get right - with our heads, hearts, and hands if we truly desire to shed terror and its connected ills.

Time

What we consider time is that indefinite and continuous duration regarded as that in which events succeed one another. Time constitutes one of the distinguishing features of humankind, for all animals - save for human - live in the continual present. It seems continuous (with no stoppages), in a direction (from past to future), and objective (we note its effect nearly everywhere). Its presence proves meaningful in our lives, so great minds contributed to our understanding of what time is, and how it is rightly understood and applied in our lives. Here, we discuss how significant thinkers have approached time. We focus particularly on Augustine, Kant, and Einstein. We then discuss time as pertaining to us as subjects and the idea of time and mind. Finally, we address how time conditions us.

In the 5th century, Parmenides maintained that change is illusion - that past and future distinctions were imaginary. This contrasted directly with Heraclitus who contended that change is all that exists. Zeno offered some thought experiments via paradoxes that structured a portion of our understanding of both time and space until Plato made his presence felt in the 4th century. He defined time as the period of motion of heavenly bodies. And, owing to his connections to various mystery schools, held that a great cycle of 25,800 years was a complete cycle. Aristotle offered time as an attribute of movement, relative to the motions of things. He called it the numeration of continuous movement, or the number of change in respect to before and after. For him, time was a measurement of change. It could exist without succession or change and it requires a soul to think it. Space was assumed to be finite but time infinite. Finally, Aristotle held that the universe has and will always exist. Time, then, was divisible, continuous, and infinite.

Other ancients noted time and questioned as to its form: linear or cyclical, and its duration: endless or infinite. The Cult of Mithra believed in a 12,000 year cycle while the Zoroastrians denoted time as the duration of the battle of good and evil. Augustine broke with precedent and, instead, offered Greek thought applied via the Christian concept of God. God is outside of time (which exists inside a created universe). God perceives the universe but time is viewed differently by finite beings within the constructed universe. Augustine was prescient with his ideas. His approach heralded some of the work of Einstein, and the ideas of the Big Bang and quantum mechanics. Augustine's self-referential arguments and circular reasoning could not elicit certainty as evidenced when Augustine writes, "And I confess to thee, O Lord, that I am still ignorant as to what time is." He concludes by offering time as a product of mind.

The thinkers of the 17th and 18th centuries gauged time's character as real versus that of an intellectual concept. Newton identified time as a dimension via a realist perspective. Time was absolute, existing independently of a perceiver. It had a constant pace throughout the universe, was imperceptible, and understood only mathematically. The philosopher Leibniz adopted an anti-realist perspective. For him, time was an intellectual concept that allows us to sequence and compare events. Therefore, no objects means there is no such thing as time. Concepts of space and time are merely products of the way we represent to ourselves. This parallels the larger empirical perspective of the time. The world exists, generally, as a product of our senses and experience.

Immanuel Kant offered his *Critique of Pure Reason* in 1788. He identified space and time as *a priori* (meaning: without or before experience) notions necessary to comprehend sense experience. They are part of a necessary, systematic framework that was transcendentally ideal. William James offered an idea called the specious present; which held that the present is composed of both earlier and later parts. He said that time could not be instantaneous, and that it occurs in intervals. With this line of thought, what was initially thought to be the present could only be past due to the delay of sense receptors and the involvement of our own our cognitive faculties. Later thinkers questioned how intervals could overlap, or how a combination of intervals made a stream of consciousness possible. 19th century physicist and mathematician Henri Poincare held that the whole of reality rests on convention. Convention refers to rules and standards of conduct or behavior. Conventions of society vary per culture, and region, but all people take note of, and use time, albeit in different fashions. The Conventionalist approach identified the speed of light as a convention. With it as a starting point, we would be wise to note how convention plays an immense part in physics. Husserl's Phenomenology in the late 19th-20th century contended how there is no perception of present sans experience of the past or the expectation of a future. Bergson identified time as duration, shown incompletely and indirectly, grasped through the simple intuition of the mind. Myriad tiny temporal particles (akin perhaps to Leibniz's monads) pieced together by consciousness made time known via sensory experience. Heidegger's *Being and Time* stated that *we are time*. Meaning: time is inseparable from human experience. We are, in fact, time travelers. At any given point, we can recall the past or anticipate the future. By engaging time via memory or concern/expectation we can connect with time at will.

Albert Einstein's work with special relativity established how time and space are relative. As a start, general physical descriptions are incomplete sans a third dimensional reference; time is necessary. Also, subjective frames of reference make for relative status. Light always moves at the speed of light, no matter the reference frame. Einstein shows how time dilates and length contracts to compensate. Essentially, when something is moving fast enough through space, it can alter its passage through time. Time decreases, or increases are predicated on movement. It passes differently depending on the frame of reference. Also, there is no universal concept of simultaneity. Observers in different frames of reference can have different measurements of whether a given pair of events happened at either the same time or at different times. Further, if something is moving relative to you, its height in the direction that it is moving will seem shorter than it would if it were not moving. Length is affected similarly, according to motion. Because length contraction is not something we see in everyday life, it is not a part of our intuitive sense of physics. We are used to seeing the world at much, *much* slower speeds than light. Time is a relative concept and, with space: can not serve as a constant.

Newtonian, quantum and phenomenal approaches to time have demonstrated how the idea of time affords or makes possible multiple dimensions, or multiple takes on time, and paradoxes that result. That parallel universes *may* exist is reason enough to engage the subject matter as more than grist for songs, movies, and countless episodes of Dr. Who. More to the pertinence of tangible and everyday concerns of our own lives in this here and now, time plays a conditioning role in our society. What is interesting to note is how connected we once were to time as a shift in stars and season. We were once intimately connected with the movements of the heavens and the shift of the year agriculturally. Because communities were once very involved with their own food production, they were also similarly connected with time. As more and more people departed rural life for urban civilization, our connection with the local, living community, and our food waned. Now we are inordinately tied to social constructs. Our education system is broken into subjects and classes per scheduled durations. The conditioning prepares people for working the paralleled 8 a.m. to 4 p.m. or the classic 9-5 shift. School schedules parallel the ordering of work shift schedules. The less we are connected to time in the natural world, the more we are tied to controlled routines situated in urban centers by the powers that be.

Augustine and Einstein notably characterized the relativity of time. What a difference of perspective exists as we sit eating ice cream in contrast to time spent sitting in a dentist's chair! Time really *does* fly while we are having fun! An earlier entry concerned the present. For this particular entry concerning time, we substantiated the imperative to be present, and mindful of the opportunity of the now. A sense of tenses allows us to extrapolate from the past in order to live well in the present and to develop as we progress, or proceed via intervals or durations into a plausible future. Our conscious sense of time connects us to every living thing, and meaningfully. We reach an age where we recognize its passage as we note its affect on living things. We ourselves, age, change, and pass. We live by the 'fact' that our time is limited, or that time terminates for mortals. Society establishes time as a limited commodity and, until we decide otherwise and break with particular convention, we need approach time on conventional terms, at the subjective and objective level to make good use of our lives.

"It's being here now that's important. There's no past and there's no future. Time is a very misleading thing. All there is ever, is the now. We can gain experience from the past, but we can't relive it; and we can hope for the future, but we don't know if there is one." — **George Harrison**

Ticking away the moments that make up a dull day Fritter and waste the hours in an off hand way.
Kicking around on a piece of ground in your home town Waiting for someone or something to show you the way
...
Tired of lying in the sunshine staying home to watch the rain.
And you are young and life is long and there is time to kill today.
And then one day you find ten years have got behind you. No one told you when to run, you missed the starting gun.

So you run and you run to catch up with the sun but it's sinking Racing around to come up behind you again. The sun is the same in a relative way but you're older Shorter of breath and one day closer to death.
Every year is getting shorter; never seem to find the time. Plans that either come to naught or half a page of scribbled lines. Hanging on in quiet desperation is the English way
The time is gone, the song is over
Thought I'd something more to say.
-Lyrics to the song, *Time* by Pink Floyd.

"Time is currency. Whatever you spent your time on is what you bought." – **Unknown**

"The trouble is, you think you have time." – **Buddha**

"The tirelessness in you is aware of life's timelessness; and knows that yesterday is but today's memory and tomorrow is today's dream." –
Kahlil Gibran

"If you love life, don't waste time, for time is what life is made up of." - **Bruce Lee**

Touch

Touch refers to coming into contact with and perceiving something. We focus here on the benefits of touch and contact as social creatures. We also explore how we can touch others, emotionally, with positive behaviors. The sense of touch is vital. As we explore the world as infants, our sense of touch informs us as to good and bad sensations of pleasure and pain. The contrast between physical contact and social isolation, or a lack of appropriate touch, is very revealing. Different levels of the hormone oxytocin are released per different types and amounts of touch and contact. A fleeting touch releases little as compared to a holding of hands or a long and extended hug. Touch and oxytocin reduces stress hormones. Gentle, supportive touch and affectionate caresses aid and facilitate health. Studies have shown how those who have engaged more hugs are healthier than those who do not. The greatest point here regards contact. Maybe we do not desire constant human companionship or embraces and touch. Pets can afford the opportunity to address loneliness and address healthy needs of affection. What a joy to experience how pets love unconditionally! Consider the availability of massage as another means of contact. Generally, touch makes a most significant difference for those that desire to be happy and healthy in the presence of coordinated, inclusive social groups.

Tradition

The handing down of statements, beliefs, legends, customs, information, etc. from generation to generation, especially by word of mouth or by practice, is tradition. They establish commonality of experience and promote a shared identity. This is done at the greater objective level of nation-states and also at the private/personal subjective level of families and individuals. States will have public holidays, sing national anthems, or feature specific cuisine, as in the case of hamburger, hot dogs, and apple pie for Independence Day celebrations, for example. Families and individuals establish traditions for similar functions. To maintain shared identity, they engage in shared activity and practices. A routine Saturday barbeque might connect family and friends across generations. The cutting of the annual Christmas tree at a farm could provide the means of facilitating unity and togetherness. People structure routines and implement personal traditions according to their own sense of meaning. We can greet the stars on the eve of our birthday, take a walk as a New Year activity, or maybe attend Burning Man as a means of significance or commemoration, as well. Traditions vary per individuals, households, groups, communities, nations, and cultures. The establishment and perpetuation of tradition enables cultural and subjective identity and is a very complex structure involving both subjective and objective meanings.

Transcendent

Something is transcendent when it exceeds usual limits. In Philosophy, it is understood as being beyond the limits of all possible experience and knowledge. It can also refer to universal applicability or significance as with the case of human rights or liberty as transcendental ideas. It is important to recognize the difference between the terms transcendent and transcendental. The former refers to that which lies beyond what our faculty of knowledge can know. The latter is a climbing, or going beyond the philosophical concept or limit. The concept is significant in the scope of intellectual history, as it pertains to ontology, epistemology, and value theory, or ethics, among perhaps all realms of philosophy. We explore concepts and traditions related to transcendence and we identify its application in real world contexts.

In the 1820s and 1830s, Transcendentalism was an American religious and philosophical movement that contrasted with the intellectual, and spiritual cultural standard of the time. It focused on the ideal spirit and state that transcends the physical and empirical. It was comprised of the combination of English and German romanticism, the transcendental philosophy of Immanuel Kant, the skepticism of David Hume, and elements from Swedenborg and the Upanishads. It contended that man was inherently good and, that people are at their best when they are self-reliant and independent. They emphasized subjective intuition over objective empiricism. Focus was on free conscience and the value of intellectual reason. Adherents longed for a more intense spiritual experience. Prominent Transcendentalists included Ralph Waldo Emerson, Henry David Thoreau, and Walt Whitman. Critics deemed it mysticism for mysticism's sake and identified its philosophical position as transcending even sanity and reason!

Kant's Transcendental Idealism (TI) concerned how human experience of things is similar to the way they appear to us. This makes use of a subject-based component that mediates perception rather than a direct activity of perceiving objects as themselves. For Immanuel Kant, it is how we intuit things and how we account for space and time. This contrasted with Leibniz, who saw space and time as relations of objects/things, and Newton, who demarcated space/time as things having real substance. Kant utilized space/time as forms of intuition by which we perceive objects. They are the subjective but necessary preconditions of any given object insofar as this object is appearance, and not a thing-in-itself. To Kant, the main point of TI concerned the way we can possibly know objects even before experiencing them. Space and time are the means that make *a priori* knowledge possible. TI transformed the realms of epistemology and ethics radically. The notions or literature offered by the Transcendentalists remain poignant if not beautiful and moving. The importance of transcendental values need be identified. While we have addressed key or core values/virtues, transcendental values undergird, if not surpass even those hallowed ideas.

Transcendental ideas exceed the spectrum if not serve as poles. The presence, or the lack thereof, in our community is a pertinent concern. Most values are now very egocentric, or concern merely narrow self-interests. Transcendental values concern a greater experience if not the greater community. They are inclusive and pertain to the whole in contrast to the myopic focus or emphasis on the self. While it is necessary to entertain, much less apply such values, the good of *much* larger broader, encompassing values can not be emphasized sufficiently. Implementing such a perspective equates to the largest of views, or the widest of scope. Should transcendent values rise to prominence and esteem in the community, we stand to benefit immensely.

Trauma

Trauma is deeply disturbing or distressing experience. Trauma can be physical or psychological. Pertaining to the former, the severity of an injury and how fast it receives sufficient address is the difference between a prolonged disability and even death. Prompt and proper response makes the difference of saving life and limb! Psychological trauma is the key point of this entry as its effects and presence is of tremendous significance.

Psychological trauma is damage to the mind. Overwhelming amounts of stress over the course of one or many experience elicit an inability to cope. Trauma plays an important role in United States society, today. Here we address the causes and symptoms of trauma, along with suggestions for making use of treatment and discovering solutions.

Trauma is different between individuals. It is remarkably subjective. Different things affect different people but people also cope and manage their stress and affairs in disparate manners. Because someone encounters trauma does not equate to a traumatized percipient. A witness to or a participant in a traumatic event can cope with stress, integrate emotions and progress with their life seamlessly. Knowing how to cope is built of temperamental and environmental factors. Exposure to activities that structure resilience and the seeking of resources or help makes a significant difference as to addressing trauma meaningfully. These habits are learned and developed skill sets. They amount to a countering of negative events with positive balancing behaviors. The maintenance and care of the self in the face of extreme adversity is an important ability. Mitigating or managing stress is a life skill and so is remaining functional, and well - even in the face of absolute devastation. Trauma can be wrought by physical elements such as terrorism, car accidents, and natural disasters like earthquakes, tsunamis, and tornadoes. Physical forms including attack and rape are traumatic incidents. Verbal barrages or, perhaps, the inability to process and integrate emotions that are associated with different stress responses can elicit psychological trauma.

Severity of psychological trauma depends on the person, the type of trauma, and the support received. The experience is very subjective. Individuals can experience anxiety, anger, sadness, or post-traumatic stress disorder (PTSD). Some might encounter difficulty sleeping well, physical pain, relationship issues, and concerns regarding self-esteem. Experience is very subjective, and individuals might experience one reaction or none at all. Re-engaging or recurring trauma occurs due to trauma reminders, or triggers. They may be conscious or unconscious. Recurring episodes demonstrates the body/mind struggling to cope. Individuals may have nightmares, insomnia, or sudden fits of anger. Trauma can register in the genetics of individuals, and be passed over generations.

In the present tense, exhaustion, despair, and depression can result if psychological trauma is left untreated. One of the worst consequences of trauma is the harsh critique of the self and calling into question the identity. Self-esteem, self-confidence, and the self-concept are of tremendous significance, especially as pertaining to trauma. For an individual who views their own person with honor, respect, and care will be healthier and more resilient. An honored self is cared for, and is viewed with reverence. It will be maintained, but it remains ever vulnerable to the incisive inquiry of a particularly stressed and overwhelmed mind.

Trauma requires prompt and sufficient care. Regarding psychological traumas, avoid alcohol and recreational drugs. Seek medical attention, or the care and attention of loved ones. Exercise, sleep, and engage in active self-care. As far as treatment is concerned, therapy is a common solution. Different methods are available for the spectrum of maladies, and the goal is processing stress, and integrating emotions in order to remain a thriving, engaged, and fully functional individual. As an important note, trauma need not define an individual. An incredible number of people live amazing lives even after suffering staggering loss or experiencing spectacular trauma. These individuals define their lives by persevering and remaining meaningfully engaged. People experience accidents, lose their families, suffer through torture, war, and an array of tragedies, but *still* demonstrate resiliency in order to adapt and overcome these specific encounters with adversity.

Our nation and communities are burdened by daily stress, but also trauma. We are barraged by terrorism, natural disasters, financial turmoil, and the existential concerns born of politics and strife. We are a people that is beset by trauma of different varieties, rendering us insecure and overwhelmed. As our trauma is not addressed for what it is, most posed solutions are offered as external, available as an array of topical and superficial approaches. Should we as a people continue to neglect our traumatized condition, we will suffer generalized PTSD as a matter of standard cultural conduct.

Trouble

A state or condition of distress, annoyance, or difficulty is trouble. Over the course of your years, you will encounter adversity and problems. Trouble may be internal, or external. You will have health issues, and need to care for head, heart, and hands. BE PROACTIVE, so as to minimize the opportunity of ill health or issue. External troubles include everything else. Conflict with others and events on the moment-to-moment basis can amount to serious difficulty. Awareness is a primary skill that serves to help us avoid unnecessary incidents and travails. In order to sidestep such occurrences, keep your head on a swivel, and be mindful of your surroundings. Keep track of your responsibilities. The more data you can both perceive and process, the better the chance for preparedness for opportunities and relative safety and security. In the case of encountering trouble, though, refer to the following problem-solving/trouble shooting steps:

-Gather information. Note related symptoms, and special circumstances.
-Eliminate unnecessary variables.
-Check common causes.
-Explore separate parts/components/entities/institutions. Be aware of series, or inter-related parts.
-Adjust, repair, revise, or replace.
-Repetition, with variation per result.

Strive to avoid trouble by remaining vigilant, and aware. Be proactive and address what needs attention before issues arise. This applies equally to maintaining a car, and maintaining a relationship. The more care and concern put forth, the better the results, more often than not.

Trust

A firm belief in the truth, ability, or strength of someone or something is trust. It is an assumed reliance, one in which confidence is played. Trust is a dependence on something as a future reliance. For example, because someone has demonstrated care and concern as a standard characteristic, one would trust those same standards to persist. Trust is faith in someone that they will abide by that same character. The absence of trust undermines relationships. A loss of trust equates to a lack of confidence. A breach or a loss of trust, is a consequential trespass. Regaining trust is a difficult task so steps need be enacted to maintain and build trust, as a first option. A healthy relationship can not be maintained with one-sided trust, or a total absence.

Some ways to establish and build trust include:
-Work to earn it. Under-promise and over-deliver. Match your words to your deeds
-Keep promises.
-Keep items, issues in confidence.
-Communicate openly, in person.
-Respect one another, and each other's differences without judgment.
-Share and live your truth. *Be authentic.*
-Forgive: accept apologies and proceed in the present instead of dwelling in the past.
-Engage personal growth in lieu of stagnating, remaining as you are. Be dynamic, concerned, and engaged.
-Be supportive of another in *any* relationship.
-Disagree in private with mature, measured exchanges of information.

Approaching self and others with respect and understanding makes for a meaningful relationship. Do what you say you are going to do and build trust by maintaining that standard.

Truth

Truth refers to the body of real things, events, and facts. It is a transcendent fundamental, or spiritual reality. It was with great difficulty that we define truth without referencing it. It has elements of faithfulness, fidelity, loyalty, sincerity, veracity, and it is an agreement with fact and/or reality. Truth is the aim of belief. Without it there is no standard – period - nor any reason *whatsoever* to life. There is no greater concept in the western tradition than truth. It stands as the benchmark as far as discussions concerning philosophy, art, and religion, and its power is applied in the consequential realms of science, law, and journalism. The entire foundation of western civilization is based on truth as a significant, if not the most meaningful characterization of good. It is the power or presence that, when applied to chaos, steers reality to the fore. It is an idea that permeates, if not guides ancient Judaism and Greek thought. If truth is applied to potential/chaos, the result is a good one.

Truth stands as the most foundational premise of our society. There is nothing more powerful than the power of truth. It is said that all of life is suffering. No matter the final outcome, we are vulnerable and exposed creatures and we will face serious challenges, adversity, and suffering. Truth is the means of the balance to chaotic life. It is living in accordance with reality. There is a strength provided by living in truth. It commands a power across immense communicative networks and all of reality. Truth resonates; it *feels* good, even if first it need be substantiated and/or proven. The act of offering untruths, or lying, has a dissociative feeling, akin to that of cognitive dissonance. Lying dissociates us at the center of our being. Truth to self is authenticity, and integrity. Even if the truth is a painful one, it still commands more power than a lie, for there is reality undergirding it. That which is based on reality can only be powerful as it is founded – it has substance.

Since truth matters, it need be pursued and applied. Acting with reality, insisting on what is true is a demand for the right and good. It is always a risk to expose oneself or to be vulnerable by speaking. By standing up and speaking truth, we claim power of our most authentic and real self. In order to do so, we need be mindful and aware of reality. We need be engaged, pursue, and insist upon its perpetuated presence. The truth brings about heaven on earth, or at least works to alleviate a portion of hell, or suffering from the terrestrial plane. Stand in truth.

Craft words that are true. Engage power and achieve standing as a person by acting in opposition to falsehood. The consequences of doing so may yet prove painful but the benefit of living in reality is a profound existential reward.

"Whoever is careless with the truth in small matters cannot be trusted with important matters." - **Albert Einstein**

"Honesty is the first chapter in the book of wisdom." - **Thomas Jefferson**

"No legacy is so rich as honesty." - **William Shakespeare**

"For every good reason there is to lie, there is a better reason to tell the truth." - **Bo Bennett**

"On the mountains of truth you can never climb in vain: either you will reach a point higher up today, or you will be training your powers so that you will be able to climb higher tomorrow." - **Friedrich Nietzsche**

"I'm for truth, no matter who tells it. I'm for justice, no matter who it's for or against." - **Malcolm X**

"Be Impeccable With Your Word. Speak with integrity. Say only what you mean. Avoid using the word to speak against yourself or to gossip about others. Use the power of your word in the direction of truth and love." – **Don Miguel Ruiz**

"A lie told often enough becomes the truth." - **Vladimir Lenin**

"In a time of universal deceit - telling the truth is a revolutionary act." – **Unknown**

Chapter 21

Underlying

'What lies beneath' is something that is underlying. It refers to latent, unrevealed, or concealed matters. Keep in mind how not all subjects are merely topical issues should they lack underlying concerns. Underlying features can serve as the foundations upon which an idea, person, place, or thing exists. Such matters need not be sinister issues kept from the light and maintained in secret. Underlying subjects can be political, emotional, intellectual, and physical, among other possibilities. The subjects upon which things are predicated need not all be investigated and publicized. It *is* important to note, however, that everything has a rationale upon which initiative or action is taken. These are underlying issues and they are the contributing, significant factors to ethos and behavior. They can be comprised of personal experience and broader culture. What lies beneath the presentation are the values, sentiments, and experience that give rise to it.

Be aware of the spectrum of possibility when addressing underlying subjects of interest. The investigation into why people, places, things and ideas are the way they are, or why they do the things they do, is a complex venture into an incredible array of applied concepts. Also, be very aware as to how you engage this behavior daily, if not on a very regular occasion. The philosophical inquiry of 'why' will command a fair portion of our mind. For we *are* curious – it is our very nature to want to understand. You will continue to address that concern of what lies underneath behavior as you continue to live and engage an external reality. Enjoy this particular enterprise and investigation.

Unity

The state of being united or joined as a whole is unity. It is the case of disparate parts to be joined for a purpose. Philosophically, the concept has been addressed by pre-Socratics including Anaximander, Heraclitus, Anaximenes, as well as Parmenides, Pythagoras via Cicero, and moderns like Descartes, Kant. Unity is sufficiently important as to be included in our national motto; 'e pluribus unum' or, 'out of many, one' (refers to the 13 colonies being joined under the aegis of one nation). Unity contrasts with plurality, and for this particular reason, is an idea that has held the attention of philosophers and statesmen since ancient times.

Pre-Socratic Philosophers Heraclitus and Anaximander are some of the first to engage the idea of unity and they both addressed an idea of the unity of opposites as underpinnings of greater metaphysical reality. Within the latter's idea of the *apeiron,* the meeting or conflict of opposites occurred. Anaximenes offered a continuum of change, to oppose the strict confrontation of opposite poles/concepts. Parmenides held that all of reality was a unity. Change is impossible and existence is then timeless, uniform, necessary, and unchanging. Sensory perception leads to mistakes and to complete the cosmogony: Parmenides denied the existence of a void. Because a unity is reality, it is the lone object of knowledge. The unreality of variety is embodied by opinion which represents but a limited aspect of the whole and truth. Later, Cicero applied the Pythagorean idea of happiness to cite the unity of family and social bonds as the origin of societies and states. Both Descartes and Kant contributed via their approach of the unity of consciousness. Kant's Transcendental Unity of Apperception makes experience possible, uniting coherent consciousness from different inner experiences.

The concept pertains to metaphysics, epistemology, logic, aesthetics, and ethics: every significant realm of philosophy. Its consequence remains apparent in the 'practical' realm of our own nation.

In 1795, the United States adopted its motto. From thirteen original colonies was birthed this sole, united country. This country is known as a tapestry of different thread, a melting pot, or a crucible of various pluralities and lesser distinctions. The promise of the country was that the unity of colonies and disparate people elicited a state, and a singular, unified entity that amounted to something greater than the sum of its parts. The unity made possible by the establishment of the country allowed for the realization of important liberties and freedoms, the achievement of a structured balance of rights and responsibilities never before experienced in human history. The principal element unity is its contrast with plurality, the idea of one among many. The unity of parts is meant for the satisfaction of a larger concern or goal. A nation was established to protect individual interests and rights. In doing so, trivial distinctions of identity were of minimal importance when compared to the greater project concerning the national character. Subjective wants and needs were addressed so long as individuals enjoined in the greater united effort.

The concepts of unity and togetherness are lofty ones, indeed. Individuals benefit should the unity make use of substantial actions and meaningful, inclusive words and deeds. Those ideals are consequential and remain worth something when they are supported. Should a unity become onerous, or even burdensome, it will be questioned, if not revised or dissolved. Its power and strength lie in the offer of promise that supersedes pluralities and identity. It is our responsibility as participants in our communities to ensure that our national unity elicits larger, inclusive benefits and rewards. Our nation exists on a sliding scale continuum of structures, or institutions. We have alternatives to this particular unity, and chaos or anarchy (literally: without a ruler), are not lone, polar alternatives. It is our opportunity and privilege to create of our selves worthy, able parts of this greater experiment of social cohesion and unity. Along those same lines, we need make certain that the principles, or the goals of the united structure, serve us well. It does no good to be passive participants ruled by conventions. We need be certain that our unity serves us, and the greater global community, too. Are we served by the unity that is the United States? How can this arrangement or structure be bettered by and for its constituents?

Utility

The concept of utility: the state of being useful, profitable, or beneficial, has been addressed in numerous sections, including that of ability, (being) capable, and others, besides. The idea pertains to self and others, and connects to time as a concept, as well. Simply: our lives need be useful. If we have no specific, subjective purpose for our presence here, we are wasting the resources that will elicit favorable returns in the form of abilities and skill sets. We need first have a use for our own selves. This ties to meaning. Our sense of meaning and self-worth are intimately connected. Our lives – our very person - need first matter to ourselves in order to earn the attention of our own address and investment.

When we recognize our own subjective value, we can move to increase and maximize our subjective happiness. And we do that not by passing time and merely existing. We elicit benefits and positive returns by being of use and structuring a self that is of greater utility. Having experience is certainly a good. But applicable skill sets or a useful set of experience imparts concrete value because one's specific resources are brought to bear meaningfully. We are no good to others, or the greater community, then, until we are of value *to ourselves* and we demonstrate that by making something of ourselves: something worthy, useful to our own purposes, but also to others and the community.

Chapter 22

Valor

Valor is great courage in the face of danger, especially in battle. It has an honored position among other concepts; societies bestow medals as recognition of particular acts of valor. The Congressional Medal of Valor is awarded in the United States while other states award similar awards. Demonstrating acts of *great* courage deserve public acknowledgement and recognition. For valor lies several orders greater than a typical application of courage. The latter is exercised on the playground, or in school, or in the workplace. People demonstrate courage by addressing peers or speaking truth to power, though of course, the concept is present on a battlefield, or when confronting a serious threat even on the street. Valor is more specifically situated in that the consequences are far more significant than others but the particular behavior is above and beyond a typical response. Valor takes place in dangerous situations, those in which the threat of serious injury, if not death, is very real. Valor consists of two primary elements. The first is the presence of the fight or flight mode. The second element of valor is the rational element that moves or persuades the individual to apply valor and address or confront the dangerous ills or harm involved in the scene.

Courage becomes valor when the stakes, or the consequences of the context, grow to dangerous proportions. The situational awareness of the situation necessitates escape or confrontation. Despite the presence of serious danger, or the prospects of injury, or death, the individual who utilizes valor is the entity who forgoes the safety of escape and, instead, addresses very real threats and harm in order to serve a greater need. This may consist of the health and well-being of others or the larger community. Police officers are commended for valor for engaging in a firefight in order to save lives. Those in the military are honored for their display of valor when they sacrifice for their colleague or for a specific campaign, or initiative. Imagine a soldier taking fire in order to cover the escape of his peers when he knows full well that the likelihood of his survival is minimal. It is a very particular situation that requires the application of valor. The sacrifice of the self may be the best if not only means of ameliorating a situation. Individuals who give their lives so that others may continue living is an act that is honored publicly, across many cultures and societies. I hope you never have to sacrifice your own self, though in the case that you do consider it as an option– be *very* mindful of the elements and factors at play. There are things that are worth dying for though there is so very much to live for, as well. Valor does not require death or sacrifice. It requires shouldering significant, imminent harm in order to lessen the likelihood of others' suffering. The instances inviting the application of valor is an intense and very particular one. Be aware of components of situations and be mindful of your own values and principles as you decide among very consequential behaviors and initiatives.

Values

For the purposes of this text, values are principles or standards of behavior that display one's judgment of what is important in life. A significant portion of this work has addressed or included the concept of values, for they play a role in *everything*. Values are one's raison d'etre - aside from biological drives and natural urges. Values can inform or guide us as to how to deal with these organic inclinations. They are called values, for they are regarded as important and worthy. There can be lower or base values; greed, exclusion, and violence are all values of a lesser standard (though there might perhaps be the context in which they serve greater, if not the greatest good). While it might be difficult to imagine *these* three as potentials for good, violence could save lives, and prove most meaningful. Point being, the higher order values are those that individuals select as guidelines, or significant principles.

Personal values are also known as common core principles. They structure the means and ways in which we lead our lives. Only certain values are core, or critical, for if all values are shared similarly, then nothing is a priority. We will recognize values at play in all settings. As we prepare to live as mature, independent individuals, we need decide upon those values and principles and then behave in such a way to demonstrate them to the external world. Two reasons for unclear depictions of values are a lack of thoroughly grasped principles and when principles are intentionally dynamic. Values are profoundly important. They need be grasped and engaged for the good of both the individual and the community. For an individual requires values to move ahead and make use of their life. Should they lack a fixed array of values, they become like buoys barraged by waves, stuck having to react to the world. The greater community need accept the values of the individual. It will not, and can not tolerate or accept an individual who makes use of anti-social, aggressive values in violent behavior at the expense of greater social unity and cohesion. In the case where someone changes their values, they will be recognized by their new activity and behavior. A person with no fixed set of values is an opportunist, one who aligns their sails to the next wind that blows. Unprincipled individuals are opportunistic, seeking rewards available in the next moment-to-moment circumstance. Should they lack inclusive values, these individuals can only value themselves and, even then: that is not a necessary condition, either. They will not honor or respect others before personal gains and benefits are satisfied.

Make use of worthy values and apply them in the course of a life well lived. Core values include:

-authenticity	-achievement	-authority	-balance
-beauty	-boldness	-compassion	-challenge
-creativity	-fairness	-faith	-fun
-peace	-happiness	-honesty	-influence
-knowledge	-leadership	-love	-meaning
-optimism	-wisdom	-poise	-respect
-security	-service	-stability	

Vibration

A person's emotional state, the atmosphere of a place, or the associations of an object, as communicated to, or felt by others, is its vibration. In this particular entry, we discuss personal vibration. Aside from intellectual conceptions of the term, we recognize vibration by feelings and intuition. Vibration is ever present and always occurring. It can be positive or negative. Positive personal vibration occurs when we are pleased or inclined to feel good due to many different catalysts and motivators. We could enjoy the rewards of an achievement, the company of others, or the release a deep bellow of a laugh and become very aware of our positive state. When we have a negative vibration, we do not feel good, and we are at odds with internal or external events/catalysts. We could be disappointed by failure, on edge because of the company we keep, or feel less than best because of the food we ingest, or the lack of sleep from the previous night. One's vibration is a combination of the conditions of the head, heart, and hands. One significant excess or deficiency in any of the three realms can have a dramatic effect on our greater vibration. Here we discuss awareness of our vibration and how to both manage and improve that subjective level.

We note how we feel however often we perform a self-diagnostic and personal review. Unfortunately, we forego the diagnostics frequently, and we live with excessive amounts of stress, worry, and fear. So when we do touch base with our self we are likely to encounter a vibration that meets or reflects that condition or state. And what is more important: the greater world responds to our vibratory state. We have discussed frequencies, energy, and the quanta. Vibration connects with much that has been offered along the lines of those aforementioned concepts. Simply: we need be more aware of how we are, by engaging our subjective condition regularly. That means taking several (if not many!) occasions during the day to pause, reflect, and feel, or intuitively investigate and discern as to our mental, emotional, and physical states. Upon establishing it as a habit, we will come to recognize with relative ease our own vibration. We will feel our own positive or negative energy. If we choose to be mindful of our condition, we can take care and proper responsibility for it. Noting how we are negative, we can address those items that contribute to the less than ideal state. We can change our mind or focus on other things. We can listen to or play music. We can sleep, eat, or connect and interact with others in order to lift our spirits and vibration. When we recognize how we are offering a positive vibe, we can repeat those methodologies that elicited the original pleasant condition, and strive to continue or perpetuate that higher vibration. Another way to apply your awareness is to feel, or intuit the scene or context in which you are situated. If you practice how to recognize and respond ably to the different energies of people, places, and ideas, you will benefit from a specialized form of intuition. A key to vibration is the mind. Should we desire to feel better, we need first direct our attention to items that will facilitate a more positive state.

Control or exercise those faculties or aspects that influence and color your subjective well-being. When you harness resources for the positive, your vibration will demonstrate that positive condition. As a contrast, some maintain how a higher, positive vibration is not the optimum state or level. Walter Russell contended how

Mind convolutes/creates reality. An increase of vibration/mind only leads further away from truth, rest, and balance at the fulcrum. Russell maintained that lower vibes were the way to go! We have yet to reach definitive understandings of energy and our own energies and vibrations, specifically. Explore and be mindful of your own vibration and general state. Managing your vibration is a significant component of self-care and it is a life skill worth developing.

Violence

According to the World Health Organization (WHO), the intentional use of force or power, threatened or actual, against oneself, another person, or against a group or community, which either results in or has a high likelihood of resulting in injury, death, psychological harm, mal-development, or deprivation is known as violence.[24] It can be against the self, or interpersonal - between individuals - or collective, as in the case of gang or state warfare. For this concept, we note causes of violence. We review a historical perspective of violence and note how it is inherent in man. We explore the necessity of violence in society and maintain that it is a very specific communicative ability that has a particular use and application. We look at violence as an art, and conclude by addressing the farcical idea of a state monopoly on violence, and the presence of violence in our national community.

Many different factors contribute to violence, including poverty, income, inequality, alcohol and drug usage, and the absence of safe, stable, nurturing relationships. Causes are complex, and occur at different levels. Biological and personal factors play a primary role as do close relationships, and the community context. Broader societal factors, including social/cultural norms, the criminal justice and social welfare system, social acceptability of violence, availability of weapons, and exposure to violence contribute to violence in various ways. Violence can be physical, sexual, psychological/emotional, or economic. Note how *violence need not only refer to physical harm*. When power plays a role, violence places a substantial burden on those who suffer non-physical violence.

Violence has forever been a facet of humanity. Whether it was used for self-defense, as initiative for resources - including the taking of a mate - or even sport, violence colors much of human history. Its presence differs across time and cultures as to the community's specific use of violence as a source of pride and a defense of honor. Norbert Elias references how the civilizing process has reduced the drive to violence and thinker Steven Pinker notes how the general level of violence has actually decreased. Regardless of how disparate people and cultures view violence, it will remain a fixture. For violence is another form of communication and some entities are inclined to communicate with lesser instruments in lieu of words and salient rationales. This makes violence necessary as, sometimes, it is the most viable option of conveying an immediately effective and meaningful message. Words and non-violent communication *can* defuse a tense, if not violent scene. It is often *only* violence that summarily impedes and terminates violent initiatives. For this reason, man has structured the study of violence as a discipline and art.

Violence is a necessity born of the perpetual presence of threats and aggression and the lesser applications of power and assorted resources. It communicates values. Simply, an entity is willing to implement threatening or harmful methodologies in order to realize aims. The majority of violence occurs as reactionary, knee-jerk behavior. Rarely is violence, specifically at the subjective level, the product of an even-keeled, levelheaded approach to an issue. Individuals get angry, rationality is discarded, and the remaining tools can be showcased in an unfortunate, undisciplined, and wholly unnecessary, base physical demonstration. The threat of violence necessitates an appropriate response. Given the options of how to communicate violently, practitioners of martial arts elect to communicate eloquently. Those who engage violence as a necessary life skill apply violence as a means of defending their own person, others, and the community. Martial artists view violence as a means to ending aggression and unjustified initiatives. Such individuals contrast with those who apply violence with malevolence as their motivation. These might be common thugs, thieves, murderers, or politicians. These entities are but minimally concerned with social inclusion or the affects of their violence upon others. They levy violence to achieve their aims, regardless of afflicted parties. Others who wield violence engage it as a sport. These individuals engage violence under the aegis of rules, referees, and a point system. For them it is a means of leisure or play, albeit in an insulated, structured realm as a recreational activity.

Those agents who approach violence as a discipline, or those who treat their study as an art are a special type. These individuals engage philosophies - examine virtues on a path that results in a delivery of conscious, deliberate violence. This third group of violent individuals might well be considered as guardians and warriors. They are people who choose to act by applying what they view to be appropriate at the time while others remain unwilling or unable. A principled approach to violence stands in stark contrast to the other two standards of violent actors. A community's perception of violence will color the social standing of those who engage violently. Along the spectrum of cultural values is the belief that the state maintains a monopoly of violence or that violence is a tool of the state or governing authority, alone. Wholly untenable, though, is the idea that an individual need forsake the responsibility of self-care and maintenance or some tools that facilitate health and wellness. It is nonsensical to forbid the use of a skill set that could protect life, liberty, property, and community. It is very telling how self-defense, in particular, is *not* enshrined formally as a right, because such a move would make explicit how individuals can apply their agency to counter and oppose even state violence. Then again:

> *Our rights need not be formalized in order to exist.* We do not need permission to defend ourselves against *any* threat.

The propensity of people to engage in violence motivates conscious individuals to structure a skill set that allows them to respond ably in specific circumstances. Violence can be approached as a particular form of communication and as an art. An awareness of factors that cause or contribute to violence and an ability to recognize and address violence in assorted forms can keep you and others safe should the knowledge be applied judiciously. Not all of life is sunshine, roses, love, and wonder. Some of it is base, aggressive, intense, and dangerous. Some violence need be countered, opposed, and stifled. In order to protect self, others, and the community, violent skill sets need be honed as a healthy and necessary part of the fullest human education. Be equipped with head, heart, and hands and make use of available resources in order to defend, or take initiative, as the case may be.

This last point is important. You are allowed to attack, and even strike first. Training will educate you as to strategy and principles along specific contextual guidelines.

"Violence, naked force, has settled more issues in history than has any other factor." – **Robert A. Heinlein**

"It's often been said, 'violence never solved anything.' The simple truth is that when you are slammed up against the wall and the knife is at your throat, when a circle of teenagers is kicking you as you curl into a ball on the sidewalk, or when the man walks into your office building or school with a pair of guns and starts shooting, only violence, or the reasonable threat of violence, is going to save your life. In the extreme moment, only force can stop force." – **Rory Miller**

Virtue

Much of what we have discussed concerns virtue, vice, and virtue theory. Virtues are any positive sentiment that leads to the happiness of our selves and others. These are the worthy, good qualities we have addressed. Vice is the absence of virtue, or that which does not lead to happiness. The guidelines provided by Aristotle and his teacher, Plato, guide this particular discussion. According to Aristotle, virtue was a mean between two vices, one of deficiency, and one of excess. There are ranked virtues: some are higher than others. Each virtue has a vice. The virtues are not distanced items of thought but pure feelings that are common that lead to happiness or otherwise. There is no one list of virtues, but most point toward the same principles.

Plato's virtues from his text, *Laws* via Aristotle's idea of the golden mean:

Ignorance – Wisdom – Sophistry
Abstention – Temperance – Indulgence
Unfair – Justice – Overly Fair
Cowardice – Courage – Rashness
Unhealthy – health – Overly health conscious
Too Humble – Beauty – Vanity
Fear – Strength – Overcompensation
Stinginess – Charity – Greed

Morals and values are very similar. They are the principles behind our behavior. They move us to act ethically. Ethics are further rules that work to sustain virtues while morals/virtues are foundational concepts. Plato said that goods are either divine or human. Physical, social, and political virtues are the human sort and practical morals connect to moral virtues of the divine variety. So, there are different virtues per different spheres of life. The satisfaction of the virtues elicits health and happiness as ends. Consider, though, how not all things that make us happy are particularly virtuous, for that matter. There are different perspectives on virtues, primarily on their ordering of priority. Mill, Bentham, Smith, and Aquinas - among other Catholic Schoolmen - are definitely worth examination and review. Generally, courage, moderation, duty, justice, will, and wisdom are some of the highest moral virtues, and there are lower forms, too. The basic premise of virtues asserts that, should an individual entertain good intentions, understand duty, moderation and justice, and hold fast to principles, the virtues would be present or, at least, encouraged. Holding the virtues would guide individuals to virtuous behavior, according first to Greek, and then to later Enlightenment Philosophers.

Aristotle remarked about habituation in his Nichomachean Ethics. Virtuous character is elicited by structured and disciplined routine. Continued good behavior builds good character. When a state structures life or culture according to virtue, every individual and the greater community benefits. Explore the civilizations of ancient Egypt and Greece to note how they developed their peoples along these very lines. Does this society encourage virtue, and how? A critical cultural review would be a positive initiative in order to discover a comprehensive answer.

Virtues pertain to the individual as much as to the greater community. It is the underlying point of all philosophy. The balance of virtue and vice takes place in a continuum between every initiative and activity. The application of virtue is in the present, with a view to the future, and, in fact: with a view to a significant spectrum of metaphysical ideas - good and evil included. How Plato and Aristotle constituted the soul, man, and the state is fascinating even today, and well worth the examination. Simply: a virtuous soul made the virtuous man which, in turn, was an able, engaged, valued, and contributing participant in a virtuous, just, and balanced society.

Our own cultural framework does not focus on concepts such as moderation, courage, or justice. The virtues are designated as academic concerns, while they persist, if only as the elephant (herd) in the room. That our society relegates the concept of virtues to that of a speculative activity demonstrates another portion of our national character. How are people supposed to be virtuous if the only mention of virtues comes only in the form of exclusive college philosophy discussions? Virtues have homes within us, should we decide to avail ourselves of their utility.

"Vices are simply the errors which a man makes in his search after his own happiness. Unlike crimes, they imply no malice toward others, and no interference with their persons or property." - **Lysander Spooner**

Vivacious

To be lively, animated, is to be vivacious. It takes of the same root as both vibrant and vital. To be vivacious is to be full of life. To achieve such a state is the result of a remarkably joyous and intentional endeavor. It is the particular human journey of experiencing, acknowledging, processing, feeling, and living (the same process over and over again) as we grow, develop, progress, and hopefully: improve! A fungus merely lives. It consumes and grows. But we have the capability, if not the responsibility, to consciously and critically engage in order to create meaning and contribute to the scene. We can do so much more than feed and age. We have the opportunity to do something special and, in that doing, we achieve vivacity and that fullest flavor and energy of life. ENJOY! There is no limit to it, if you apply yourself well.

The Void, The Abyss

The concept of the void or the abyss is a very interesting one. It could refer to the universe as it was pre-matter, according to Parmenides. We could refer to it along the lines of the Shadow and adopt the perspective of Nietzsche, perhaps. It can operate as that space that can give rise to zero point energy, if not the emergence of the God-particle. Subjectively, we can understand the concept as an absence of another, or a space that is lacking a significant component. The abyss can mean an emotional chasm elicited by trauma or extreme strain and stress. The ideas of the void, or the abyss depict a deficiency of some sort. It is a space of nothing. Its component of lack is generally a negative, though we note that an investigation and address of the Shadow is wholly necessary. In contrast, an examination of the void, specifically, might not fall into the realm of metaphysics and be aided by a shaman or a guide. Whether we are referring to ethics, to black holes, to a specific science fiction movie from the 1980s, Parmenides or Nietzsche, we can diversify and flesh out our understanding of the human experience by engaging these specific concepts.

"He who fights with monsters should be careful lest he thereby become a monster. And if thou gaze long into an abyss, the abyss will also gaze into thee." – **Friedrich Nietzsche**

Chapter 23

Warrior, Warriorship

A warrior is a person who is experienced in conflict, struggle, and warfare. Warriorship consists of practices, or status as a warrior. Examples of warriors include Hoplites, Spartans, Visigoths, Samurai, and Filipino Escrimadors. Warriors are the products of their culture. A warrior is trained and disciplined, cultivated to address and engage conflict against others, typically in the physical realm via combat. Historical precedent differs as to means and ends. Generally, a warrior is an individual apart from the rest of the community; it takes a special entity to be a warrior. Among the necessary qualities are strength, courage, determination, being action-oriented, principled, and having mental toughness and an acuity of mind. A warrior typically adheres to a code of conduct, but not necessarily. Not all have the inclination to serve, protect, or defend the weak and defenseless. Not all warriors entertain higher order ethical concepts and values. The idea of the warrior is an ancient one, which holds pertinence in today's modern setting. For this entry we address how the concept applies for individuals in a society that values contrasting concerns and concepts.

Our society makes mere adjectival use of the term 'warrior,' and warriorship. The understanding is distanced due to its irregular occurrence and minimized presence in our culture. There is a remarkable distinction of values between our community and others that hold warriors in high esteem. The emergence of a warrior in a warrior society/community, such as ancient Sparta, was an important rite of passage. Consecrated and honored was that path, for it was an extremely esteemed position. The role was tasked with an important responsibility of care and protection of the community in the face of aggression, violence, and even death. Warriors were structured and conditioned to address the very real dangers and threats of invaders, brigands, and even local criminals. It is a special role, as precious few are inclined to engage violence, much less study it as an art, and direct a significant portion of time and other resources to satisfaction that is realized through constant vigilance, the careful application of violence, and practices that promote and encourage the presence of guiding principles including virtues and mores.

Few are inclined to address art as it requires and demands. The dedication, focus, and sacrifice involved are characteristics of rare individuals, indeed. Few put forth the necessary hours, consideration, and abandonment of a more regular routine in favor of a nearly all-encompassing practice. Warriorship is defined as an art for the same reasons. It takes a tremendous individual to be a warrior. They are not a common fighter, brawler, or combatant in mixed martial arts competitions, *though they could be warriors, too*. Warriors adopt a disciplined approach, elicited by principles, vigorous training, and engagement. A warrior is not an occupation, nor is it realized in the fulfillment of a role or service. So law enforcement and military personnel are not necessarily warriors, either.

Being a warrior requires the discipline and mastery of the head, heart, and hands. Thoughts need be guided by principles. An awareness is structured by a receptive and open mind. A warrior's most important tool is this cognitive faculty and their sense of perception. Sans these most important tools, a lesser brawler engages haphazardly, lacking distinctions and a discerning perspective. These specific resources lend themselves to propriety and a balanced approach to situations, not just violent or dangerous ones. Importantly, these resources provide the means of distinguishing between effective types of engagements, saving the considerate warrior other important resources when such conflicts prove petty or trifling. Mindfulness and meditation exercises are the means of situating and centering the warrior's mindset.

The warrior's heart is a special resource, one like no other. A warrior puts his or her self into harm's way. They dedicate themselves to a task that will result in aggression, violence, even self-sacrifice, or death. A warrior cares enough to commit to the responsibility. An individual, who trains unceasingly, lives critically, vigilantly, virtuously has care and concern for others at the core of their being. A warrior is one of the best people because their own cultivation is made with others, and the greater community, in mind. Warriorship entails the destruction of lower traits, and the lowest self, in order to serve for the community both an example of higher ideals but also a safer existence. The application of the warrior's heart is one of the most pure demonstrated forms of care. The individual who addresses the bully on the block exemplifies it, as does the individual who enters a perilous fray to protect others, or right a serious wrong. The warrior's heart delays a strike, and even takes into consideration the wrong or individual being corrected. A stayed hand might be a better tool in some instances than the closed fist landing a blow. A component of aikido (literally: the way of peace) is known as the path. A warrior can elect to be brutally efficient and stunningly adept at bringing pain to bear or they can apply a gentler route and apply other, less harmful resources in the moment. Peace is not passivity. It is forbearance and discipline – even in the face of physical adversity. It requires heart, and a special type of care to relent and apply such honed resources and skills so ably.

The warrior is a finely tuned instrument. Their complete physical person is a tool to be wielded. A key distinction, here: their person, and ability need not be the tool of another. A warrior will not permit himself or herself to be used as a pawn of others. They must be very principled and cautious as to who or what is served by their engagements. They are careful not to allow themselves to be used for unjust causes, or by unworthy individuals. In the interests of structuring a viable physical skill set, a warrior trains their physical person in a variety of ways, with a diversified spectrum of arts in order to format a character that is capable of impeding or eliminating an existential threat. Martial arts and the building of abilities via calisthenics, weight training, and yoga, among other physical endeavors, prepare a warrior for the next necessary entanglement. A dedicated routine of rest as well as a nourishing diet deliver meaningful results. As with all other activities, breath and breathing exercises need retain proper consideration and application. Breathing is integral to stamina, and general self-regulation and is so very important to the ideal warrior.

Bushido's 8 Virtues, the 9 Noble Virtues, o, the 7 Cardinal Virtues play but minor parts in our United States culture. An array of other concepts and ideas can guide a virtuous, disciplined individual while they dedicate themselves to the life of a warrior. Warriorship in this country is a very specific concern, considered only by the precious few who can grasp its consequence as a necessity in *any* society. The way of the United States American warrior is a subjective route, rather than an objective cultural reality. Still, the means of structuring and refining a warrior ethos is an endeavor undertaken by a serious minority. Those individuals are one of the necessary means of caring for the community. Should you feel stirred, or obligated to protect others and address trespasses and wrongdoing, the way of the warrior might be for you, though if and only if you are willing to shoulder the responsibilities of such an incredible role. Remember, too: this culture lacks a proper understanding of warriors and warriorship. A herd of sheep generally resent the presence of the sheepdog until that presence becomes necessary. And because evil never rests, vigilant entities need rise to the occasion by living, serving as warriors.

Water

While it is more than a passing concern, an address of water receives but minimal treatment *here*. As an important component of greater biological and human health: more than 70% of both the globe and the human body are comprised of water. We would do well to conserve and protect this most precious natural resource. The seas are the maligned filters of the planet. When we take into consideration the results of the experiments of Dr. Masaru Emoto, we note that we are maligning our bodies' waters similarly. Participants in the study blessed or cursed containers of water. Water changed its molecular structure according to the treatment received. Water responded to mental forces!

As a people, we are stressed, overly self-abusive, and lacking significant components of self-respect. While addressing these concerns may not start, nor end with blessings directed and applied towards our selves, the activity could not hurt. That we are a majority of water means that our own waters could react similarly. We need provide the stimulation that elicits a favorable return of our resources! Water is an integral component of our earth and our own selves. Should we respect earth, and desire to continue our own existence on this plane, we need drastically revise how we approach water as a natural resource. That corporate entity Nestle denies it as a human right and some pertinent thinkers consider the next global wars to concern water availability means that time is of the essence. We will experience serious consequences should we fail to be proactive, and engage meaningfully.

Wholeness

Wholeness is a harmonious unity. It refers to all aspects of human nature, especially as a composite of one's physical, intellectual, and spiritual aspects. When we previously engaged the concept of the self, we flirted with the idea of wholeness. Integrating the disparate elements and experiences of a lifetime results in wholeness. In order to attain a whole character, it is necessary to enjoin in an education that addresses the entire person. Such an endeavor is the responsibility of the individual. When an individual cares sufficiently as to want to develop across the realms of the head, heart, and hands, they will seek those resources that facilitate a holistic, or comprehensive sense of self. With this text you have been given the means of enlarging what you know in an effort to widen your perspective, and transform your mind. It is hoped that it guides you to improve your condition and the quality of your thoughts, feelings, and behavior. Wholeness is a significant portion of health across realms: intellectual, emotional, and physical. Foster wholeness within your person by diversifying activities that impart worthwhile and meaningful skills. Recognize that the search for wholeness does not pertain to external goods. As it is, you have the complete means at your disposal to make of your own self all that you desire and need. Structure and enjoy a life that makes use of integrity and wholeness as significant components.

The Will

At any moment of decision, the will chooses the strongest desire. The will, then, is a mechanism for choosing. With reason and understanding, it is a distinct part of the mind. The will is central to ethics. For this concept, we emphasize the will's part in self-definition and self-mastery as we review how it has been addressed through time by better thinkers. An important portion of the concept pertains to free will, the idea that our choices are not predetermined or fated to occur.

A prominent line of philosophers and thinkers has addressed will. Aristotle addressed it in his *Nicomachean Ethics*. Books III and VII provide discussions that have influenced and structured the topic for all else. He ultimately associated it as a means of self-mastery.

Augustine deemed will to be the "mother and guardian of all virtues." Aquinas followed his predecessors' example and, in his *Summa Theologica*, outlined a remarkable treatise concerning the concept. Modern philosophers including Spinoza, Locke, and Hume considered all will to be free, hence the term 'free will' amounted to verbal confusion. Schopenhauer's identification of will as *the* thing-in-itself, in response to Kant's Transcendental Idealism, marked a new standard. He contended that we are made of endless drives and all other phenomena is will. It is primary, and makes use of knowledge to satisfy cravings and urges. The historical record of investigations pertaining to will is important, for it concerns volitional acts and decision-making; associated realms include the consequential ones of law and psychology. We identify individuals as strong- or weak-willed, as having the capacity or discipline to make restrained decisions or not. We note the idea of *akrasia*: the behavior of acting against one's own best interests. The unconscious mind sometimes exerts control over and substantially influences the exercise of will.

A portion of mental health is comprised of the ability to control thoughts and impulses. Will selects between unconscious drives in accordance with the manifest desires and values of an individual. The will steers behavior to the strongest-held desire. Controlling the mind and developing impulse control are imperative. Applying a strong will means one applied a meaningful approach to their subjective desires. A strong will elicits behavior that is in line with values while weak-willed initiatives cede to temptation and lesser inclinations. Will is at play in every activity: what we will is what occurs. So when faced with the option of sleeping in, or rising with the alarm clock to address goals and responsibilities, our will demonstrates our resolve, our foundational principles in that moment. A strong will elicits behaviors and decisions that align with considered, subjective values. A weak will demonstrates lesser values. We *all* give in to temptation and base drives. Sometimes we engage hypocritically - contrary to how we present ourselves as principled. For example, we might get angry at others for texting while driving but we might still engage the same practice. Or hypocrisy is demonstrated by those who champion farm workers' rights, but complain about the high prices of food at the market.

Will is a demonstration of strength of conviction. It is courage in the face of your own self as adversity. We might lapse in our good habit or demeanor, but that failing in the moment does not characterize our person, totally. Strength of will or will power is tested on a moment-to-moment basis as it is our repeated adherence to principles and an insistence on particular subjective values via prioritized behaviors that demonstrates the general character of a person. Developing a strong will elicits benefits of self-control, firm convictions, determination, and motivation. A strong will helps us persevere in the face of adversity and temptation and it is an invaluable resource. Pursuing goals and holding measured values necessitates the presence of will. The irresolute character of a weak will is spineless and such a standard is beneath the level of good and worthy people.

Wit

Wit refers to mental sharpness, keen intelligence, wisdom, and sagacity. A quick wit can impart levity. Keeping one's wits about them means remaining in a state of readiness, in the case intellectual resources need be brought to bear suddenly. Wittiness refers to the ability of someone to apply wit via a clever comment, quip, or wisecrack. A battle of wits occurs when entities use their intelligence and wits to defeat one another. Wits are an intellectual concept. It is the application of what is known in an insightful, maybe comedic manner. Wit involves being able to connect or associate known things in a particularly novel fashion. Not everyone has a sharp or quick wit. Some are deemed dull, slow, or dim-witted. Being a systematic thinker with the ability to connect and synthesize disparate bodies of information lends itself to social dynamics as well as instances requiring problem-solving skills.

Studying and making use of the incredible array of material across cultures, religions, time, and place deliver a portion of wit. The crucial element of wit, though, is to be gained via experience with others. Wit is a communal exercise. It need be shared with others in order to be recognized and appreciated. One could certainly keep their witticisms inside, to themselves, but the humor created by the amalgamation or overlap of content is worth sharing for a group to enjoy. Wit demonstrates the mind of an able thinker, a lively conversationalist, and creative perspective. It is important to know things and be intelligent. It is quite another thing entirely to integrate remarkably disparate material or find the congruity or commonality in seemingly unrelated data. Keep your wits about you, and investigate the abundance of connections across spheres of knowledge and experience! Also, as the saying goes, "do not engage in a battle of wits with an unarmed opponent."

Wonder

Surprise, mingled with admiration caused by something dreadful, unexpected, unfamiliar, or inexplicable is wonder. It is born of curiosity and the desire to behold or investigate something impressive. A child sees the world as a magical place. They have yet to experience the travails and darker elements of the world. They remain open and curious as to more components of the greater scene. This openness lends itself to pro-social behavior. A sense of wonder draws attention to the wider world and minimizes the importance of the individual in a greater scheme of life and things. Wonder is a transcendent exercise. It invites inspection, review, and participation. The person, place, or thing that elicits wonder will be addressed and included objectively – but hopefully: subjectively! Wonder brings forth our involvement. When we somehow perceive an item X, some sort of fancy is piqued, and we enjoin in a relationship. We can structure the relationship as a means to the satisfaction of intellectual curiosity. Alternatively, we can lend ourselves fully to the dynamic and explore how this Item X is in relationship – we examine what particular aspect draws our attention, and how it garners our interest.

A sense of wonder is a powerful activity in and of itself but it is also an incredible social/communal/cultural instrument. In the interests of facilitating the emergence of good character and further: aiding the coalescence of good people in a community, a sense of wonder needs be encouraged. It is necessary to ask: what are we doing culturally, that invites and instills a sense of curious wonder within the people? Or: what are we doing culturally, that reduces, minimizes, or even eliminates the prospects for, or presence of wonder? It *is* possible to situate wonder as a social norm, and a priority, at that. This would pertain to the realms of the public education system, media, and, in fact, the entire social sphere. What earns our curiosity, or piques our attention is another facet of what distinguishes us subjectively. One individual might be curious as to the dynamics of nuclear fission while another might experience wonder as they witness the transformation of seasonal crops. Every single thing can be a matter of wonder. By encouraging curiosity, and the sense of awe or ecstasy (according to Maslow), we can help produce people that are more inclined to interact, pro-socially along lines concerning community and larger matters than those pertaining only to their own subjective lives.

The concept of wonder is a philosophical one. Plato said that philosophy starts with wonder.[25] Unsurprisingly, both Aristotle and A.N. Whitehead followed suit. We can appreciate Plato's specific perspective, given his mentor's proclivity for engaging folks in the community and asking pointed questions. Wonder involves the posing of questions for investigation and review. Curiosity begets wonder which invites inquiry and exploration. Wonder involves a percipient participating with their most human of activities: the application of conceptual thought. We examine a subject and then extrapolate components for review or discover associated ideas and concepts. Wonder elicits learning and a greater sense of curiosity, which, in turn, brings about still more wondrous engagement. A sense of wonder is stifled, discouraged when items are forbidden subjects of inquiry. Dogma and extended perspective effectively curtail investigation born of wonder and curiosity. Viewing the world as composed of wondrous things means we have the ability to foster the presence of wondrous people, too.

Work

To labor, or fulfill duties regularly for wages or salary, or to exert oneself for a purpose or under compulsion is work. Different aspects of this concept influence and significantly affect our lives. We discussed labor, previously. In this entry, we address several issues related to work. First, we review the time spent at work and how it is both formative and bi-conditionally influential with the home setting. We examine the idea of meaningful work. Finally, we explore the idea of trading life for pay.

Work need be considered an influential setting as we spent a majority of waking hours there. Out of a total of 168 hours in a week, many spend close to one-third of that time at the workplace. This does not take into consideration how doctors, lawyers, and teachers spend untold hours working outside of the workplace.

> As an interesting consideration: what if teachers billed for their time, as lawyers do?

Spending such a large share of time at work influences what remaining hours are spent at home. As a particular note, work has a particularly formative affect on those just entering the work force. The barrage of broader concerns that are unrelated to the home setting affects the family and private life. Not only do people bring actual work tasks home to address, they bring their workplace issues, as well. Politics and all other elements of the work setting arrive home with the worker. It is interesting to note how folks escape their home life at work and vice versa: home becomes a refuge from work. Stresses of either realm invariably permeate barriers and color the other. The reward of work is financial means that afford other resources for the home. Given the amount of experience shared at a job, workmates become more than cubicle community members and peers at an office. A remarkable sum of hours of shared space and experience imparts a significant degree of intimacy, if not familiarity and closeness. Workmates and peers can easily become a form of family. These bonds can affect the home environment, and the individual worker, as well. The worker develops ties in an extended vocation, or position. While there are exceptions, it is difficult to imagine how an employee can remain unconnected and aloof given their extended presence as a community member at their place of employment.

The workplace, then, is a type of commons. It is shared and used by a larger communal group. Personal behaviors and values are minimized in lieu of those attitudes, beliefs, and activities that facilitate and engender cohesion along the lines of organizational creed or ethos. Maintaining a presence away from family is a significant investment. The means garnered via work are meant for the family and home. Time spent apart is a matter of trading life for pay. The exchange of salary for time and labor need be one that justifies the transaction for all parties involved. Meaningful work, complemented by an inclusive, efficient, and responsive work setting can harness the passion and interested service of engaged employees. An organization that offers work that benefits the worker beyond salary and wage will elicit loyalty and performance. Those companies that address the subjective concerns and preferences of independent workers will structure a dynamic that elicits worthwhile returns that surpass the rubrics quantified by dollar signs, ones, and zeroes.

Work is significant and meaningful in a different sense. The performance of work builds character. It instills a work ethic or a means by which subjective individuals apply themselves to tasks. Work is a powerful means of demonstrating personal values. Character is demonstrated by how we address tasks: how responsively, efficiently, and well we satisfy work says something about how we live our greater lives. If work is shirked, or performed at a shoddy standard, it shows values and elements of character. There are aspects demonstrated elsewhere but work variables speak to a generality, for work is ubiquitous and a staple of life as we know it. Meaning: a man might be courageous and brave and make a stand for justice as a protestor. But, if he, as a worker is lazy, apathetic, and unconcerned with exerting himself with tasks and responsibilities, a greater portion of his character is exposed. People are more likely to judge him for his work ethic than how he shares values elsewhere. Mature people grasp the importance of work, and of exerting oneself when facing responsibility or even adversity. It is a necessary community/cultural burden that need be confronted and handled summarily. Other approaches may leave work for others. Laziness and sloth are depicted over the course of not performing or contributing to a work cause and there are better character traits to emulate.

Work serves as an investment, and the concept of trading hours and freedom for paid labor is an important life activity. It is said, though, that 'if you love what you're doing, you will never work a day in your life.' When you structure a skill set that means something important to you, consider applying them as a vocation. Building a skill set for employers to make use of is a waste of your own personal time and abilities. When identifying those skills that resonate with you, format and implement them so that they benefit *you*. Else we run the risk of forever building skills sets for others to harness and apply. In the likely and probable case that interest wanes, the necessary consequence is the pursuit of other externally appreciated abilities. Work is a significant concept, across cultures, and for nearly all people. The trade-off of return for exchanged hours/life is a consequential one. When engaging the larger work realm, be sure to note how your principles, values, and abilities are applied. Make certain that the organization, cause, or entity you are working with/for has an interest in your continued, perpetuated well-being. Make something of your passion, and abilities, and as you work, do something you love.

Worry

We are not going to waste precious time with worry. See: **angst, anxiety**.

Self-Worth

Self-worth is the opinion you have about yourself and the value you place on yourself. A familiar approach of applying variables amounts to nil, should the individual not hold himself or herself in sufficiently high regard. However much friends and family convey their affectionate sentiments and appreciation for an individual; the same holds true: internally generated and maintained self-respect and self-love equates to an individual with a concrete, secure sense of self-worth. It need be founded on internal values and concepts as opposed to external behaviors, or the association of others. For baubles will lose their luster, people and activities change radically, and it does no good to associate with people when their morality is opposed to or lacking in regard to one's own position. Self-worth is elicited by how a person thinks about and views his or her traits, beliefs, and purpose within the world. So this text is not an equation, nor the proffered mandate from heaven. Consider: when a chef, or any creator for that matter, makes use of the best possible ingredients and resources, good is the result. Do not cheapen experience by making use of shoddy ideas or entertaining for extended periods of time lesser notions, concepts, and values. In order to experience the best, you need align with quality of the same standard. Realize that you are worth continued investment and work!

In order to develop a positive sense of self and self-worth:
-Believe in yourself.
-Live and speak your truth.
-See yourself in a positive light by engaging in positive and worthy activities.
-Be compassionate with yourself, when and if you fail or fall short of a desired aim.
-Keep moving forward.

You are capable of great things, if you engage critically, and well. You can experience and generate significant happiness – you only need consider yourself worthy of it. What you achieve and experience in this life will mirror your subjective sense of worth.

Chapter 24

X-Factor

A variable in a given situation that could have the most significant impact on the outcome is an **X-Factor**. It will become increasingly interesting to witness the remarkable spectrum of variables that play a role, or participate in different contexts. Tidbits, anecdotes, asides, persons, places, things, and ideas - among all else - provide the means of moving the world forward. To note or discover one particular component that provides the most significant impact in a situation is important. Finding a solution to circumstance or bringing resources to bear allows a context to proceed apace. In the course of building skill sets and honing abilities, we will become more and more aware of how we, as individuals, are the means of most significant impact. *We* are the X-factor. We each have a subjective x-factor, for it is that which differentiates and distinguishes us from one another. The concept can be equivocated for the translation of the French *je ne se quois*, but the x-factor is the application of the variable, and its provision of consequential effect.

Chapter 25

You

Who are You?

Who were you? Who will you become?

What do you do? What do you want?

What is the best aspect of your character?

What do you believe?

What are your goals?

When do you see yourself succeeding? Are you succeeding now?

Where are you? Where have you been? Where are you going?

Why are you the way you are?

Why do you live by your specific principles?

How will you improve?

How are you imparting Goodness in the world?

How can you be your best? How are you when you are at your best?

Chapter 26

Zeal

An extraordinary energy or enthusiasm in pursuit of a cause or an objective is zeal. Someone who is zealous or has zeal is known as a zealot. Those who are zealous entertain a nearly fanatical devotion or dedication to their cause or objective. Their zeal can prove overwhelming and maintain a primary position of importance. It can override thresholds of balance and moderation and make for a troubling issue in some cases. Energy and enthusiasm are important resources and factors of different situations. It is best to engage with them and with zeal! Remain mindful of the mean and apply zeal in moderation, lest you sway to an unbecoming extreme.

Might there be variables or causes that warrant or deserve unbridled zeal? Fanatical devotion detracts from worthy pursuits and objectives. A fervent or myopic focus on any one thing detracts attention from and inclusion of other concepts and activities. Such a limited focus or perspective excludes nearly all else. For example, a zealous regard of the family - or anything else, remember - excludes the rest of the cosmos. Such immoderation can not be healthy. Strive to remain balanced and inclusive of the greater world. When we act without regard for significant portions or components of the world, we run the risk of suffering serious consequences. Zest is a more restrained energy and enthusiasm. It features no fanatical character and is a healthier approach to life, generally.

Zenith

The time at which something is most powerful or successful is the zenith. It can also refer to a navigational point that is directly above a position or a plane, or horizon. For the purposes of this discussion, we focus on the prior definition, as pertaining to an individual. Someone achieves success, or gains power, by engaging with certainty: applying resources with initiative and strategy. While some gains are elicited by chance occurrences, generally: fortune favors the bold, and the prepared. Bringing resources to bear entails a goal or entertaining an aim in mind. Realizing success equates to applying the resources meaningfully in the face of dynamic variables. A zenith is attained after momentum is built; several successes provide the ability to achieve another level of efficiency or gain. Mounting wins provide the means of obtaining a superlative level. The zenith is achieved when there remains no further means of improvement or gain. It is the final, utmost level of achievement.

Improvement, development, and growth should be a goal of all activities. We can progress as we address both long- and short-term pursuits. A zenith, in particular, is born of continued actions and behaviors that elicit success. In the short-term, a zenith might be reached per incremental step or individuated activity. We discussed Nietzsche's consideration of the activity that is perfect, or something repeated ad nauseum. He refers to the eternal recurrence. He asks, "Do you desire *this* once more, and innumerable times more?" Separating volitional activities: our next step, blink, breath, or interaction, we can strive to make each conscious initiative the most successful, or something of notable particular power. We can reach a zenith with each considerate action. Along the lines of Zeno's Paradox, rather than making a zenith as the culmination of separate victories, what if we reached a zenith with every intentional behavior?

When pursuing a goal, applying your own personal agency, marshal your resources to achieve an aim, but be mindful of the interval steps of the process. Be centered and sufficiently engaged as to mark those intervals with poise, certitude, and clarity. A zenith need not be a distanced goal, but an attainable end to each conscious act or initiative.

Zoophilous

Zoophilous refers to having an affinity for animals. Different cultures utilize disparate approaches to the animal kingdom. Many households in the United States include dogs and cats, while those in India revere the bovine as holy. Native Americans consider animals as kin or ancestors. Ancient Egyptians considered cats to be sacred. Whatever your background, affiliation, or association, animals offer the opportunity to learn, and, in some specific cases, to love. Some animals provide a demonstration of collective or herd mentality. Their presentation of unity, solidarity, or community can be powerful. A herd of peaceful migratory grazers will coordinate to protect their young as forcefully as a nomadic wolf pack cares for its members. Utilizing a pack mentality can also elicit disaster, in some circumstances. In the human realm, it becomes mob mentality and violence often results.

What is particularly striking in the animal kingdom is the occurrence of inter-species coordination. Animals will coordinate not only to protect one of their own, but they will also take initiative to aid those of a different species; animals will sometimes aid those that are usually predators. Assorted videos present a spectrum of action: a female elephant carried a lion cub upon its tusks to a watering hole, while the mother lioness trotted beside them, en route. A bear in its zoo enclosure saved a bird from drowning. Cats save dogs, and chimpanzees mobilize to save a gazelle from the jaws of a predator, too. Mutualism, or inter-special cooperation is the way two organisms of different species exist in a relationship in which each individual benefits from the activity of the other. We would do well to mimic certain behaviors of the animal kingdom, and care for our own kind - our human brothers and sisters.

In some cases, animals provide insight as to how we humans would coordinate and care, albeit sans the restrictions and encumbrances of rational thought and significant social constructs. In other moments, they demonstrate a base savagery that parallels behavior of our own species. Note the spectrum of action and behaviors. Strive to recognize behaviors we would do well to emulate, in contrast to the initiatives that are best left to the beasts.

Conclusion

In an effort to facilitate the emergence of flourishing individuals, I offer this labor of love. Pertinent terms that apply to the intellectual, psychological, emotional, physical, and quantum realms of the individual are available for consideration and implementation. Refined thoughts, balanced emotions, and measured, or considerate behavior can result by adhering to many of these concepts. These entries - various hallmarks of the western cultural tradition - are served in accessible, digestible portions, and the food for thought is a decent appetizer to a fuller meal.

This is intended to engender care and concern for the self, others, and community. In order to enjoy better conditions comprised of improved social, economic, and environmental circumstances, we need have a basic grasp of many of these concepts. Unfortunately, the public education provided in the United States does not impart a conceptual apparatus. It is formatted to elicit a docile, separated audience, one characterized by a lack of critical engagement and wonder. It performs exactly as it is able and intended. As a result of its shortcomings and consequences manifested over generations, this text is necessary.

The list is not comprehensive, nor is it meant to be. Within the text there is little mention of aliens, nationalism, identity politics, transhumanism, bitcoin or blockchain, despite the fact that such terms shed remarkable light on disparate spheres of experience. I also neglected to write about equality, equity, and numerous other concepts, as well. It is hoped that individuals apply themselves and investigate their inner and outer worlds, in order to flesh out their own subjective existence.

May your travels be punctuated by a diverse array of people, places, things, and ideas! Contribute your own portion - something worthwhile and unique - to this wondrous human journey.

"Nothing in life is to be feared, it is only to be understood. Now is the time to understand more, so that we may fear less." – **Marie Curie**

"You can not get through a single day without having an impact on the world around you. What you do makes a difference, and you have to decide what kind of difference you want to make." – **Jane Goodall**

"Liberty cannot be preserved without general knowledge among the people." - **John Adams**

"When the mob governs, man is ruled by ignorance; when the church governs, he is ruled by superstition; and when the state governs, he is ruled by fear. Before men can live together in harmony and understanding, ignorance must be transmuted into wisdom, superstition into an illumined faith, and fear into love." – **Manly P. Hall**

Reference

The majority of definitions, unless explicitly stated, via Webster's Encyclopedic Dictionary of the English Language, New Deluxe Edition. Thunder Bay Press, San Diego, 2001.

---

[1] *See The Apology*, section 38a

[2] https://www.artofmanliness.com/articles/how-to-develop-the-situational-awareness-of-jason-bourne/

[3] See *The Gay Science*

[4] *Phaedo*, sections 61c-69e

[5] See Aristotle's *Rhetoric*

[6] *The Concept of Dread*, 1844

[7] *Cosmos*, 1980

[8] http://www.mentalhealthamerica.net/conditions/depression-women

[9] *Laws, 626e*

[10] http://www.psychologycharts.com/james-fowler-stages-of-faith.html

[11] http://apps.who.int/iris/bitstream/handle/10665/254610/WHO-MSD-MER-2017.2-eng.pdf;jsessionid=EA2F4FA6CA148047A12DD322EF34C555?sequence =1

[12] World Health Organization (2005). Promoting Mental Health: Concepts,

Emerging evidence, Practice: A report of the World Health Organization, Department of Mental Health and Substance Abuse in collaboration with the Victorian Health Promotion Foundation and the University of Melbourne. World Health Organization. Geneva.

[13] The Energetic Heart: Bioelectromagnetic Interactions Within and Between People
By Rollin McCraty, Ph.D.

[14] See Plato's *Apology,* 203-23c.

[15] https://www.forbes.com/sites/walterpavlo/2011/08/12/pennsylvania-judge-gets-life-sentence-for-prison-kickback-scheme/#d38c7a44aef0

[16] http://www.policestateusa.com/2013/annie-dookhan-crime-lab-chemist-falsified-evidence/

[17] http://bigstory.ap.org/article/fd1d4d05e561462a85abe50e7eaed4ec/ap-hundreds-officers-lose-licenses-over-sex-misconduct

[18] https://www.jonathangullible.com

[19] Utilitarianism, 1863

[20] http://liveboldandbloom.com/05/self-awareness-2/50-important-life-lessons

[21] http://fortune.com/2017/12/12/chamath-palihapitiya-facebook-society/

[22] Martin Luther King, Jr.

[23] See Ortega y Gasset's *Revolt of the Masses*

[24] http://www.who.int/violenceprevention/approach/definition/en/

[25] See *Theaeteus* 155d

Made in the USA
Columbia, SC
24 September 2020